I0320316

Scoring to Picture in Logic Pro

Explore synchronization techniques for film, TV, and multimedia composers using Apple's flagship DAW

Prof. Chris Piorkowski

BIRMINGHAM—MUMBAI

Scoring to Picture in Logic Pro

Copyright © 2023 Packt Publishing

All rights reserved. No part of this book may be reproduced, stored in a retrieval system, or transmitted in any form or by any means, without the prior written permission of the publisher, except in the case of brief quotations embedded in critical articles or reviews.

Every effort has been made in the preparation of this book to ensure the accuracy of the information presented. However, the information contained in this book is sold without warranty, either express or implied. Neither the author, nor Packt Publishing or its dealers and distributors, will be held liable for any damages caused or alleged to have been caused directly or indirectly by this book.

Packt Publishing has endeavored to provide trademark information about all of the companies and products mentioned in this book by the appropriate use of capitals. However, Packt Publishing cannot guarantee the accuracy of this information.

Group Product Manager: Rohit Rajkumar
Publishing Product Manager: Vaideeshwari Muralikrishnan
Senior Editor: Hayden Edwards
Technical Editor: Joseph Aloocaran
Copy Editor: Safis Editing
Project Coordinator: Aishwarya Mohan
Proofreader: Safis Editing
Indexer: Pratik Shirodkar
Production Designer: Aparna Bhagat
Marketing Coordinators: Namita Velgekar & Nivedita Pandey

First published: September 2023
Production reference: 1130923

Published by Packt Publishing Ltd.
Grosvenor House
11 St Paul's Square
Birmingham
B3 1R

ISBN 978-1-83763-689-1

www.packtpub.com

I would like to give thanks and glory to God for allowing me to become a film composer, working in Hollywood for many years, and now, as a result, being able to share my learned knowledge and experiences with others.

I would also like to thank Hayden Edwards for his assistance in helping me to edit and finalize the writing for this book, as well as my wife, Mary Alice, for her devoted help with editing the book and for acting in the Mercedes commercial that was produced exclusively for this book.

I'd like to dedicate this book to all aspiring film composers who are passionate about film music.

– Prof. Chris Piorkowski

Foreword by David K. Schmal

I have known Prof. Chris Piorkowski since the summer of 2016, and in that time, I have seen a man of determination, passion, and skill share his many talents and knowledge of composition, arranging, orchestration, and music production in the scholarly context at the Michael W Smith Center for Commercial Music at Liberty University School of Music. Upon arriving at LUSOM in 2016, Chris assumed a leadership role as an instructor in film scoring and music production using Logic Pro software. In this capacity, he was involved in overseeing film scoring techniques coursework and technology classes using Logic Pro as a tool for creative expression and composition.

As a response to the need of his students and the marketplace, Chris created the textbook *Scoring to Picture in Logic Pro*. As a composer of well over 50 films, including work in TV, in collaboration with composer Tommy Proffitt, as well as his experience as a sound engineer and producer at Sound City Studios in Los Angeles, Chris encapsulates his knowledge as a film composer and music producer and the experience he has gained through his work in the industry. He brings all of this expertise to the task of creating the definitive text for synchronization techniques for film, television, and multimedia composition with the industry standard for production software, Logic Pro.

In his step-by-step processes, presentations, and samples, Chris demonstrates the best practices for music production using Logic Pro. This involves the use of various audio elements such as sound design, instrumental, and media plugins and how these technological developments are applied within a real-world film scoring structure. Because of his experience, Chris is able to deliver insights into current trends regarding the role of music in film, TV, and multimedia environments. This includes developing and understanding film scoring technology and video components, setting up and syncing movie projects, tempo and beat mapping, shaping and designing film/TV and commercial projects, mixing and exporting to video, and other advanced concepts regarding elements of timing and exporting stems.

All of these elements come together to create a wide range of applications and best practices for writing high-quality film, TV, multimedia, and video game music, as well as how to best position yourself as a composer and take full advantage of an ever-evolving commercial market.

David K. Schmal, D.M.A. Coordinator of Film Scoring Professor of Music Michael W. Smith Center for Commercial Music

Liberty University School of Music

Foreword by Luciano Saber

I've known Chris Piorkowski for over a decade and worked with him on multiple feature film and television projects. I relied heavily on his counsel and expert advice while he scored my feature films and found Chris to be one of the most creative professionals in my entertainment career. I feel confident that his knowledge of all aspects of music composition far surpasses the norm in the industry.

Chris is a musical prodigy and has composed since he was a teenager, performing in Germany, France, and on other European stages. He understands how to capture an audience and bring a scene to extraordinary heights through music. Films and TV shows are visual stories that can be flawlessly executed, but without music, even the most beautifully acted, directed, and captured scene can sometimes fall flat. Music in film and television comes to life in the subconscious minds of the viewers by suggesting how the viewer should feel. It instills a feeling in the audience, and to accomplish that, it takes an incredible amount of musical talent. That's an area in which Chris excels.

I remember spending hours with Chris, sometimes way into the night hours, in his Los Angeles studio, discussing the mood of each scene and even individual shots. Chris worked diligently to make sure every note and every musical passage was perfect and communicated my directorial vision and point of view to the viewer.

Although I'm not musically inclined, Chris had the patience and gentle approach to help me understand his world and technique. Even when I was exhausted, after a ten- or twelve-hour session, Chris had the energy to stay in the studio and continue working. I found his dedication to the craft to be inspiring. I'm glad Chris decided to share his talent with aspiring composers, musicians, and the world, and I'm sure *Scoring to Picture in Logic Pro* will serve as a window into the mind of this brilliant musical talent.

Luciano Saber

Writer, Director, and Producer

Foreword by Michael M. Conti

Based on his outstanding work on films such as *The Unruly Mystic: Saint Hildegard* and *The Unruly Mystic: John Muir*, Chris's versatility as a composer allows him to seamlessly adapt to different themes and genres, ensuring that his music perfectly complements the unique storytelling for my films. Through his exceptional ability to evoke emotions, Chris creates a powerful and deeply moving connection between the audience and the subject matter, enhancing the impact of each film. How he actually does that technically is composition magic that I know nothing about, but this is what he shares in the book.

Michael M. Conti

Film Director

Contributors

About the author

Prof. Chris Piorkowski is an award-winning composer, artist, and educator. Completing his graduate studies with a major in music composition for film and multimedia, he holds a Master of Music (M.F.A.) terminal degree from Vermont College of Fine Arts.

Professor Piorkowski participated in a music performance for Pope John Paul II, performing a solo piano concert at Palais des Congrès de Paris in Paris, France with over 3,000 people present. In 1999, he was selected, because of his outstanding achievement in composition and arrangement, to score, produce, and arrange the theme song of the Boxing World Cup in Helsinki. In addition to his many composition projects, he was chosen as an orchestrator, composer, arranger, and audio engineer for German pop star and recording artist Guildo Horn (the Eurovision Song Contest, 1989).

At age 12, he received a diploma in harmony from a music conservatory in Europe. He studied orchestration with Steven Scott Smalley and received a diploma in sound engineering and music production from the Audio Institute of America in San Francisco and a diploma in media composition from Music For The Media in London. He studied Jazz piano with Walter Norris and jazz harmony with Sigi Bush at Music University Berlin, and in 1996, received a scholarship from Berklee College of Music in Boston, where he later studied film scoring and orchestration. He also studied music technology in the master's program at the University of Newcastle, Australia. He has worked on countless projects at the legendary Sound City Studios in Los Angeles, CA, and has scored over 50 feature and short films as well as many TV commercials. Among many other film trailers and multimedia projects, he has composed music for Gene Roddenberry (the Star Trek creator). His music appears on Showtime, PBS, TBN, and other network television stations.

I want to thank the people who have been close to me and supported me, especially my loving wife, Mary Alice Piorkowski.

To Packt Publishing, who motivated me to write this content, and the team at Packt for their help and support throughout the process.

About the reviewer

After his MSc in telecommunications, **Dominique Légitimus** worked in the field of underwater signal processing and pattern recognition before switching to his real passion. Since 2010, he has been an Apple Logic certified master trainer and teaches music production and film scoring in France, the French West Indies, and Africa. As well as this, he manages the audio bachelor program development and the creation of the sound design and film scoring streams for the International Film and Television School, Paris. Dominique is also a guitarist and a composer working in TV and cinema.

Table of Contents

Preface	xv

Part 1: An Introduction to Scoring to Picture

1

Understanding Film Music Industry Standards — 3

What is film music?	3	Spotting notes	8
How does the film music industry function?	4	During the meeting	9
		End of the meeting	12
A step back in time	4	What are the character qualities of a successful film composer?	12
Scoring to picture today	5		
What is a spotting session?	6	What skills are required of a film composer?	13
Understanding spotting sessions	6		
Before the meeting	6	Summary	13

2

Understanding Film Scoring Terminology — 15

What is SMPTE timecode?	15	Errors in drop frame and non-drop frame timecodes	25
What is BITC?	16		
What is a 2-pop?	19	Exploring SMPTE and BITC errors	26
What is a 3-pop?	21	Reviewing correct SMPTE timecodes in individual reels	30
What is an end pop?	22		
What is a 2 second pre-roll?	23	Reviewing timecodes with Adobe Premiere	34
What is a 3 second pre-roll?	24	Reviewing dialogue and temp music	36
		Summary	37

3

Reviewing QuickTime Video and Video Components — 39

Technical requirements	39	General	42
Opening the QuickTime Inspector	40	Video Details	44
Understanding video file components	40	Summary	46

Part 2: Project Setup and Navigation

4

Setting Up a Movie in Logic Pro — 49

Technical requirements	49	Setting up the frame rate	57
Opening, saving, and closing a Logic Pro session	51	Moving and adjusting the position of the movie	58
		Changing the movie size	60
Opening a movie file in Logic Pro	52	Adjusting the movie size aspect ratio	62
Importing a movie file	55	Saving a session with a movie file	63
Extracting audio from a movie file	55	Summary	64
Setting up the sample rate	56		

5

Syncing Logic Pro to Picture — 65

Technical requirements	65	Locking the movie	78
Reviewing visual synchronization tools	65	Saving a project session with a movie file	82
Giant Time and Beats Display settings	66	**Syncing Logic Pro with different movie files**	**84**
Logic Pro SMPTE display without subframes	67	Syncing a movie file with a countdown leader	84
Syncing Logic Pro to picture	**69**	Syncing a movie file with a 2-pop	91
Importing the movie file	69	Syncing a movie file with a 3-pop	94
Accessing and reviewing the movie project settings	70	Syncing a movie file with multiple reels	97
Accessing and reviewing the synchronization settings	77	Syncing a movie file with SMPTE Offset View	107
		Scoring a movie from any bar location	109

Creating a custom scoring to picture template	111	Summary	122

6

Working with Hit Points and Scene Markers — 123

Technical requirements	124	Creating scene markers	138
Defining hit points	124	Comparing standard, SMPTE-locked, and scene markers	139
Reviewing music spotting notes	124		
Copying the spotting notes list into Logic Pro	126	Creating and removing movie scene cut markers	143
Creating markers without rounding	126	Navigating with markers	145
Naming and renaming markers	131	Creating new marker sets	147
Changing markers to the SMPTE view position	136	Summary	149

Part 3: Methods of Scoring to Picture

7

Creating Tempo Maps — 153

Technical requirements	154	Creating a tempo map	167
Dealing with tempo in film music	154	Creating a tempo map based on hit points	174
Watching a movie with a metronome	154		
Using Tap Tempo	156	Adjusting the tempo to match the hit points	179
Reviewing the Logic Pro LCD position display	158	Summary	182
Reviewing marker positions	163		

8

Working with Beat Mapping — 183

Technical requirements	184	Creating a Tap Tempo using an instrument track	184
Understanding beat mapping	184		

Beat mapping single MIDI notes	192	Using Beat Mapping scene markers	205
Beat mapping an entire MIDI region	199	Beat mapping the hit points	216
Editing tempo points	202	Summary	221
Editing a Beat Mapping track	204		

9

Working with a Time Signature — 223

Technical requirements	223	Adding time signatures to existing marker positions	230
Understanding a time signature in film music	223	Adding time signatures to a constant tempo	243
Reviewing a time signature in Logic Pro	224	Comparing musical choices versus technical choices	251
		Summary	252

Part 4: Synchronizing Music to Picture

10

Scoring a Commercial — 255

Technical requirements	255	Choosing music choices over technical choices	257
Choosing a mood and style for the commercial	256	Reviewing the composing process and layering instruments	258
Structuring the cue	257	Summary	304

11

Shaping the Score and Exporting to Video — 305

Technical requirements	306	Shaping the sound and finalizing the basic mix	313
Evaluating the mix	306		
Setting the volume level of tracks	306	Exporting the score to video	345
Setting panning for each track	310	Summary	348

12

Advanced Concepts for Dealing with Timing in Film Music — 349

Technical requirements	350	A single frame of a 35mm film	364
Outlining structure and timings	350	Click book	365
		BPM versus FPB	365
Scenario 1 – using 120 bpm and the 3/4 time signature	354	Calculating timings using fpb formulas	367
Scenario 2 – using 120 bpm and the 4/4 time signature	356	Displaying time as feet and frames in Logic Pro	369
Scenario 3 – using 192 bpm and the 4/4 time signature	357	Displaying tempo as frame click in Logic Pro	372
Calculating timings using a DAW	358	Exploring visual synchronization methods used today	373
Method 1 – calculating timings inside Logic Pro	358	Picture cueing	373
		Digital metronome	375
Method 2 – calculating timings using formulas	360	Implementing punches and streamers today	376
Synchronizing music to picture during the Golden Age of Hollywood	363	Summary	379

Index — 381

Other Books You May Enjoy — 388

Preface

Scoring to Picture in Logic Pro is a book I have wanted to write for a long time. As a professor of film scoring at Liberty University for the last seven years, I was always in search of a textbook or materials for my students to use in their studies. I found that there are a lot of film scoring books circulating in the market, but most of them are outdated because of all of the technological developments in the last 20 years. I wanted to make sure that the most crucial aspects of film music and using Logic Pro from a film composer's perspective are covered.

I have always been passionate about writing music for film, and working on many projects in the Hollywood industry has given me valuable hands-on experience as a film composer. I'm excited to share my knowledge with all of you, in a compact format for quick learning and use. This book, from beginning to end, not only will give you a comprehensive understanding of synchronization and an overview of how film scoring works but it will also explore how to use Logic Pro in the context of film music.

There are four areas that will be covered:

- An introduction to scoring to picture
- Project setup and navigation
- Methods of scoring to picture
- Synchronizing music to picture

In this book, you will learn how to "score to picture" in Logic Pro and begin to understand the basic components of video and Logic Pro and the process of synchronization to picture using Logic Pro. I will provide scenarios and real-world examples you can work through that will give you the experience needed to take on a professional film scoring project.

You will learn what film music is and why and how it's used in film and multimedia, as well as the process of post-production and final film score delivery. You will understand the role of a film, TV, and multimedia composer. It will give you the ability to implement commonly used industry scenarios in real gig environments.

The content reflects current working practices and extensively covers the latest topical issues and some historical aspects when it comes to the synchronization of music to picture and dealing with timing.

After successfully completing and practicing the entire book content, you will be able to enter the professional market of scoring to picture with greater confidence.

Who this book is for

This book is for:

- Basic and advanced Logic Pro users who are interested in becoming multimedia composers
- Music enthusiasts, musicians, and aspiring multimedia, film trailer, and game composers
- Music supervisors, music editors, orchestrators, and advanced film and TV composers

What this book covers

Chapter 1, *Understanding Film Music Industry Standards*, provides a look at film music and the film music industry, how music blends with film in support of a picture's needs, and how to prepare for working on a real project.

Chapter 2, *Understanding Film Scoring Terminology*, provides an overview of film scoring terminology to help with working and setting up a movie file in a Logic Pro session.

Chapter 3, *Reviewing QuickTime Video and Video Components*, provides an overview of QuickTime video components and how to handle and use them in Logic Pro.

Chapter 4, *Setting Up a Movie in Logic Pro*, provides an overview of how to work with a movie file in Logic Pro.

Chapter 5, *Syncing Logic Pro to Picture*, provides an overview of how to align and set up a movie, as well as how to sync Logic Pro to picture.

Chapter 6, *Working with Hit Points and Scene Markers*, provides an overview of how to create and lock markers to SMPTE.

Chapter 7, *Creating Tempo Maps*, provides an overview of how to deal with tempo in Logic Pro.

Chapter 8, *Working with Beat Mapping*, provides an overview of how to align markers and lock them in at specific locations.

Chapter 9, *Working with a Time Signature*, provides an overview of how to deal with meter and how to implement time signatures with an existing tempo map.

Chapter 10, *Scoring a Commercial*, provides an overview of how to score a commercial, based on a pre-composed example.

Chapter 11, *Shaping the Score and Exporting to Video*, provides an overview of how to customize and develop sound that supports and benefits the picture mood.

Chapter 12, *Advanced Concepts for Dealing with Timing in Film Music*, provides an overview of advanced concepts and methods of how to work with synchronization of music to picture and timing calculations in film music.

To get the most out of this book

Before reading this book, you should have a basic knowledge of Logic Pro, music theory, composition, and film scoring.

Software/hardware covered in the book	Operating system requirements
Logic Pro 10.6.1 and up	macOS Catalina and up

Download the project files

You can download the project files for this book from the following link: `https://packt.link/hxCer`

If there's an update to the project files, they will be updated through that link as well.

All audio and video files included in this book were specifically created to be used in conjunction with this book for educational purposes only. None of the project files are permitted to be used or distributed in any form without legal permission under the law.

Conventions used

There are a number of text conventions used throughout this book.

Bold: Indicates a new term, an important word, or words that you see onscreen. For instance, words in menus or dialog boxes appear in **bold**. Here is an example: "In the **Instrument** section, from the drop-down menu, select **Sampler (Multi-Sample) | Stereo**."

> Tips or important notes
> Appear like this.

Get in touch

Feedback from our readers is always welcome.

General feedback: If you have questions about any aspect of this book, email us at `customercare@packtpub.com` and mention the book title in the subject of your message.

Errata: Although we have taken every care to ensure the accuracy of our content, mistakes do happen. If you have found a mistake in this book, we would be grateful if you would report this to us. Please visit `www.packtpub.com/support/errata` and fill in the form.

Piracy: If you come across any illegal copies of our works in any form on the internet, we would be grateful if you would provide us with the location address or website name. Please contact us at `copyright@packt.com` with a link to the material.

Share Your Thoughts

Once you've read *Scoring to Picture in Logic Pro*, we'd love to hear your thoughts! Scan the QR code below to go straight to the Amazon review page for this book and share your feedback.

https://packt.link/r/1-837-63689-3

Your review is important to us and the tech community and will help us make sure we're delivering excellent quality content.

Download a free PDF copy of this book

Thanks for purchasing this book!

Do you like to read on the go but are unable to carry your print books everywhere?

Is your eBook purchase not compatible with the device of your choice?

Don't worry, now with every Packt book you get a DRM-free PDF version of that book at no cost.

Read anywhere, any place, on any device. Search, copy, and paste code from your favorite technical books directly into your application.

The perks don't stop there, you can get exclusive access to discounts, newsletters, and great free content in your inbox daily

Follow these simple steps to get the benefits:

1. Scan the QR code or visit the link below

```
https://packt.link/free-ebook/9781837636891
```

2. Submit your proof of purchase
3. That's it! We'll send your free PDF and other benefits to your email directly

Part 1: An Introduction to Scoring to Picture

In this first part, you will get an overview of film music, looking at the industry and how it functions, as well as what working in the industry can look like. You will also become familiar with film scoring terminology. Additionally, you will become familiar with QuickTime video and its components.

This section contains the following chapters:

- *Chapter 1, Understanding Film Music Industry Standards*
- *Chapter 2, Understanding Film Scoring Terminology*
- *Chapter 3, Reviewing QuickTime Video and Video Components*

1
Understanding Film Music Industry Standards

Before we learn how to score to picture in Logic Pro and how certain software components function, we will look at film music and the film music industry. We will talk about how to prepare for working on a real project and delivering the final score, how music blends with film in support of the picture's needs, and the role of a film composer as a storyteller to heighten the audience's emotions.

The intent here is to prepare and equip you for what can be a challenging and constantly evolving task of being a film composer.

So, in this chapter, we will cover the following topics:

- What is film music?
- How does the film music industry function?
- What is a spotting session?
- How can a film composer effectively express emotion through music?
- What are the character qualities of a successful film composer?
- What skills are required of a film composer?

What is film music?

When it comes to understanding this industry, understanding film music is perhaps the best place to start. **Film music** is music written to serve and support the elements of a film. It is not for the audience to enjoy as they would when they go to a concert or music venue; instead, it is created specifically and solely to serve the picture.

It can incorporate familiar genres of music such as classical, jazz, or pop, taking just a single style or a combination of styles to enhance what's on the screen. The music should not draw attention to itself but instead evoke emotion in the viewers. When properly coupled with a film, film music helps the viewer become more deeply involved in the film, without even realizing that the music is there.

It is also important to know that film music is not to be composed as, let's say, a symphony would be, including a sonata followed by three movements, or a pop song, which includes verses, choruses, and bridges, or any other structure that you would see in different music genres. Since film scoring is crafted based on a specific mood, story, events, characters, scene cuts, and tempos, you are not limited to a specific structure or defined parameters – this is the exciting part of film music.

Next, it's important to look at the film-music industry and understand how it functions, starting with film production.

How does the film music industry function?

Film production goes through multiple stages of development, including pre-production and then production, before entering the phase of post-production. This phase is where film music comes in, along with other musical elements to be added, such as finished songs, Foley, SFX, sound design, and underscores. Together, all these elements contribute greatly to the final experience of moviegoers.

Let's quickly look at the history of the film-music industry.

A step back in time

Back in the days when legendary film composer John Williams was scoring/composing music for iconic films such as Star Wars, Jaws, and Indiana Jones, things were done a little differently.

Originally, the composer would sit at a piano with a pen and a blank sheet of music paper while watching film excerpts on the tiny screen of a Moviola projector. A common workflow would involve complex time calculations and conversions to make sure the composer's initial ideas were in sync with the picture, all of which was done by hand. At the same time, the composer would meet with the film director so that they could watch the film together and swap ideas so that the composer could understand the director's vision (this meeting still happens today, and we will explore this shortly).

After the completed score had been sketched out, which commonly consisted of five or six staffs on a single sheet of music paper, it was then passed to the film's orchestrator. The orchestrator expanded the written sketch and filled out all the required instrument parts for a full orchestra before preparing it for the live orchestra recording session. When the entire score was successfully recorded, the music was then mixed and sent over to a dubbing stage, where the dialogue, SFX, and music were mixed. Once approved by the director and producer, the entire mix was attached to the picture and the film was ready for distribution.

This process required the film composer to have strong synchronization skills, and the film director also had to trust and understand the film composer's ideas. As a lot of film directors didn't (and often still don't) have much music education, they didn't know what the score would sound like outside of just a piano until they heard the final score.

It was this uncertainty on the director's part that led film composers to come up with the idea of creating something called orchestral mockups. This was developed in the 80s with the introduction of the **Music Instrument Digital Interface (MIDI)**. MIDI allows the sequencer to connect and communicate with many synthesizers and samplers to create and emulate the sound of a real orchestra. As you can imagine, this process was very costly and cumbersome, and stacking countless synthesizers, sound modules, and samplers loaded with recorded orchestral samples never seemed to be a fully satisfying experience because of the sound quality limitations. However, it was good enough for the film director to make the final decision to accept or reject the composed score and so it was used.

Scoring to picture today

As the music industry continued developing ways to achieve better-sounding mockups, in the 90s, well-known film composer Hans Zimmer decided to create a custom-made software sampler by recording the London Symphony Orchestra. This huge move forward in the development of music technology set new standards in the music industry. The usage of computers and software samplers took over and found themselves in countless film composers' studios during the late 90s and more so at the beginning of the 2000s.

The well-known software sample library EastWest, developed in 2001, provided a great-sounding sampled orchestra that was available to film composers worldwide. The orchestral sample libraries are installed and streamed on multiple computers, to offload the heavy RAM and CPU consumption, so that a vast amount of great-sounding orchestral instruments were at the film composer's fingertips. This was a game changer for so many film composers at the time. It was one step closer to achieving great-sounding orchestral mockups. Film composers were thrilled and so were film directors and producers.

Since then, going ahead in time just over 20 years to today, film composers can still use one, two, three, or more computers networked together to accomplish the demanding task of scoring to picture. Specifically, they use **Digital Audio Workstation (DAW)** software (such as Logic Pro!), which allows them to load a movie file and synchronize music to picture. It can also load multiple patches of different virtual libraries, instruments, and countless audio files.

Music is prepared "in the box" using a computer with a DAW such as Logic Pro. This is often logistically less problematic since there's no live orchestra involvement. Today, more than ever, the samples of live instruments sound excellent, making this the choice of many young film directors, who do not have funds for live players.

Additional ways of scoring to picture can be achieved using an iPad or iPhone, though it might be a little challenging because of the many limitations that those devices present. For example, these portable standalone devices and their software and hardware components are not equipped with enough power to handle demanding tasks like Mac computers can. Within that context, there are many other types of iOS music software available today for composers, such as notation programs, but again, there are limitations because they are only phone devices. Despite the iPhones' and iPads' existing software ability to control Logic Pro, which can help in the film scoring process, they can't handle the complete task of scoring.

As you experience and learn about this constantly evolving industry, you'll decide what method will work for you, either by using sheet music and sketching out your music ideas first or going directly into Logic Pro. Scoring is subjective, and what method works for someone else may not work for you, and that's okay.

Now that we've explored the history of scoring, let's start talking about the meeting between the composer and director. This meeting happens before you start scoring to picture.

What is a spotting session?

Given the same script, two different film directors would likely create quite different versions of a scene of a film. So, too, would two film composers likely score a scene differently. Both film directors and film composers bring their unique creativity to a project; however, collaboration and clear communication are essential to realizing a creative outcome in which the composer's score seamlessly supports the film director's vision. The film director and film composer must find a common artistic language to envision what a film needs. This often begins with what is called a spotting session.

Understanding spotting sessions

A **spotting session** is a meeting where the director and composer (though others can be involved too) determine and agree on what type of music will need to be composed and where the music will need to be placed within the movie timeline.

The composer's task is to translate the emotional aspects of scenes into the music of the film score. This "translation," though, must fit into the director's overall vision. It can be counterproductive for the composer to make any decisions related to the score before they understand what the director is seeking. Without such understanding, the composer is shooting in the dark. This can lead to a lot of time spent on music that doesn't support the director's true vision and, therefore, is a waste of time. This is why the spotting session is so important.

Before the meeting

Before the meeting, the film editor and/or film director preselects existing music, called the **temp track** or **temp music**. This music gives them an idea of what they're looking for or what the film may need before they meet with the film composer.

Temp music is not normally a film composer's first choice because they have to emulate the audio examples to the point of nearly copying the temp track, instead of being able to create their own new and fresh score. This is an additional challenge for the film composer. What makes it more challenging is that the film composer needs to have the skill to follow the director's request, retain the feel and the style of the temp music, and, at the same time, compose an original score.

The film composer will be sent a movie file with the temp track attached to it before the first spotting session. It is helpful to know your computer system so that you can ask the director or video editor to provide you with a movie file based on your computer system.

Since working in small movie chunks is more efficient, today, film directors and composers have found a way to work with one another by cutting the entire movie file into so-called reels. Take a look at the following diagram:

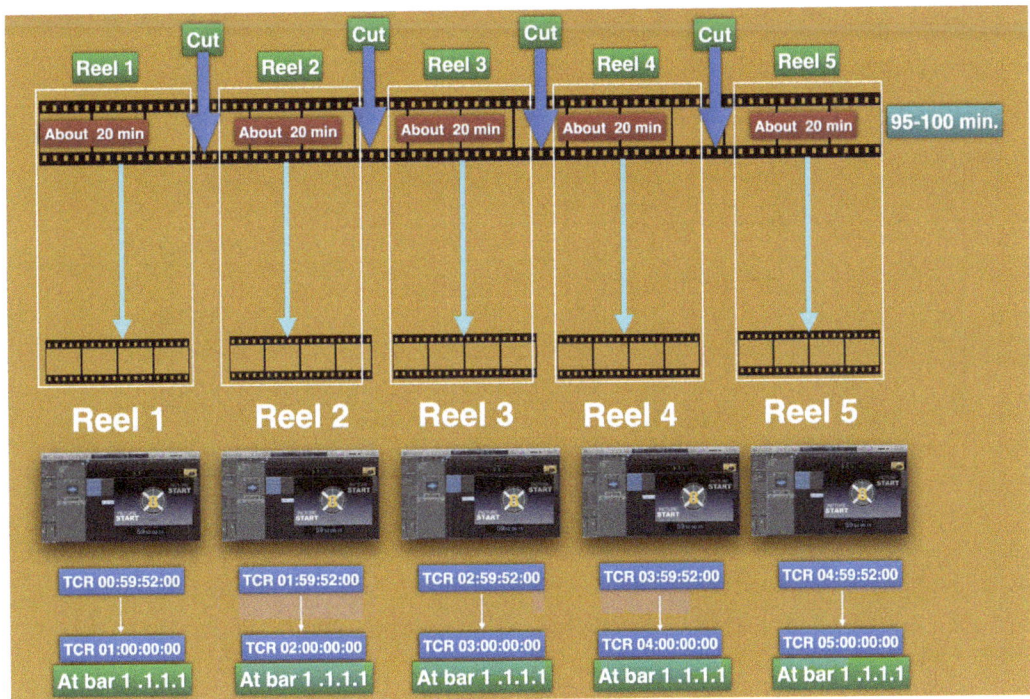

Figure 1.1: Film reels

So, if you are scoring 95-100 minutes of film, for example, you may want to ask the film director to cut the footage about every 20 minutes or so. The film director, however, makes the cuts based on the events and the story flow in the film, so they will not cut the reel in the middle of the story. In this example, you would end up with five reels in total.

In the case of a 60-minute film, you can request the director to cut the movie into 3 reels of 20 minutes each. You will work on one reel at a time. When you start composing to picture, you might end up with many different cues (or music pieces) inside the reel. Each cue might have a different revision until the director is completely satisfied with your score. Once the director is completely satisfied with each cue within the reel, including all the final revisions, and they've been approved, then you will move on to the next reel.

Next, we will examine how a film director or editor shares their notes on temp music and the directions that the film composer will need to follow.

Spotting notes

Spotting notes, also commonly known as **cue sheets**, are a list of important film cuts and descriptions that discuss the type of music that the film director is looking for. Cuts are also known as hit points, or spots where music needs to line up with important events in the film.

These spotting notes or cue sheets may or not be provided by the film director, depending on how the film company likes to work, but film composers will always have to make notes. If the film director doesn't provide the written notes ahead of time, either way, the film composer will have to make notes during the spotting session meeting.

The following figure shows an example of some spotting notes:

Cue	Time Code In (music start time)	Time Code Out (music end time)	Music Description/ Mood	Reference/Temp Music
1m1	01:00:00:00	01:03:43:18	Orchestral dark theme	In the temp track
1m2	01:03:51:18	01:04:11:17	Short quirky mood	In the temp track
1m3	01:05:57:21	01:08:30:24	Celtic mood	In the temp track
1m4	01:08:33:11	01:11:13:07	Irish mood	In the temp track
1m5	01:11:15:07	01:12:34:05	Orchestral epic mood	In the temp track
1m6	01:13:05:05	01:14:05:03	Orchestral happy mood	In the temp track
1m7	01:18:18:21	01:20:26:18	Orchestral adventure	In the temp track

Figure 1.2: Cue sheet example

This cue sheet example presents a general idea of what type of information should be included at a minimum (some cue sheets may be more elaborate or different based on what film company you are working with).

As we learned earlier, a feature film can be divided into, for example, five reels. In the preceding cue sheet example, in the **Cue** column, you can see a description of **1m1**. Here, the first number represents the reel, **m** stands for music, and the second number represents the cue. So, **1m1** means reel one, music cue one; **1m2** means reel one, music cue two; and so forth.

The list of time codes in the **Time Code In** and **Time Code Out** columns is where the music should start and end for each cue. Time codes will be discussed in more detail in the next chapter.

For each music cue, you should know what the director's intentions are. The fourth column, **Music Description/Mood**, describes what the music's intended feel/mood should be at specific points in the film. Since most film directors are not familiar with music terminology, they will tell you what they want via emotions or feelings they want to evoke, or what style and genre of music they want. This is often discussed during the meeting.

During the meeting

During the spotting session, both the film composer and director watch the film together, go through the spotting notes, and talk about the film director's vision for the film and the role that the music will play in it. This is an important time for you to ask as many questions as you need to understand the director's vision and get the job done.

In the meeting, you will open a movie file that should be synced in Logic Pro, along with the **burnt-in timecode (BITC)** window that the editor will give you so that you can make specific notes about the film's events. The film director will point to a specific timecode location and, from that, you will write a specific music cue.

In the following BITC example, you can see that the window shows **TC 01:00:00:00**. TC stands for timecode, the first two numbers refer to hours, the next two for minutes, followed by seconds, and then frames. So, if the director asks for the music to start at this timecode, they are asking for music to start exactly at the 1 hour, 0 minutes, 0 seconds, 0 frames mark:

Figure 1.3: Movie with BITC example 1

As another example, the director may ask you to write music 13 seconds into the film. This would be reflected by a timecode of **TC 01:00:13:00** – that is, 1 hour, 0 minutes, 13 seconds, 0 frames:

Figure 1.4: Movie with BITC example 2

Without the timecode window in the movie, you will not know whether your DAW is synced to the picture. This process will be discussed in more detail in the next chapter.

The process of reviewing spotting notes might also involve looking at the provided temp track list from the cue sheet. The two of you will likely consider questions such as the following:

- Where should music be playing and where should there be silence?
- What should the music be doing in this or that scene?
- What does the director want the audience to feel?

The film director will use mood descriptions, also referred to as buzzwords, instead of musical terms to describe how they want the music to be. For example, they may ask you to compose music that is magical and, at the same time, mysterious. For reference, the following chart lists some commonly used mood descriptions:

Figure 1.5: Moods in film music

The film director may also send you additional YouTube links as examples, to help describe the mood, and you should include those in the Reference/Temp Music column (shown in *Figure 1.2*). The film composer should take notes of these descriptions while reviewing the film.

Using music to convey complex emotions while using moods

Expressing moods in music composition can be challenging – the film composer has to use the music to convey a very complex set of emotions to the audience, in a way that is effective yet subtle, and that does not draw too much attention to itself. If the music is too obvious, the score is no longer effective, and the audience will be focusing on the music rather than the story.

The composer uses tools such as musical instruments, sample libraries, and recording equipment to reflect the emotional state of a character or scene in support of the underlying drama. The film score can greatly deepen the visual experience by providing "the right sound" that triggers emotions in the viewers. It helps viewers absorb all of what a complex scene presents.

When watching a movie, have you noticed that when the main character appears, a specific musical phrase will play each time they appear? Each main character can have a musical theme known as a **leitmotif** (this comes from a German term that means "leading motive"). Think of the menacing music that plays when Darth Vader appears in Star Wars. That signature sound or so-called leitmotif helps the audience identify characters with ease amid sound effects, dialogue, action, the main score, and more.

End of the meeting

The end of the meeting is a good time to ask the director how the final score needs to be delivered. This means either scoring using a computer (commonly referred to as "in the box") or utilizing a live orchestra. Scoring "in the box" is relatively inexpensive compared to a live orchestral session. The director's choice, based on the film production's budget, will determine the outcome.

Now that we've discussed the spotting session and how the composer will know exactly what the music needs to do, next, we'll talk about what character traits will greatly impact the quality of your work.

What are the character qualities of a successful film composer?

A composer who can write brilliant music for a performance may not be able to write equally brilliant music for a film if they are lacking in some of the areas outlined here.

The following are important character qualities that a film composer should possess:

- **An open mind**: The ability to follow directions and take on other people's ideas without holding on to or forcing your own ideas and thinking
- **Full of inspiration**: Taking initiative and coming up with helpful and creative ideas that will contribute to the film director's overall vision
- **Empathy**: The ability to relate to others' experiences in many different life situations
- **Spiritually inclined**: This enables you to focus more on others than yourself, and helps you sense and understand the needs of others
- **Intuitive**: The ability to anticipate situations that may come up so that you can be a contributor instead of a spectator
- **Good listener**: Being attentive to what is being said will help you interact and execute what is being asked of you
- **Attention to detail**: The ability to execute all the tasks successfully and thoroughly no matter how small or large the project is and deliver it without any problems
- **Positive attitude**: Easy to get along with, agreeable, diplomatic, motivated, humble, not dwelling on problems and difficulties, learns from mistakes, and confident
- **Motivated**: Having an attitude of taking challenges as opportunities is a key to repeated clients

As important as it is to work on your character traits, it's equally important to work on your technical level of expertise. We will look at this next.

What skills are required of a film composer?

In a constantly evolving film industry, the expectations and challenges for film composers require certain preparation and skill levels. Here are some:

- Able to play at least one musical instrument
- Strong music theory, harmony, and improvization skills
- Efficiently arrange and orchestrate music
- Write music quickly for delivery
- Strong knowledge in using computer technology such as Logic Pro (DAW)
- Mix your own music
- Create orchestral mockups
- Compose a variety of different styles and genres of music
- Able to score to picture in Logic Pro (DAW)
- Create music with a limited amount of time and resources
- Good time management and organization skills
- Good knowledge of the business of music, including the costs of orchestras, recording sessions, and budgeting

You don't need to have all of these skills right away as you venture into film music, but you'll want to keep working on these areas to help you reach your desired potential.

Summary

Thus far, we have taken time to understand what film music and the film music industry are by touching on the history of scoring, what a spotting meeting is, what cue sheets are, and having a very brief look at delivering a score. We also reviewed the challenging aspect of conveying emotion through music to the audience, as well as the character qualities and skills that are expected of a film composer.

In the next chapter, we will be looking at film scoring terminology, as well as how to use film and music components when scoring to picture.

2
Understanding Film Scoring Terminology

To further prepare yourself for the challenging tasks of a film and multimedia composer, familiarizing yourself with film scoring terminology is vital. Not only do you need to know this terminology when you're working in Logic Pro but you also need to be able to communicate clearly with the industry professionals that you're going to be working with.

In this chapter, you will learn film scoring terminology that will help you to set up a movie file in a Logic Pro session.

We will cover the following topics:

- What is SMPTE timecode?
- What is BITC?
- What is the academy leader?
- Errors in drop frame and non-drop frame timecodes
- Exploring SMPTE and BITC errors
- Reviewing correct SMPTE timecodes in individual reels
- Reviewing dialogue and temp music

What is SMPTE timecode?

SMPTE stands for **Society of Motion Picture and Television Engineers**. This society created a timecode clock that allows both components of audio and video to synchronize with one another, referred to as **SMPTE timecode**.

SMPTE timecode is a format for labeling and identifying frames in a video and serves as a reference point for all involved in the post-production stage. It is referred to as absolute time because it has a constant, unchanging speed as compared to music where the speed can vary, referred to as relative time, when scoring to picture.

Here is an example: **01:03:07:15**. This group of numbers gives each frame in a film a specific location. The first group of 2 numbers (01) are the hours, the second 2 numbers (03) are the minutes, the third 2 numbers (07) are the seconds, and the last 2 numbers (15) are the number of frames. So, this timecode represents 1 hour, 3 minutes, 7 seconds, and 15 frames into the film.

> **Note**
> In the United States, the timecode starts with the first movie frame at 01:00:00:00, whereas in Great Britain, the timecode starts with the first movie frame at 10:00:00:00.

Additionally, you may find some other details provided to you by the film director before the timecode. There is no difference between any of them; it's just that the company may use these different labels, based on their preferences:

- **TC 01:07:03:14**: TC simply stands for timecode
- **TCR 01:07:03:14**: TCR stands for timecode recorded
- **John Smith 01:07:03:14**: Here, John Smith is the name of the composer

Now that we understand what SMPTE timecode is, next, we will look at what we call it when this timecode is superimposed on a movie.

What is BITC?

BITC stands for **Burnt-In Timecode**. It is also referred to as "burn," "window burn," "burn in," or "burnt in," depending on who you're working with. BITC is the SMPTE timecode superimposed on top of a movie, which you can see in *Figure 2.1*:

Figure 2.1: Movie file with the BITC

The SMPTE timecode is the group of numbers on the clock; the BITC is the numbers superimposed on a movie file. The following figure shows how the SMPTE timecode becomes a BITC:

Figure 2.2: SMPTE timecode and BITC

SMPTE timecode and BITC are synchronization tools used to help sync your movie in Logic Pro, which will allow you to sync your music to the film accurately. We will discuss how to use these tools in Logic Pro from *Chapter 4* onward.

Next, we will talk about the academy or universal leader, which is also a tool used for synchronization.

What is the academy leader?

The **academy leader** (also known as the universal leader, countdown leader, movie header, or countdown clock) is a movie file with a countdown clock on it, placed at the start of the movie, and is generally 8 seconds in length. It tells you when the movie will start by counting down from the number displayed in the middle of the movie window. In some instances, the composer may receive the countdown clock with the BITC included on it.

Figure 2.3 is an example of a movie window with the 8-second countdown clock and the BITC at the bottom of it.

Figure 2.3: Movie window with the 8-second academy leader

In the past, it was added to the beginning of the movie and used to synchronize movie reels with one another on multiple projectors. Today, it is mostly used to help synchronize the movie file with the score.

Sometimes the countdown clock will have the words **PICTURE START** at the beginning of the countdown clock rather than a number, but it is still an 8-second countdown clock.

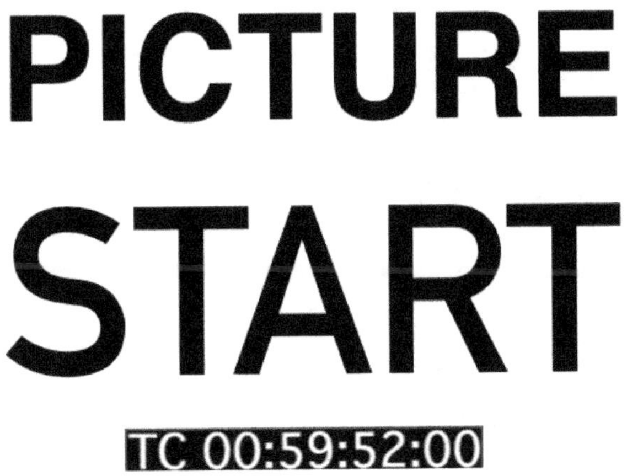

PICTURE START

TC 00:59:52:00

Figure 2.4: Movie window with the 8-second PICTURE START academy leader with BITC

It's also possible for the words **PICTURE START** to be replaced with any other images or words (this is less common though), but still, it is an 8-second countdown clock.

> **Note**
> The synchronization process and all topics here, including how the countdown clock is implemented and applied inside Logic Pro, will be discussed in more detail in later chapters.

Next, we will be discussing the audible pops that occur within the countdown clock.

What is a 2-pop?

A **2-pop** (also known as a sync pop) is a 1 kHz tone that is placed at the end of the countdown clock. It is usually found within the audio track, and it occurs 2 seconds before the first frame of the film. As mentioned earlier, the first movie frame starts at **TC 01:00:00:00**, so the 2-pop occurs at **TC 00:59:58:00** during the countdown. Often, but not always, you will receive a movie file from the film director with a 2-pop in it to help with synchronization.

Figure 2.5 is an audio track with an arrow marking the location of the 2-pop:

Understanding Film Scoring Terminology

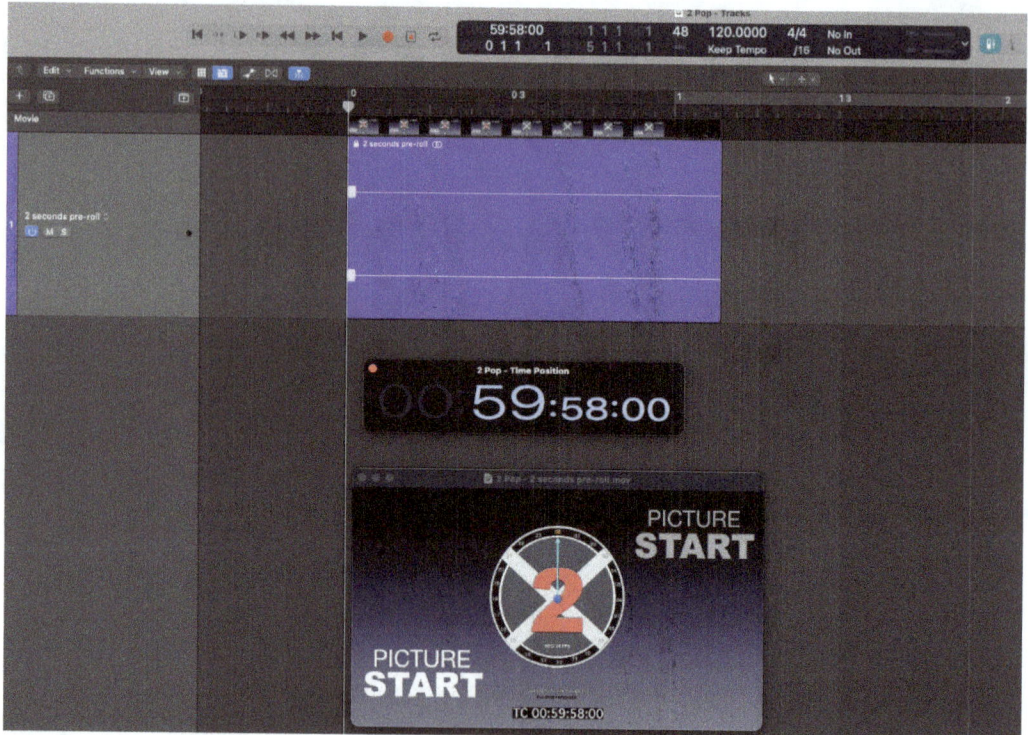

Figure 2.5: Audio file with 2-pop

When you send the director your first reel for approval, this will be in the form of an exported audio file of your score. The 2-pop inside of the audio file will allow the film director to accurately sync the audio file to their timeline in the video editing software.

After receiving your music with the 2–pop, the director will zoom in so that they can see the audio as a block, and that makes it easier to line up the 2-pops. *Figure 2.6* is an audio file with the 2-pop and the director's timeline that the audio file will be synced with:

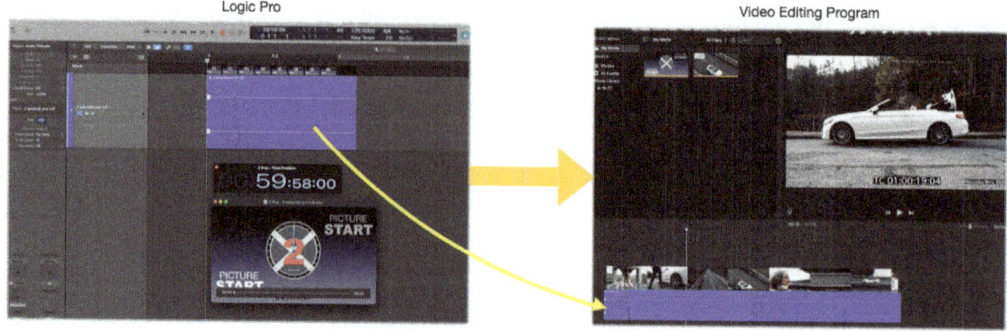

Figure 2.6: Audio file with a 2-pop and the Final Cut Pro timeline

When you are writing an action cue, for example, there may be a lot of tempo and time signature changes, so if your 2-pop is in the right spot, and correctly exported for the director's review, then that will help to keep everything in sync.

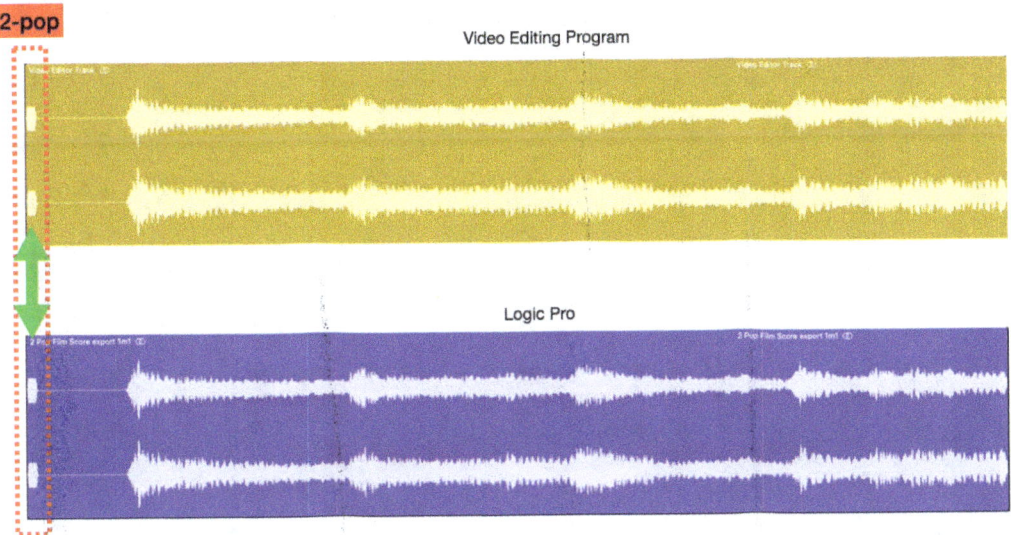

Figure 2.7: Film director's timeline with 2-pop sync

As another example, if your music starts off softly, without the 2-pop, the director would not be able to line up the music to their film accurately.

What is a 3-pop?

A **3-pop** is 2 short-sounding 1 kHz tones occurring one after the other that are placed at **TC 00:59:57:00** – 3 seconds before the first frame of the movie. The 3-pop is generally used in TV programs. Where the audible pops occur will depend on the preferences of the film director.

The 2-pop follows the 3-pop, occurring at **TC 00:59:58:00**. This can also be referred to as a 3-2 pop.

Figure 2.8 shows an audio file with the location of the 3-pop (also referred to as a double pop or 3-2 pop). The blue area in the following screenshot represents an audio file with a 3-pop and a 2-pop. Under that is the movie file with the BITC followed by an internal Logic Pro timecode display.

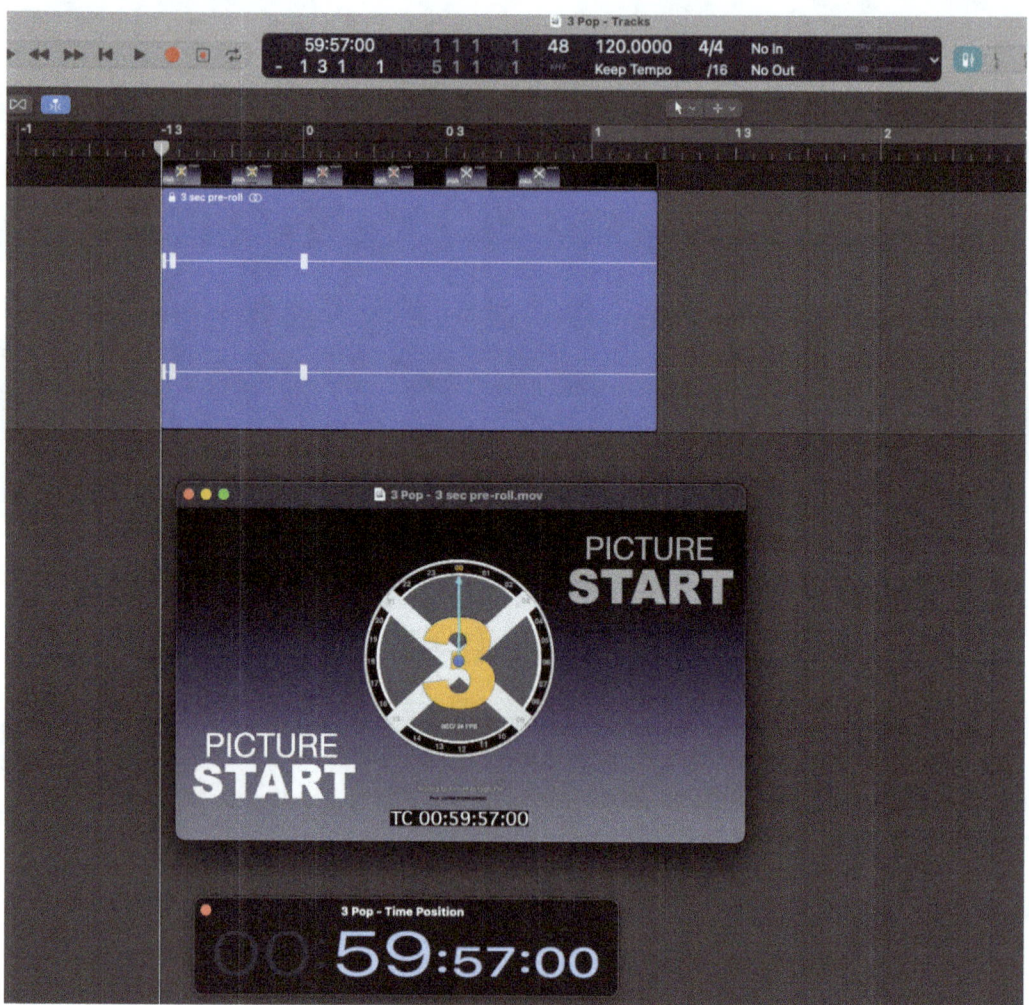

Figure 2.8: Audio file with a 3-pop

What is an end pop?

An **end pop** occurs at the end of a reel, 2 seconds after the reel ends. When the film director cuts the movie for the film composer in five different reels, for example, they add an end pop to mark the location of the cuts between the reels. Its main purpose, when exporting your final score for the post-production house, is to help them synchronize your music with the main picture cut.

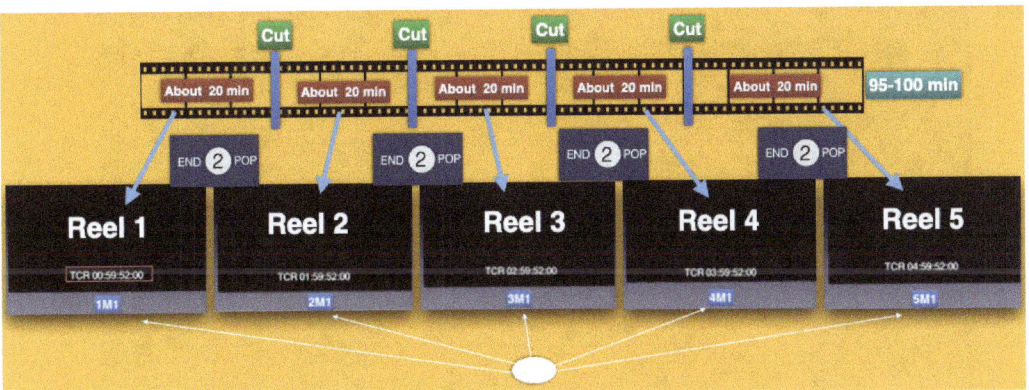

Figure 2.9: Five reels with end pops

The variety of available 1 kHz tones is essential in the process of working with film music or television since they provide a solid platform for synchronization.

By default, film editing companies don't always provide an end pop in a film for the film composers. If you want to have an end pop included in a film, you may have to request it from the director.

Next, we will talk in more detail about 2 and 3 second pre-rolls. A **pre-roll** is a vehicle that carries the 1 kHz tone for synchronization purposes. Pre-rolls are also used to share the progress of your work with the film director so that they can perfectly align your work with their footage.

What is a 2 second pre-roll?

A **2 second pre-roll** is a movie file that is attached to the front of the movie and is 2 seconds in length. The 2-pop occurs at the beginning of the pre-roll, at the 2 second mark, before the timecode turns **TC 01:00:00:00**. The purpose of the pre-roll is to help with synchronization, as long as the 2-pop is included in it.

Figure 2.10: A 2 second pre-roll with 2-pop

The 2 second pre-roll is commonly used in the world of advertising, but advertising companies may or may not send the film composer the movie file with the 2 second pre-roll. So if they don't provide you with a pre-roll, you will need to ask for it, making sure that it has a 2-pop attached to it.

What is a 3 second pre-roll?

A 3 second pre-roll is a movie file that is attached to the front of the movie and it's normally 3 seconds in length. It can have either a double pop or a 3-2 pop. The purpose of the pre-roll is to help with synchronization, as long as it has a double pop or 3-2 pop included in it.

Figure 2.11: A 3-second pre-roll with 3-pop

The 3 second pre-roll is commonly used in the world of TV production. However, television companies may or may not send the film composer the movie file with the 3 second pre-roll, so if they don't provide you with a pre-roll, you will need to ask for it, making sure that it has a 3-pop in it.

It's recommended that the 1 kHz tone be included with a pre-roll, which is provided by the film director, because that will allow for more accurate synchronization.

Next, we will talk about errors in a BITC, which involves drop frame and non-drop frame rates.

Errors in drop frame and non-drop frame timecodes

Timecodes are a labeling system, and the frame rate is the speed of **frames per second** (**fps**). The speed of black and white TV broadcasting in the USA was originally 30 fps as a non-drop frame. When color TV was introduced in 1953, the speed of the frame rate was slowed down to a 29.97 fps drop frame, so that the millions of people who had black and white TVs could also receive color TV programs without any visible artifacts.

With the invention of electronic video tape editing in the 1960s, SMPTE timecode was introduced and allowed each individual frame to be labeled. The frame number of the timecode was dropped in the labeling system without any changes to the frames of the video itself. It was done by dropping 2 frames each minute, except every 10th minute, in the SMPTE timecode labeling.

For the film composer, it is important to identify and check with the film director/editor what the correct frame rate is. Let's review the drop and non-drop frame timecodes.

The **drop frame** (**DF**) rates are identified by either a semi-colon or a period between the seconds and the frames in the timecode, as shown in *Figure 2.12*.

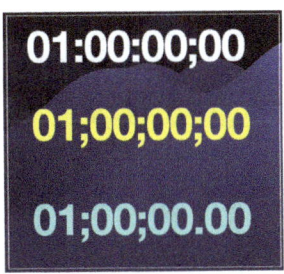

Figure 2.12: BITC with DF rates

The **non-drop frame** (**NDF**) rates are identified with all colons, as shown in *Figure 2.13*.

Figure 2.13: BITC with NDF rate

Sometimes, when a film director is preparing a movie file for a film composer and typing in the timecode numbers, they may put a semi-colon instead of a colon, or vice versa, in error. The most commonly used timecodes are used with non-drop frame rates so if anything is different in the BITC, you should verify with the film director whether it is valid or not. We will talk more about frame rates in *Chapter 3*.

Next, we will take a look at some errors that can occur when you receive a movie file from a film director, including incorrect SMPTE, BITC, and 2-pop placements. Knowing this information will help to identify and correct the movie file before you start working on it. It will also help you to know what to request from the film director.

Exploring SMPTE and BITC errors

As mentioned earlier, the countdown clock counts down 8 seconds as a pre-roll before the movie starts. Errors occur when the film director places the BITC in the "wrong" part of the film. This is the result of an incorrect SMPTE timecode. When the SMPTE timecode is incorrect, then the BITC will display the incorrect timecode and will be placed in the wrong part of the movie.

> **Note**
> Here, we're assuming that the timecode is wrong as an example, but some composers don't have a problem working with these errors and don't consider them errors at all.

Figure 2.14 is an example of a window "burnt in" with the incorrect timecode of **TC 01:00:00:00** (it should say **TC 00:59:52:00**):

Figure 2.14: BITC with incorrect timecode

As a result of this incorrect timecode placement, there will now no longer be a traditional pre-roll, with the 2-pop at **TC 00:59:58:00**. Instead, the 2-pop will occur at **TC 01:00:06:00**, as shown in *Figure 2.15*.

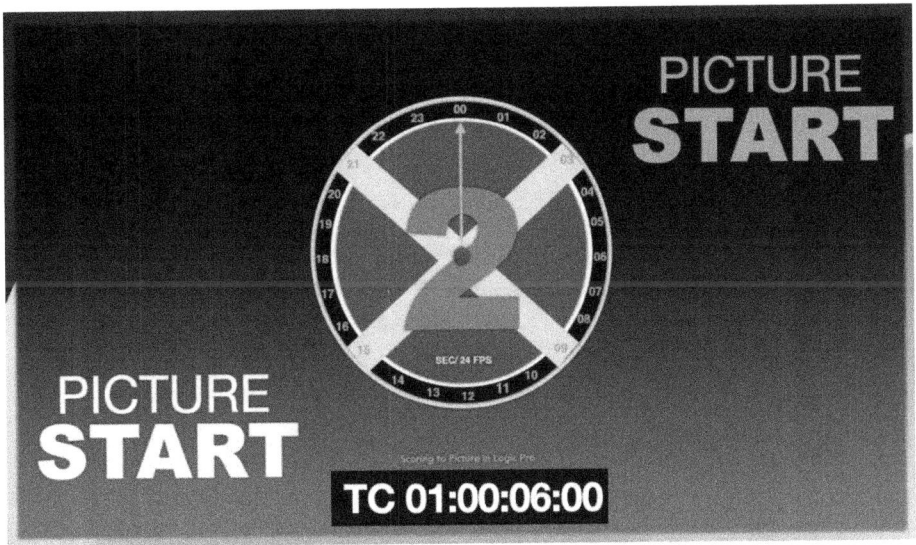

Figure 2.15: BITC with incorrect 2-pop

Since the Adobe Premiere software adds additional test footage of 2 or sometimes 3 seconds prior to the countdown, we'll have to consider and review the movie file to see what length it is and make sure the BITC is correct. Sometimes the film director may share a movie file with the film composer that has an incorrect placement of the BITC, so it's important to be aware of that.

Next, we will review examples of Adobe Premiere movie files with incorrect and correct BITC placements. *Figure 2.16* is an Adobe Premiere movie file with 2 seconds of additional footage, plus the 8-second countdown, which totals 10 seconds, with an incorrect BITC.

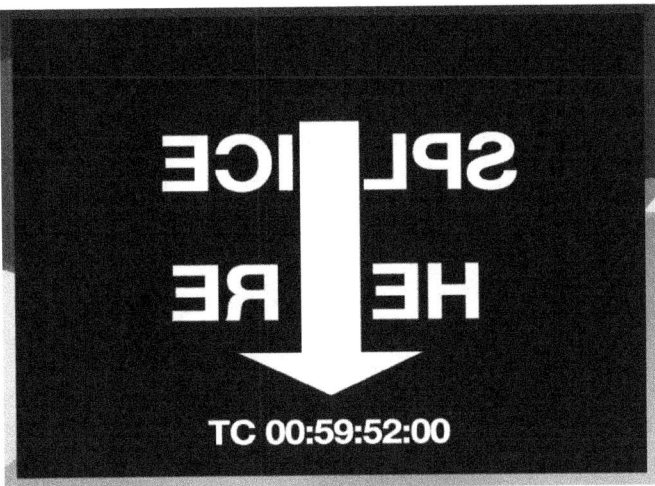

Figure 2.16: Adobe Premiere countdown with incorrect BITC

With the 2-second test footage added to the countdown, the BITC is shown as **TC 00:59:52:00**, which is incorrect. The correct BITC should be shown as **TC 00:59:50:00**, as shown in *Figure 2.17*:

Figure 2.17: Adobe Premiere countdown with correct BITC

Figure 2.18 is an Adobe Premiere pre-roll with 3 seconds of additional footage, plus the 8-second countdown, which totals 11 seconds, with an incorrect BITC:

Figure 2.18: Adobe Premiere 11-second pre-roll and countdown with incorrect BITC

With the 3-second test footage added to the countdown, the BITC is shown as **TC 00:59:52:00**, which is incorrect. The correct BITC is **TC 00:59:49:00**, as shown in *Figure 2.19*:

Figure 2.19: Adobe Premiere 11-second pre-roll and countdown with correct BITC

Often, when working on a movie file to be exported to a film composer, directors do not pay attention to, and may neglect, the correct timecode implementation; even if you get a movie with what seems to be the correct timecode implementation, you have to check both the beginning timecode of the film and the BITC of the 2-pop to make sure they are both correct.

In *Figure 2.20*, we can see that the BITC reflects the correct timecode of **TC 00:59:50:00**, with 2 seconds of added test footage plus the 8 seconds of the countdown, totaling 10 seconds:

Figure 2.20: Adobe Premiere pre-roll with correct BITC

As the film continues and you're observing the BITC progress, you would expect to see the BITC at **TC 00:59:58:00**. However, *Figure 2.21* shows the 2-pop occurring at **TC 00:59:57:00**, which is an error because the 2-pop doesn't match the BITC window.

Figure 2.21: Adobe Premiere pre-roll with incorrect 2-pop

It's important that the BITC and the 2-pop are in the right location to ensure proper synchronization.

When you recognize SMPTE and BITC errors, there are a couple of things you can do:

- If you want to make changes by yourself, and if you own Final Cut Pro or the Adobe Premiere software, you could re-embed the correct timecode window and share that with the director
- You could also mention it to your film director and ask for another copy of the movie files with the correct timecode placement

In the previous sections, we learned about the different types of errors that may occur in movie files and what to avoid when you receive a movie file from a film director. In the next section, we will look at how timecodes are correctly added to different reels.

Reviewing correct SMPTE timecodes in individual reels

In this section, we will review correct SMPTE timecodes in individual reels so that you know what they should look like and what you should ask for when working on multiple reels. Knowing this information will prepare you to score your film in Logic Pro more efficiently.

As mentioned previously, a feature film can be sliced into separate cuts or reels. *Figure 2.22* shows five different reels with different timecodes:

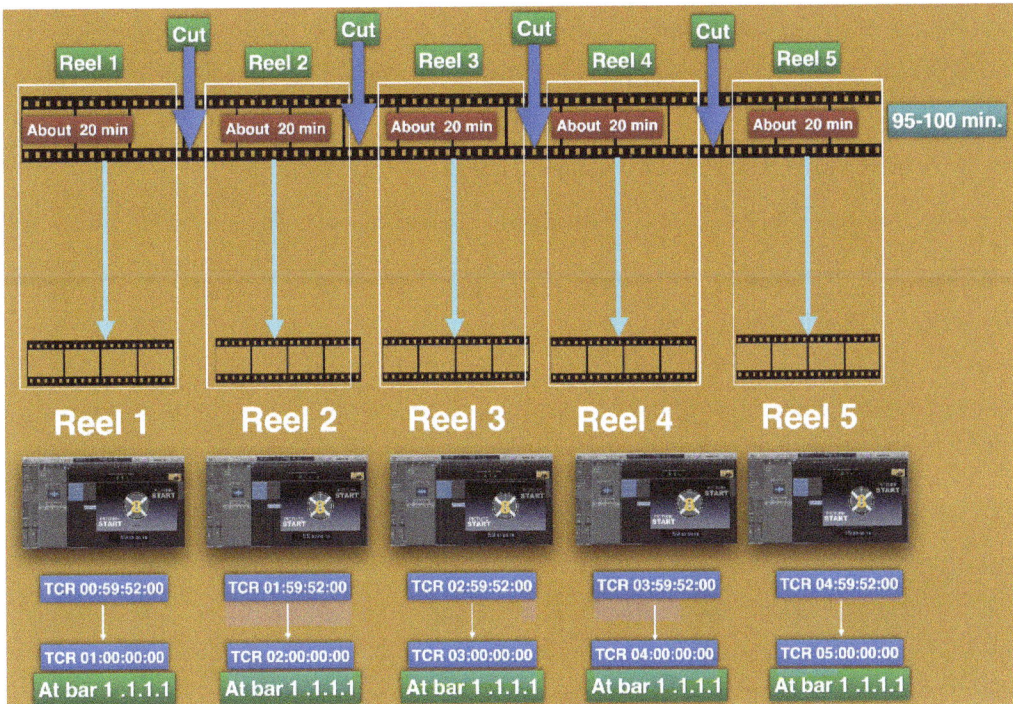

Figure 2.22: Film reels

We will now examine each individual reel with its BITC timecode, so that you know how to request reels with the correct BITC placement and 2-pop.

Figure 2.23 shows a countdown of Reel 1. The image on the left side shows the movie at the beginning of the reel, starting at **TC 00:59:52:00**. The image on the right side shows the passing of the 8-second countdown and the first frame where the film begins, at **TC 01:00:00:00**. Therefore the 2-pop should occur at **TC 00:59:58:00**.

Figure 2.23: Beginning of Reel 1 and the first frame of the movie in Reel 1

As a reminder, when you start composing music in Reel 1, for example, your consecutive cues can be indicated as **1m1**, **1m2**, **1m3**, and so on. When it comes to changes or revisions, you can rename them as **1m1_ver2**, and so on. This nomenclature for revisions helps you to chronologically track your changes and is crucial to have in the final delivery stage of your score so that each cue is properly labeled for export. This format and nomenclature should be applied to all reels.

When a film composer, for example, is finished writing all the cues for the film, each of the reels will be assembled with each consecutive cue per reel and delivered to the postproduction house for mixing. The postproduction house will gather all the music cues for all the reels and assemble them with the main footage for final mixing.

Figure 2.24 shows a countdown of Reel 2 with the BITC and the movie start time with the BITC. The second reel countdown starts at **TC 01:59:52:00** and the first movie frame starts at **TC 02:00:00:00**. Therefore the 2-pop should occur at **TC 01:59:58:00**. The timecodes in *Figure 2.24* remind us that we're still in Reel 2 because **TC 02:00:00:00** is always the timecode in the second reel.

Figure 2.24: Beginning of Reel 2 and the first frame of the movie in Reel 2

Renaming the hour section of the BITC timecode in each reel helps to maintain clear spotting notes for each reel and helps to keep track of revisions. It also helps the director or producer to track the reel you're working on while you're presenting your reel for approval.

Figure 2.25 shows a countdown of Reel 3 with the BITC and the movie start time with the BITC. The third reel countdown starts at **TC 02:59:52:00** and the first movie frame starts at **TC 03:00:00:00**. Therefore the 2-pop should occur at **TC 02:59:58:00**. The timecodes in *Figure 2.25* remind us that we're still in Reel 3 because **TC 03:00:00:00** is always the timecode in the third reel.

Figure 2.25: Beginning of Reel 3 and the first frame of the movie in Reel 3

Figure 2.26 shows a countdown of Reel 4 with the BITC and the movie start time with the BITC. The fourth reel countdown starts at **TC 03:59:52:00** and the first movie frame starts at **TC 04:00:00:00**. Therefore the 2-pop should occur at **TC 03:59:58:00**. The timecodes in *Figure 2.26* remind us that we're still in Reel 4 because **TC 04:00:00:00** is always the timecode in the fourth reel.

Figure 2.26: Beginning of Reel 4 and the first frame of the movie in Reel 4

Figure 2.27 shows a countdown of Reel 5 with the BITC and the movie start time with the BITC. The fifth reel countdown starts at **TC 04:59:52:00** and the first movie frame starts at **TC 05:00:00:00**. Therefore the 2-pop should occur at **TC 04:59:58:00**. The timecodes in *Figure 2.27* remind us that we're still in Reel 5 because **TC 05:00:00:00** is always the timecode in the fifth reel.

Figure 2.27: Beginning of Reel 5 and the first frame of the movie in Reel 5

After reviewing the BITC and the movie start time with the BITC of each reel, you will know what specific timecode you'll need when requesting reels from the film director. For example, when working on a film, to start with, you will want to reach out to the film director and request that they cut the entire film into five reels. You will also need to ask them to add to each reel a BITC with the correct timecodes as listed here:

- Reel 1: **TC 00:59:52:00**, with the first movie frame starting at **TC 01:00:00:00**
- Reel 2: **TC 01:59:52:00**, with the first movie frame starting at **TC 02:00:00:00**
- Reel 3: **TC 02:59:52:00**, with the first movie frame starting at **TC 03:00:00:00**
- Reel 4: **TC 03:59:52:00**, with the first movie frame starting at **TC 04:00:00:00**
- Reel 5: **TC 04:59:52:00**, with the first movie frame starting at **TC 05:00:00:00**

Additionally, you will want to ask the film director to provide you with the correct 2-pop placement, as described earlier.

Reviewing timecodes with Adobe Premiere

Individual reel timecodes that are provided to the film composer and created in Adobe Premiere will look slightly different, so here we will review a movie file that was created in Adobe Premiere and look at the correct SMPTE timecodes in individual reels.

In Adobe Premiere, before the countdown starts counting down the 8 seconds, the video editor might give you an additional test picture pre-roll attached to it that has 2 or 3 seconds before the countdown. In *Figure 2.28*, we can see the BITC start time of **TC 00:59:50:00**. That means that the entire length including the 2-second test footage and the 8-second countdown is 10 seconds in total.

Figure 2.28: Adobe Premiere countdown

When working with a film director who works in Adobe Premiere, you should request, as mentioned in the previous section, that they cut the entire film into five reels. Similarly, you will also need to ask them to add to each reel a BITC with the correct timecodes, as listed here:

- Reel 1: **TC 00:59:50:00**
- Reel 2: **TC 01:59:50:00**
- Reel 3: **TC 02:59:50:00**
- Reel 4: **TC 03:59:50:00**
- Reel 5: **TC 04:59:50:00**

Keep in mind that when you receive the Adobe Premiere file format video, as previously described, each reel will have 2 seconds of test footage and an 8-second countdown.

If the Adobe Premiere file format video has 3 seconds of test footage, you will have to ask the director to set the timecode as **TC 00:59:49:00** at the beginning of the footage, because now there will be 3 seconds of test footage with the 8-second countdown, so there will be 11 seconds before the timecode turns into **TC 01:00:00:00**.

Figure 2.29: Adobe Premiere with a 3-second pre-roll and an 8-second countdown

As you can see, there are often differences in how you receive a movie file. As long as the beginning timecode and the 2-pop location are in sync, you're good to go. That also means that you will need to set up your Logic Pro sessions properly to match this BITC window. That's why it is important to know what you need, how you're going to work, and how you're going to deliver the final approved music score.

After reviewing the countdown with a 2-pop and the correct BITC placement within the movie file, what follows is the task of adding dialogue and temp music.

Reviewing dialogue and temp music

Occasionally, you may receive from the film director a countdown that looks slightly different from the previous examples.

After the film director provides the movie file with the countdown and correct BITC, it is recommended that the dialogue and temp music be added to the audio track as a split track, with the dialogue being placed in the left channel and the temp music placed in the right channel.

In *Figure 2.30*, you can see that the director indicated the dialogue and temp music placement, as well as the reel number, the length of the reel, the frame rate, and the small window countdown.

Figure 2.30: Movie file with additional info and split audio channels

Unless you request this format, the film director might send you the dialogue track and the music cues separate from the film, or send you the dialogue track and YouTube temp music links.

If the audio file included with the movie file is a stereo file and has dialogue and temp music on it but not on separate audio channels, this will not allow you to separate the files from one another. This is crucial, since you always want independent control of the dialogue and the temp music and it will definitely improve your workflow.

We'll discuss importing a movie file into Logic Pro and extracting dialogue and music out of the film in more detail later in the book when synchronizing Logic Pro to picture.

Summary

In this chapter, we discussed general film scoring terminologies. We also learned how to identify errors and how to communicate with the director to receive the correct file.

Understanding the terminology will help speed up the process of using Logic Pro and help you to communicate within the general film industry before starting your project. It will also help you to be more efficient when working on film projects.

All the tools covered in this chapter will equip you to do all tasks in Logic Pro – you may or may not use all of these tools; it's up to each composer to use them as they see fit.

In the next chapter, we will discuss working with QuickTime Video.

3
Reviewing QuickTime Video and Video Components

Film directors will always give you a QuickTime movie file and so it's important that you understand the file type and how to handle and use it.

In this chapter, we will look at QuickTime video and its properties, including video codec, video size, and sample rate. We will also discuss QuickTime Video components, including video file types, codec, and movie file resolution, as well as audio sample rate, in detail, so that you will be prepared to use digital movie files properly in Logic Pro.

In this chapter, we will cover the following topics:

- Opening the QuickTime Inspector
- Understanding video file components

Technical requirements

To follow along with this chapter, you will need a Mac computer with Logic Pro and QuickTime software installed.

Opening the QuickTime Inspector

The QuickTime Inspector is a menu containing the movie file's properties. To open it, navigate to the upper taskbar and click **Window**, then **Show Movie Inspector**. Alternatively, you can use the *Command + I* keyboard shortcut. The movie file **Inspector** window will open as a black, floating dialog box:

Figure 3.1: Open QuickTime Video with the Inspector window

Now that we know what the QuickTime Inspector is, we will look at a few of the components that are included in the **Inspector** window.

Understanding video file components

In this section, we will take a look at two of the main components of the **Inspector** window – **General** and **Video Details** – looking at the settings that are most useful to a film composer.

For reference, *Figure 3.2* is a closer look at the **Inspector** window with its components:

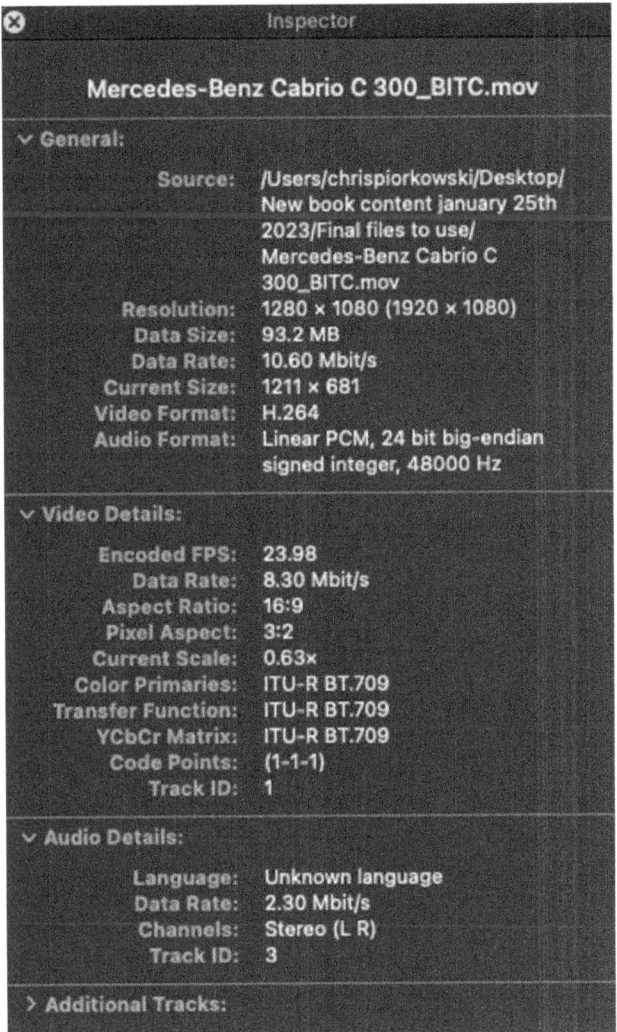

Figure 3.2: QuickTime Inspector window

Now, let's review the components that are important for a composer to understand.

General

Under **General**, we will look at four main settings – **Resolution, Data Size, Video Format**, and **Audio Format**.

Resolution

Video file resolution is referred to as the dimensions of a video file with x number of pixels. The **Resolution** section in *Figure 3.2* shows the video dimension as **1280 x 1080** for this movie file; that means the movie file is 1,280 pixels wide and 1,080 pixels high.

The more pixels the movie has, the larger the file is. For example, if you want to view your movie file on an external 50-inch TV, you will probably want to use a higher pixel ratio so that the movie file doesn't get blurry or pixelated. As another example, if you're using a laptop to view the movie file and you're concerned about the file size, disk space, and so on, then you may want to use a lower pixel ratio.

Once you decide what movie file resolution will work best for you, you could then either request a new movie file from the film director with the desired resolution or you could use a video program such as Final Cut Pro that will allow you to edit and change the movie file resolution yourself.

Data Size

The **Data Size** setting tells us how much space the movie file will occupy on your hard drive. The size of a movie depends on the duration of the entire movie file, and it could be 3 GB or 8 GB in size, for example. As we can see in *Figure 3.2*, it is **93.2 MB**.

When requesting a video file from the film director, keep in mind that an uncompressed movie file can be larger in size, based on its length, and a compressed movie file, in general, is smaller in size. You will want to be mindful of your computer system specifications so you know what movie file size will work best for you and your system.

If you're concerned about working with a larger-sized movie file, you could reduce the file size by using the Mac video compressor, iMovie, QuickTime, or Final Cut Pro applications.

If the movie file is streamed directly from the same disc that your Logic Pro project is using, it is recommended that you use an external SSD drive. *Figure 3.3* is an example of an external SSD drive connected to a MacBook Pro.

Figure 3.3: MacBook Pro with an external SSD drive

The SSD drive offers a faster way of streaming the movie file and also offers faster and more reliable performance. A traditional hard drive has a slower performance and is not as reliable because, on average, the longevity of the drive is around 2-3 years. It's important to consider the data size versus video compression of the movie file before opening it up in Logic Pro to make sure that your system can handle it, and so that your workflow is not interrupted.

Video Format

A video file format is a single metadata file within a video, referred to as a container, that holds media files, audio data, and the frame rate. There are different types of containers, and they are identified by different extensions, such as .mov or .dv, for example.

A so-called video codec is included in the video container and refers to how compressed or uncompressed the video files are. The most commonly used video file formats in the industry are .mov, .mp4, QuickTime Movie, MPEG-4, m4v, MPEG-2, MPEG-1, AVI, Motion JPEG, and DV. The most commonly used video codecs in the industry are MPEG-4, H.264, Apple ProRes 422, DV, Photo JPEG, Sorenson Video 2, and Sorenson Video 3. In *Figure 3.2*, **Video Format** is listed as **H.264** video codec.

As a film composer, understanding the basics of video file formats and video codecs can help you to manage storage space and to have a smooth and efficient playback on your computer system.

Recommended video file formats

The film director will give you a movie file that will be either compressed or uncompressed. In general, it is recommended to work with uncompressed movie files because a compressed movie file has to be uncompressed during playback, and that may use a substantial amount of the CPU, resulting in slower disk speed and less efficiency. For example, if you're working on a laptop that only has 8 GB of RAM and it does not have the fastest processor, you will want to request from the film editor or director a movie file format that has no compression.

The downside of an uncompressed movie file is that it might be large in size, but since there is now a significant amount of space available on a hard drive, that shouldn't be a problem. Saying that, when working with a computer that has a single hard drive, I would highly recommend that the movie file be saved in your Logic Pro project folder on an external SSD drive. This will free up more resources on the main drive of your computer and will result in better performance during your Logic Pro session playback. We will discuss saving the movie file within Logic Pro in *Chapter 4*.

A few of the video codecs that are uncompressed are Apple ProRes 422, DV, Photo JPEG, and Sorenson. In comparison, the H246 codec, which is the most used compressed movie file format, can put a lot of stress on your computer, because the main hard drive can become easily overloaded and then the movie file may play back a bit jittery. You should test your machine by opening different movie files of different lengths and different codec types to see how well your computer will perform. You will need to decide what movie file formats and video codecs will work best based on your computer system's specifications.

Audio Format

The **Audio Format** setting displays the **audio sample rate**. Looking at *Figure 3.2*, we can also see the audio sample rate, which is 48000 Hz (48 kHz). When working with video files, 48 kHz is the standard used in the industry today. Sometimes, however, the film director may send you a movie file with a different audio sample rate and so you will want to check with the director to make sure that the audio sample rate they gave you is correct. We will discuss the audio sample format in more detail in *Chapter 4*.

Video Details

Under **Video Details**, we will just look at one setting: **Encoded FPS**.

FPS stands for **Frames Per Second**. A frame represents a single still (not moving) image. In the example shown in *Figure 3.2*, the **Encoded FPS** rate is **23.98**. This means the movie file has 23.98 still images occurring sequentially per second.

When you open a movie file in Logic Pro software, Logic Pro automatically identifies the frame rate of the movie file. However, it's important to make sure that the frame rate on Logic Pro matches the one that the film director gives you.

Logic Pro software has a list of available frame rates, shown in *Figure 3.4*, and you will want to select the frame rate from the list that matches the movie file frame rate:

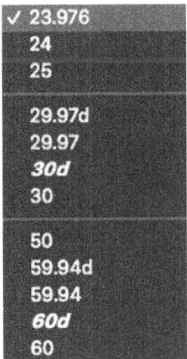

Figure 3.4: Frame rates

> **Note**
> There's one exception that is not available from the list, however. When you receive a film with 23.98 fps, since this frame rate is not in the list of available frame rates in Logic software, you will need to select the **23.976** fps.

As you can see, some of the numbers have the letter **d** at the end, such as **29.97d**. The **d** means that it is a drop frame rate. It's important to check with the film director to confirm whether the frame rate is a drop frame or a non-drop frame rate (discussed in *Chapter 2*), and then select the correct frame rate from the list.

Most popular DAWs, such as Logic Pro, are equipped with multiple frame rate options to match frame rates in a movie file. For reference, here is a list of frame rates most commonly used in the film and TV industry worldwide:

- 23.96 fps (and 23.98 fps), used for HD film
- 24 fps, used as standard for films in the USA
- 25 fps, used as standard for films in Europe
- 29.92 fps, used as standard for TV color video
- 30 fps, was used for black and white TV, but is now used as an HD format
- 50fps, 59.94fps, and 60 fps are commonly used in GoPro video

Each project has a different frame rate, so before scoring, it's important to set up Logic Pro with the same frame rate as the video you'll be working with. This will ensure that your music is perfectly in sync with the video.

Summary

In this chapter, you have learned how to open, review, and understand the QuickTime Player Inspector and its components. Understanding all of the components that were discussed will help you when opening a movie file in Logic Pro and will also help you to synchronize the movie file with Logic Pro.

In the next chapter, we will explain how to start and set up our first project, as well as how to open and synchronize a movie file within Logic Pro.

Part 2: Project Setup and Navigation

In this part, you will get an overview of the importance of aligning an imported movie file within a Logic Pro session, how to set up a movie file in Logic Pro, and how to sync Logic Pro to picture.

This part will also cover visual events, known as hit points, in a movie, including how to identify them correctly, how to put them together in lists, and how to represent them as SMPTE-locked markers.

This section contains the following chapters:

- *Chapter 4, Setting Up a Movie in Logic Pro*
- *Chapter 5, Syncing Logic Pro to Picture*
- *Chapter 6, Working with Hit Points and Scene Markers*

4
Setting Up a Movie in Logic Pro

In this chapter, we will go over how to set up a movie file in Logic Pro. It's important to know how to set up a movie file properly, including how to import a movie file, remove or replace an existing video, change the movie size, extract an audio file from a movie, and review movie project settings, to make sure everything works smoothly.

Knowing how to work with movie files in Logic Pro also helps improve and optimize your working environment for greater efficiency.

We will cover the following topics:

- Opening, saving, and closing a Logic Pro session
- Opening a movie file in Logic Pro
- Importing a movie file
- Saving a session with a movie file

Technical requirements

To follow along with this chapter, you will need a Mac computer with Logic Pro and QuickTime software installed. You will also need to use movie files provided with this book: https://packt.link/hxCer.

For easier access, before beginning the Logic Pro session, you can place the Logic Pro icon onto the dock on the desktop. To do this, navigate to the **Applications** folder, shown in *Figure 4.1*, and locate the Logic Pro app.

50   Setting Up a Movie in Logic Pro

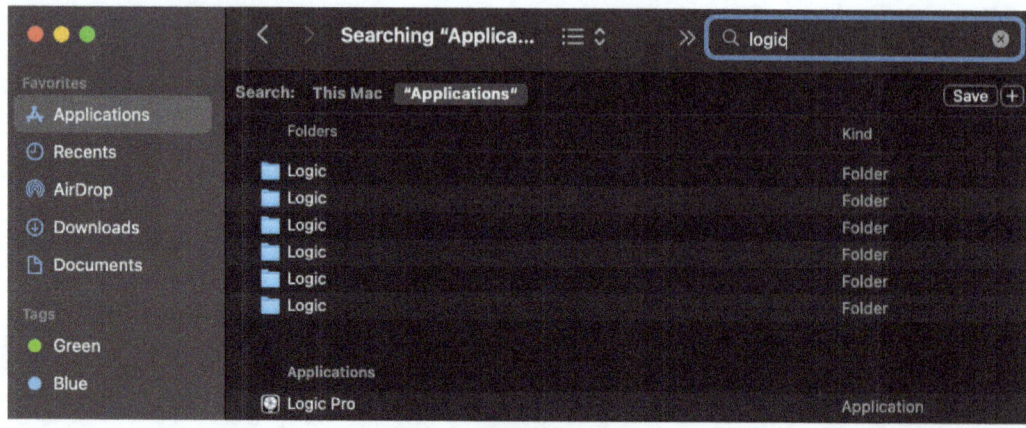

Figure 4.1: Applications folder

Next, drag and drop the Logic Pro icon onto the Apple dock, like so:

Figure 4.2: Logic Pro in the Apple dock

Opening, saving, and closing a Logic Pro session

To launch Logic Pro, double-click on the Logic Pro icon in the dock.

A Logic Pro session and a dialog box will open. Click on the **Audio** tab in the dialog box and set the **Number of tracks** field to 1. Then click **Create**.

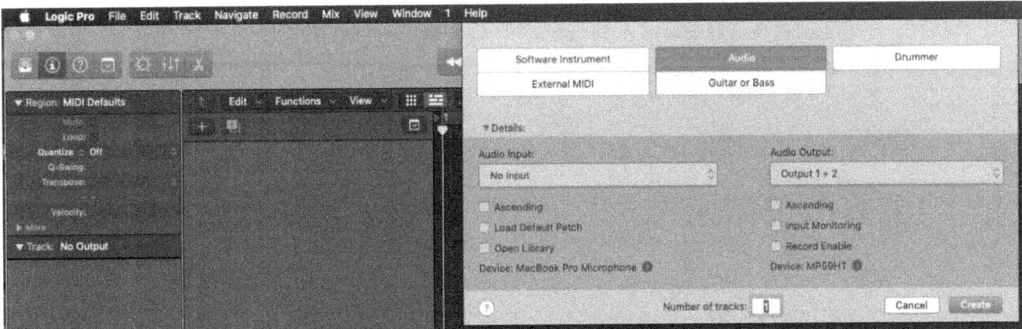

Figure 4.3: Logic Pro session dialog box

Logic Pro will create a single audio track:

Figure 4.4: Open the Logic Pro session with a single audio track

The next step is to save the Logic Pro session. To do this, go to **File** and hit **Save**. Give the session a name and select the location of where you want the file to be saved.

Once the session is saved, to close and quit, click on Logic Pro in the upper left corner and hit **Quit Logic Pro** from the drop-down menu.

Now that we've reviewed how to open, save, and close a Logic Pro session, next we will go over how to open a movie file in Logic Pro.

Opening a movie file in Logic Pro

There are a few ways to open a movie file in Logic. Let's look at them:

- The first option is to simply drag and drop the movie file into the Logic Pro workspace:

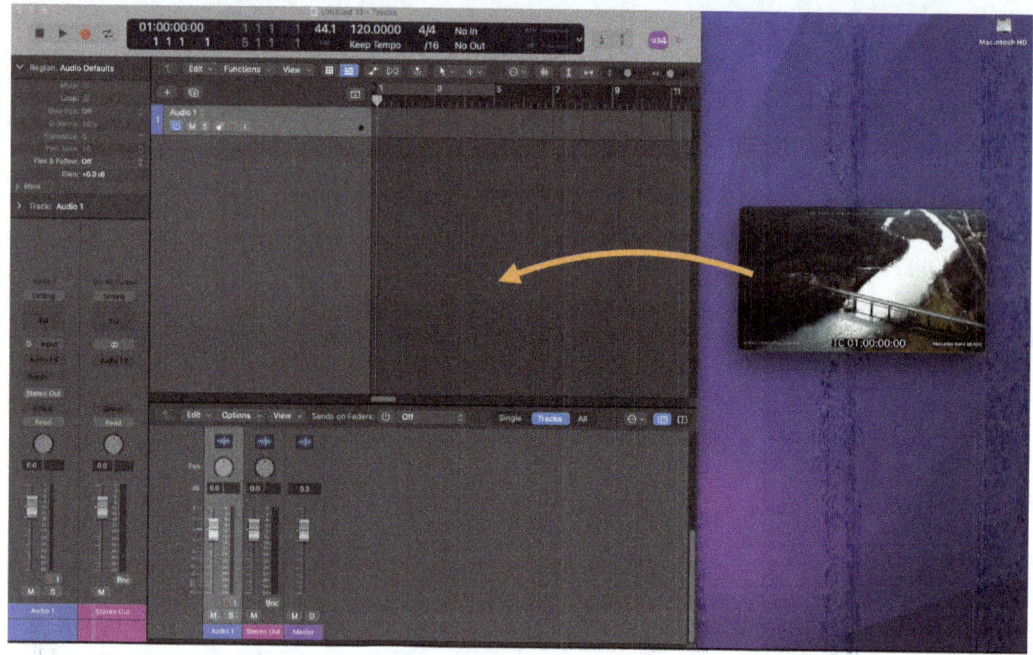

Figure 4.5: Dragging a movie file into a Logic Pro session

- The second option is to go to the Logic Pro menu and click on **File**, then **Movie**, then **Open Movie** (or use the shortcut *Option + CMD + O*):

Opening a movie file in Logic Pro   53

Figure 4.6: Logic Pro file menu

- The third option is to open **Global Tracks** (using the shortcut *G*) and then right-click on the global tracks and select **Movie** from the pop-up menu. This will make your movie track visible. An additional way to open the movie track is to hit *Option + G* and click on the box next to **Movie**. Then click on the up and down arrows on the movie track to open the menu, shown in *Figure 4.7*, and select **Open Movie…**:

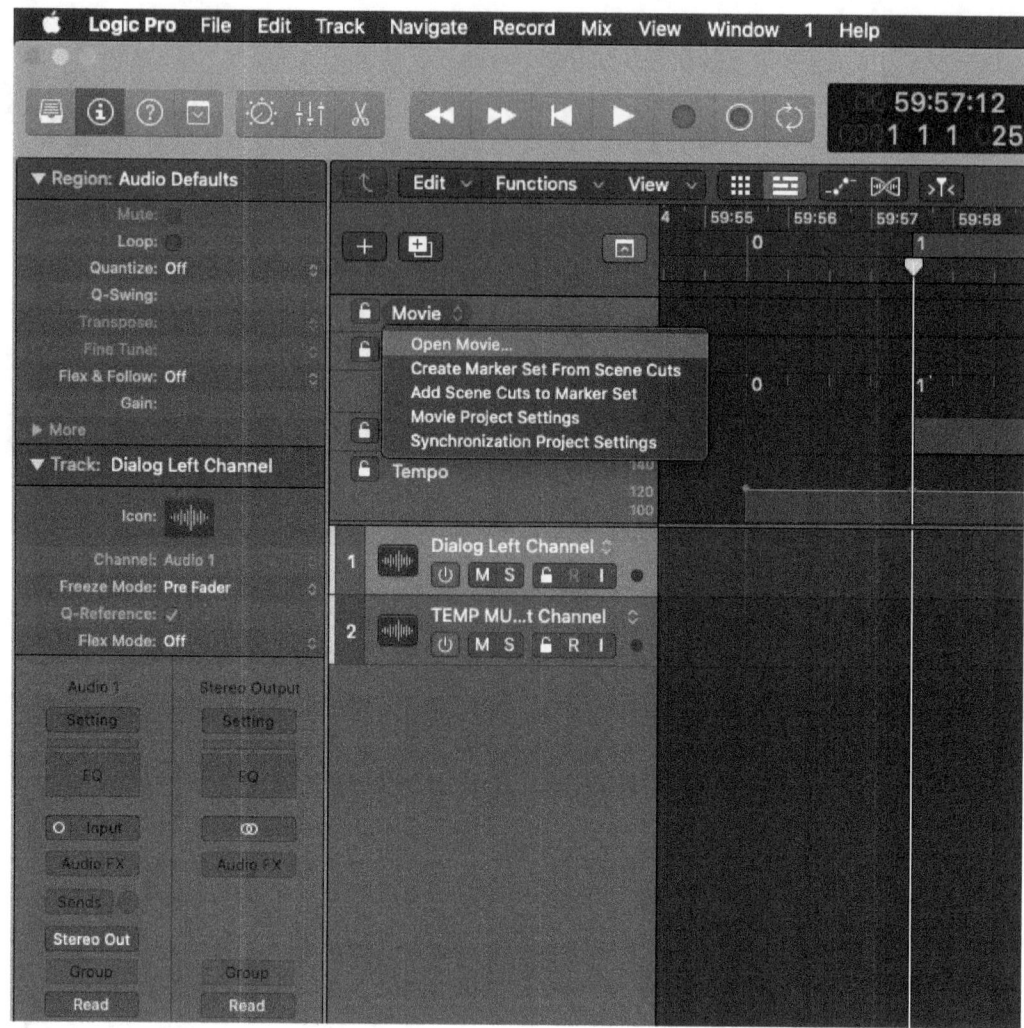

Figure 4.7: Opening a movie in Global Tracks

Once the movie is loaded, you then have a choice to remove and replace the movie. In order to remove the movie, click on the up and down arrows to open the menu, shown in *Figure 4.8*, and select **Remove Movie…**:

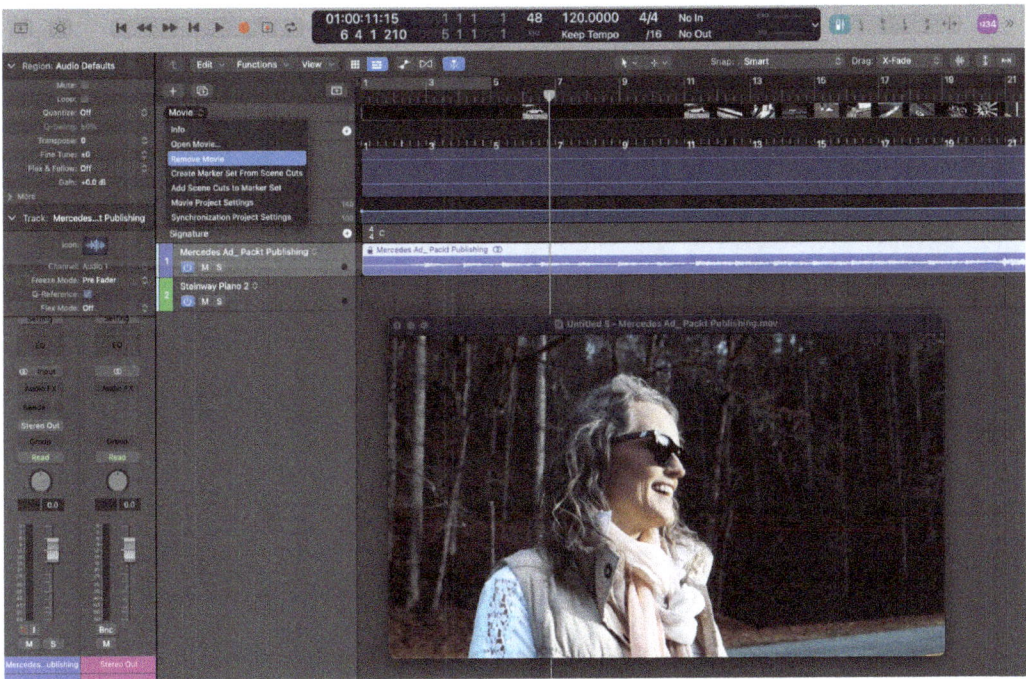

Figure 4.8: Removing a movie in Global Tracks

Now that we've discussed the three different ways to open a movie file, next, we will go over the entire process of importing a movie file step by step, including extracting the audio and setting up the sample and frame rate.

Importing a movie file

To review the entire movie file process, we will use the `Mercedes-Benz.mov` file, which you can find through the link in the *Technical requirements* section. You can import the file using any of the three methods we discussed, before moving on to the first stage.

Extracting audio from a movie file

After opening the movie file, an **Open Movie** dialog box will appear. As shown in *Figure 4.9*, Logic Pro gives you options to open or not to open a movie file, and the option to extract or not extract the audio track.

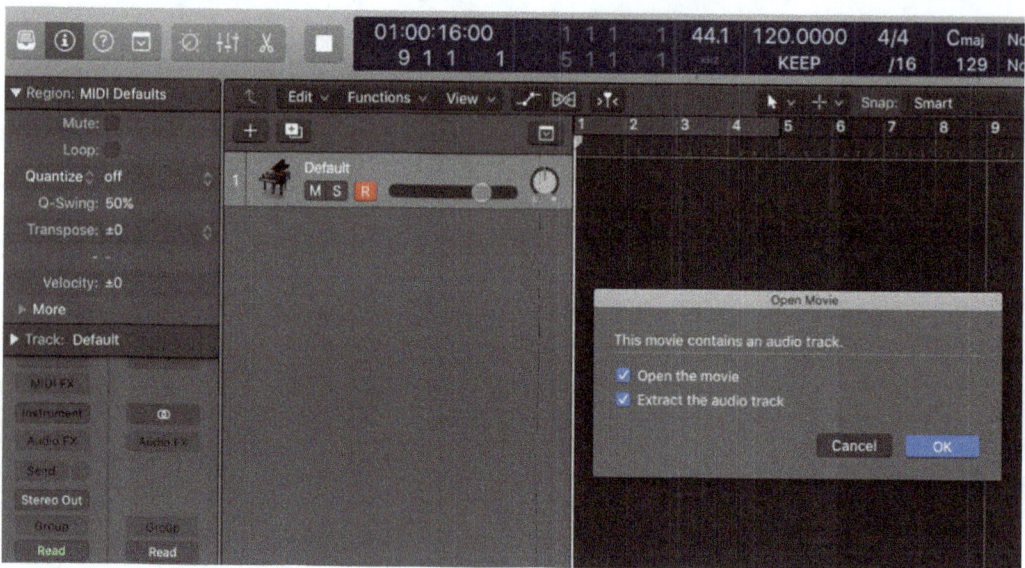

Figure 4.9: Open Movie dialog box

There may be times when only the audio file needs to be extracted without opening the movie and vice versa, but in general, **Open the movie** and **Extract the audio track** should be checked. Make sure that you do that now.

Setting up the sample rate

After selecting the option for opening the movie and extracting the audio track, Logic Pro will open another dialog box, prompting you to confirm the correct sample rate, as seen in *Figure 4.10*. Even though Logic Pro identifies the sample rate automatically, you should still keep in mind and know the sample rate of the audio file you will be importing, so that you select the matching sample rate.

Figure 4.10: Sample rate dialog box

If your prior Logic Pro session was, for example, set to 44.1 kHz, Logic Pro will ask whether you want to use that setting or change to 48 kHz for this session. In this example, you should click on **Use 48.000 Hz** (48.000 Hz equals 48 kHz).

Setting up the frame rate

After confirming the sample rate, Logic Pro will identify the frame rate of your movie file using another dialog box. If your prior Logic Pro session was using a different frame rate, Logic Pro will ask whether you want to use that frame rate or change to the suggested frame rate.

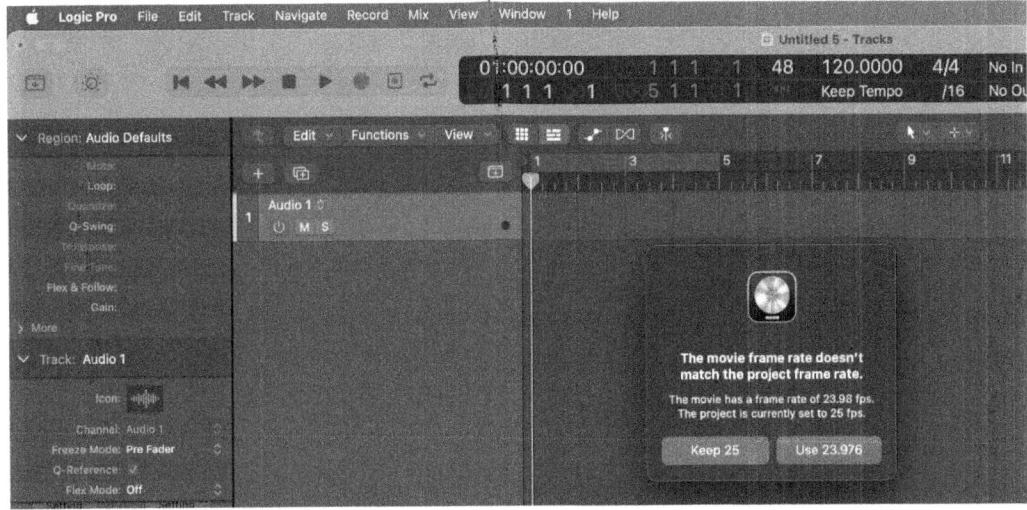

Figure 4.11: Frame rate dialog box

It's important you know the original move file frame rate before opening the movie file and confirming the correct frame rate. Logic Pro is mostly accurate when recognizing the movie frame rate, but there are times when it may not be accurate.

Confirm the frame rate of the imported movie file and click **Use 23.976**.

Moving and adjusting the position of the movie

When you open a movie, Logic Pro displays a movie region on the movie track and the accompanying audio region below the movie region with the padlock icon as SMPTE locked. That movie file can be moved on the Logic Pro timeline as a regular region, but the movie region can't be edited.

Sometimes when you drag and drop a movie file into a Logic Pro session, Logic Pro doesn't automatically place the movie file at the beginning of the session. In order to move the movie to the beginning of the session, place the playhead at bar 1:

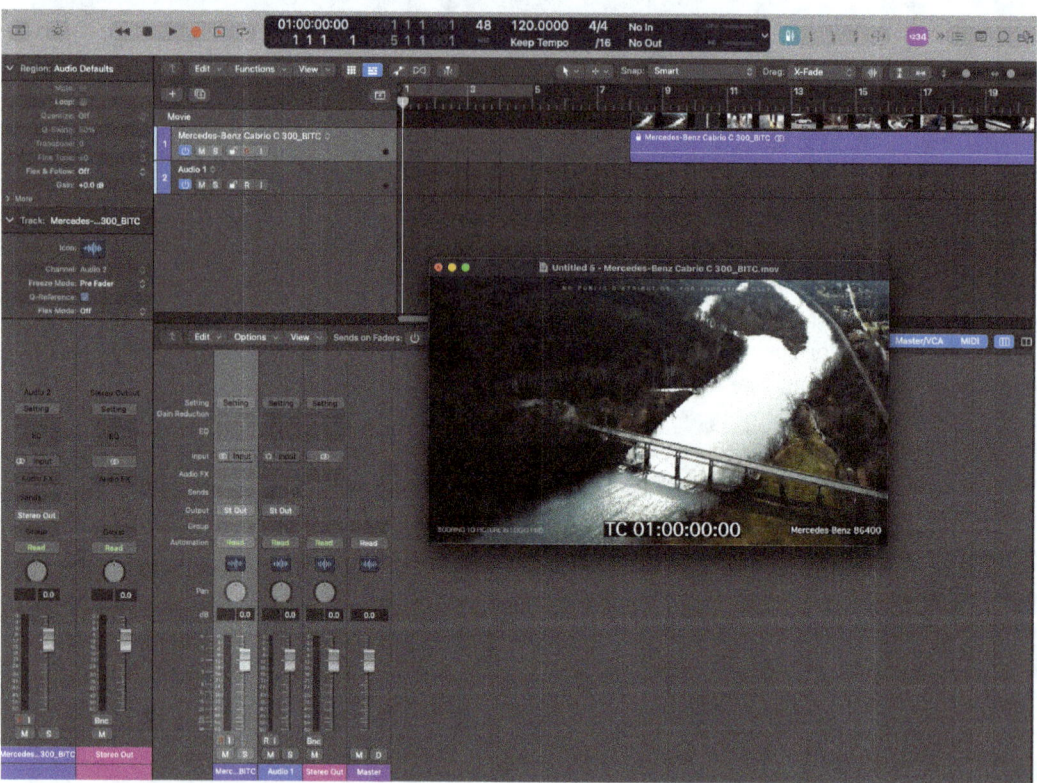

Figure 4.12: Playhead at bar 1

Once the playhead is at bar 1, hover your mouse over the movie track, right-click on it, and select **Move Movie Region to Playhead** from the drop-down menu:

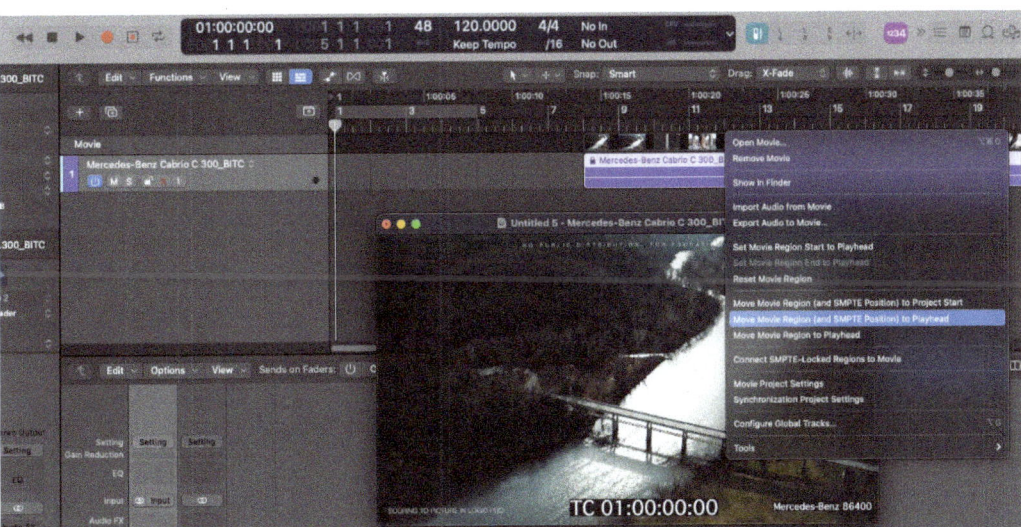

Figure 4.13: Move Movie Region to Playhead

Another way to move the movie file to the playhead is to right-click on the movie file window and select **Move Movie Region (and SMPTE Position) to Playhead**.

The movie file and the audio file are linked together and will then snap to the bar 1 location. There will also be a padlock on the audio region, showing that the movie is locked into position:

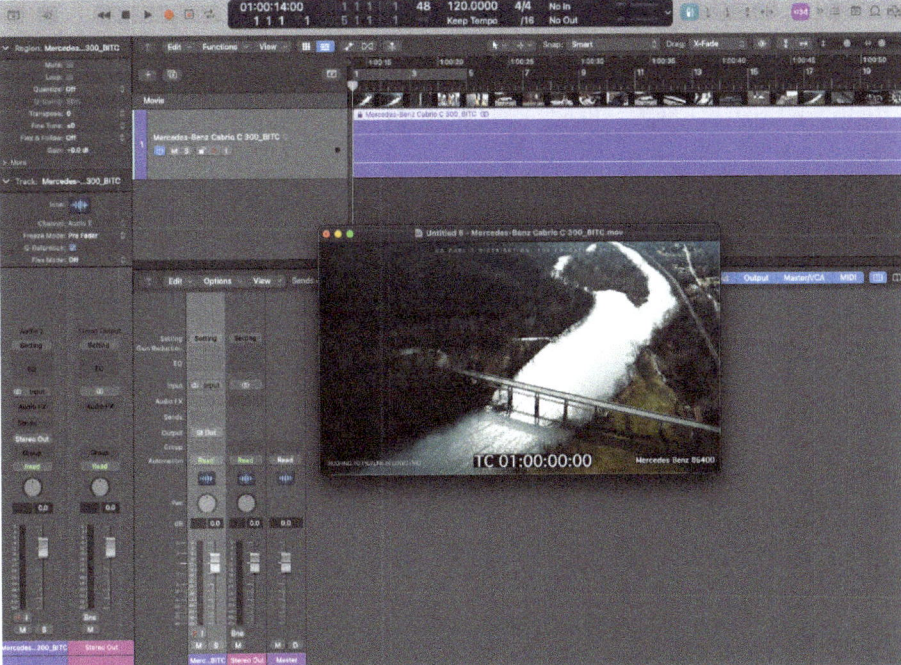

Figure 4.14: Movie file moved to the bar 1 location

When moving a movie file, sometimes the movie and the audio file can become out of sync. To correct this, right-click on the audio region and select **Unlock SMPTE Position** from the menu. Then, manually move the audio to line it up with the movie, right-click on the audio region, and select **Lock SMPTE Position**:

Figure 4.15: Unlocking the region SMPTE position

If audio and video regions continue to be out of sync, you may need to reimport the movie again and repeat these steps.

Now the movie file and the audio file should be in sync.

Changing the movie size

Logic Pro allows you to move the position of the entire movie by moving the floating window out of the **Arrange** window (as seen in *Figure 4.16*) and into the **Inspector** window, which makes it a smaller size.

Importing a movie file 61

Figure 4.16: Floating movie in the Arrange window

To move the movie out of the **Arrange** window, double-click on the movie window and the movie will move to the **Inspector**, located on the left side of the Logic Pro window (as seen in *Figure 4.17*).

Figure 4.17: Moving the movie window to Inspector

The reason to move the movie out of the **Arrange** window is to create space to record music into the **Arrange** window, so it will be more efficient to work with multiple tracks. There will be multiple tracks visible in the **Arrange** window, and so moving the movie into the **Inspector** area declutters the view.

If you want to move the movie back into the **Arrange** window, double-click on the movie file in the **Inspector**. The movie file will appear as a floating window, and the window can be moved to any location in the Logic Pro window.

Adjusting the movie size aspect ratio

Another way to resize the movie file is to right-click on the floating movie window and select **Movie Project Settings**.

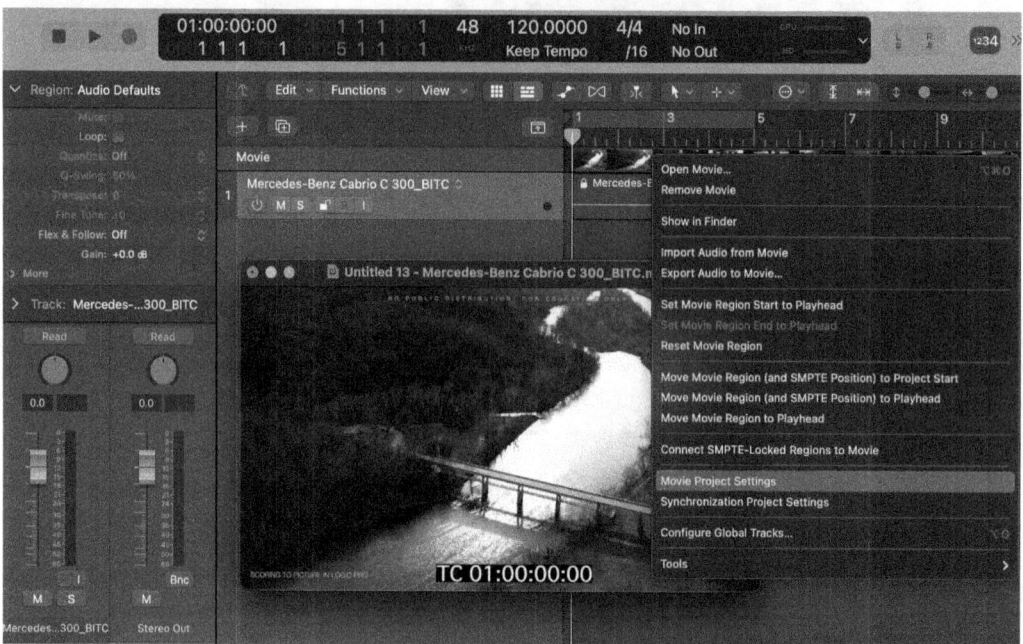

Figure 4.18: The Movie Project Settings menu

In the **Movie Project Settings** menu, you can change the movie size by selecting a size option from the menu. The size you select will depend on your preference for how you want to view and work with the movie file:

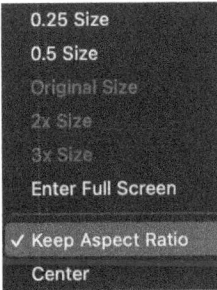

Figure 4.19: Movie size option menu

If you are using multiple computer monitors, for example, adjusting your ratio to a full-screen view on one of the monitors can be helpful because it will allow you to view Logic Pro on one monitor and the full movie on the other.

Now we have gone through multiple stages of importing and setting up our movie file, let's quickly look at how to save it.

Saving a session with a movie file

Make sure to save your session with a movie file. To do so, go to **File**, then **Save** (or use the shortcut *CMD + S*). In the **Save** dialog box, give your movie a name, save it in a place where you can easily find it, and make sure that **Movie file** is checked (you can see this option at the bottom of *Figure 4.20*):

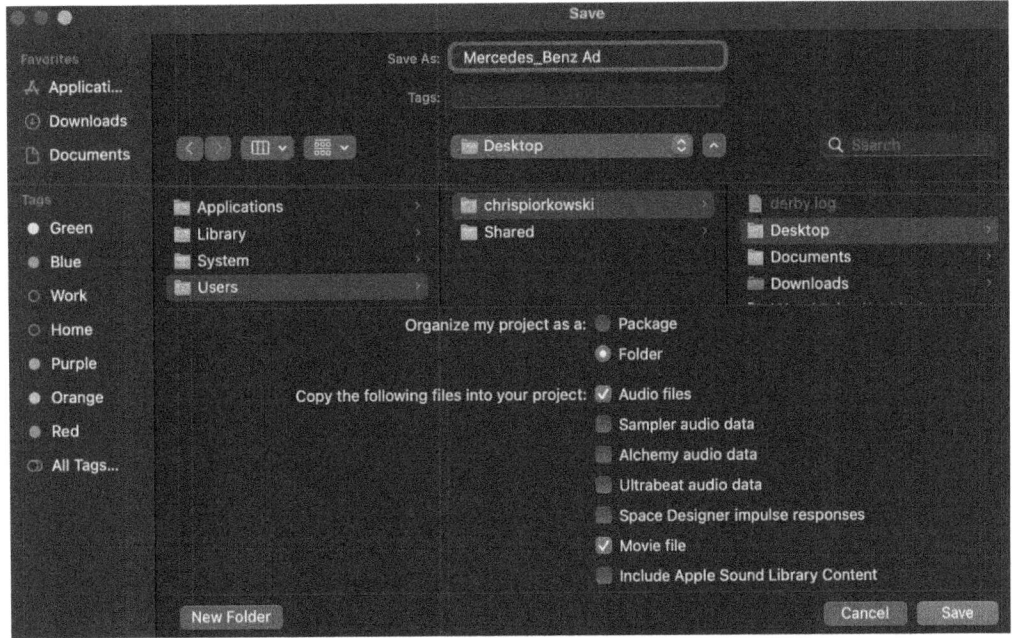

Figure 4.20: Saving a session with a movie file

After the Logic Pro session with the movie file is saved, every time you open an existing project, Logic Pro will automatically load the same movie into the session, without having to search for it on the hard drive. Doing this will improve and speed up your workflow.

After saving the session, close and quit the Logic Pro session by going to **Logic Pro**, then **Quit Logic Pro**:

Figure 4.21: Quitting a Logic Pro session

Summary

In this chapter, we discussed how to open and launch a Logic Pro session. We also discussed how to open a movie file, extract an audio file that was attached to the movie file, adjust and set up the sample and frame rate, and change the movie size aspect ratio.

Understanding these steps and processes will help you to work more effectively with a movie file in Logic Pro.

In the next chapter, we'll learn how to properly align the movie file and sync Logic Pro to picture.

5
Syncing Logic Pro to Picture

In this chapter, we will learn how to properly align and set up a movie, and how to sync Logic Pro to picture. To do this, we will go over the options on how to import a movie file, work with different displays and settings, and also walk through the steps of syncing Logic Pro to picture using the different types of movie files most commonly used in the industry.

We will also apply what we learned from *Chapters 1* to *4* in this chapter, including opening and saving a movie file, dealing with SMPTE, BITC, frame rates, and the academy leader. We will also implement QuickTime video and its components, dialog, and temp music.

Learning and applying all of this content is crucial to be as efficient as possible in dealing with the challenges when scoring to picture, as well as properly preparing you for real gig situations.

In this chapter, we will cover the following topics:

- Reviewing visual synchronization tools
- Syncing Logic Pro to Picture
- Syncing Logic Pro with different movie files
- Creating custom scoring to picture template

Technical requirements

To follow along with this chapter, you will need a Mac computer with Logic Pro and QuickTime software installed. You will also need to be able to access the movie files provided with this book: `https://packt.link/hxCer`.

Reviewing visual synchronization tools

Before we begin the steps of synchronizing Logic Pro to picture, we will review a few visual tools that are helpful for synchronization.

Giant Time and Beats Display settings

The **Giant Time** and **Beat Display** are extra-large visual representations of the timecode and bar and beat numbers. Even though these numbers are listed on the LCD display, being able to see them enlarged helps to make the comparison with the BITC easier during the synchronization process.

To open the **Giant Time Display**, on the right side of the LCD display, click on the down arrow:

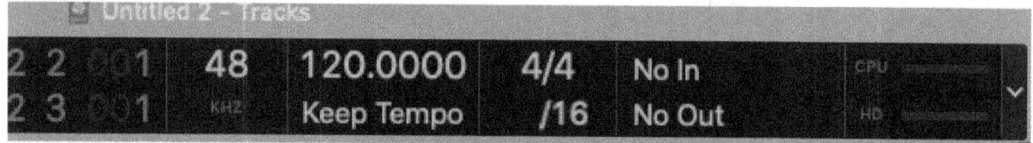

Figure 5.1: Logic Pro LCD Display

From the pop-up menu, click on **Open Giant Time Display**:

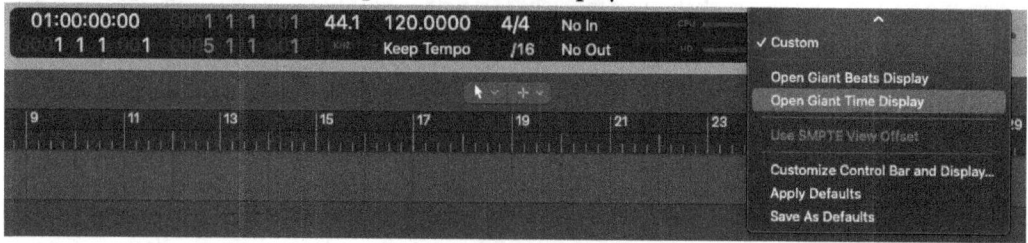

Figure 5.2: LCD pop-up menu

Logic Pro will open a floating **Giant Time Display** on the screen. The display can be resized or moved inside of the **Arrange** window, or it can also be dragged over to an extended monitor if you have one connected to your Mac.

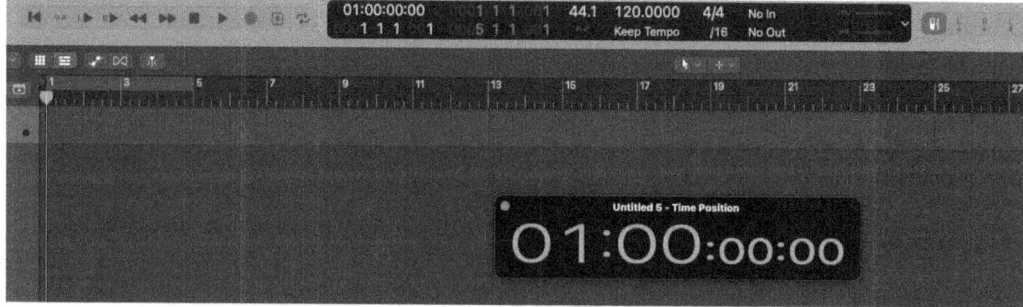

Figure 5.3: Logic Pro Floating Giant Time Display

To open the **Giant Beats Display**, click on **Open Giant Beats Display** from the **LCD Display** menu:

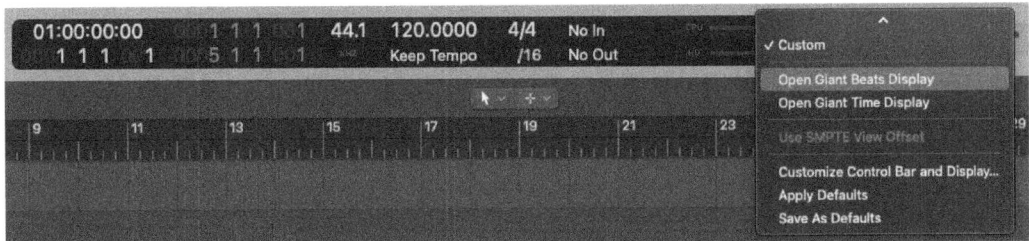

Figure 5.4: LCD pop-up menu

Logic Pro opens a floating **Giant Beats Display** on the screen. Again, the display can be resized or moved inside of the **Arrange** window, or it can also be dragged over to an extended monitor, if you have one connected to your Mac. The **Giant Beats Display** reflects the bar and beat positions at the playhead location:

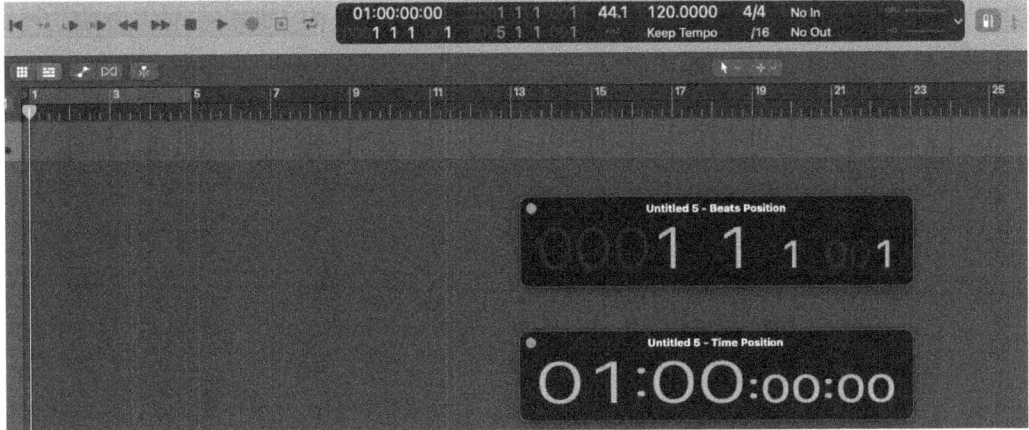

Figure 5.5: Logic Pro floating Giant Beats Display

Now that we've reviewed floating giant displays, we will review a Logic Pro SMPTE display without subframes.

Logic Pro SMPTE display without subframes

By default, Logic Pro sets up the SMPTE display with subframes. Generally, in film scoring, since we only use hours, minutes, seconds, and frames, the subframe numbers do not need to be displayed.

To change to the SMPTE display without subframes, go to **Logic Pro**, then **Preferences** (in Logic Pro 10.7, **Preferences** was replaced with **Settings**), and then **Display**:

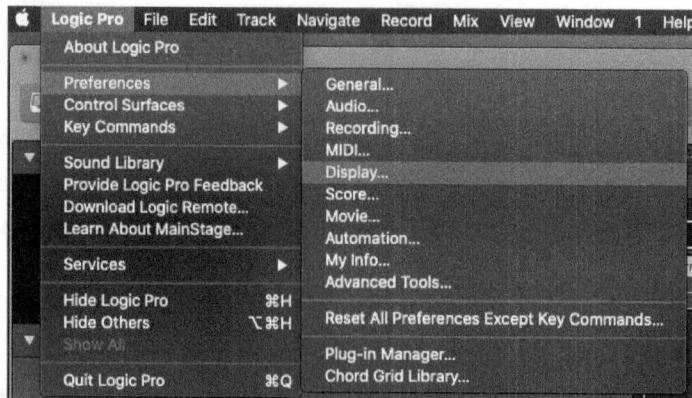

Figure 5.6: Logic Pro Preferences with the Display pop-up menu

In the **Settings** window, click on the **General** tab, and then go down to the **Displays** section and find the **Display Time As**, which will be set as **SMPTE/EBU with Subframes**.

Instead, we want to click on the **Display Time As** drop-down menu and select **SMPTE/EBU Without Subframes**:

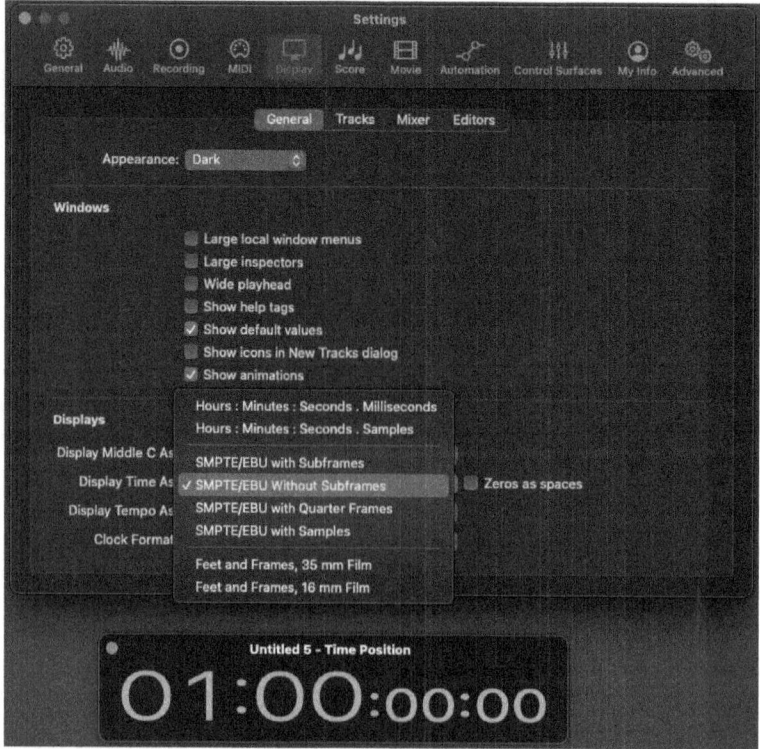

Figure 5.7: Logic Pro Display window Without Subframes selection

After changing the SMPTE view to **Without Subframes**, Logic Pro will display only four groups of digits – **01:00:00:00**.

Now that we have reviewed some visual tools, we will cover how to sync Logic Pro to picture.

Syncing Logic Pro to picture

In this section, we will go step by step through the process of how to sync Logic Pro to picture, including importing the movie file, as well as accessing and reviewing the movie project settings and synchronization settings. Additionally, we will cover aligning the movie file with Logic Pro so that the BITC of the movie file and the Logic Pro timecode are in sync with one another.

Importing the movie file

To begin, import the `Mercedes-Benz 300C_BITC.mov` movie file in Logic Pro, along with the audio file, and confirm the frame and sample rate of the imported movie.

Then, make sure that the movie file is placed at bar 1. As mentioned back in *Chapter 4*, when you drag and drop a movie file into Logic Pro, the movie file might not drop at the beginning of your session. If the movie file is not placed at bar 1, place the playhead at bar 1, right-click (or *Ctrl* + click) on the movie track, and select **Move Movie region to Playhead**.

The movie file should now be moved to bar 1 at the playhead position, as shown here:

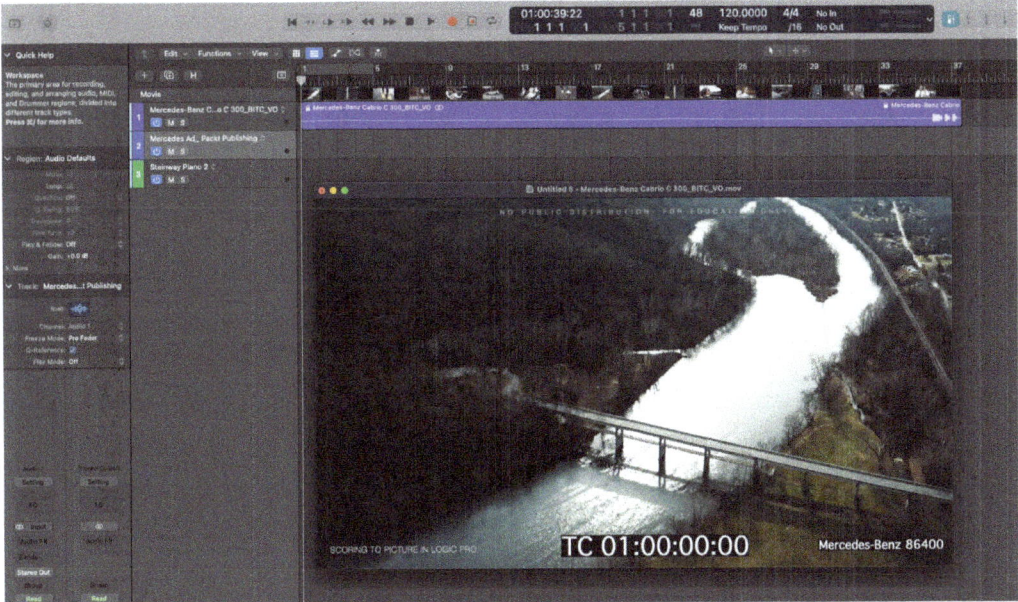

Figure 5.8: Logic Pro Arrange window with the movie file at the playhead position

At this point, the movie file in Logic Pro is not in sync yet, so the next step is to go over the movie project settings and synchronization settings. We will start with the movie project settings.

Accessing and reviewing the movie project settings

The **Movie Projects Settings** window is used to input the movie BITC and to start aligning the movie BITC with Logic Pro. There are five different ways to access the movie project settings:

- The first option is to go to **Logic Pro**, then **Preferences**, and then **Movie…**:

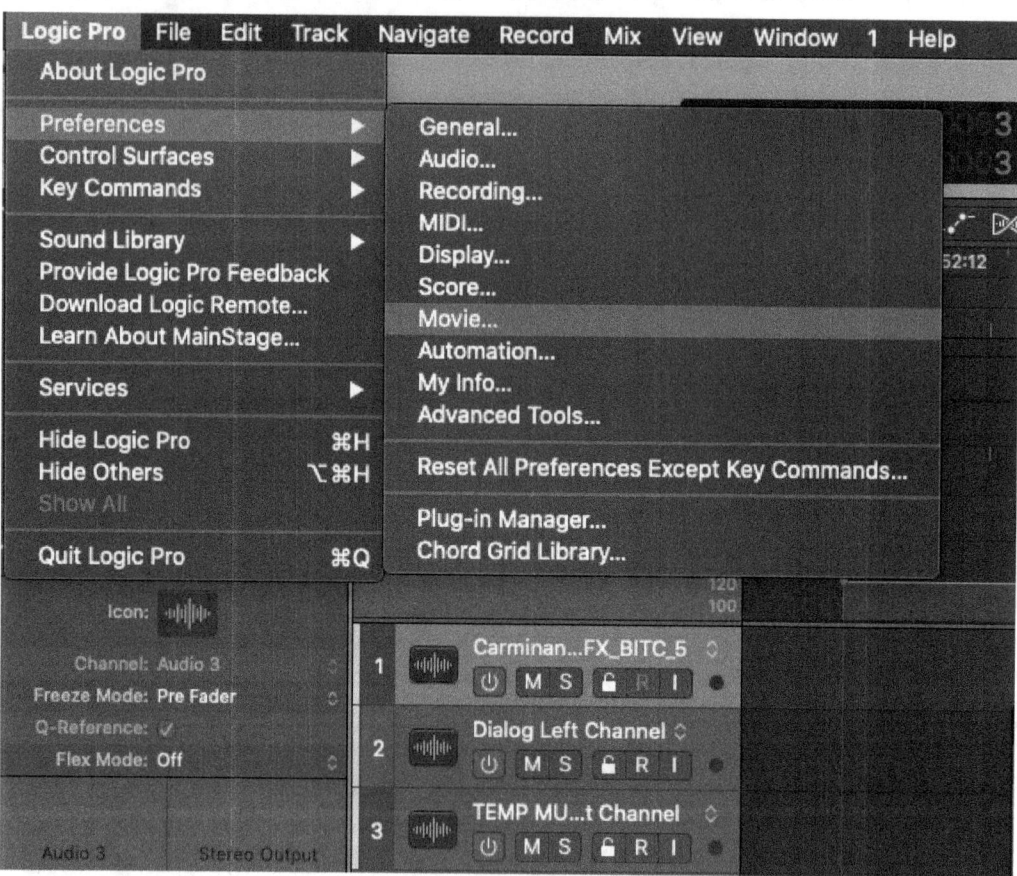

Figure 5.9: Logic Pro Preferences drop-down menu

Then, in the **Preferences** window, click on **Movie Project Settings…**:

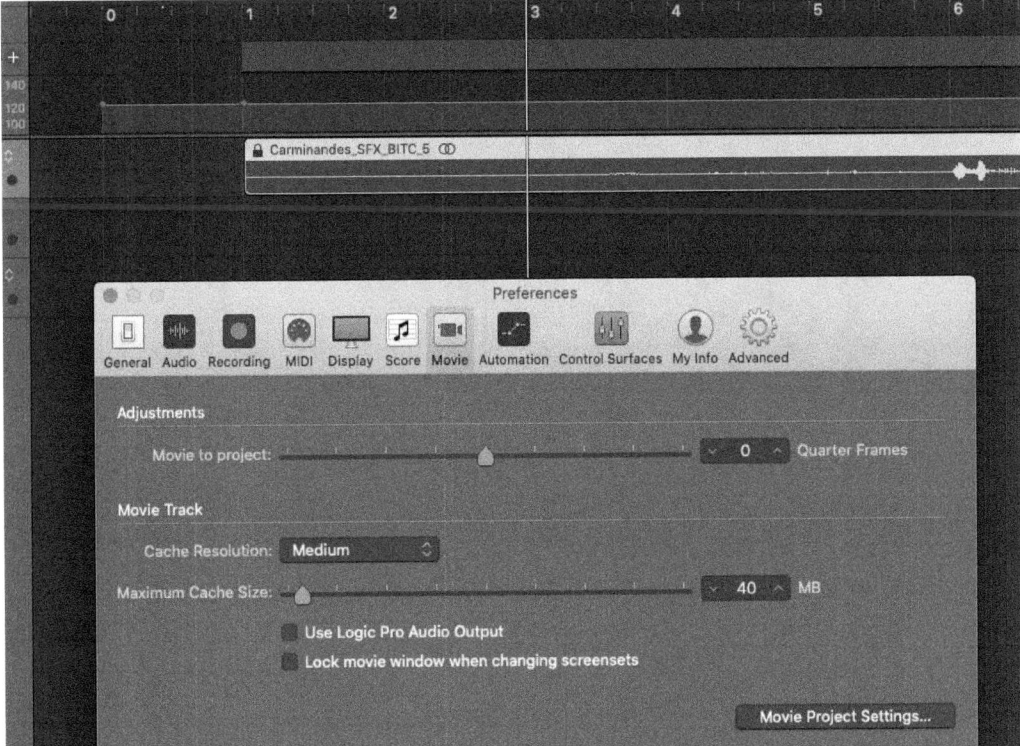

Figure 5.10: Movie Preferences window

- The second option is to click on the movie track in the global tracks and select **Movie Project Settings**:

Syncing Logic Pro to Picture

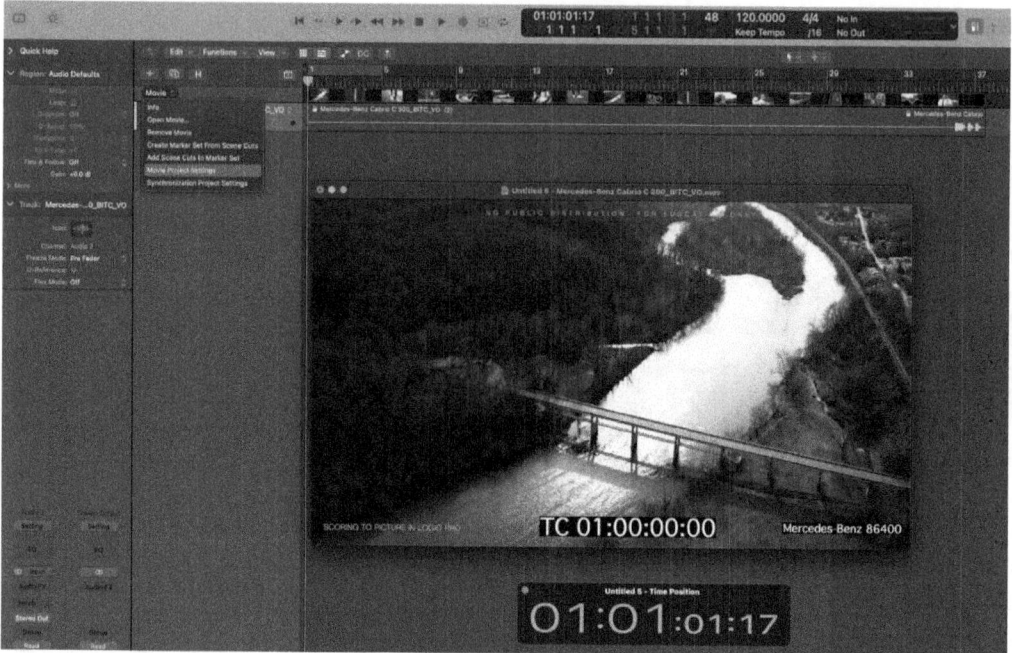

Figure 5.11: Global movie tracks drop-down menu

- The third option is to right-click directly on the movie track and select **Movie Project Settings**:

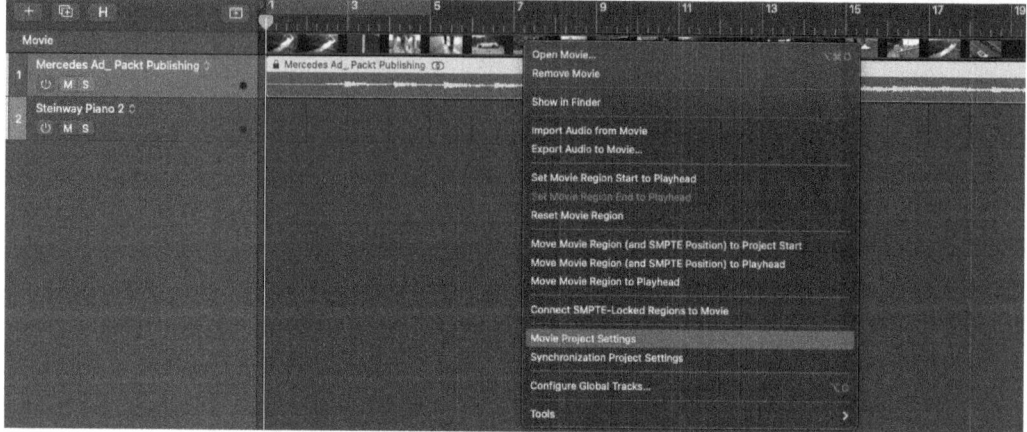

Figure 5.12: Movie Track pop-up menu

- The fourth option is to click on the floating open movie window and select **Movie Project Settings**. Then, make sure to open the **Giant Time Display** and place it below the floating movie.

Figure 5.13: Floating movie with the pop-up menu

- The fifth option is to click on **File**, then **Project Settings**, and then **Movie**.

Now that you know how to access the **Movie Project Settings** window, we will continue with the synchronization steps, looking at the movie project settings. This is to make sure that the **Movie** timecode window matches the timecode of the imported movie, and that the **Region Borders** timecode also reflects the same timecode numbers.

After clicking on the **Movie Project Settings** pop-up menu, Logic Pro opens the **Movie Project Settings** window, as shown in *Figure 5.14*:

Figure 5.14: Floating Movie Project Settings window

The movie we're working with has a BITC start time of **TC 01:00:00:00**. However, currently, the internal Logic Pro SMPTE timecode and the Movie BITC do not match, meaning they are not in sync:

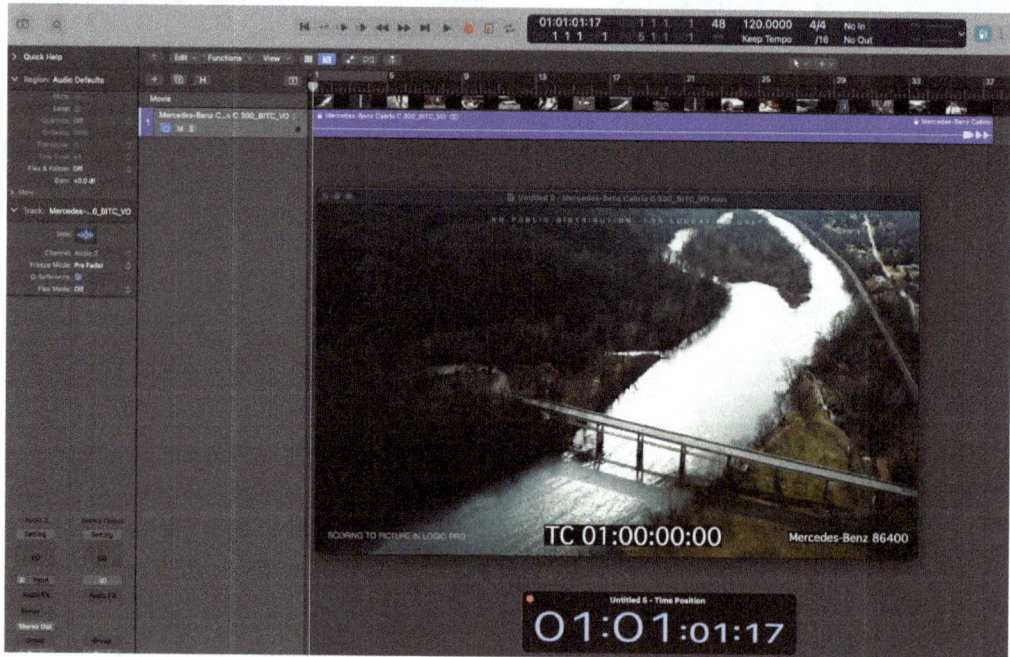

Figure 5.15: Movie file and Logic Pro SMPTE not in sync

We need to adjust the movie timecode numbers in the Logic Pro **Movie Project Settings** window to match the movie file BITC. In the **Position** section, you can see the **Movie** field displays the movie timecode as **01:00:24:00**. To change this, click inside the **Movie** field (which will become highlighted in blue) and type in the following numbers without spaces – 01:00:00:00 (the timecode window needs to match the BITC of the movie file). Then, hit *Enter*.

Figure 5.16: Floating Movie Project Settings window

Additionally, in general, the **Region Borders** movie **Start** timecode should match the **Position Movie** timecode. If the **Region Borders** start timecode is different from the movie start time, then the movie will, in a way, "fold into itself."

For example, in *Figure 5.17*, the **Region Borders** movie **Start** timecode shows **TC 01:00:12:00**, and it's different from the **Position Movie** timecode. The movie will still start at **TC 01:00:00:00**, but the movie border region will only be visible at the 12-second mark. In the movie track, in *Figure 5.17*, you can see the movie is not present for the first seven bars, even though it's playing from bar 1.

Syncing Logic Pro to Picture

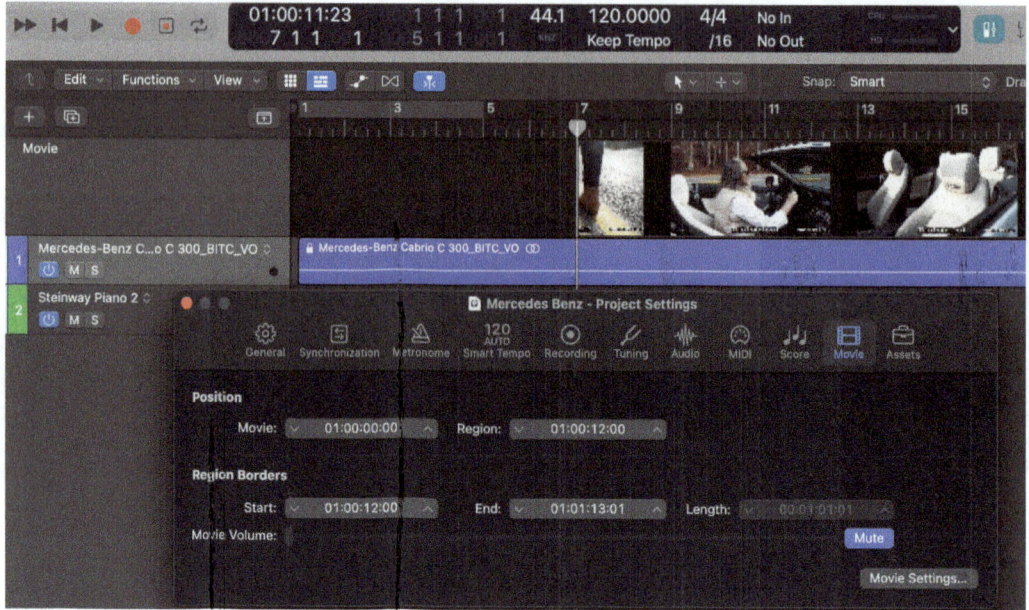

Figure 5.17: Movie position and region borders not matching

When it comes to changing the synchronization settings, and when entering or re-entering different synchronization settings, Logic Pro can make adjustments to the movie's region border that makes the movie appear truncated. At first, it may look like part of the movie vanished somehow, but it's simply that the movie position and the movie region border have changed and do not match. This is why it's important to make sure that the movie position and the movie region border match.

Below the **Regions Borders** section are the **Movie Volume** slider and the **Mute** button:

- The **Movie Volume** slider is used when you do not import the audio file of the movie to your project session; in this case, the QuickTime movie player will play the audio in the background. You can then adjust the overall movie volume setting by sliding the lever from left to right.

- You will also want to make sure that the **Mute** button is off (highlighted gray). By doing this, you don't have the ability to control the volume of the movie file as you would if you imported the audio file to your session.

> **Note**
>
> It is important to know that when removing and opening another movie in the same session, Logic Pro will unmute the movie volume.

Once the movie project settings are set, the next step is to go over the synchronization settings.

Accessing and reviewing the synchronization settings

To access the synchronization settings, in the **Movie Project Settings** window, click on the **Synchronization** icon in the upper-left corner, and then select the **General** tab:

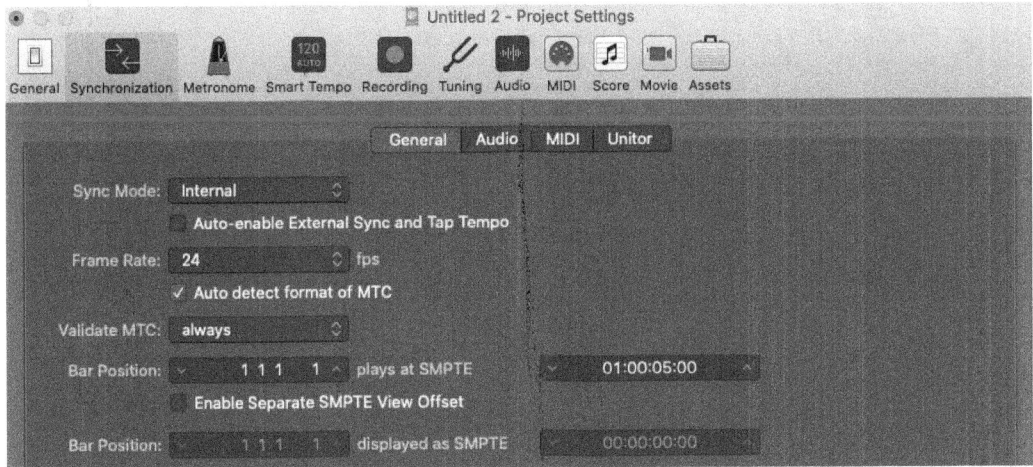

Figure 5.18: Synchronization settings window

First, make sure that the **Frame Rate** matches the movie frame rate; for our example, this is **24 fps**.

Next, make sure that the movie starts at bar 1 with the startup BITC of the movie file. The **Bar Position** setting needs to be at **1 1 1 1**, and **plays at SMPTE** should be set to **01:00:00:00**. To change **plays at SMPTE**, click in the box and make sure that all of the numbers are highlighted. Once all of the numbers are highlighted, type 01 and hit *Enter*. Logic Pro will then display the **01:00:00:00** timecode at bar 1.

Figure 5.19: Synchronization window – plays at SMPTE

Now, close the **Synchronization** window. The **Arrange** window will now show that the Logic Pro timecode, in blue, matches the BITC of the movie file.

In order to make sure that Logic Pro and the movie are in sync with one another, it's helpful to place the playhead at the last couple of bars at the end of your movie and hit **Play**. If the Logic Pro timecode and the movie BITC stay identical as it plays, then everything is synced properly, like so:

Syncing Logic Pro to Picture

Figure 5:20: Arrange window displaying Logic Pro and the movie in sync

Now that we've reviewed synchronization settings, we will go over how to lock the movie.

Locking the movie

Once the movie and Logic Pro are in sync, it's important to lock the movie so that it doesn't shift when you begin working with different time signatures and tempos (we will cover working with time signatures and tempos in depth in *Chapter 6*).

To do this, right-click on the track header and select **Configure Track Header…** (or use the *Option + T* shortcut):

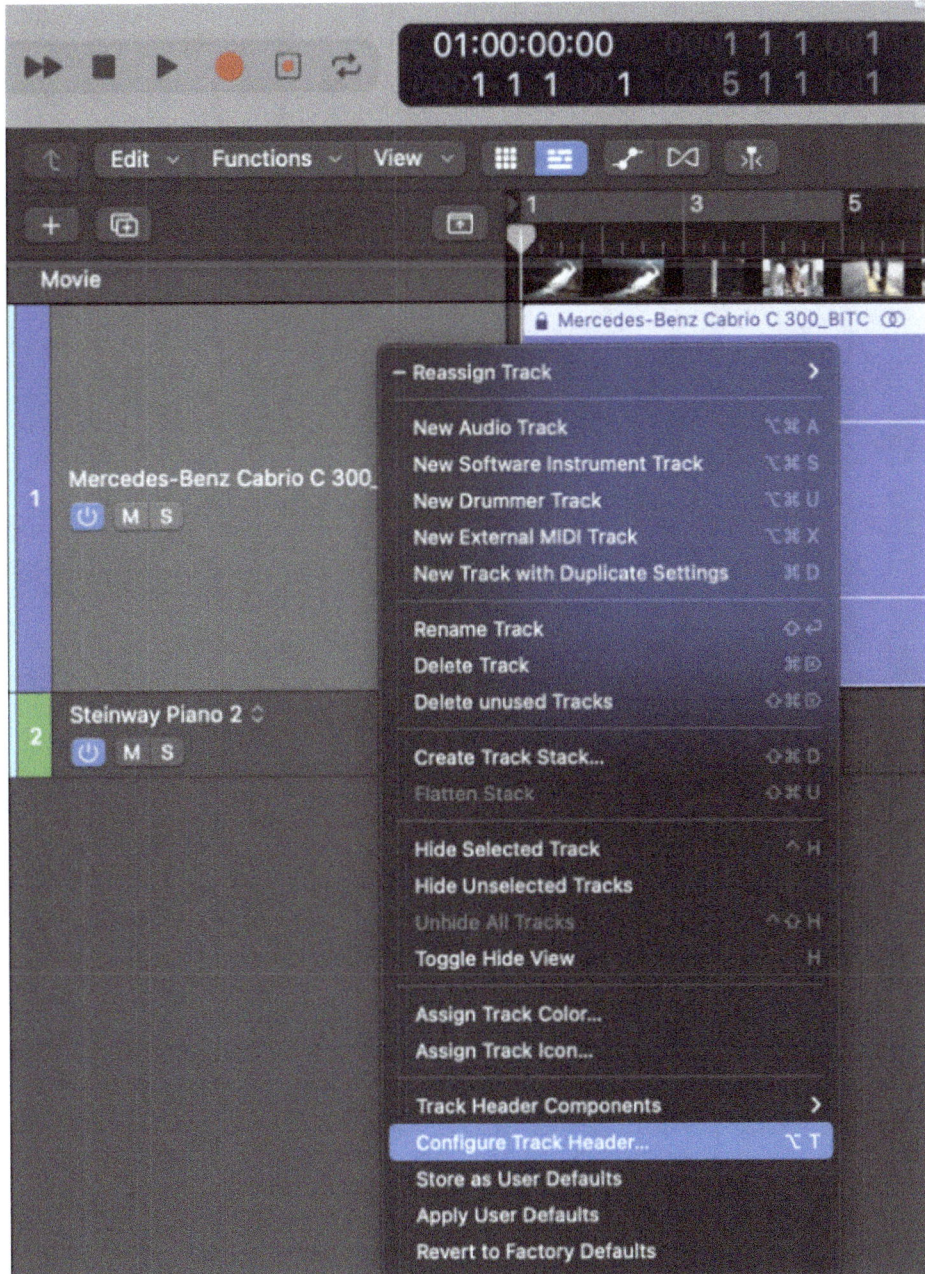

Figure 5.21: Configure Track Header drop-down menu

Then, in the **Track Header** window, select **Protect** (the green padlock icon):

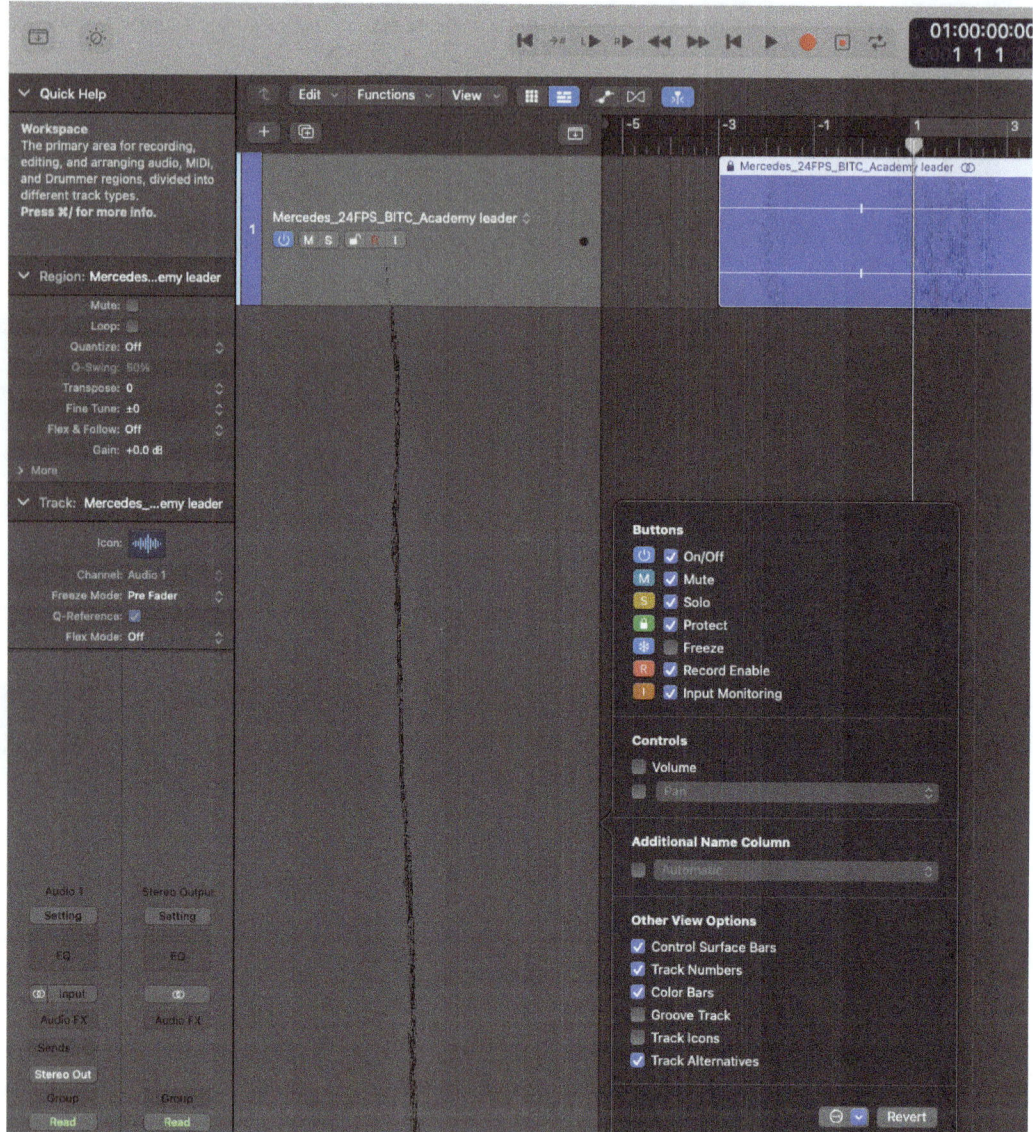

Figure 5.22: Track Header window with Protect enabled

After enabling **Protect**, click anywhere in the **Arrange** window to close the menu. Then, make sure that the global tracks are open (by using the `G` shortcut). If **Protect** was enabled, the unlocked padlock icon should be visible on the movie track inside the global tracks:

Syncing Logic Pro to picture

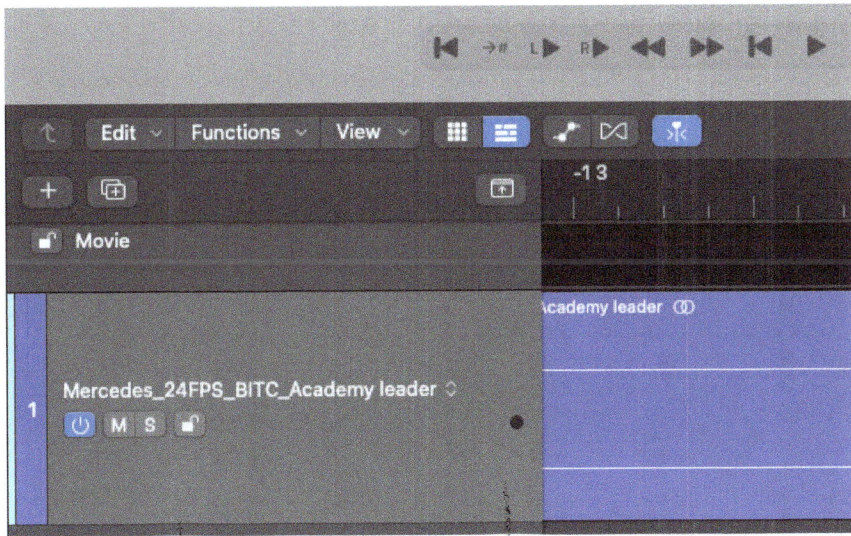

Figure 5.23 Unlocked movie track

Next, click on the padlock icon in the movie track. The icon will turn a green color and the movie track will be locked:

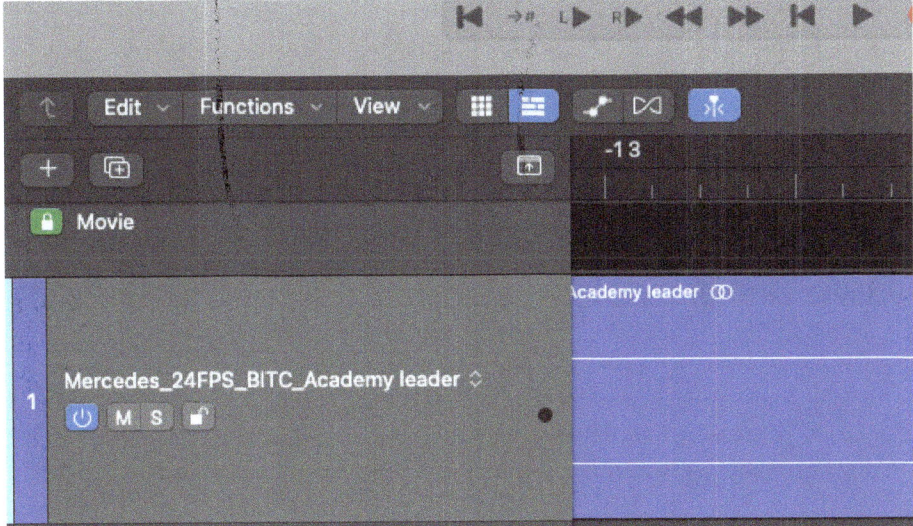

Figure 5:24 Locked movie track

When you try to move the movie file, Logic Pro will prompt you with a message saying that the movie is protected.

Next, we will review another film-scoring tool that can be helpful during the process of synchronization.

Accessing and reviewing the Movie Track Info panel

The **Movie Track Info** panel is a quick way to access the movie QuickTime properties. Here, you can check the movie file frame rate, format, duration, audio sample rate, and data size, without opening the movie file on a desktop.

To access it, from the **Global Tracks** window, click on the drop-down menu arrows next to **Movie**, and then select **Info**:

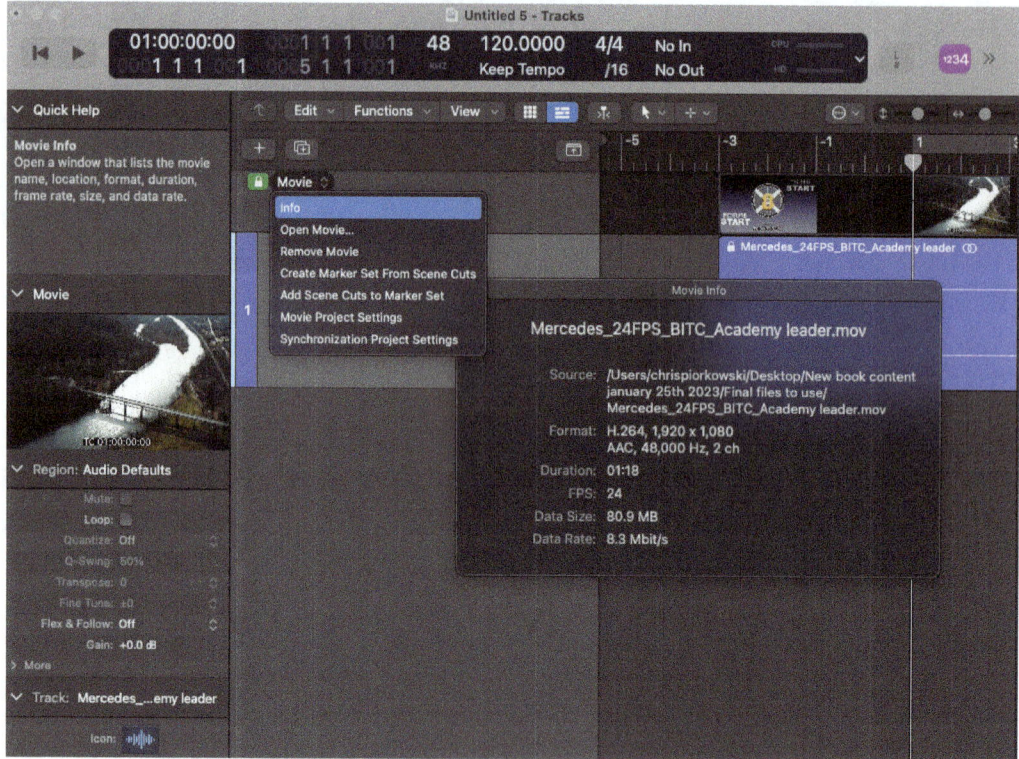

Figure 5.25: Movie Track Info panel

The panel is helpful particularly when reimporting movie files because it allows you to quickly confirm that the settings are set up as intended.

Saving a project session with a movie file

After everything has been synced, to finish the Logic Pro project, save it by going to **File** and then **Save** (or by using the *CMD + S* shortcut). This will open the **Save** dialog box:

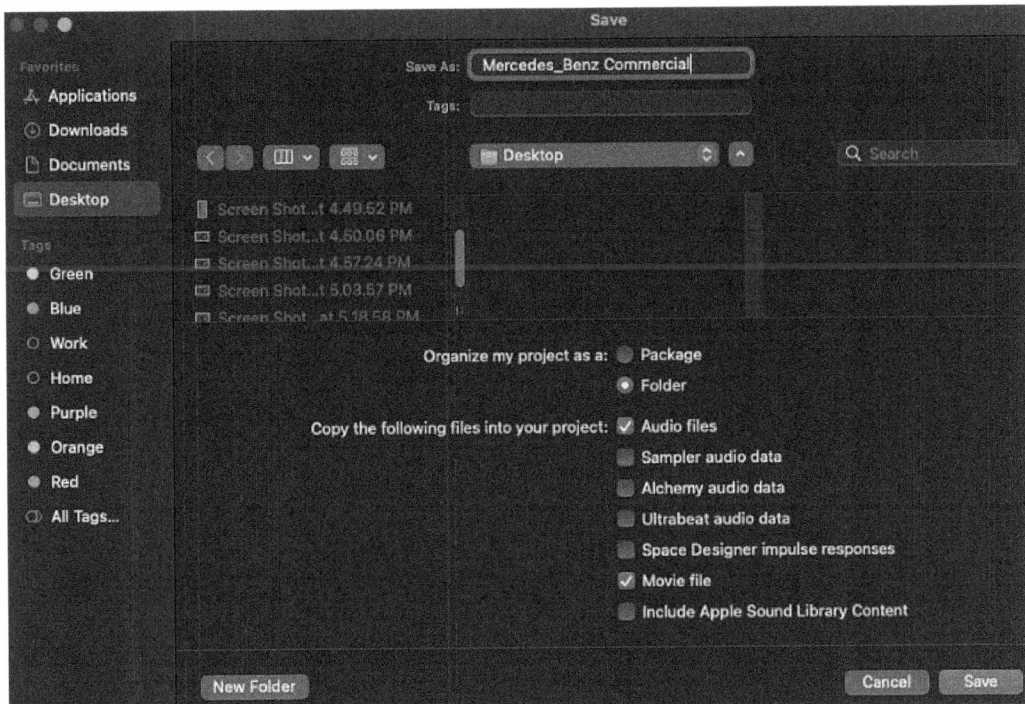

Figure 5.26: Save dialog box window

Here, name the file, then make sure to select **Organize my project as**, and choose **Folder**. Also, from the **Copy the following files into your project** list, select **Audio files** and **Movie file**; this way, all of your audio files and your movie file will be easily accessible from that one folder.

Once done, hit **Save**, and Logic Pro will create a folder on your desktop or your specified location.

In *Chapter 4*, we introduced a basic way of saving a project with a movie file, but now we're covering how to save your project in a more organized way that will track your progress chronologically. This will help your session versions, when working continuously throughout a project, to be easily found. For example, when working on a feature film, you may be dealing with five reels, and each them may take five to nine different cues. Each of the cues in the reel will most likely have to have a revision version, and sometimes multiple versions of those revisions. Therefore, keeping a clear structure of your progress, throughout all the reels, is vital to finishing your job successfully.

Whether saving project sessions or working with project alternatives, which can be buggy sometimes, though, is up to how the film composer prefers to work. In my experience, working with large, orchestral sessions with multiple reels, using a couple of slave computers running **Vienna Ensemble Pro (VEP)** software, and saving project versions in chronological order is more streamlined.

When working on your projects, any changes or revisions need to be clearly labeled so that when the film director wants to get an earlier or later version of the project, it can be easily found. The next time you save a new version of the Mercedes commercial project, you can save it as `Mercedes_Benz Commercial _01, _02`, and so on, and when dealing with a revision, you can then save it as `Mercedes_Benz Commercial _01_rev_01, _02_rev_01`, and so on. Also, when you save the file in the folder, your Mac will add a time and a date stamp, allowing you to track the date and time you worked on it.

Now that we know how to synchronize a movie in Logic Pro, as well as save a project with multiple reels, we will explore how to synchronize Logic Pro to picture with other types of movie files. We will look at different movie files that are commonly worked with in the industry.

Syncing Logic Pro with different movie files

In this section, we will look at how to sync Logic Pro with different movie files, including the following:

- A movie file with a countdown leader
- A movie file with a 2-pop
- A movie file with a 3-pop
- A movie with multiple reels
- A movie file with SMPTE offset view

We will also look at syncing a movie from any bar location. So, let's get started.

Syncing a movie file with a countdown leader

First, we will learn how to open and synchronize a movie file with a countdown leader. To begin, open a new Logic Pro session and import `Mercedes_24FPS_BITC_Academy leader.mov`:

Figure 5.27: Arrange window with an open movie file

Now, hover your mouse on top of the ruler, above the global tracks. The pointer will turn into a left bracket shape with arrows on both sides:

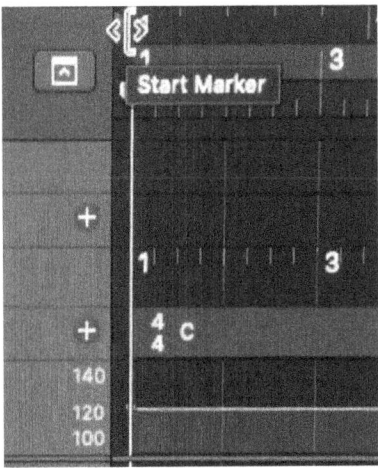

Figure 5.28: Arrange Window with the Ruler view

Once the bracket appears, hold and drag the mouse to the left side of the **Arrange** window to reveal the negative bars. *Figure 5.29* shows the negative bars to the left of the playhead, starting with 0, -1, -2, -3, and so on, going from right to left.

Figure 5:29: Arrange window with negative bars

Logic Pro, by default, has an existing environment that is set up to help with the synchronization of a movie countdown. For example, any movie that has a countdown leader with a BITC of **TC 00:59:52:00** can utilize Logic Pro's negative bar section to match the movie countdown leader BITC.

In order to properly synchronize Logic Pro with the movie file countdown leader, Logic Pro has to have the same matching BITC numbers. Since the LCD display bars and numbers are currently small, we want to open the Giant Time and Beats display:

Figure 5.30: Arrange window with the Giant Time and Beats display

Right-click on the movie file and select **Movie Project Settings**. In the **Movie** tab, under the **Position** section, click the value in the **Movie** box. This will highlight all the numbers in blue. Now, type the movie timecode, `00:59:52:00`, and hit *Enter*:

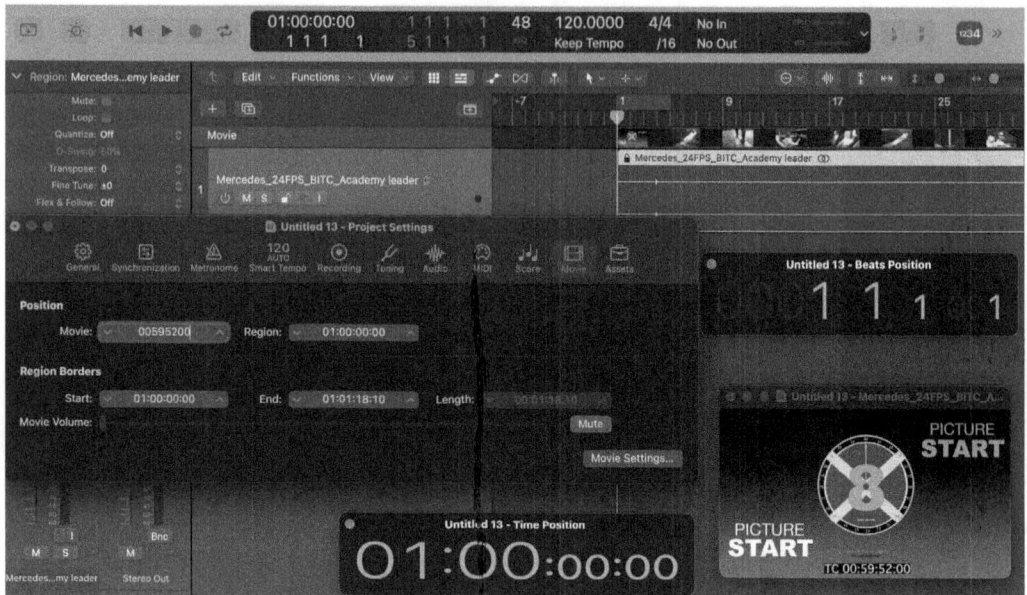

Figure 5.31: Movie Project Settings window

With the playhead at bar 1 and the numbers input correctly, you should now see that the timecodes match. And, since the countdown took place in the negative bars, the first frame of the movie will end up starting at bar 1:

Figure 5.32: Arrange window with the Movie Project Settings window

To confirm that everything is synchronized, in the **Movie Project Settings** window, click on the **Synchronization** icon. There, make sure that the **Frame Rate**, **Bar Position**, and **Plays at SMPTE** settings are as intended.

Figure 5.33: Arrange window with the Synchronization window

The last step is to make sure that the audio 2-pop within the countdown leader is in the correct location. To do this, close the **Synchronization** window and play the movie from the beginning. Make sure that you can hear the audio 2-pop at location **TC 00:59:58:00**, which will be visible in the negative bar area.

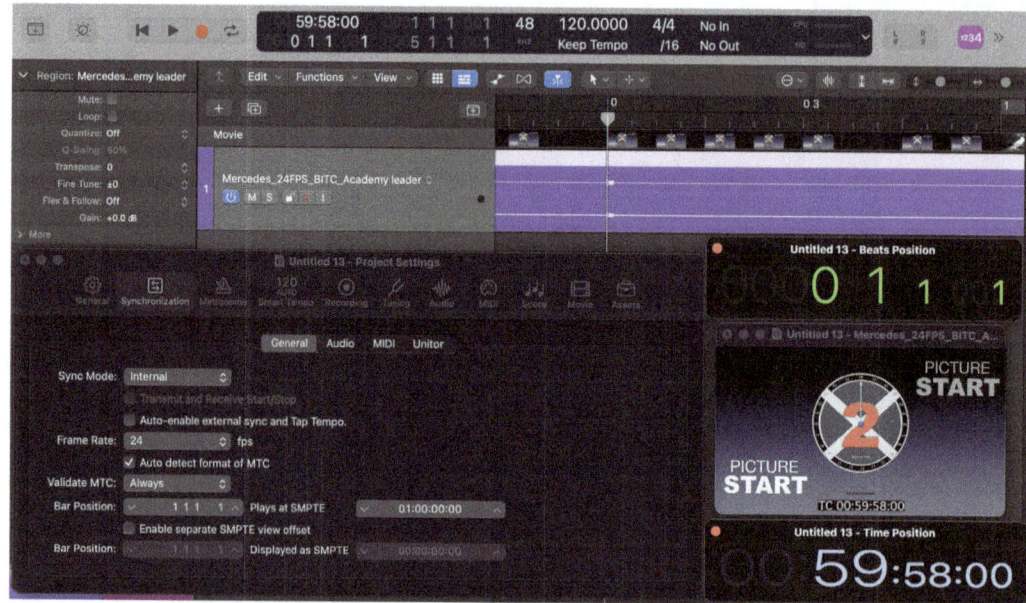

Figure 5.34: Logic Pro playhead at the 2-pop location

Syncing a movie file with a 2-pop

In this section, we will learn how to open and synchronize a movie file with a 2-pop. To begin, open a new Logic Pro session and import `JFHTH_AD_BITC_2_pop.mov`:

Figure 5.35: Arrange Window with a 2-pop movie file

Right-click on the movie file and select **Movie Project Settings**. In the **Project Settings** window, go to the **Position** section, click in the **Position** box, type in 00:59:58:00 (without spaces), and hit *Enter*:

92 Syncing Logic Pro to Picture

Figure 5.36: Arrange Window with the Movie Project Settings window

The Logic Pro timecode should now match the movie BITC:

Figure 5.37: Movie project settings with matching timecodes

Next, click the **Synchronization** button, and in the window that appears, make sure that bar 1 is set so that **plays at SMPTE** is **01:00:00:00**:

Figure 5.38: Synchronization window with matching timecodes

Then, close the **Synchronization** window and place the playhead at bar 1. The Logic Pro timecode should now match the movie timecode of **TC 01:00:00:00**:

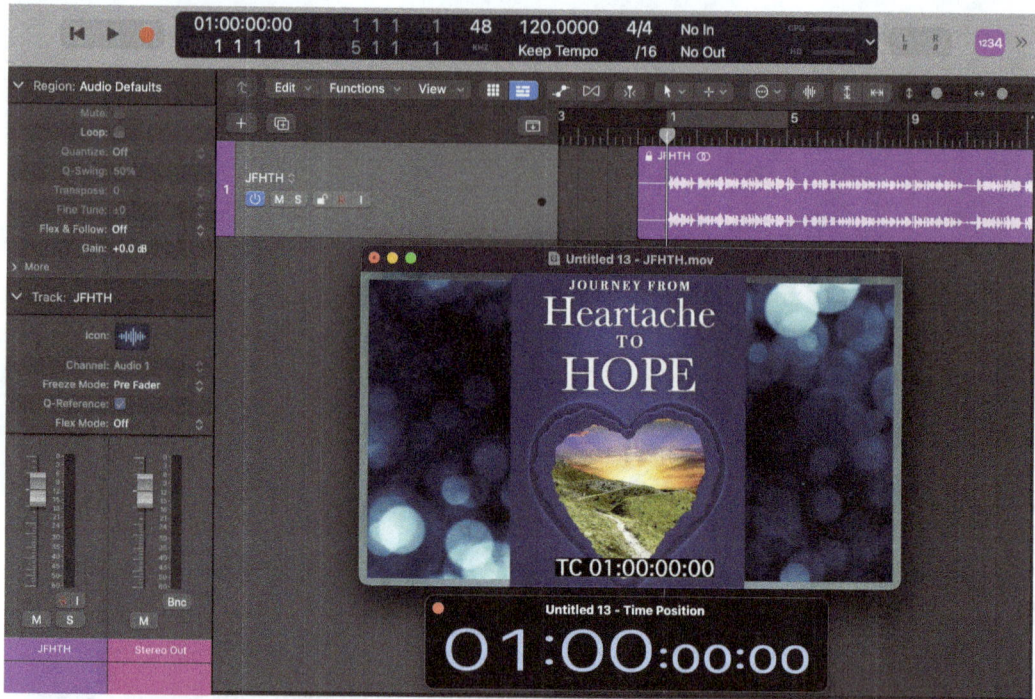

Figure 5.39: Arrange window with matching timecodes

To make sure Logic Pro and the movie are in sync, play your movie file at the beginning and right before the end. If the numbers stay identical as it plays, then everything is synced properly.

Syncing a movie file with a 3-pop

In this section, we will learn how to open and synchronize a movie file with a 3-pop. We'll begin by opening a new Logic Pro session and importing `Journey Add_BITC_3-pop.mov`:

Syncing Logic Pro with different movie files   95

Figure 5.40: Arrange window with a 3-pop movie file

Right-click on the movie file and select **Movie Project Settings**. In the **Movie Project Settings** window, go to the **Position** section, click in the **Position** section box, type in 00:59:57:00 (without spaces), and hit *Enter*:

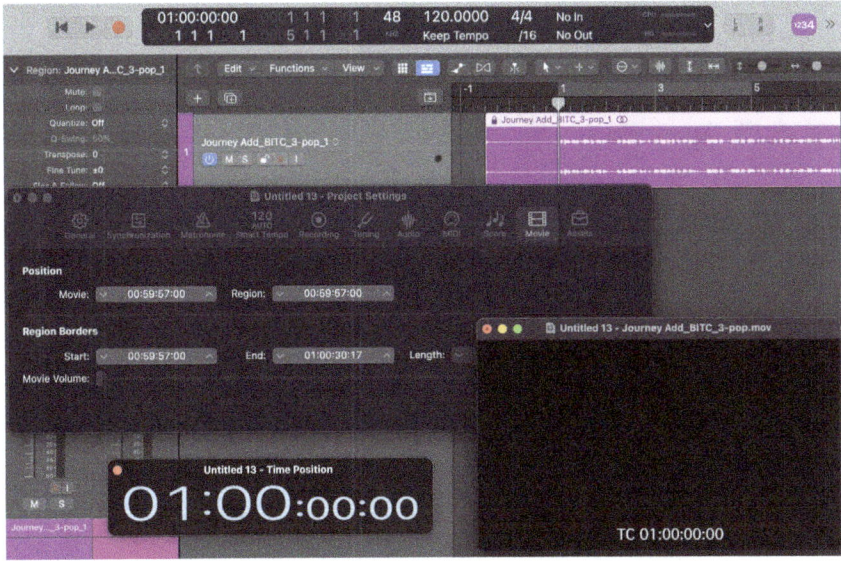

Figure 5.41: Arrange window with the Movie Project settings window

Next, click the **Synchronization** button, and in the window, make sure that bar 1 is set so that **plays at SMPTE** is **01:00:00:00**:

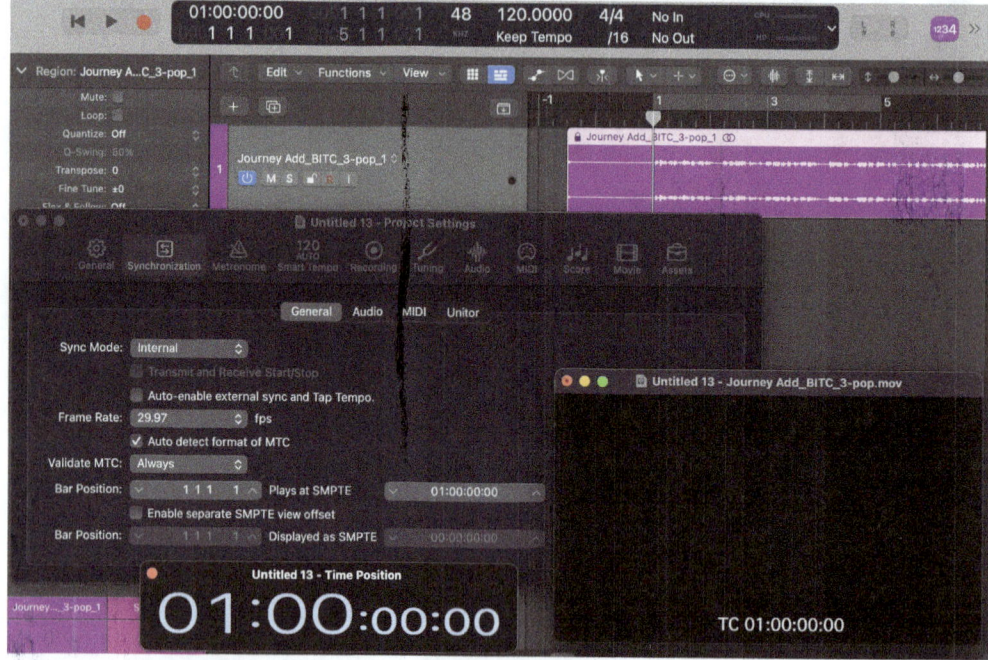

Figure 5.42: Arrange window with the Synchronization window

Close the **Synchronization** window and place the playhead at bar 1. The Logic Pro timecode should now match the movie timecode of **TC 01:00:00:00**:

Figure 5.43: Arrange window with the movie and Logic Pro in sync

By placing the playhead anywhere in the timeline of the **Arrange** window, the Logic Pro timecode should now match the movie BITC:

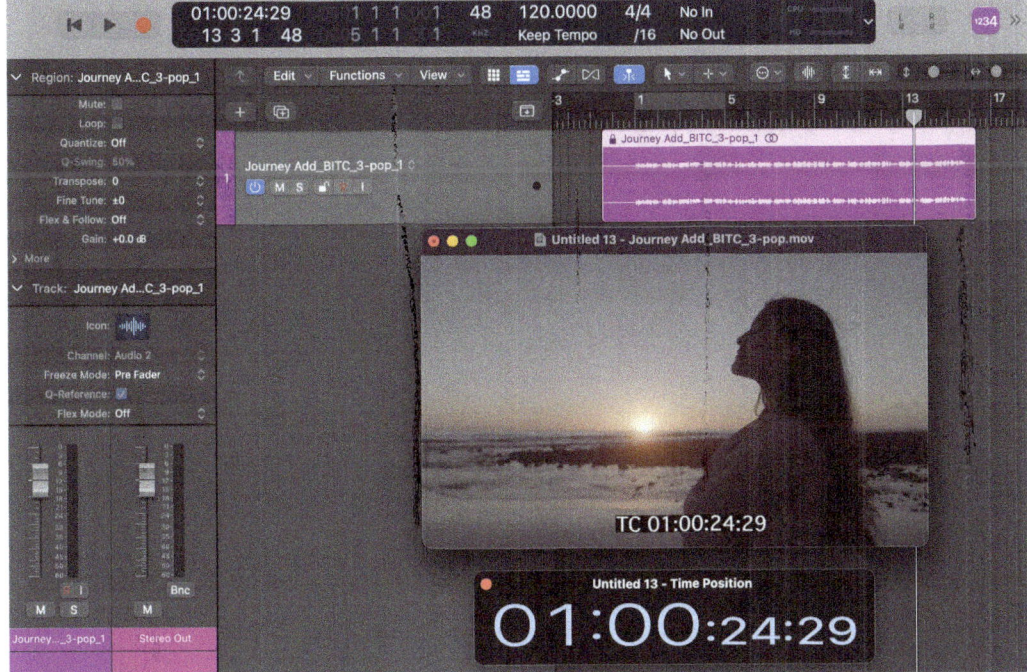

Figure 5.44: Arrange Window with matching timecodes

Syncing a movie file with multiple reels

In this section, we will review how to set up Logic Pro when working with multiple reels. As discussed in previous chapters, when working on a film that, let's say, is 95 minutes, the film composer will work on split movie cuts called reels. In the following example, we will work on five `Mercedes Reel` files. Let's get started.

Setting up Reel 1

Begin by opening a new Logic Pro session and importing `Mercedes Reel 1.mov`. Then, right-click on the movie file and select **Movie Project Settings**. In the **Movie Project Settings** window, within the **Position** section, click in the box and make sure that all of the numbers are highlighted. Then, type in `00:59:52:00` (without spaces) and hit *Enter*.

Next, click on the **Synchronization** icon. In this window, make sure that the bar position is **1 1 1 1** and **Plays at SMPTE** is set to **01:00:00:00**. Additionally, make sure that the audio track 2-pop happens at **TC 00:59:58:00**. At this point, you should see that Logic Pro and the movie are in sync:

Figure 5.45: Reel 1 Synchronization Settings window

Setting up Reel 2

Begin by opening a new Logic Pro session and importing `Mercedes Reel 2.mov`. Right-click on the movie and select **Movie Project Settings**. Then, in the **Movie Project Settings** window, in the **Position** section, type in `00:59:52:00` for the timecode and hit *Enter*.

Even though the Reel 2 BITC is **01:59:52:00**, you still have to enter `00:59:52:00` because if you enter `01:59:52:00` in the **Position** section of the **Movie Project Settings** window, Logic Pro will place the movie 1 hour, 59 minutes, and 52 seconds ahead in your sequencer timeline. This is an exception from what we did previously with other movie files because we are working now with multiple reels:

Figure 5.46: Movie project settings with Reel 2

Next, click on the **Synchronization** icon to get to the synchronization settings. Here, make sure that the upper **Bar Position** section is displayed as **1 1 1 1** and the **Plays at SMPTE** section is set to **01:00:00:00**. Additionally, make sure that the audio track 2-pop happens at **TC 00:59:58:00**.

The next important step is to select **Enable separate SMPTE view offset**. Then, make sure that the lower **Bar Position** section is displayed as **1 1 1 1** and the **Displayed as SMPTE** section is set to **02:00:00:00**:

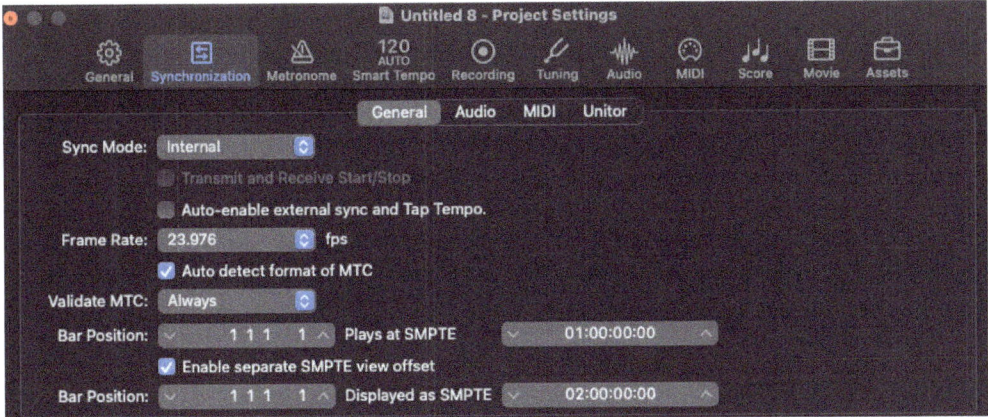

Figure 5.47: Reel 2 Synchronization Settings window

Now that the Logic Pro timecode in blue, **02:00:00:00**, matches the BITC of Reel 2, the movie and Logic Pro are properly synced:

Figure 5.48: Reel 2 and the Logic Pro matching timecodes

Setting up Reel 3

Begin by opening a new Logic Pro session and importing `Mercedes Reel 3.mov`. Right-click on the movie and select **Movie Project Settings**. In the **Movie Project Settings** window, in the **Position** section, type in `00:59:52:00` for the timecode and hit *Enter*.

Even though the Reel 3 BITC is **02:59:52:00**, you still have to enter `00:59:52:00` because if you enter `02:59:52:00` in the **Position** section of the **Movie Project Settings** window, then Logic Pro will place the movie 2 hours, 59 minutes, and 52 seconds ahead in your sequencer timeline.

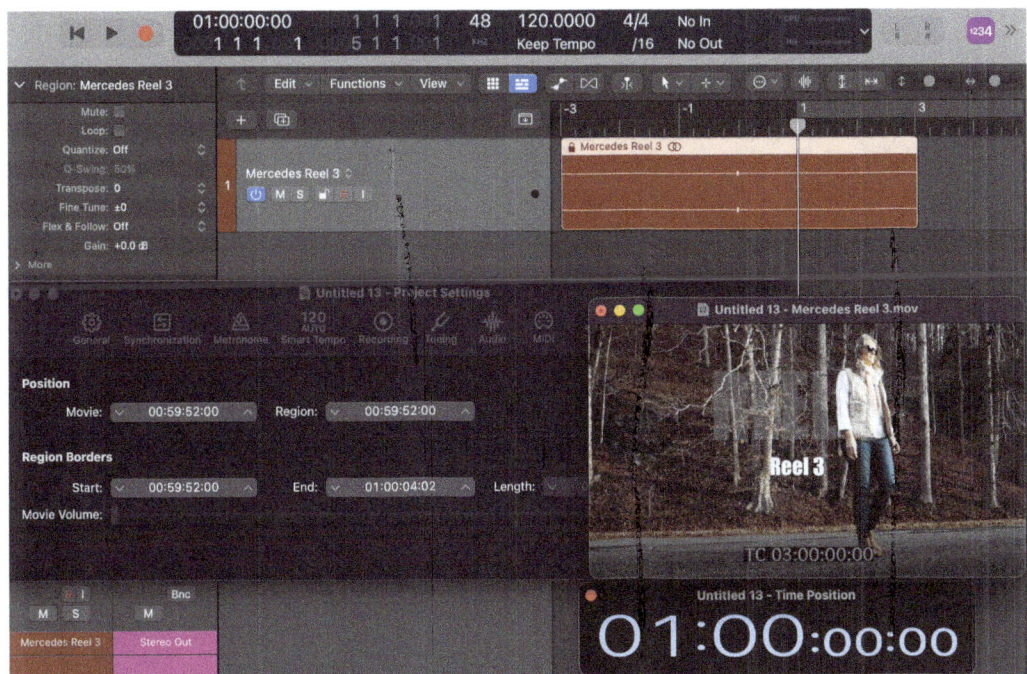

Figure 5.49: Movie project settings with Reel 3

Next, click on the **Synchronization** icon to get to the synchronization settings. Here, make sure that the upper **Bar Position** section is **1 1 1 1** and the **Plays at SMPTE** section is set to **01:00:00:00**. Additionally, make sure that the audio track 2-pop happens at **TC 00:59:58:00**.

Then, select **Enable separate SMPTE view offset**. Make sure that the lower **Bar Position** section is displayed as **1 1 1 1** and the **Displayed as SMPTE** section is set to **03:00:00:00**.

Now that the Logic Pro timecode in blue, **03:00:00:00**, matches the BITC of Reel 3, the movie and Logic Pro are properly synced:

Figure 5.50: Reel 3 and the Logic Pro matching timecodes

Setting up Reel 4

Begin by opening a new Logic Pro session and importing `Mercedes Reel 4.mov`. Right-click on the movie and select **Movie Project Settings**. In the **Movie Project Settings** window, in the **Position** section, type in `00:59:52:00` for the timecode and hit *Enter*.

Even though the Reel 4 BITC is **03:59:52:00**, you still have to enter `00:59:52:00` because if you enter `03:59:52:00` in the **Position** section of the **Movie Project Settings**, then Logic Pro will place the movie 3 hours, 59 minutes, and 52 seconds ahead in your sequencer timeline.

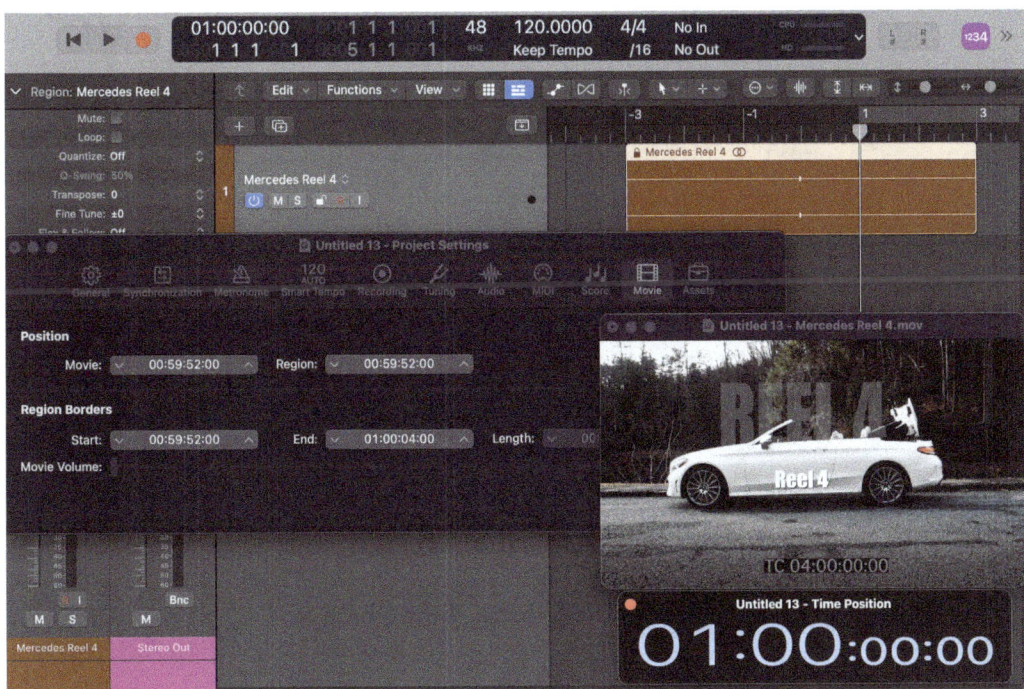

Figure 5.51: Movie project settings with Reel 4

Next, click on the **Synchronization** icon to get to the synchronization settings. Here, make sure that the upper **Bar Position** section is **1 1 1 1** and the **Plays at SMPTE** section is set to **01:00:00:00**. Additionally, make sure that the audio track 2-pop happens at **TC 00:59:58:00**.

Then, select **Enable separate SMPTE view offset**. Make sure that the lower **Bar Position** is displayed as **1 1 1 1** and the **Displayed as SMPTE** section is set to **04:00:00:00**.

Now that the Logic Pro timecode in blue, **04:00:00:00**, matches the BITC of Reel 4, the movie and Logic Pro are properly synced:

Figure 5.52: Reel 4 and the Logic Pro matching timecodes

Setting up Reel 5

Begin by opening a new Logic Pro session and importing `Mercedes Reel 5.mov`. Right-click on the movie and select **Movie Project Settings**. In the **Movie Project Settings** window, in the **Position** section, type in `00:59:52:00` for the timecode and hit *Enter*.

Even though the Reel 5 BITC is **04:59:52:00**, you still have to enter `00:59:52:00` because if you enter `04:59:52:00` in the **Position** section of the **Movie Project Settings**, Logic Pro will place the movie 3 hours, 59 minutes, and 52 seconds ahead in your sequencer timeline.

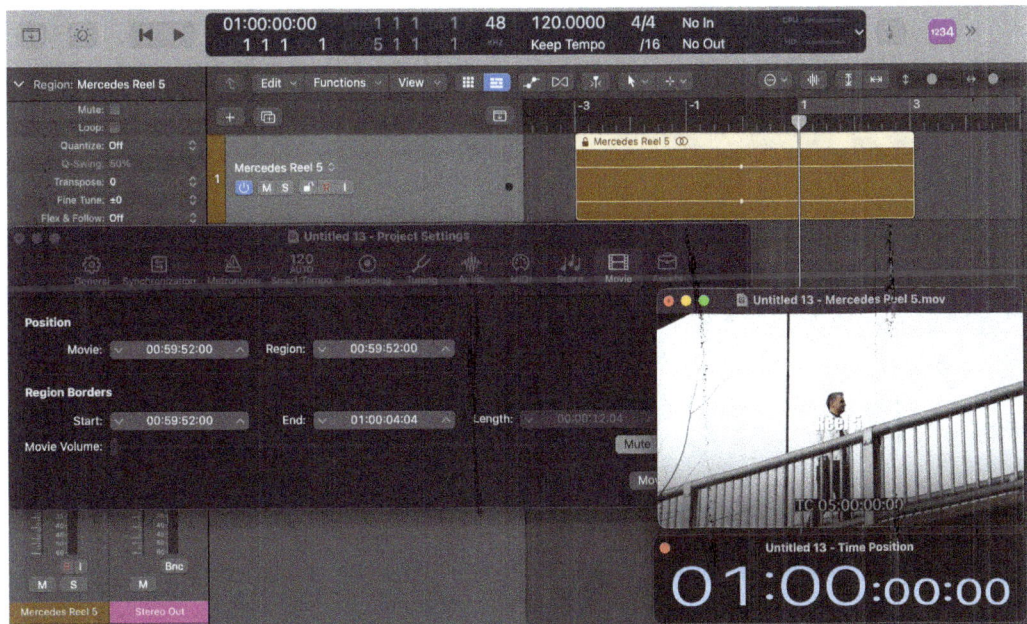

Figure 5.53: Movie project settings with Reel 5

Next, click on the **Synchronization** icon to get to the synchronization settings. Here, make sure that the upper **Bar Position** section is **1 1 1 1** and the **Plays at SMPTE** section is set to **01:00:00:00**. Additionally, make sure that the audio track 2-pop happens at **TC 00:59:58:00**.

Then, select **Enable separate SMPTE view offset**. Make sure that the lower **Bar Position** section is displayed as **1 1 1 1** and the **Displayed as SMPTE** section is set to **05:00:00:00**.

Now that the Logic Pro timecode in blue, **05:00:00:00**, matches the BITC of Reel 5, the movie and Logic Pro are properly synced:

Syncing Logic Pro to Picture

Figure 5.54: Reel 5 and the Logic Pro matching timecodes

To summarize, when working with multiple reels, the timecode in the **Movie Project Settings** window will always need to be **00:59:52:00**, no matter what reel you're working on. Let's look at the following table:

Reel	Reel Start Timecode BITC	Setting Timecode in Logic Pro	Setting Offset view in Logic Pro at bar 1 1 1 1 to the Following:
1	TC 00:59:52:00	TC 00:59:52:00	No offset
2	TC 01:59:52:00	TC 00:59:52:00	TC 02:00:00:00
3	TC 02:59:52:00	TC 00:59:52:00	TC 03:00:00:00
4	TC 03:59:52:00	TC 00:59:52:00	TC 04:00:00:00
5	TC 04:59:52:00	TC 00:59:52:00	TC 05:00:00:00

Figure 5.55: Five movie reels with a timecode offset view

To break this table down, the first column shows the five different reels. In the second column, we see different timecodes for each of the five reels. Each reel starts with a different hour at the beginning of the timecode (00, 01, 02, etc.). In the third column, we see the same timecode numbers that will need to be put into the **Movie Project Settings** window for each reel. In the fourth column, we see a corresponding timecode window with the Logic Pro offset view. That window needs to be changed to match the movie BITC of the corresponding reel. Additionally, when working with movie reels with countdowns that start at **TC 00:59:50:00** or **TC 00:59:49:00**, for example, those numbers would need to be entered in the **Movie Project Settings** window, for each reel.

Syncing a movie file with SMPTE Offset View

In this section, we will learn how to open and synchronize a movie file using SMPTE Offset View. The offset view is when the original movie start time has a new start time, so you're viewing the movie with the new start time instead of the original movie start time.

Sometimes, film directors will want a film composer to start from the beginning of the movie, and sometimes from a specified location. In this section we will use an example of how to sync the movie from a specified location, using the SMPTE Offset View, and in this example, the film director requests that the composer start scoring at **TC 01:00:15:12**, which would be 15 seconds and 12 frames into the movie.

To begin, open a new Logic Pro session and import `Mercedes-Benz Cabrio C 300_BITC.mov`. Make sure that the movie and Logic Pro are synchronized properly.

Next, press the forward slash (/) button on your keyboard to open a floating **Go To Position** window. In the second box to the right of **New**, enter the timecode numbers `01:00:15:12`:

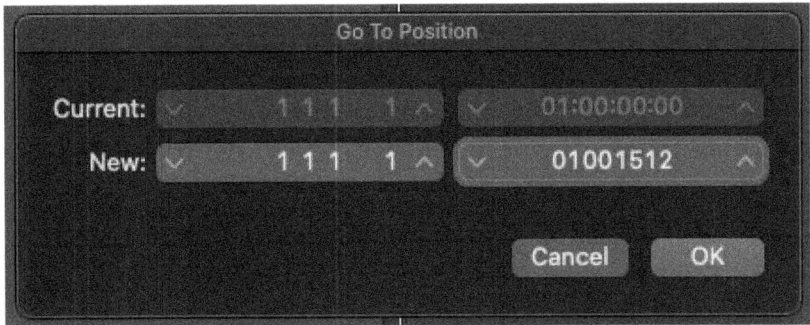

Figure 5.56: Go To Position window

After typing the timecode location in the **Go To Position** window, Logic Pro will move the playhead to that position. In the following screenshot, Logic Pro shows the playhead at **TC 01:00:15:12**, bar 8, beat 4, but we want to set up Logic Pro to start scoring at bar 1:

Figure 5.57: Arrange window with the Beats and Time display

To fix this, right-click on the movie and select **Synchronization**. As seen in *Figure 5.58*, with the bar position as **1 1 1 1**, type 01:00:15:12 in the **Plays at SMPTE** section and hit *Enter*. Logic Pro will adjust the movie position and create an offset view by moving the movie file to the bar 1 position.

Figure 5.58: Arrange Window with SMPTE Offset View

As a reminder, make sure to enable **Protect** in the movie track and lock the movie.

Scoring a movie from any bar location

In this section, we will learn how to open and synchronize a movie file using any bar location. This is useful, as some film composers may prefer to start scoring from bar 3, 5, or any other bar location.

Begin by opening a new Logic Pro session and importing `Mercedes_24FPS_BITC_Academy leader.mov`. Make sure that the sample rate and frame rate match the movie rate. Then, drag and drop the movie to the bar 5 location and place the playhead at bar 5.

Figure 5.59: Movie file starting at bar 5

Right-click on the movie and select **Movie Project Settings**. In the **Position** section, type in `00:59:52:00` for the timecode and hit *Enter*.

Figure 5.60: Movie Project Settings window

Next, click on the **Synchronization** icon. In the **Bar Position** section, type `5 1 1 1`, and in **Plays at SMPTE**, type `01:00:00:00`:

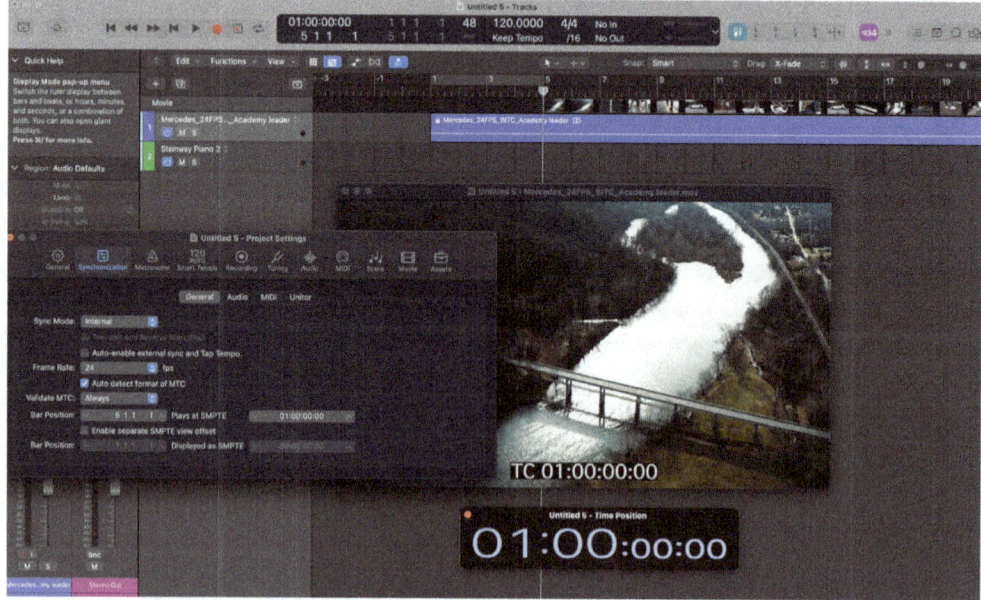

Figure 5.61: Synced SMPTE Offset View at Bar 5

Once again, make sure Logic Pro and the movie are in sync with one another by playing your movie and observing the movie and Logic Pro timecodes, making sure that the numbers match as it plays. In this example, you will now be able to start scoring from bar 5.

The task of synchronizing Logic Pro to picture can take some getting used to, so practice and repeat the synchronization process. If the Logic Pro and movie timecodes are drifting apart for more than plus or minus two frames (for example, **TC 01:15:21:05** plus two frames would be **TC 01:15:21:07**, and minus two frames would be **TC 01:15:21:03**), then you will want to check the reason for why they're getting out of sync. A possible cause could be streaming too much data from the disk. The solution would be to move the project folder with the movie file, or to move and relocate the internal Logic Pro sound library to an external SSD drive. This could improve the performance of your Logic Pro sequencer and prevent out-of-sync problems.

Now that we've covered different methods of synchronizing a movie with Logic Pro, we will go over how to create a variety of scoring to picture templates that will help speed up the workflow.

Creating a custom scoring to picture template

With so many different possible ways of scoring to picture, it is helpful to create different film scoring templates. Using custom templates allows you to have prepared working environments suitable for different film scoring tasks, which will speed up the working process.

To create a custom template, begin by opening a Logic Pro session and creating two audio tracks.

Rename the first audio track `Dialog Left Channel`, and turn the **Pan** knob all the way to the left. Then, rename the second audio track `TEMP MUSIC Right Channel`, and turn the **Pan** knob all the way to the right:

Figure 5.62: Renamed audio tracks for Dialog and TEMP MUSIC

Hover your mouse over the LCD display area, click on the drop-down menu arrow, and select **Customize Control Bar and Display…**:

Figure 5.63: LCD Display window drop-down menu

In the next window, there are many options for you to choose from that can be used for customization, based on personal preference. Under **LCD**, click on the **Beats & Project** drop-down menu and select **Custom**, then check the box next to **Sample Rate**. Next, under the **Transport** section, select **Capture Recording**.

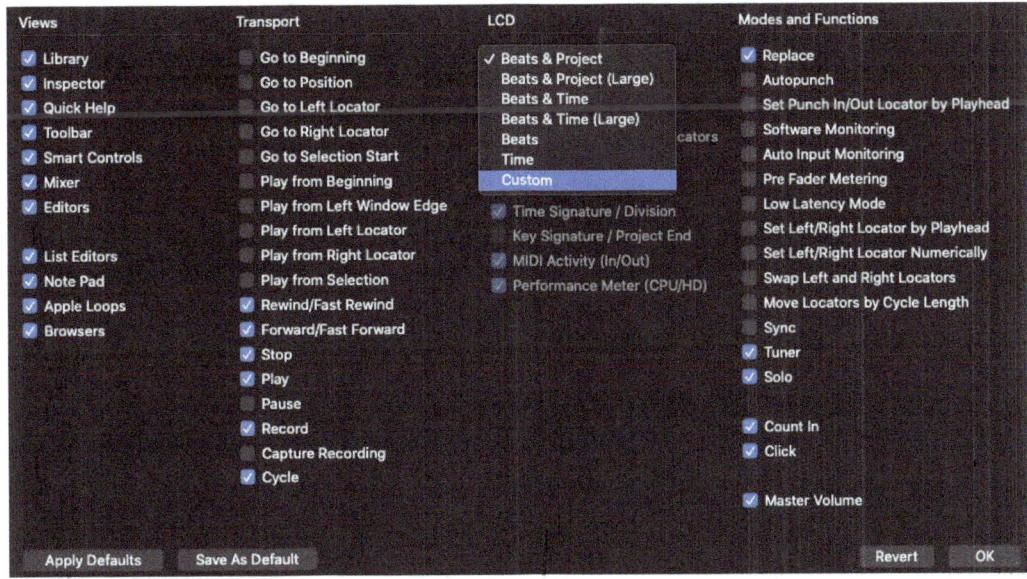

Figure 5.64: LCD drop-down menu

You can customize this window by selecting any additional parameters that will be helpful in improving the workflow. Once you've made your selections, click **OK** to confirm your selections and close the window. The large LCD display will now show your selections; you can click on any of them to make changes:

Figure 5.65: Customized view of the LCD display

Next, click on **View**, and from the drop-down menu, select **Secondary Ruler** and **Marquee Ruler**:

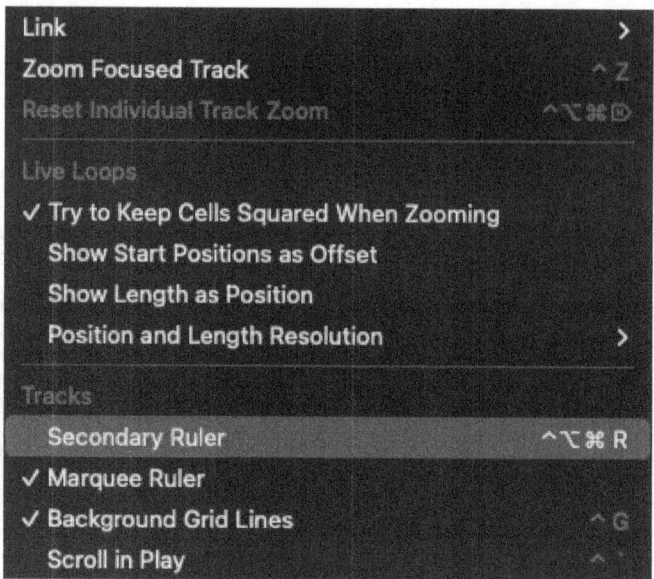

Figure 5.66: View drop-down menu

The **Secondary Ruler** and the **Marquee Ruler** are now visible:

Figure 5.67: Secondary and Marquee rulers

Next, open the global tracks (using the *G* shortcut) and right-click on any of the visible tracks. From the menu, in addition to the **Movie** track, enable the **Marker**, **Signature**, **Tempo**, and **Beat Mapping** tracks:

Creating a custom scoring to picture template   115

Figure 5.68: Global tracks

Reorganize the tracks by holding and dragging them up or down. For this example, align them from top to bottom, in this order – **Movie**, **Marker**, **Beat Mapping**, **Signature**, and **Tempo** (as shown in *Figure 5.69*):

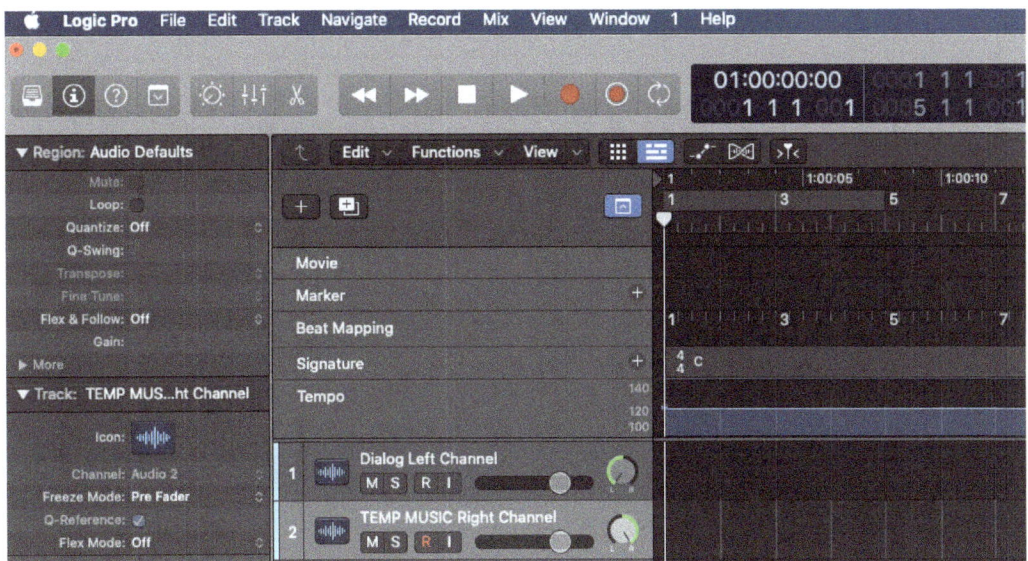

Figure 5.69: Global tracks view

Next, hover your mouse over the upper ruler portion. The pointer will turn into a left bracket shape with arrows on both sides, just like back in *Figure 5.28*. Drag the bracket cursor to reveal the negative bars. Expand the view and drag the bracket cursor a little past the negative three (**-3**) bar location:

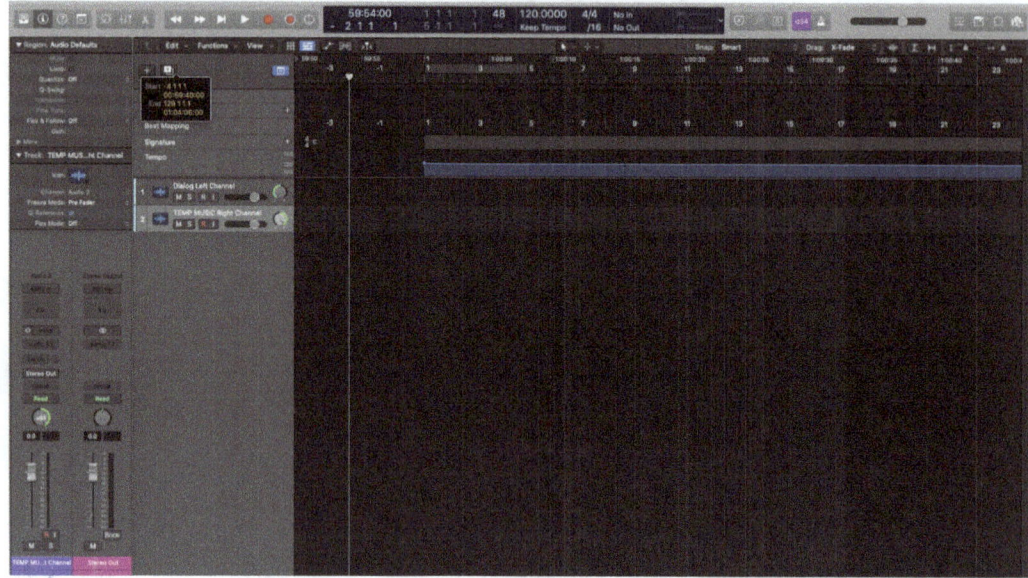

Figure 5.70: Expanded view of the negative bars

Next, open the **Tempo** window (using the *Shift + Option + T* shortcut), or hit the **Editor** button (using the *D* shortcut) and click on the **Tempo** tab. As a default setting, Logic Pro will display a tempo node of **120** bpm, at position **1 1 1 1**. Next, place the playhead at bar 0, and in the **Tempo** window, click the + icon:

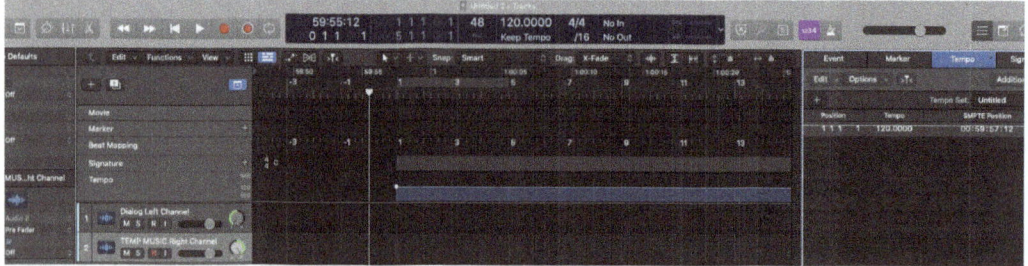

Figure 5.71: Global tracks and the Tempo window

Logic Pro will create a tempo node of **120** bpm at bar **0 1 1 1**.

Creating a custom scoring to picture template   117

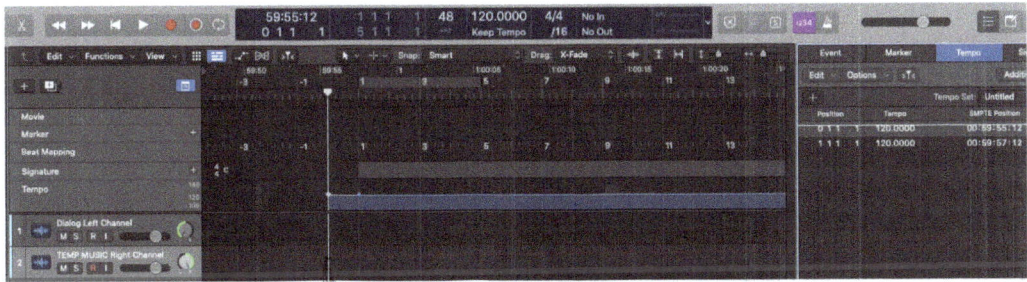

Figure 5.72: Tempo node at bar 1 location

Now, zoom in horizontally (*CMD* + the right arrow) and place the playhead at bar **1 1 1 21**. Click the + icon in the **Tempo** window again, and Logic Pro will create an additional tempo node.

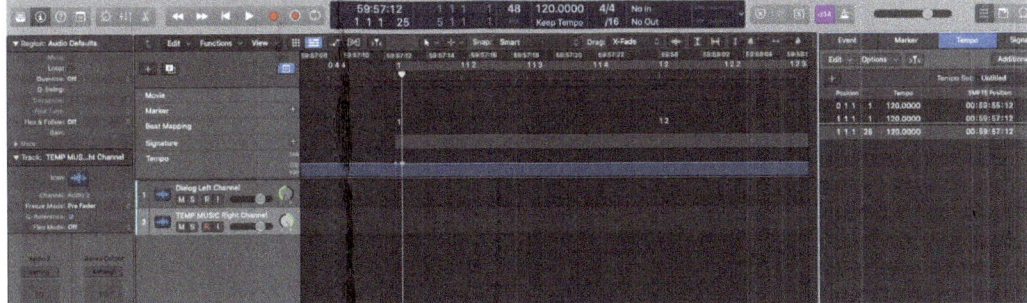

Figure 5.73: Tempo node at bar 1 location

Creating additional tempo nodes at the beginning of a Logic Pro session can help the synchronization process to be more efficient when dealing with many tempo calculations. It's specifically helpful when using bars, locked markers, and beat-mapped hit points. All of these film-scoring terminologies will be covered in more detail in the next chapter.

Next, right-click on the track header and select **Configure Track Header** (or press *Option* + *T*). Then, select **Protect**, **Track Numbers**, **Color Bars**, and **Track Alternatives** (you can select any additional options as needed):

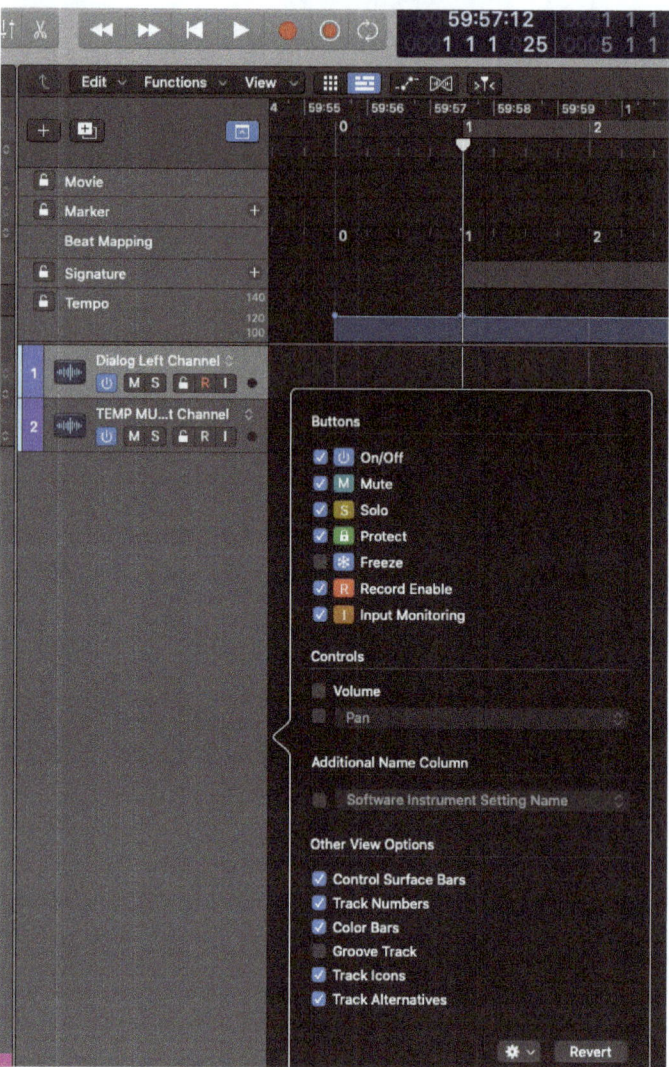

Figure 5.74: Track Header window with selections

When you put a checkmark next to an icon in the track header menu, that function will be visible on all the tracks.

Now, open the toolbar, then right-click in the toolbar area, and click on **Customize Toolbar**:

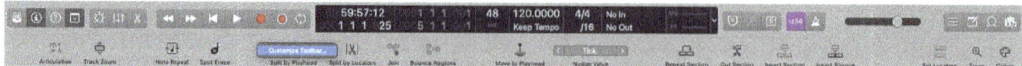

Figure 5.75: Customized toolbar

Select any tools that will be helpful in your workflow, based on your personal preferences. Then, click **OK** to confirm your selection and close the **Toolbar** window:

Figure 5.76: Toolbar menu options

Next, save this Logic Pro session as a template by selecting **File**, and then **Save as Template**.

Name the template with your preferred convention, including a version number, a date, or the type of template in the name. Remember not to change the provided project template folder location. Then, hit **Save**.

Figure 5.77: Naming your Template window

When starting a new Logic Pro session, you can decide how Logic Pro will open the session. You have the option to work from a custom template or the default template each time you launch Logic Pro. In order to change Logic Pro's behavior at startup, click on **Logic Pro | Preferences | General**:

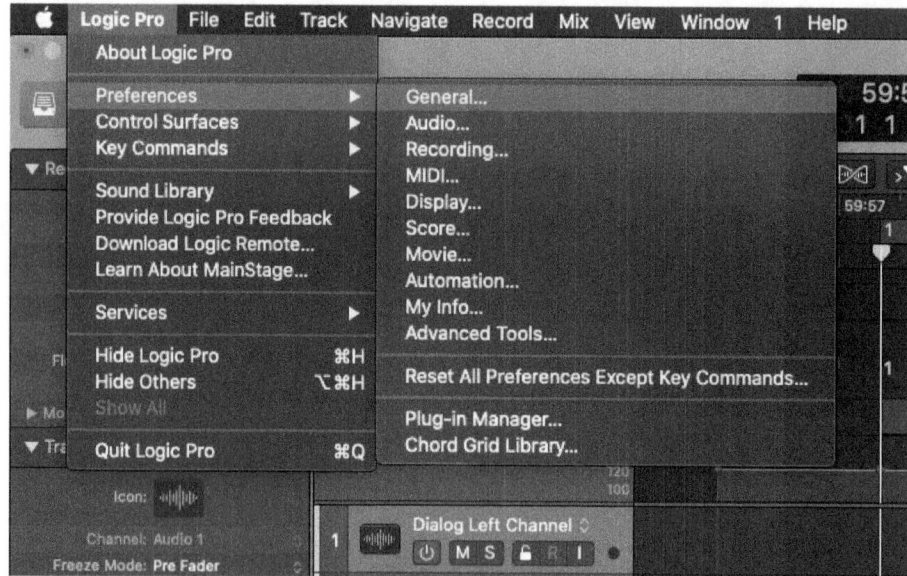

Figure 5.78: Logic Pro Preferences menu

In the **Preferences** window, go to the **Project Handling** tab, where you will see **Startup Action** and **Default Template**:

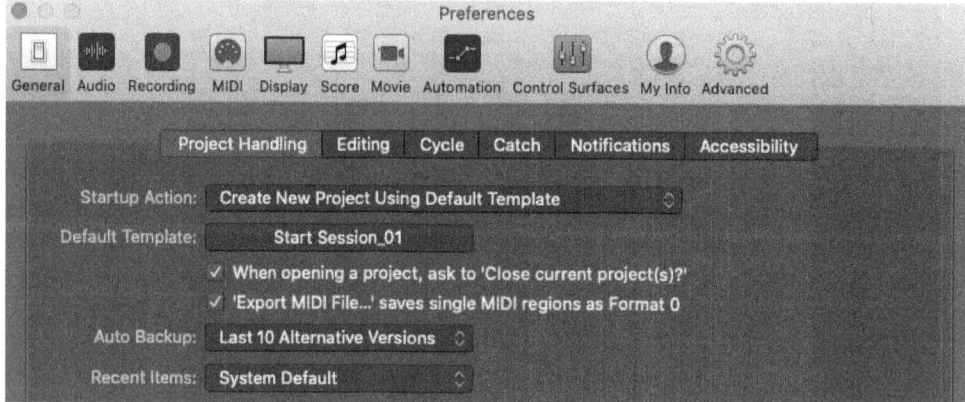

Figure 5.79: Project Handling section

Click on the **Startup Action** drop-down menu arrows and choose how you want Logic Pro to handle your project. For this example, select **Create New Project Using Default Template**:

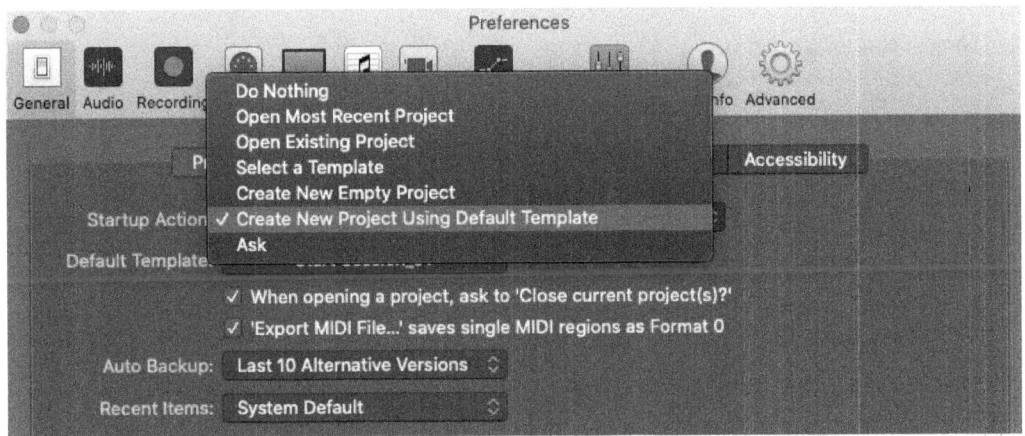

Figure 5.80: Startup Action drop-down menu options

Next, click on the **My Templates** folder on the left-side panel and select the desired template:

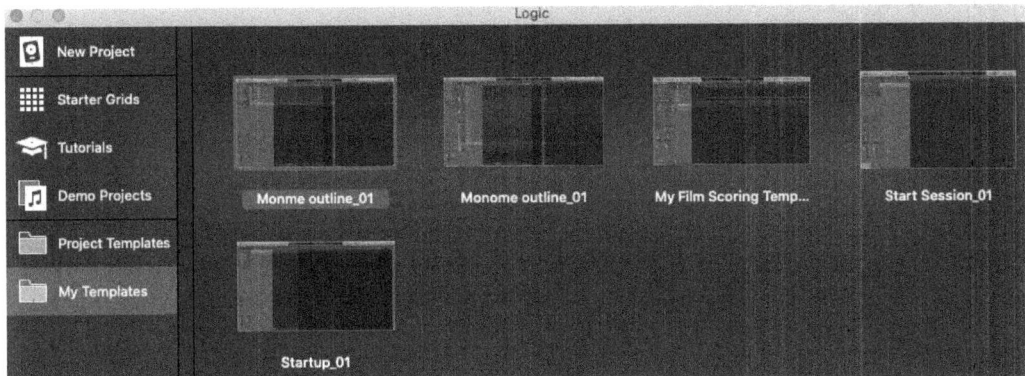

Figure 5.81: My Templates thumbnail window

In the **Project Handling** section, from the **Startup Action** drop-down menu, select **Create New Project Using Default Template**. Then, from the **Default Template** drop-down menu, select **My Film Scoring Template_01** (you can select any template from the drop-down menu to use as the default template):

Figure 5.82: Preferences window with the selected Startup Action template

Every time you start a new Logic Pro session, whatever template you select will be what Logic Pro will start your project with. You can always change how Logic Pro handles your project at startup.

Since there can be many different ways of how you prefer to work, based on different types of film scoring tasks, creating as many usable templates as possible will speed up the workflow process.

Summary

In this chapter, we learned how to synchronize Logic Pro to picture, covering all aspects of the process, including how to use movie project settings and synchronization settings. We also covered how to synchronize different types of movie files to Logic Pro, and how to create and use a film-scoring template.

It's important to cover all these so that you, as a film composer, learn all the different methods of scoring to picture and can select the one that works best for you.

In the next chapter, we will discuss working with markers when scoring to picture.

6
Working with Hit Points and Scene Markers

In the previous chapter, we learned how to align and sync a movie with Logic Pro. The next task is to create markers that will represent specific events on the movie timeline.

In this chapter, we will cover visual events, also known as hit points, in a movie, including how to identify them correctly, put them together in lists, as well as how to represent them as SMPTE-locked markers.

Since we're dealing with tempo and time signature changes, working properly with markers in Logic Pro will make the task of scoring to the picture much smoother and more efficient without compromises.

So, in this chapter, we will cover the following topics:

- Defining hit points
- Reviewing music spotting notes
- Copying the spotting notes list into Logic Pro
- Creating markers without rounding
- Naming and renaming markers
- Changing markers to the SMPTE view position
- Creating scene markers
- Comparing standard, SMPTE-locked, and scene markers
- Creating and removing movie scene cut markers
- Navigating with markers
- Creating new marker sets

Technical requirements

To follow along with this chapter, you will need a Mac computer with Logic Pro and QuickTime software installed. You will also need to be able to access the movie files provided with this book: `https://packt.link/hxCer`.

Defining hit points

Hit points, also referred to as sync points, visual points, visual events, or cuts, are specific spots in a movie where the music needs to adapt to or acknowledge the events while being synced with the movie in a logical way. The events could be, for example, scene cuts, dialog lines, specific actions on screen, and so on.

In film music, identifying those hit points is crucial when scoring to picture because they point out where in the movie the music needs to emphasize that precise event or moment. Hit points will be reflected in Logic Pro as scene markers and we will go over how to create scene markers later on in this chapter.

Reviewing music spotting notes

In *Chapter 1*, we discussed how to create a cue sheet, or a music spotting notes list. Generally, the film director will provide you with the music spotting notes list. If a music spotting notes list is not handed to you by the director, then the director will communicate the cuts, important events, and hit points during the spotting session, and the film composer will need to make notes accordingly. The music spotting notes list is a helpful guide for not only analyzing and identifying specific cuts or events but also finding the most important hit points that will need special attention.

To see an example, let's open the Word document `Mercedes Benz_Music Spotting Notes List.docx`. This list shows all the events from the start to the end of the Mercedes commercial that we saw previously in the book.

When you have the list, the first step is to observe all of the listed events in the movie. Review the music spotting notes list while watching the commercial on your computer desktop, observing the specific locations, and reading the scene descriptions.

Music Spotting Notes List
Film Production: *Mercedes-Benz Commercial C-300*

CUT	"Hit point"	Time Code	Scene Description	Music Description
01		01:00:00:00	Movie starts	
02		01:00:02:15	Cut to over-the-bridge shot	
03		01:00:04:20	Cut to a girl	
04		01:00:07:06	Cut to a girl - medium shot	
05		01:00:07:07	Cut to walking	
06		01:00:08:11	Cut to car shots	
07		01:00:10:16	Cut to a girl - medium shot	
08		01:00:17:05	Cut to car open top	
09		01:00:24:05	Cut to the bridge car passing	
10		01:00:27:04	Cut to a girl walking	
11		01:00:28:21	Cut to a guy - medium shot	
12		01:00:30:13	Cut to a guy walking on the bridge	
13		01:00:31:23	Cut to aerial wide shot	
14		01:00:35:07	Cut to car interior shot	
15		01:00:38:12	Cut to aerial wide shot	
16	**Yes**	**01:00:39:20**	**Cut to over-the-bridge shot**	
17		01:00:41:12	Cut to car driving over the bridge	
18		01:00:43:20	Cut to a girl driving car- medium shot	
19		01:00:44:21	Cut to car passing the bridge	
20		01:00:46:06	Cut to a guy in the rearview mirror	
21		01:00:47:03	Cut to a guy driving car- medium shot	
22		01:00:48:08	Cut to car interior	
23		01:00:49:10	Cut to car passing the bridge	
24		01:00:51:16	Cut to the sun	
25		01:00:51:21	Cut to car driving across the bridge	
26		01:00:53:07	Cut to over-the-bridge shot	
27	**Yes**	**01:00:54:14**	**Cut to couple driving car over-the-bridge**	
28		01:00:59:03	Cut to a girl walking up the stairs	
29		01:01:01:09	Cut to a girl looking out medium shot	
30		01:01:02:14	Cut to couple driving car over-the-bridge	
31		01:01:03:09	Cut to couple driving - interior shot	
32		01:01:05:09	Cut to front car lamp	
33		01:01:06:14	Cut to front car logo	
34	**Yes**	**01:01:07:20**	**Cut to couple standing outside**	
35		01:01:09:19	Cut to black	

Figure 6.1: Music spotting notes list

Now that we have reviewed all of the spotting notes, next we will go over how to make them available directly in Logic Pro.

Copying the spotting notes list into Logic Pro

Making the spotting notes list available in Logic Pro is a helpful way of reading and accessing all of the notes without having to go in and out of a Word document.

Before copying the spotting notes list into Logic Pro, the movie file needs to be opened and synchronized to the picture. So, open the movie file `Mercedes-Benz Cabrio C 300_BITC.mov`, make sure that the movie and Logic Pro are in sync, and save the project.

Next, open the `Mercedes Benz_Music Spotting Notes List.docx` Word document again. After the document is open, select all of the content using the *CMD + A* shortcut and then use the *CMD + C* shortcut to copy all of the content selected.

Back in Logic Pro, click on the **Notes** button (or use the *Option + CMD + P* shortcut). Then, in the **Notes** window, click on the **Project** tab, and click on the **Aa** button in the upper-left corner of that window. Once Logic Pro displays a blinking cursor, click in the window and use the *CMD + V* shortcut to paste the spotting notes list into Logic Pro Notes.

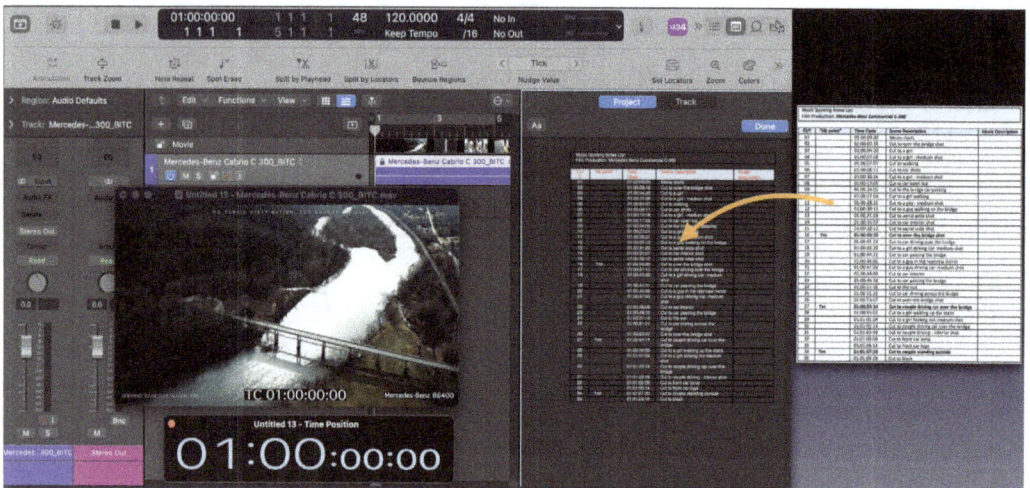

Figure 6.2: Music spotting notes list in Logic Pro Notes

Having all of the spotting notes inside Logic Pro is going to be very helpful for creating markers. In the next section, we will go over how to create markers.

Creating markers without rounding

In Logic Pro, we can create regular markers and markers without rounding. The difference between the two is that when you create a regular **marker**, Logic Pro will place it at the nearest bar and beat, whereas a **marker without rounding** can be placed anywhere in the ruler without being rounded to the nearest bar and beat.

For this reason, markers without rounding are mostly used in scoring to picture. We will use the spotting notes that have been copied into Logic Pro notes as the pointers for creating markers.

First, let's open the previously saved Logic Pro session with the `Mercedes-Benz Cabrio C 300_BITC.mov` movie file and the imported spotting notes list.

Next, open **Global Tracks** (shortcut *G*) and enable the marker track. If the **Marker** track is not visible, right-click on the movie track and select **Marker** from the drop-down list.

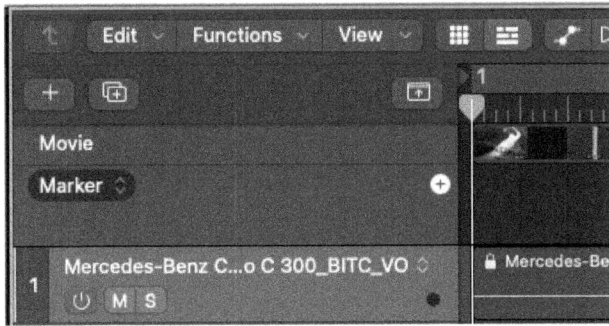

Figure 6.3: Marker track

Next, create a marker without rounding by clicking on the + icon in the **Marker** track, or by using the *Ctrl* + *Option* + ' (apostrophe) shortcut. Another way to create a marker without rounding is by going to **Navigate | Other** and clicking on **Create Without Rounding** from the drop-down menu.

> **Tip**
> To create a regular marker, use the *Option* + ' key command. To create a marker without rounding, use the key command: *Control* + *Option* + '. You can create custom key commands for markers by going to the **Key Command Assignment** window (*Option* + *K*) and renaming existing shortcuts or creating new ones.

Our goal is to create markers without rounding for all of the timecodes listed in the Logic Pro Notes window. Place your playhead at bar 1, beat 1 by clicking on the + icon on the marker track to create your first marker.

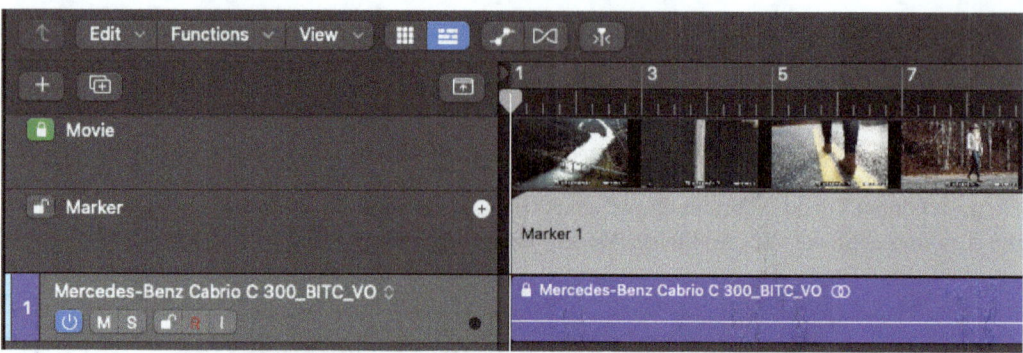

Figure 6.4: First marker without rounding

To create the second marker, go to the **Notes** window in Logic Pro and copy the timecode **01:00:02:15** (to select any content in the **Notes** window, make sure to click on the **Aa** button first).

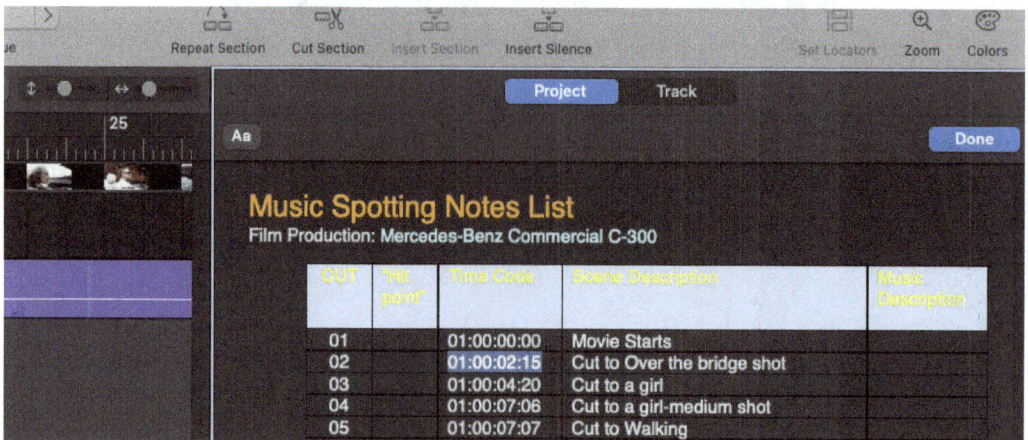

Figure 6.5: Logic Pro Notes window with spotting notes list

Next, open the **Go To Position** panel (shortcut /) and paste the timecode into the lower-right box.

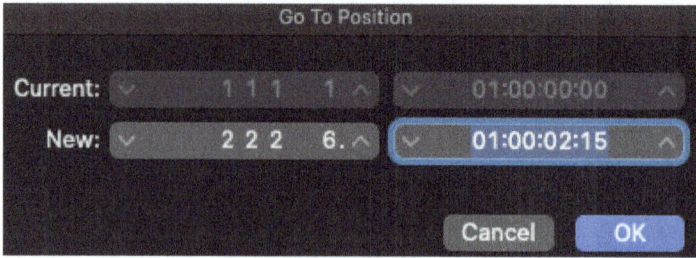

Figure 6.6: Go To Position window

Hit *Enter* or click **OK** and Logic Pro will place the playhead at the exact location of **TC 01:00:02:15**:

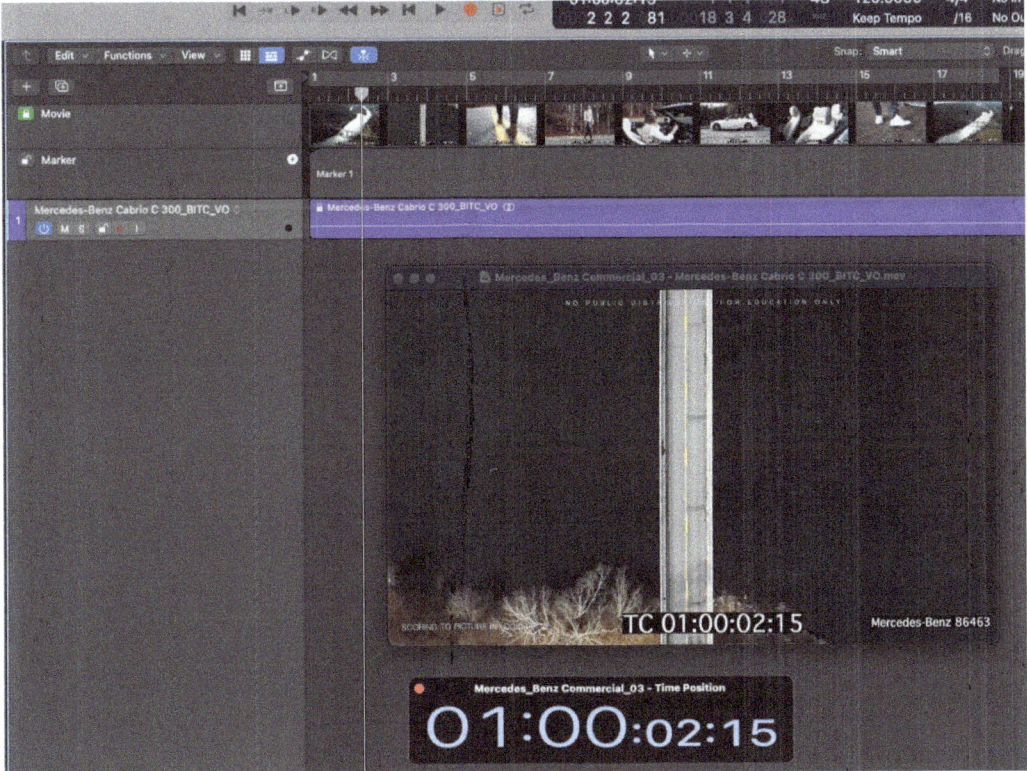

Figure 6.7: Playhead positioned at specified location

Next press *Option* + ' (apostrophe) and Logic Pro will create a second marker without rounding at the exact location of **TC 01:00:02:15**:

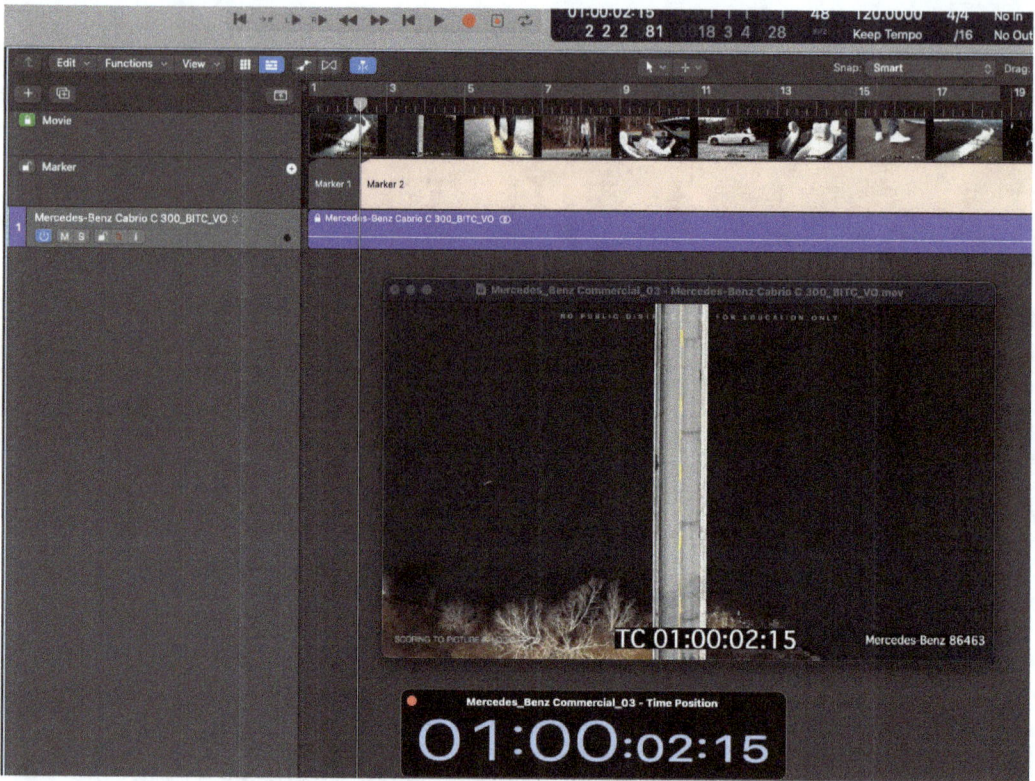

Figure 6.8: Second marker without rounding

Now, to create the third marker without rounding, let's try a slightly different method. Instead of using **Go To Position**, use the **Giant Time Display** to move the playhead to a specific location. You can adjust the timecode numbers by hovering your mouse over the **Giant Time Display** and dragging the mouse, adjusting the timecode numbers individually to match the marker timecode locations. As the playhead moves to the following location of **TC 01:00:04:20**, create the third marker without rounding.

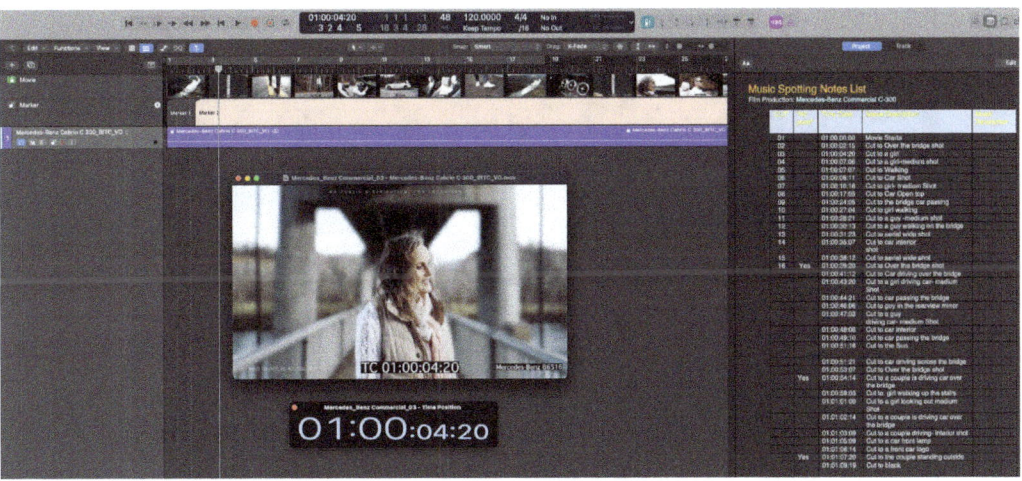

Figure 6.9: Big Time Display – playhead location adjustment

Use the previous instructions to create markers without rounding for all the timecodes listed in the Logic Pro notes section. Your **Marker** track with all 36 markers should look like so:

Figure 6.10: Filled-out Marker track

> **Tip**
> Like in the previous figure, you can color each marker individually by using the *Option + C* shortcut. This will help visually differentiate the markers.

Now that we know how to create markers and markers without rounding, next, we will go over how to name and rename markers.

Naming and renaming markers

To better identify markers when scoring to the picture, instead of using generic names such as Marker 1, Marker 2, and so on, we will use the imported spotting notes list in Logic Pro to name them. This will help to see clearly the events of the spotting list in the ruler within the scene cuts.

To do this, click on the **List Editors** button (shortcut *D*) and then click on the **Marker** tab:

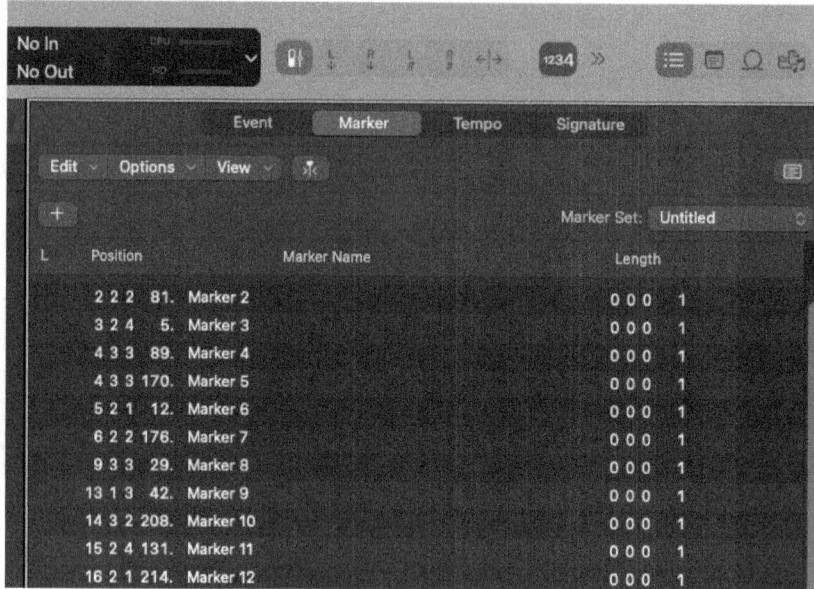

Figure 6.11: Marker window

With the **Marker** tab now blue, click, hold, and drag it to the middle of the Logic Pro **Arrange** window. When you let the window go, Logic Pro will create a floating **Marker** window.

Figure 6.12: Floating Marker window

Next, click on the **Notes** tab and you should see Logic Pro notes and the floating **Marker** window:

Figure 6.13: Floating Marker window with notes window open

From the spotting notes list, select and copy the marker name from the **Scene Description** column. Then, highlight the corresponding marker in the floating window and paste the name into the bottom areas of the window shown in the following figure. This will rename the marker.

Working with Hit Points and Scene Markers

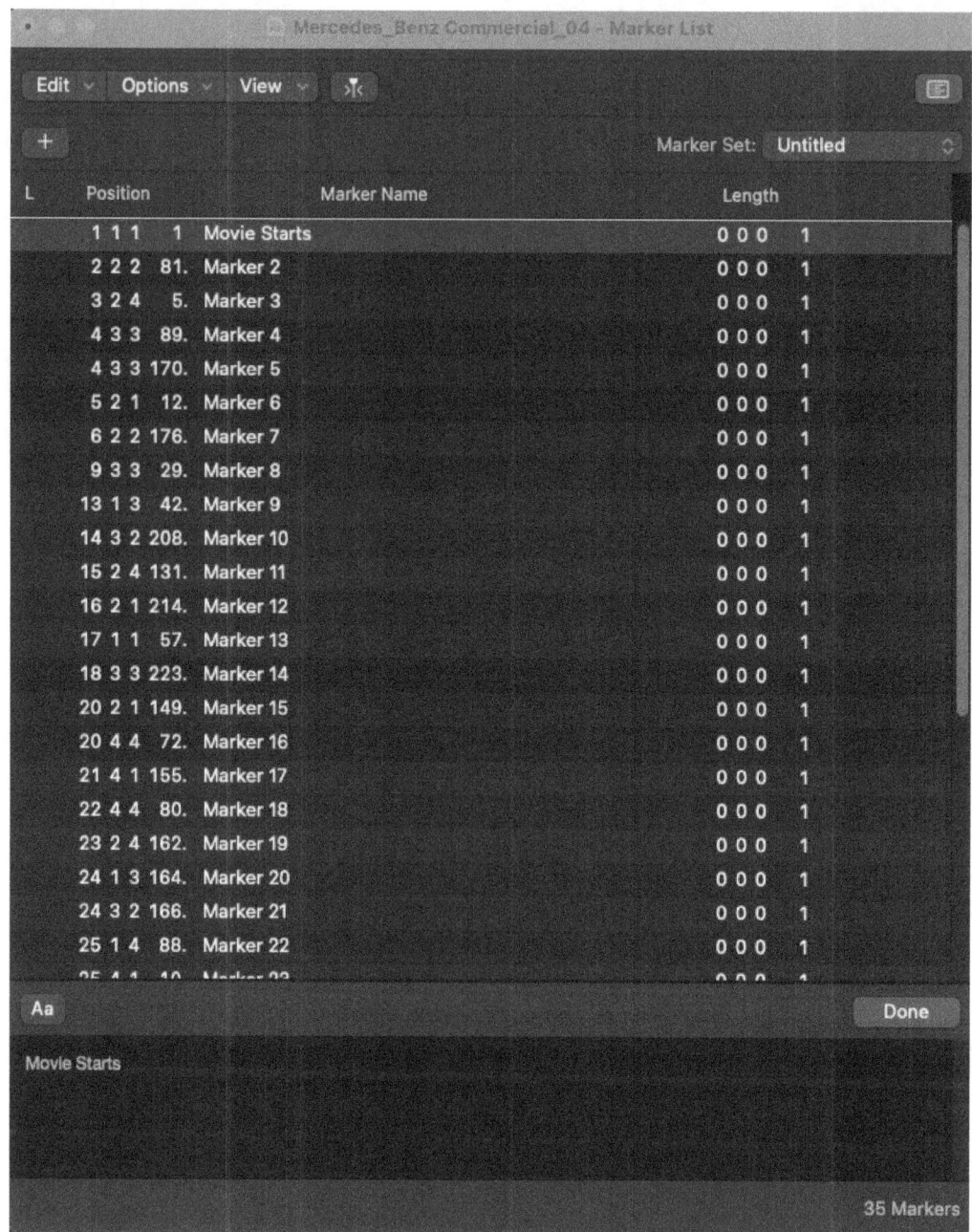

Figure 6.14: Floating Marker window with notes window open

Repeat these steps to rename all markers. You can see the result here:

Figure 6.15: Renamed markers list window

After renaming all the markers in the **Marker** window, the marker names in the **Arrange** window should now match.

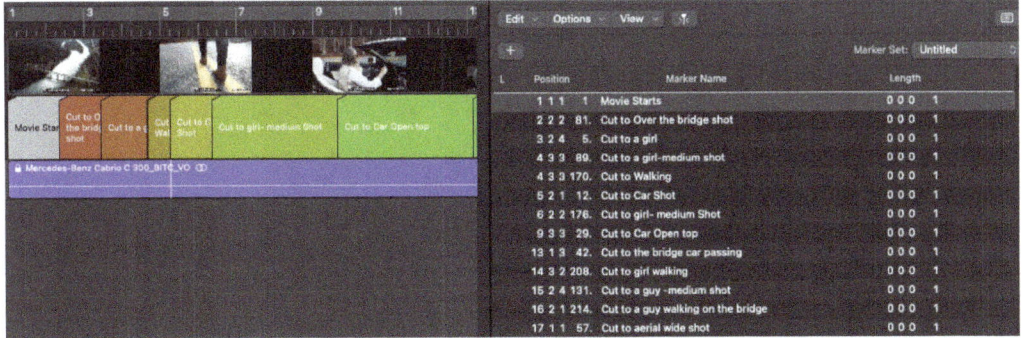

Figure 6.16: Renamed markers

Working with Hit Points and Scene Markers

Now that we've learned how to name and rename markers, next, we will go over how to convert markers to reflect the SMPTE position in the **Marker** window.

Changing markers to the SMPTE view position

In the previous section, the markers only reflected the bars and beats position, but now we will change the view to a SMPTE timecode view. The reason why we're changing the view of the markers in the **Marker** window is to make sure they match the timecodes of the cuts and hit points in the spotting notes list. We can then visually compare the timecode description of the markers in the window with the spotting notes before locking them to SMPTE.

Select all the markers by using *CMD + A*, then right-click (or *Ctrl* + click), and select **Event Position and Length as Time** from the drop-down menu:

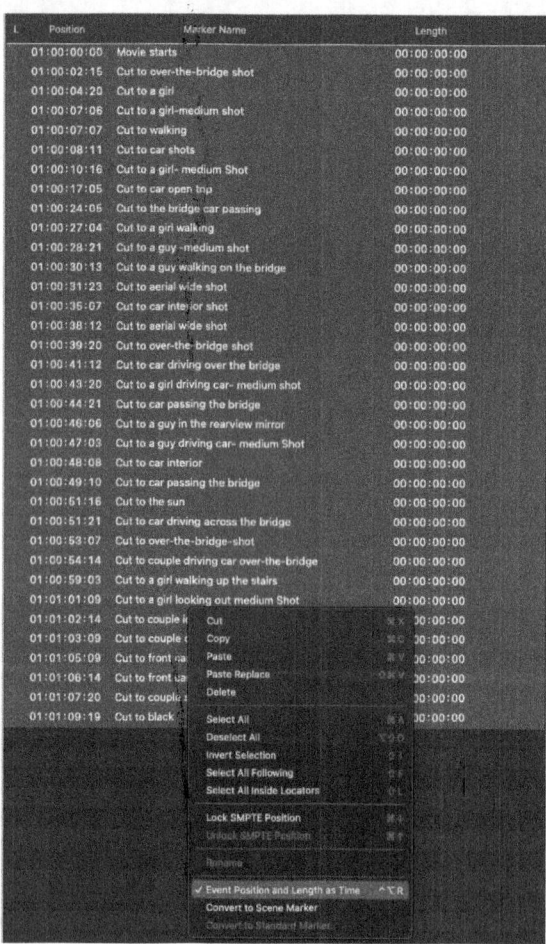

Figure 6.17: Markers pop-up window menu

After converting the markers from the bars and beats view into a SMPTE timecode view, now all of the markers' positions match the timecodes in the spotting notes list.

Logic Pro also displays the marker length by default, as an infinite value of **00:00:00:00**. Changing the marker position and adjusting the marker length will also be reflected in those numbers.

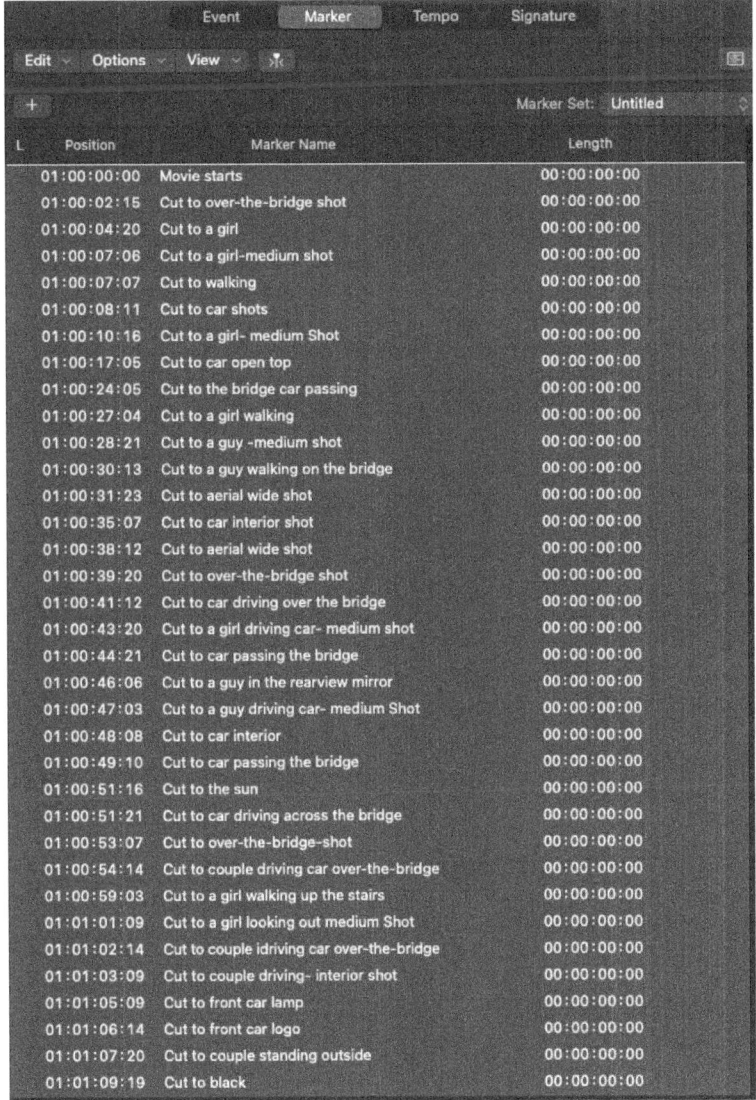

Figure 6.18: Marker SMPTE view position window

Now that we've learned how to change the markers from the bars and beats position view to the SMPTE view, next, we will need to lock them to the SMPTE location.

Creating scene markers

As mentioned before, markers are either locked or unlocked. Scene markers, by default, are SMPTE-locked markers. Logic Pro allows you to lock the position of the markers so that no matter what musical changes occur during the process of scoring to the picture, the markers will be locked into place. If the markers are not locked to an SMPTE position, any type of tempo or time signature change can cause the position of the markers to shift.

To create scene markers, open the **Marker** window and use *CMD + A* to select all the markers. Then, right-click (or *Ctrl* + click) in the window and select **Convert to Scene Marker** from the drop-down menu:

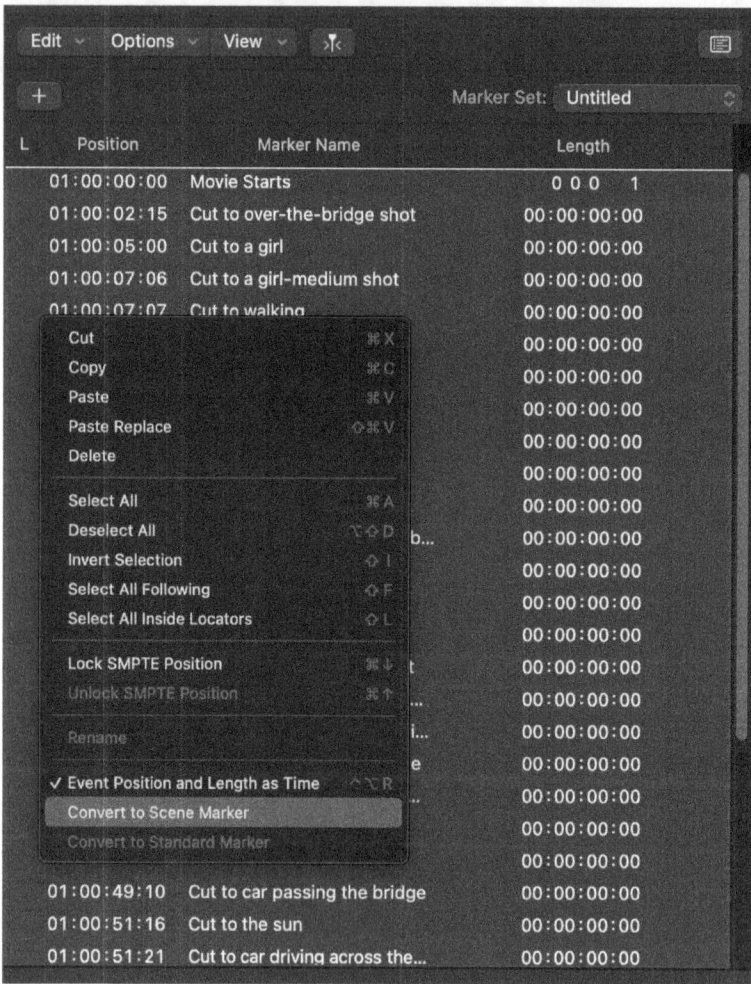

Figure 6.19: Convert to Scene Marker drop-down menu

Logic Pro will convert all the selected markers into scene markers, and each of those markers will receive a clock icon placed on the left side of the SMPTE timecode. Additionally, all the markers in the **Arrange** window will have a padlock icon visible indicating their locked SMPTE position.

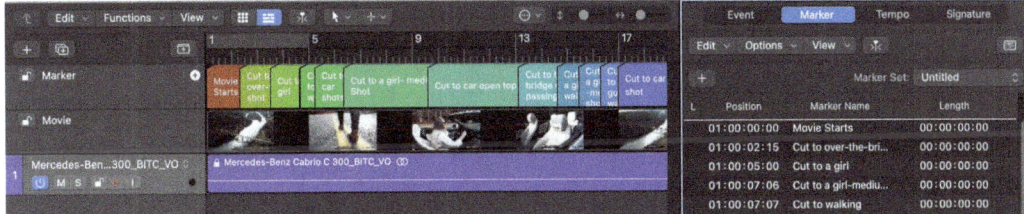

Figure 6.20: Locked scene markers

Now that we understand how to change the position from bars and beats to the SMPTE view position and to SMPTE-locked Scene markers, next, we will examine the differences between the markers and their usage. Until now, what we've seen is the step-by-step process of creating scene markers before scoring to picture. In general, once these steps are completed, you are then ready to score to picture. These steps should be repeated and practiced.

In the next section, comparing the markers will help prepare you for other additional scenarios when scoring to picture.

Comparing standard, SMPTE-locked, and scene markers

Standard markers could be either regular markers or markers without rounding. The standard markers by default are not SMPTE-locked.

It is important to notice that by clicking on the plus button located in **Global Tracks** on the marker track, Logic Pro creates a marker without rounding. When clicking on the + button in the **Marker** window, Logic Pro will create a standard marker not rounded to the nearest bar and beat.

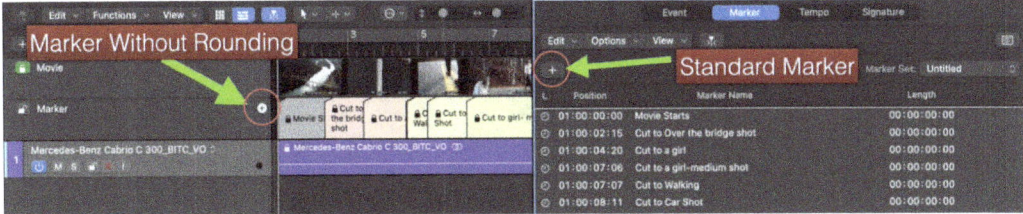

Figure 6.21: Standard marker and marker without rounding buttons

In the **Marker** window, a standard marker can be converted into a SMPTE-locked marker and vice versa. To create a standard marker, click the + button in the **Marker** window, or open the **Options** tab and select **Convert to Standard Marker** from the pop-up menu.

Working with Hit Points and Scene Markers

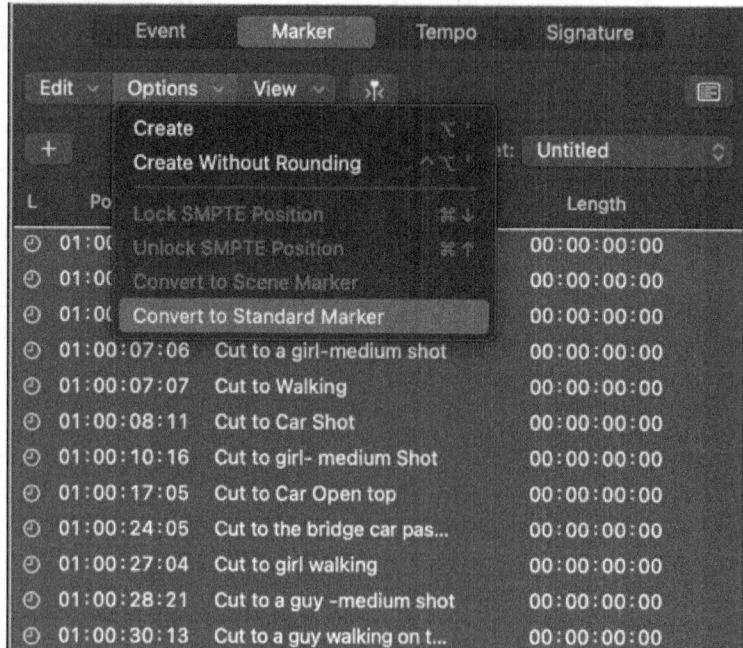

Figure 6.22: Options drop-down menu

Logic Pro will display regular standard markers like so:

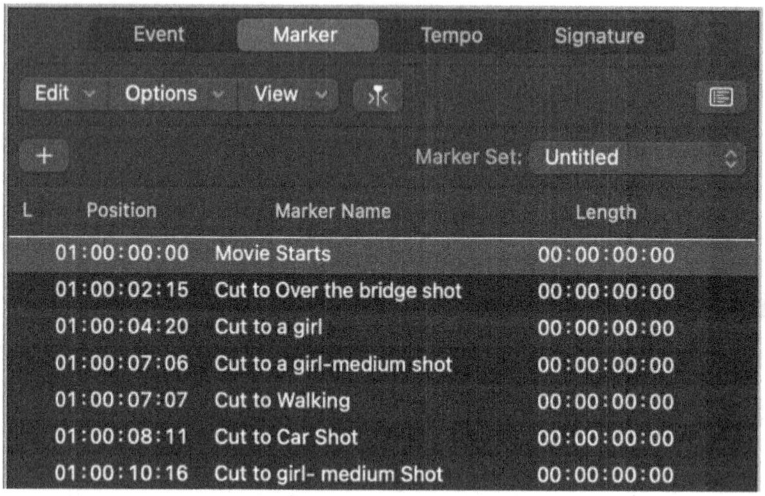

Figure 6.23: Converted scene markers into standard markers

To create a SMPTE-locked marker, click on the **Options** tab in the **Marker** window and select **Lock SMPTE Position** from the drop-down menu.

Comparing standard, SMPTE-locked, and scene markers | 141

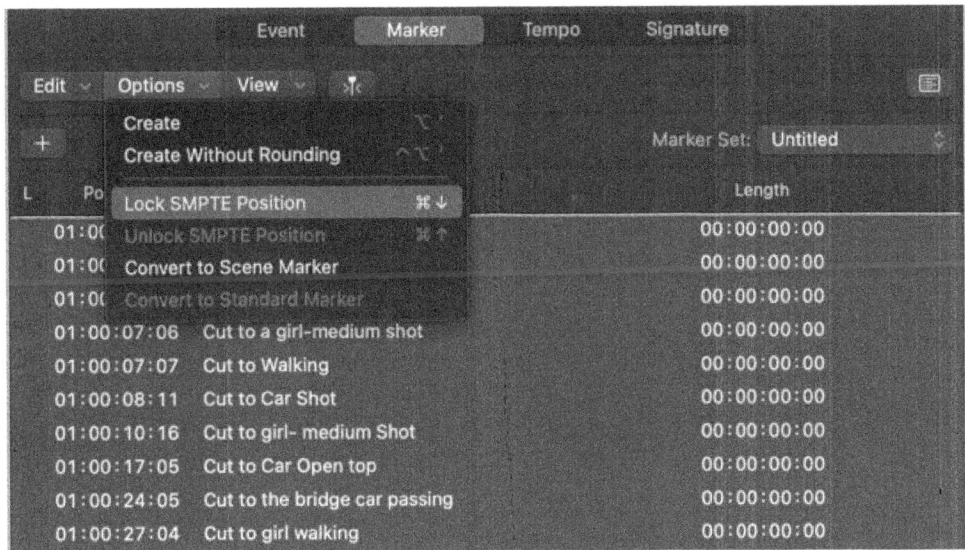

Figure 6.24: Converting standard markers to locked SMPTE position markers

The locked SMPTE position markers will be identified with a padlock icon on the left of the panel:

L	Position	Marker Name	Length
🔒	01:00:00:00	Movie Starts	00:00:00:00
🔒	01:00:02:15	Cut to Over the bridge shot	00:00:00:00
🔒	01:00:04:20	Cut to a girl	00:00:00:00
🔒	01:00:07:06	Cut to a girl-medium shot	00:00:00:00
🔒	01:00:07:07	Cut to Walking	00:00:00:00
🔒	01:00:08:11	Cut to Car Shot	00:00:00:00
🔒	01:00:10:16	Cut to girl- medium Shot	00:00:00:00
🔒	01:00:17:05	Cut to Car Open top	00:00:00:00
🔒	01:00:24:05	Cut to the bridge car passing	00:00:00:00

Figure 6.25: Marker window with locked SMPTE position markers

Scene markers and locked SMPTE position markers are both SMPTE-locked. The slight difference between them is when removing the movie file from a Logic Pro session – when removing a movie with scene markers, Logic Pro gives you the option to remove the markers entirely or keep them by selecting **Don't Remove**.

142   Working with Hit Points and Scene Markers

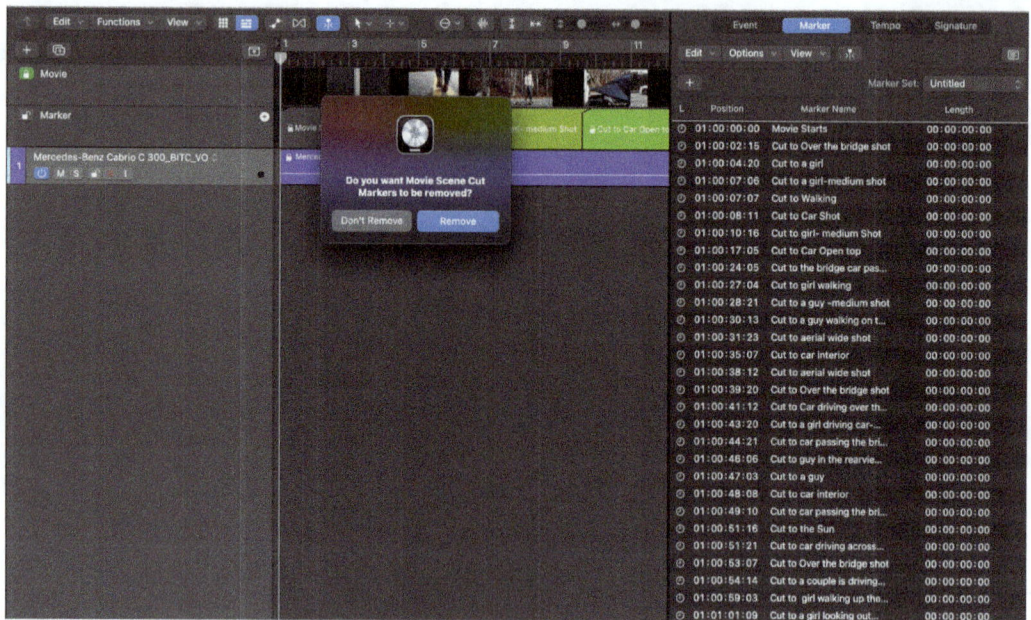

Figure 6.26: Removing a movie with scene markers

When removing a movie with locked SMPTE Position markers, Logic Pro will remove the movie right away and keep all the SMPTE-locked markers in place as shown here:

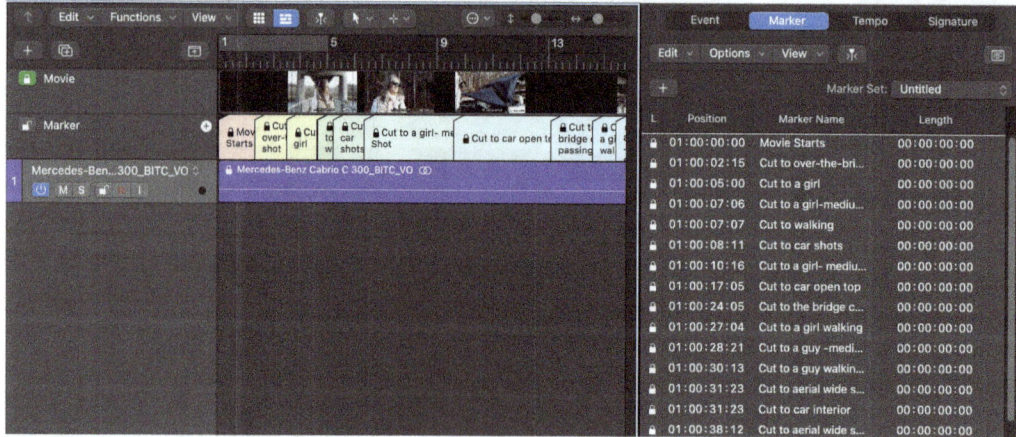

Figure 6.27: Removing a movie with SMPTE-locked markers

Now that we've discussed the different types of markers and how to create them, next, we will look at an additional way to create markers all at once instead of individually.

Creating and removing movie scene cut markers

Instead of creating the markers manually, Logic Pro can extract the markers from the entire movie or from a selected area. The markers that are created are referred to as **movie scene cut markers** and are SMPTE-locked.

To create markers based on an entire movie, go to **Navigate | Other | Create Movie Scene Cut Markers | Entire Movie**:

Figure 6.28: Logic Pro Navigate menu – Create Movie Scene Cut Markers

Logic Pro will analyze the entire movie for all the scene cuts and create movie scene cut markers that are locked to a SMPTE position.

However, creating movie scene cut markers by selecting a smaller, specific range is more commonly used because extracting markers from an entire movie will create a countless number of random markers that are not all usable. Using a smaller section of a movie will give more precise and better results in the end.

To create scene markers based on a selected area, in the Logic Pro Ruler, select a range of bars. For this example, make a selection from bar 27 to 31. Then, go to **Navigate | Other | Create Movie Scene Cut Markers | Cycle Area**:

Working with Hit Points and Scene Markers

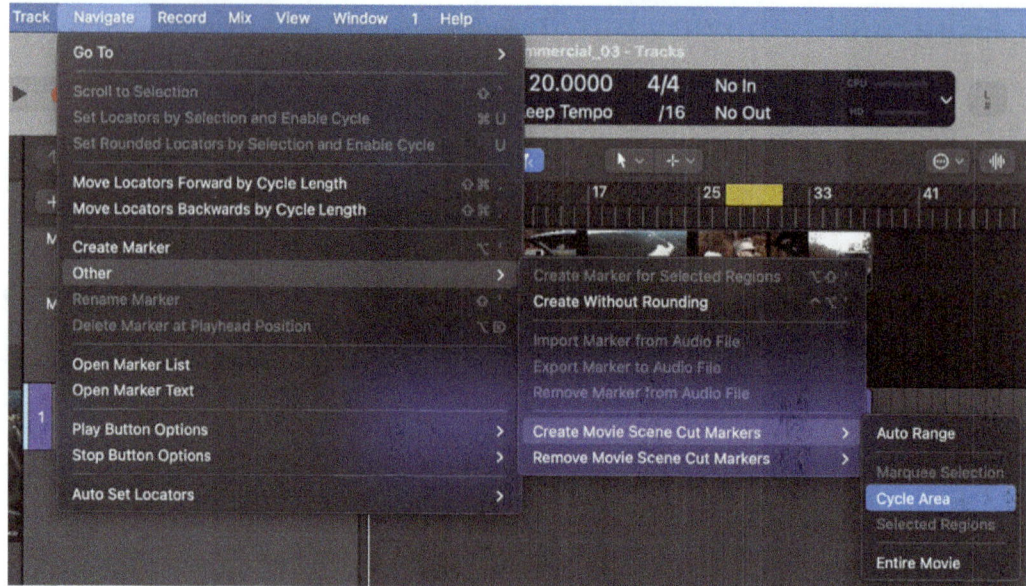

Figure 6.29: Logic Pro Navigate menu – Create Movie Scene Cut Markers

Now, Logic Pro will create markers from bar 27 to 31:

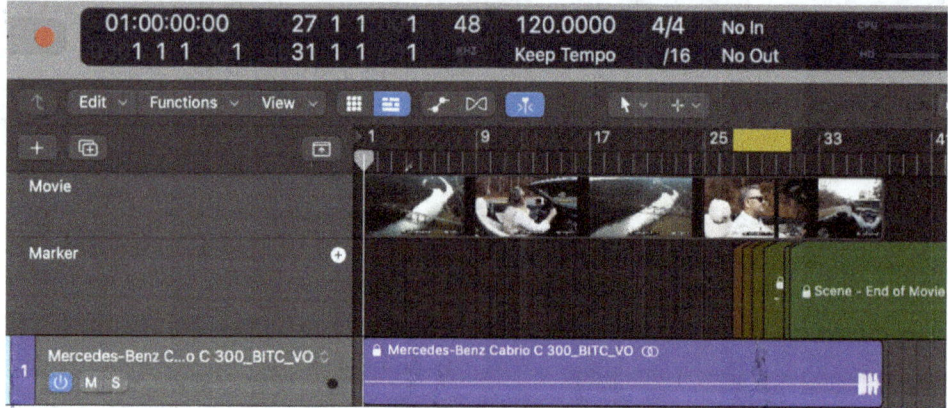

Figure 6.30: Logic Pro Navigate menu – Create Movie Scene Cut Markers from Cycle Area

Additionally, you have the option to create movie scene cut markers based on the **Marquee Selection** or **Selected Regions**. Logic Pro will create movie scene cut markers in conjunction with any existing marquee, selection regions, or cycle area (the option we selected in the instructions).

Moving on, there may be situations where you need to remove a marker. Logic Pro provides the options to remove markers based on **Marquee Selection**, **Cycle Area**, **Selected Regions**, or **Auto Range**, or by removing **All Scene Markers**.

To do this, go to **Navigate | Other | Remove Movie Scene Cut Markers** and select the option that is suitable for your workflow:

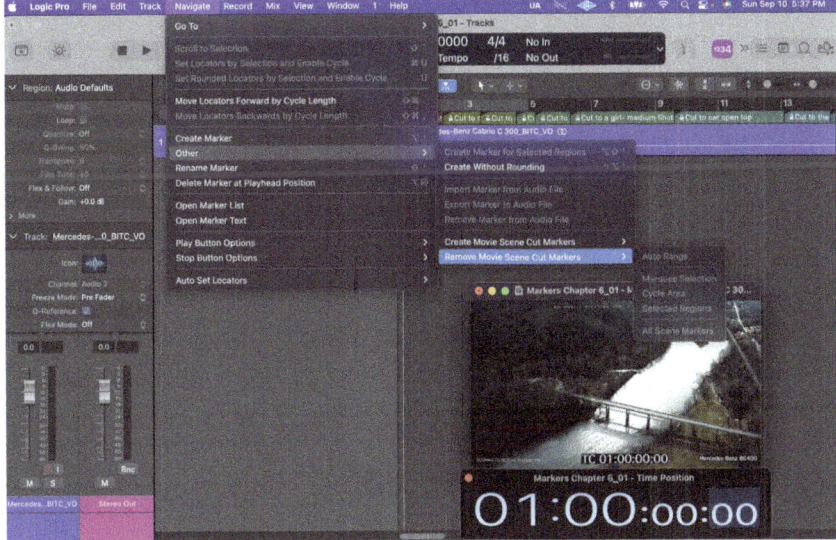

Figure 6.31: Removing movie scene cut markers

Now that we know how to create and remove movie scene cut markers, next, we will look at how to navigate with markers.

Navigating with markers

Logic Pro has a few tools that you can use that help with navigating easily and efficiently between markers, which will help to speed up your workflow. Let's look at three different options:

- To select a specific marker from the list, hold down *Option* and click on the name of the marker in the marker list. The Logic Pro playhead will move to that selected location.

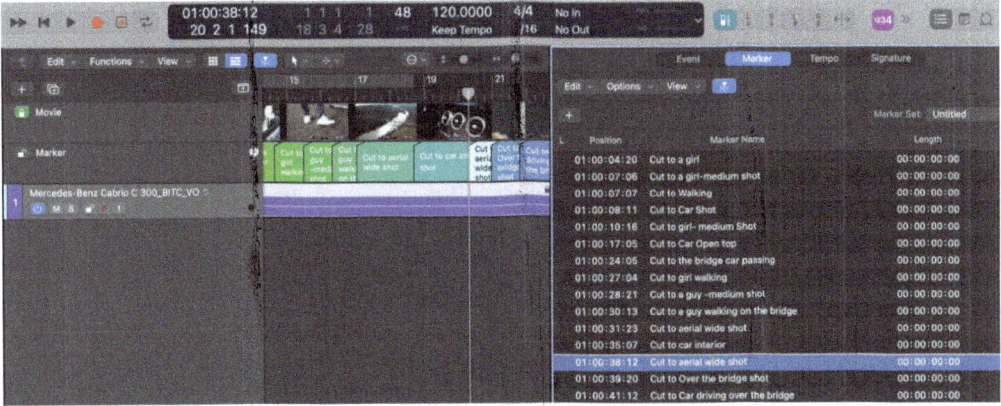

Figure 6.32: Navigating with markers

- Use the *Option + /* key command to open the **Go To Marker** window. Type the number of the marker and hit **OK**. Logic Pro will move the playhead to the marker location. You can navigate between markers by typing the marker number on the numeric keypad.

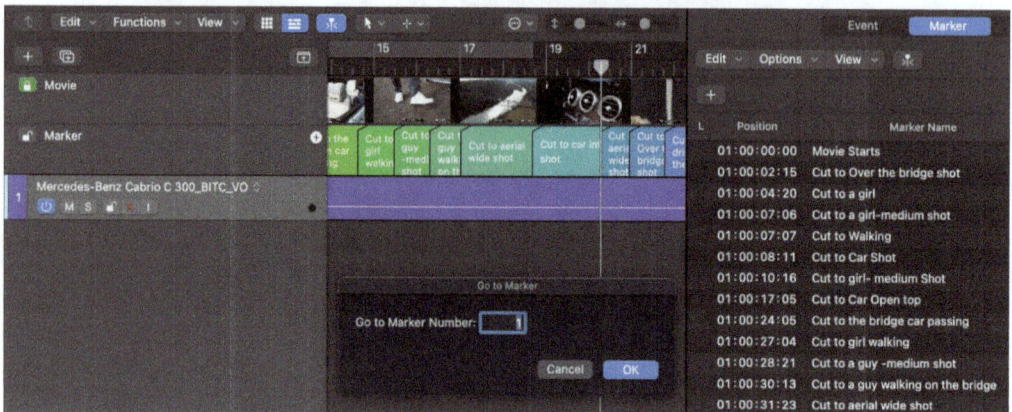

Figure 6.33: Go to the Marker window

- Open the **Key Command Assignments** window by using the *Option + K* shortcut. In the upper search window, type `marker` to see assigned and unassigned key commands.

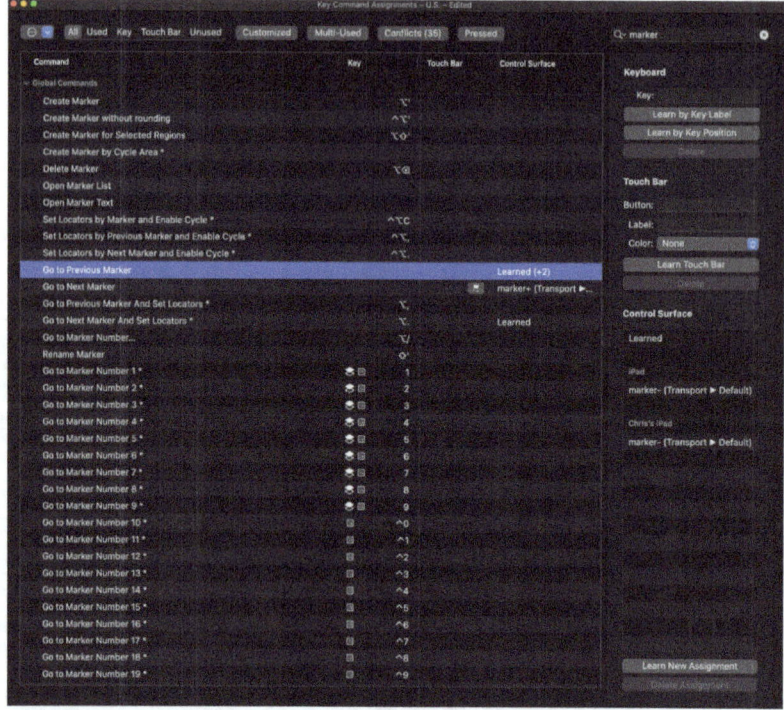

Figure 6.34: Key command assignment window

Now that we know how to navigate the markers, next, we will look at how to create new marker sets.

Creating new marker sets

If you are not getting the results that you want, or the film director or editor gives you a new, edited movie version that has new cuts, you may need to create a new marker set. Logic Pro has a great option for creating a new marker set in the existing session. A new **Marker Set** is a marker subtrack that lays beneath an existing marker or marker track.

This can be very useful in many scoring-to-picture situations since the film director will mostly give the film composers new changes or cuts to the movie. As a result, the film composer would need to work with new cuts and new markers. Therefore, a new marker set can be copied and reused to create a new additional marker set.

To create a new marker set, click on the **Marker** menu in **Global Tracks** and select **New Set…**. You can rename an existing or new marker set, for example, Reel 1 version 1, Reel 1 version 2, and so on to help keep track of all the changes when scoring to picture.

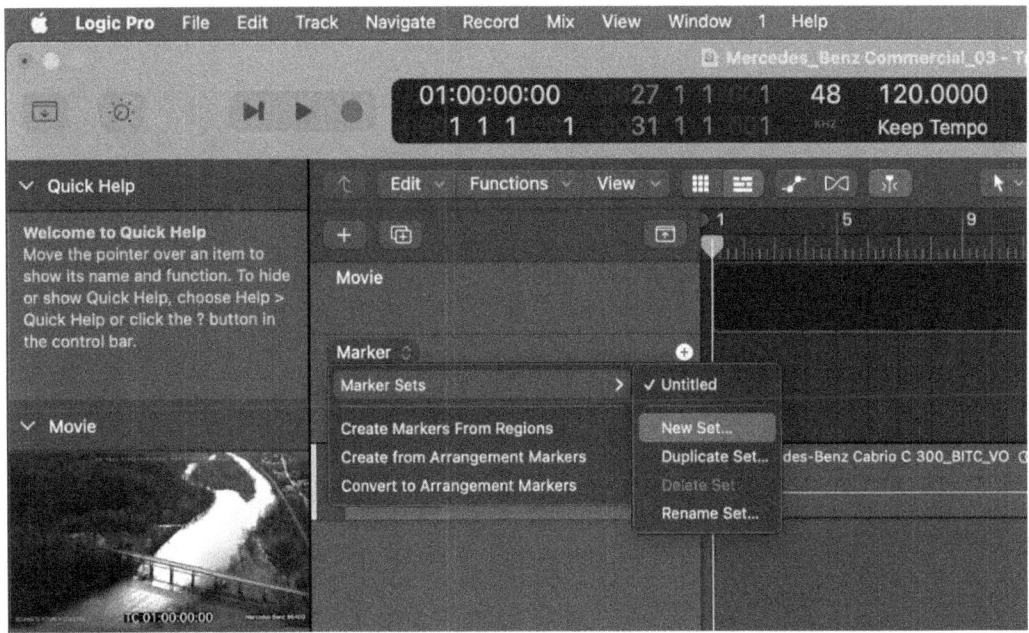

Figure 6.35: Creating a new marker set

To create an additional new marker set, click on the **Marker** track, and select **New Set…** again. When you click on **New Set…**, a marker track becomes an empty track that you can populate with new markers.

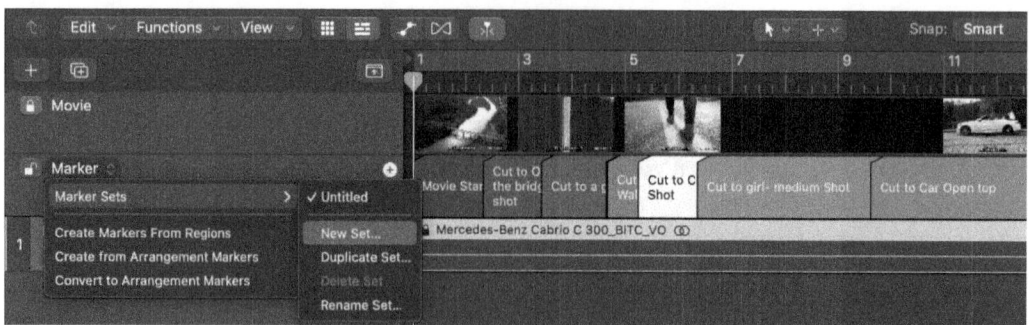

Figure 6.36: New marker set

Since we're creating new marker sets, it's recommended to name each set. In the example here, we named the first marker set `Reel 1`, and the next additional marker set is named `Reel 1 revision`. If you don't name each set, they will be listed as untitled. In the drop-down menu, you have the option to duplicate, delete, or rename a set.

You can repeat these steps continuously and rename each marker set based on the film revision notes, for example.

Figure 6.37: Additional new marker set

Marker sets are helpful when dealing with new movie cuts and revisions. The film composer can reuse existing marker sets to create new ones or start with a brand-new marker set depending on the complexity of the project.

Summary

In this chapter, we discussed hit points and the music spotting notes list. Then, we learned about markers, including the differences between the various types, how to manually add them, how to navigate using them, and how to remove them.

We also explored how Logic Pro can create movie scene cut markers from an entire movie or by a certain selection, as well as how to create new marker sets.

Dealing with markers is essential when it comes to scoring films. They function as a reflection of the spotting notes and in conjunction with the movie events, mark the spots where the music should reflect the occuring events, the mood, and in general what's on the screen.

In the next chapter, we will discuss different methods of scoring to picture, referred to as "laying out the cue," by using hit points and different types of markers.

Part 3: Methods of Scoring to Picture

In this part, you will get an overview of the entire process of finding and working with tempo. In addition, you will discover different methods of finding a suitable tempo for a film, including using the Logic Pro Beat Mapping function and techniques, as well as different ways of adding and dealing with time signatures.

This section contains the following chapters:

- *Chapter 7, Creating Tempo Maps*
- *Chapter 8, Working with Beat Mapping*
- *Chapter 9, Working with a Time Signature*

7
Creating Tempo Maps

In the previous chapter, we learned how to deal with a spotting list and creating different types of markers, as well as how Logic Pro can extract markers from a movie.

One of the first, most important, and challenging steps when getting ready to score to picture is finding the appropriate tempo that best suits the film. The entire process of finding the tempo before scoring to picture is referred to as "**laying out the cue**".

In this chapter, we will cover how to find an appropriate tempo and how to create a tempo map, by using SMPTE locked markers. We will also evaluate and look at the markers' position numbers and their bar and beat locations along with the overall tempo. Additionally, we will explore different methods of finding the suitable tempo for a film and we will look at the benefit of using the Logic Pro tempo operation window.

So, in this chapter, we will cover the following topics:

- Dealing with tempo in film music
- Watching a movie with a metronome
- Using Tap Tempo
- Reviewing the Logic Pro LCD position display
- Reviewing marker positions
- Creating a tempo map
- Creating a tempo map based on hit points
- Adjusting tempo to match hit points

Technical requirements

To follow along with this chapter, you will need general knowledge of using the Logic Pro DAW and a Mac computer with Logic Pro and QuickTime software installed. You will also need to be able to access the movie files provided with this book: `https://packt.link/hxCer`.

Dealing with tempo in film music

Film has its own cuts and pace, and music has a supporting role that needs to acknowledge, evaluate and follow the pace of the film. Music will adapt to the pace of the film cuts and transform them into a rhythmic form that can then be utilized during the scoring to picture process. After reviewing a scene, a film composer will figure out the tempo of the scene with the overall content and pace of the story and how the music and rhythmic choice can support the scene.

The tempo of the music can greatly affect how a scene feels. If the final finished score is too slow, it could drag the flow of the film, or if the tempo of the music is too fast, it could be jarring and ineffective for the viewers. Either way, if the music is not in sync with the pace of the movie, it will not serve the film optimally.

By carefully watching and analyzing the film cuts, the film composer can feel the rhythmical pulse that exists based on the scene cuts. It takes countless hours of practice watching different types of films to become aware of the tempo behind them. This is a skill every film composer needs to develop.

In this section, we are just touching on this since it's a topic that is covered in film composition studies in depth. Even if the film composer is inexperienced with identifying cuts and reinterpreting them into the form of a tempo, beginning with a simple metronome click will help to get started with this concept – this is what we will see in the next section.

Watching a movie with a metronome

Before deciding what the music in your film will do or how it will serve the picture, the first step is to simply watch the movie. In this section, we will watch a movie with the metronome (also referred to as click) on.

Open the movie file `Mercedes-Benz Cabrio C 300_BITC.mov` that you saved in *Chapter 6*, with the SMPTE locked scene markers. Make sure that the movie and Logic Pro are in sync, then name and save the project (for example, I will choose `Tempo mapping_01.`).

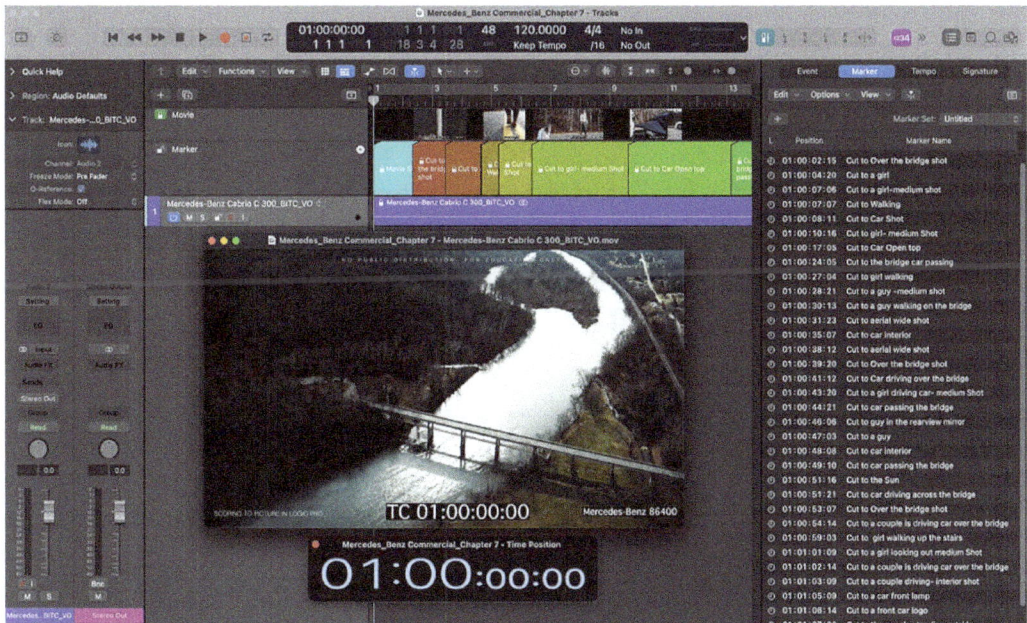

Figure 7.1: Arrange window with spotting notes list

The next step is to lock the movie track and the marker track by clicking on the padlock icon; this will prevent the markers and the movie from shifting when changing the tempo or time signature:

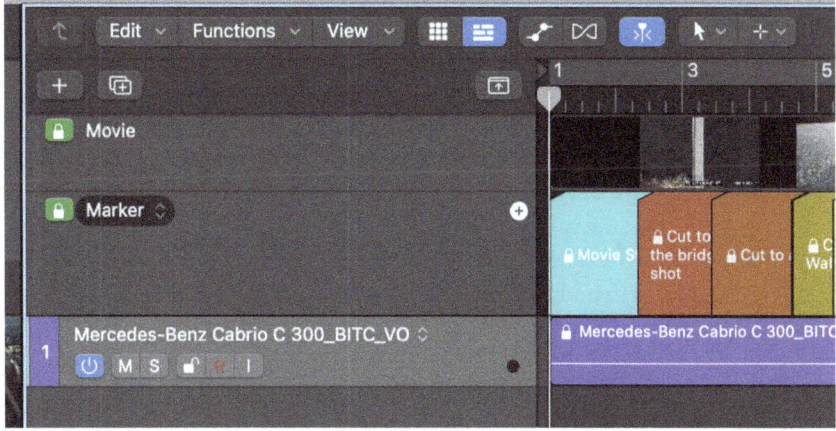

Figure 7.2: Locked movie and marker tracks

Next, turn on the metronome by using the shortcut (*K*) and view the entire film with a click.

Watch the entire movie from the beginning to the end and observe the default tempo while listening to the click track and getting an overall feel of the tempo. Currently, the default tempo of our session is set at 120 bpm.

After viewing the entire movie with the metronome, we want to change the time signature. To change this, go to the LCD display and hover and click the mouse on the **Time Signature** section. From the drop-down menu, change the time signature from the default **4/4** to **1/4**, as shown here:

Figure 7.3: Logic Pro LCD display with time signature

Switching the time signature to **1/4** will create a steady beat with no particular emphasis on a specific beat, offering just a simple click.

Next, watch the movie again with the **1/4** time signature and tempo set to **120** bpm, while observing the tempo and movie cuts with the metronome. Observe the selected tempo with the metronome against the pace of the movie, to see whether the rhythmic cuts of the movie closely match the selected tempo of Logic Pro. The goal is to find the tempo that will best match the majority of the film cuts.

While watching a movie, adjusting the metronome settings involves stopping the DAW. Next, we will go over a function that Logic Pro offers called **Tap Tempo**, which is a smoother way of adjusting Logic Pro's tempo during a film preview.

Using Tap Tempo

Tap Tempo allows you to tap a key on the computer keyboard to change Logic Pro's tempo. This is helpful when watching a movie and trying to experiment with different tempos.

By default, **Tap Tempo** doesn't have an assigned keyboard shortcut. To create a custom keyboard shortcut, press *Option + K* to open the **Key Command Assignments** window. Then, in the upper-right corner, type Tap Tempo. Now select **Tap Tempo** from the **Global Commands** list and assign a keyboard shortcut of your choice. In this example, we've assigned the keyboard shortcut *F19*.

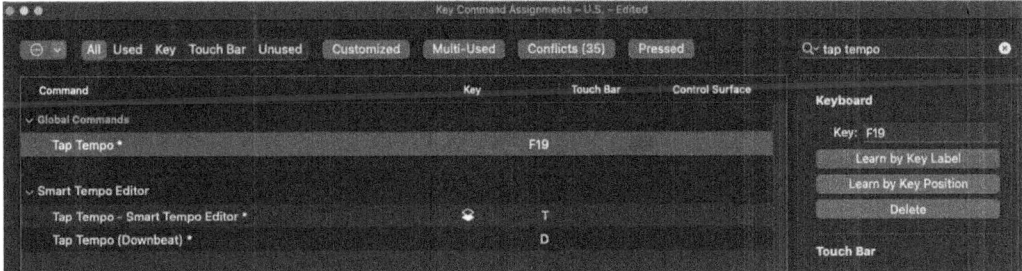

Figure 7.4: Key Command Assignments window

To check whether the assignment worked, hit your newly created keyboard shortcut. A window will open asking you to enable the **Tap Tempo** function. Simply click **OK** to confirm.

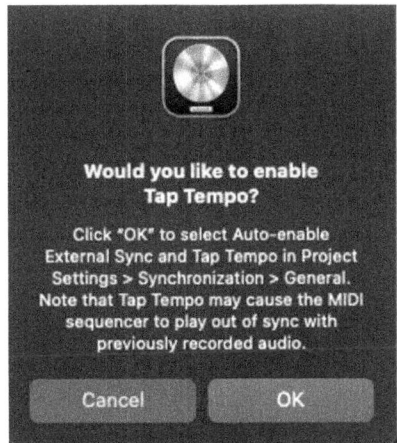

Figure 7.5: Enable Tap Tempo window

After enabling **Tap Tempo**, Logic Pro changes the playhead color from white to blue for easy identification.

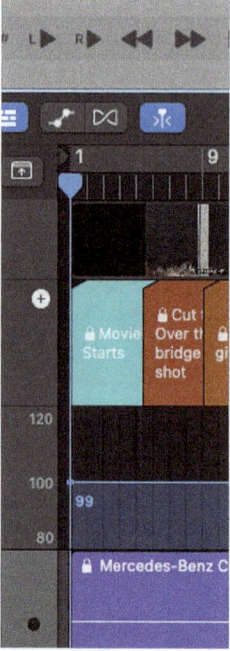

Figure 7.6: Tap Tempo blue playhead

Watching the movie and experimenting with multiple tempo settings can greatly assist the film composer by offering many ideas that will help find the best suitable tempo. Using **Tap Tempo** allows the user to follow visual cuts that can be reinterpreted as beats without starting and stopping the sequencer. Tapping the tempo against the picture allows the film composer to match the visual events and achieve finding the desired tempo much faster.

After finding the desired tempo, even though it may work for some cuts, it may not work for others. This is where the **Temp Operation** window will assist with calculating tempo based on the marker position, as we'll explore later in this chapter.

Before we review the marker positions, we will look at the Logic Pro position and the grid display that deals with bar, beat, division, and tick position.

Reviewing the Logic Pro LCD position display

Logic Pro users learn about position and grid settings using bars, beats, divisions, and tick functions during the beginning stages of exploring Logic Pro, and it is considered essential Logic Pro knowledge. Here, we are going to review this content again because it will help prepare for the complex task of creating a tempo map. This will help with reading and identifying the specific position of the marker, which will help with determining how close the marker is to the nearest bar and beat.

In *Figure 7.7*, you can see the LCD display and the **Giant Beats Display**, showing the playhead location at **1 1 1 1**, meaning *bar 1, beat 1, division 1, and tick 1*.

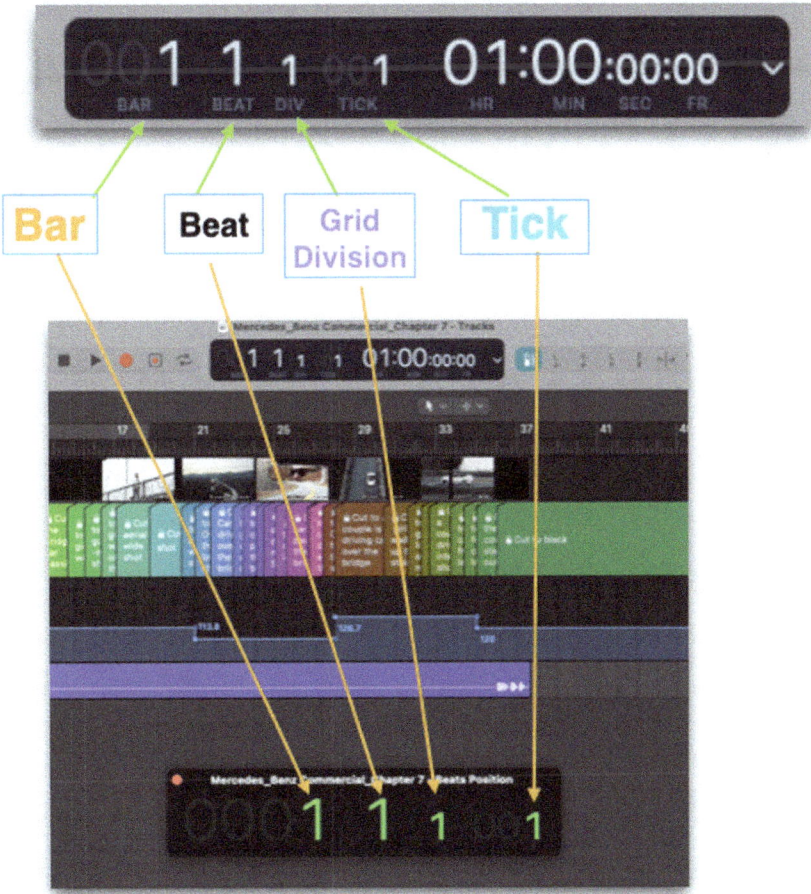

Figure 7.7: Position numbers with explanation

Next, we're going to look at a specific marker from the spotting list, with a default tempo of 120 bpm, and review how to read the position of the marker in the marker window.

In *Figure 7.8*, the current position of the selected marker is **3 2 4 34**. That means that the beginning of this marker is positioned at bar 3, beat 2, division 4, and tick 34. We can see the selected marker position in the **Marker** window, also reflecting the exact same position numbers in the **Giant Beats Display** and the LCD display.

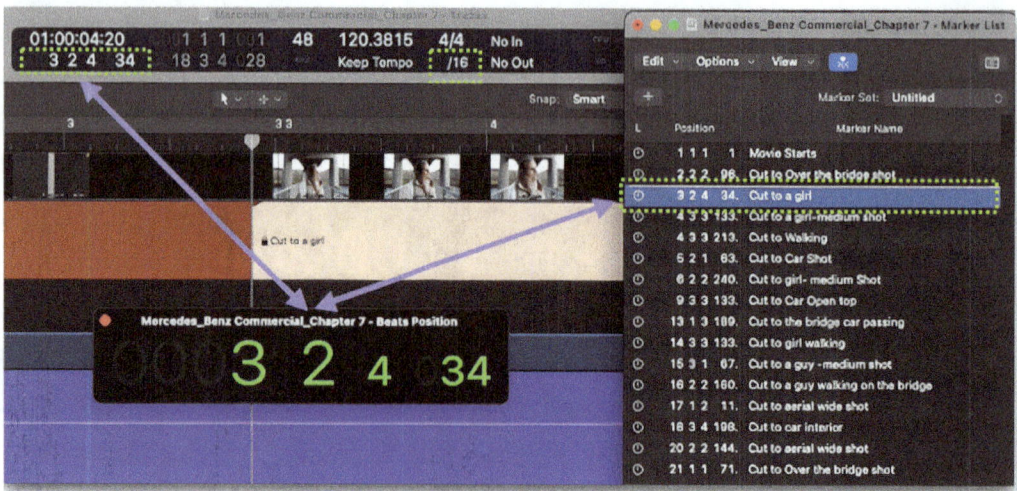

Figure 7.8: Highlighted position marker

Next, we will continue reviewing the marker position numbers that can be affected when changing the grid settings.

A single bar can be divided into beats, divisions, and ticks, based on the type of time signature and grid division that is set up in the **Arrange** window.

In *Figure 7.9*, the ruler in the Logic Pro **Arrange** window is zoomed in and is showing a grid setting of 1/16th in the LCD display (see the red circle). All of the **Giant Beats Displays** are showing the playhead in different locations and positions.

Starting at the beginning of the ruler, the first **Giant Beats Display** shows bar 1, beat 1, division 1, tick 1. Then, moving from left to right, we see the next **Giant Beats Display** showing bar 1, beat 1, division 2, tick 1, then bar 1, beat 1, division 3, tick 1, and then bar 1, beat 1, division 4, tick 1.

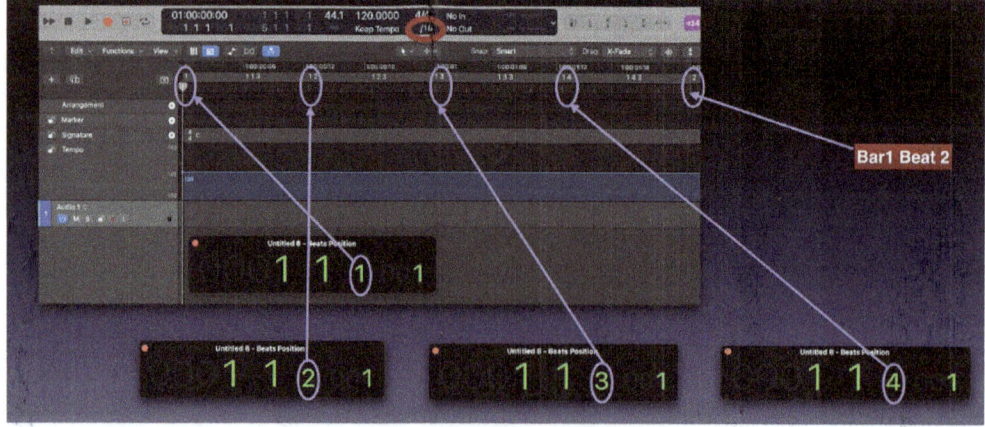

Figure 7.9: Arrange window with position and grid display

Next, we will review the division and ticks inside of a single beat, with a specific grid setting.

Figure 7.10 is based on the specific grid setting of 1/16th in the LCD display. In addition to the positions with purple arrows, we can see above the positions, the maximum of 240 ticks per division in a beat. In the bar 1, beat 1, division 1 section, there is a maximum of 240 ticks before bar 1, beat 1, division 2, and tick 1 occur. The same thing applies to all of the divisions in one beat. This all occurs inside of one beat. At the end of the **Arrange** window, on the far bottom-right side, we can see the position **of 1 2 1 1**, meaning the bar 1, beat 2, division 1 position.

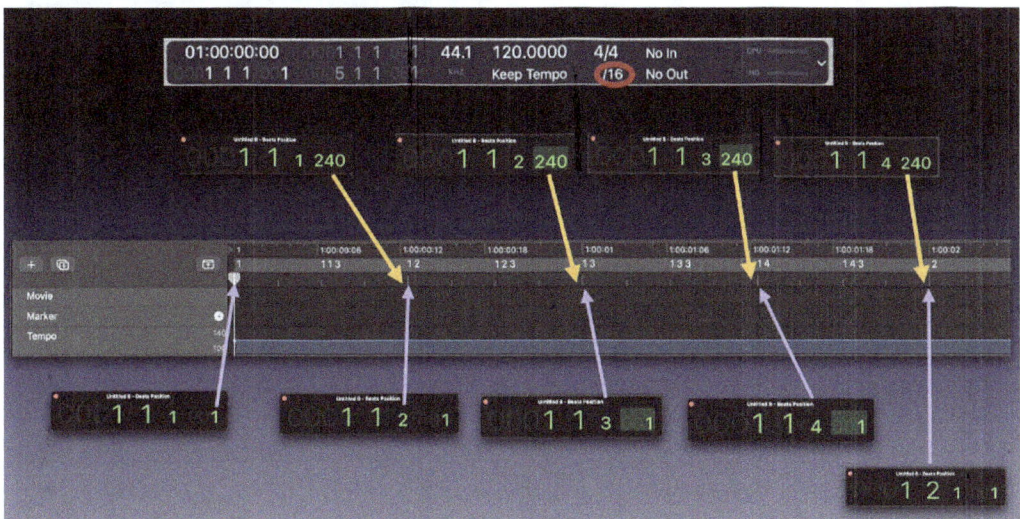

Figure 7.10: Logic Pro ruler with position and grid display

Now that we have reviewed the division and ticks inside of a single beat, with a specific grid setting, next, we will review other grid settings and how they affect the division and ticks position view.

In *Figure 7.11*, we see three **Arrange** windows with **Giant Beats Displays**, with the playhead placed in the same position but showing different grid settings.

Creating Tempo Maps

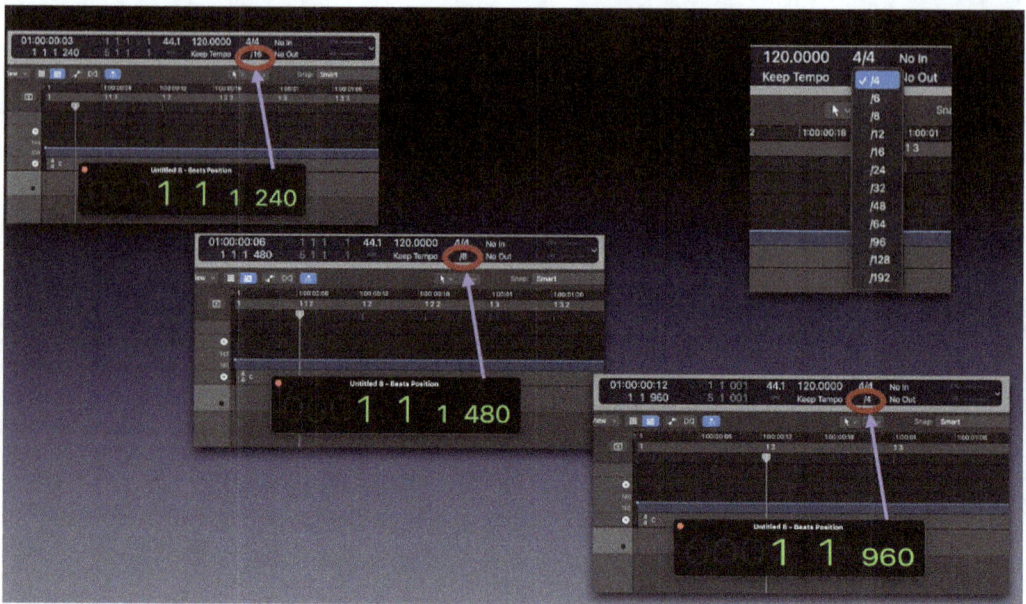

Figure 7.11: Arrange windows with different grid settings

In the top **Arrange** window example, we can see **1 1 1 240** meaning bar 1, beat 1, division 1, 240 ticks. This position is 1 tick away from position **1 1 2 1**, meaning bar 1, beat 1, division 2, tick 1. This is with the grid setting set to 1/16th.

If we switch the grid setting to 1/8th, the maximum ticks available will be 480, as shown in the middle **Arrange** window.

The grid setting of 1/4th shows the maximum ticks available as 960 at the bottom right of the **Arrange** window example.

The window with the drop-down list, in the upper-right corner of *Figure 7.11*, shows the different grid setting options that are available. As we just mentioned, changing the grid settings alters the ticks and division numbers, related to the position of a playhead or region. It allows the user to see in greater detail the position of a playhead or marker, therefore allowing the playhead or the marker to be moved in smaller increments. The larger the number of the grid setting, the more detailed the view of the location. The smaller the grid setting number is the less detail there is.

Now that we have reviewed how Logic Pro deals with bars, beats, divisions, and ticks, as well as grid settings, next, we will explore the **Marker** window and review the marker positions from the spotting list we used in *Chapter 6*.

Reviewing marker positions

In this section, we will review the marker positions and the meaning of the numbers, to determine their precise location in relation to the bar and beat positions. Understanding the position numbers of the markers will help to know exactly where they fall on the beat grid.

To see the marker positions, first, go to the **Marker** window, click on the marker name plate, and drag it to the **Arrange** window. The floating **Marker** window will show the bar and beat positions for every marker listed.

Figure 7.12: Position markers and SMPTE locked markers windows

Next, we will review two adjacent marker positions and where they fall in relationship to the beginning of a bar. After understanding the marker positions, we can then determine how far away the marker is from the downbeat of a bar.

In *Figure 7.13*, we can see that the first marker starts at the **1 1 1 1** position, and the second marker is located at bar 2, beat 2, division 2, tick 80. We can also see the two floating marker windows, with their bars and beats, division, and ticks display, as well as a floating marker with the locked SMPTE position. Plus, we can see that the second marker falls close to the middle, between bar 2 and bar 3.

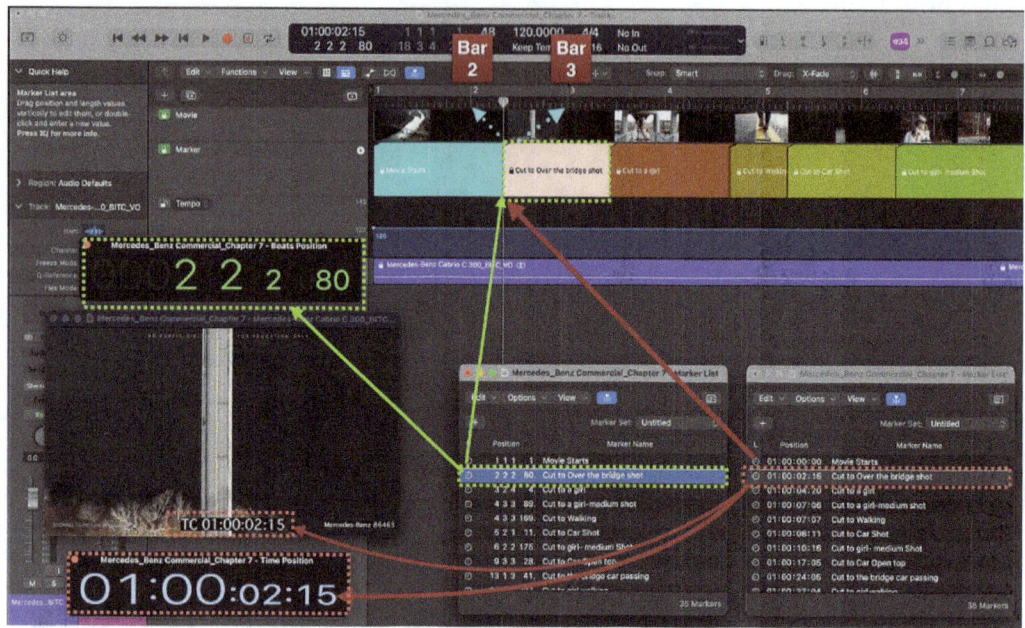

Figure 7.13: Arrange window with floating markers

In *Figure 7.14*, we see that the grid setting is 1/16th, the marker position indicated in the **Giant Beats Display** and their corresponding SMPTE position, **TC 01:00:02:15**, in the **Marker** window.

Reviewing marker positions 165

Figure 7.14: Arrange window with 1/16th grid setting

If the grid setting is changed to 1/8th, the **Giant Beats Display** shows the position as bar 2, beat 2, division 1, tick 320, and the same corresponding SMPTE position of **TC 01:00:02:15** in the **Marker** window.

166 Creating Tempo Maps

Figure 7.15: Arrange window with 1/8th grid setting

If the grid setting is changed to 1/4th, the **Giant Beats Display** shows the position as bar 2, beat 2, tick 320, and the SMPTE position of **TC 01:00:02:15** stays the same again, in the **Marker** window.

Creating a tempo map   167

Figure 7.16: Arrange window with 1/4th grid setting

Now that we understand what the marker position numbers represent, we can better determine their bar and beat position in relationship to one another. This will help with the process of creating a tempo map, which is what we will review in the next section.

Creating a tempo map

Tempo mapping is the process of outlining and confirming tempo or tempo changes for existing SMPTE locked markers, based on the selected grid setting. Any type of tempo changes for those markers within Logic Pro, when scoring to picture, can be referred to as tempo mapping or "laying out the cue."

During the process of creating a tempo map, the film composer needs to compare marker positions with one another to make sure that the markers fall on the downbeat of a bar. As a result, Logic Pro will adjust the markers so they land on the downbeat of a bar by retaining their SMPTE locked position and will suggest a new tempo to accommodate this.

This process is a Logic Pro task, a technical skill that needs to be practiced. The ability to make technical choices is important before making any musical choices. We will talk more about technical choices versus musical choices in *Chapter 9*.

In this section, we will go over how to create a tempo map and how you can use Logic Pro to help create a tempo. The first step is to switch the previously used session time signature back to **4/4**. Then click on the **Tempo** tab, to the right of the **Marker** tab:

Figure 7.17: Tempo window

In this tab, click on **Options** and select **Tempo Operations** from the drop-down menu.

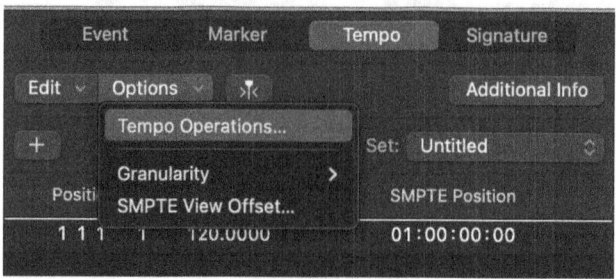

Figure 7.18: Tempo Operations drop-down menu

In the **Tempo Operations** window, select **Create Constant Tempo**.

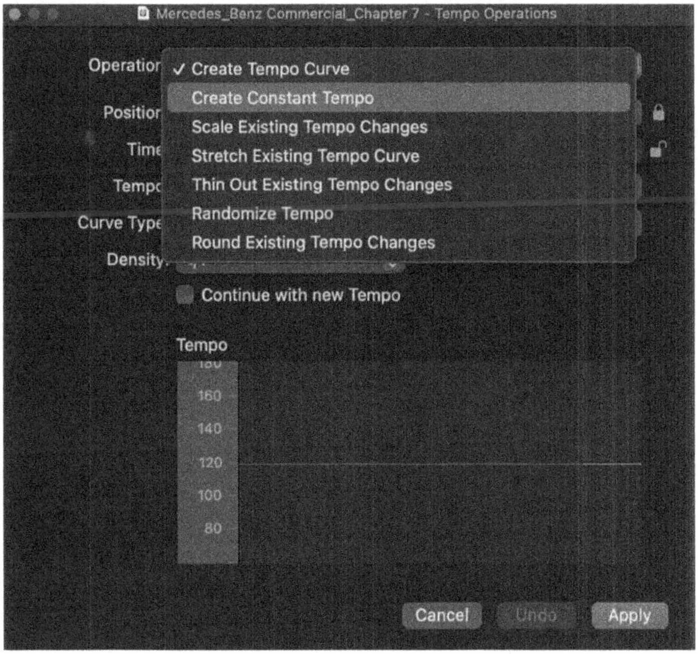

Figure 7.19: Tempo Operations drop-down menu

Keeping the **Tempo Operations** window open, click on the **Marker** window and drag it to the **Arrange** window, so that it shows as a floating window. In the **Arrange** window, you will now see the **Tempo Operations** window on the left, the floating **Marker** window with their positions in the middle, and the **Marker** window with the SMPTE timecode positions on the right.

170 Creating Tempo Maps

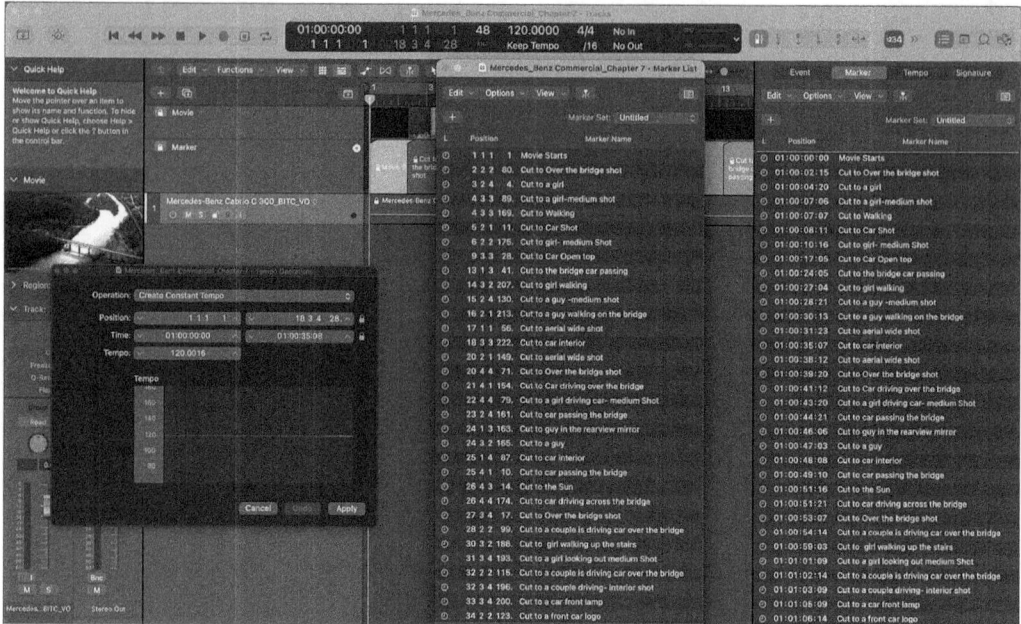

Figure 7.20: Arrange window with the Floating Tempo and Marker windows

When working with a constant tempo, the timecode section has to have a padlock (has to be locked) in order to enter the SMPTE time. So, next, make sure that both padlocks on the right side of the **Tempo Operations** window are locked.

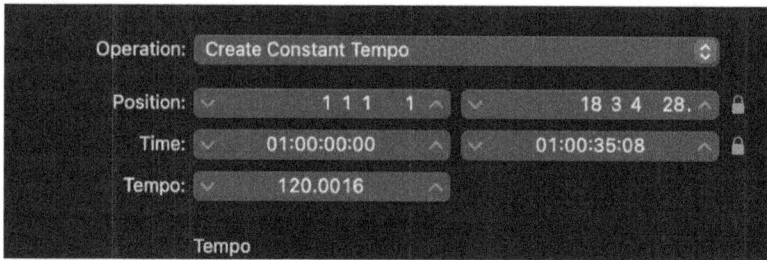

Figure 7.21: Tempo Operations window

The next step is to compare the first and the second markers' bar and beat positions. In the floating **Marker** window, in the **Position** section, the first marker is located at **bar 1 1 1 1 (Movie Starts)** and the second marker falls on **bar 2 2 2 80 (Cut to over the bridge shot)**. Since the second marker almost falls on bar 2 beat 1, we will let Logic Pro change the second marker to the bar 2 beat 1 position.

Creating a tempo map | 171

In the following example, the first marker position is **1 1 1 1**, and that marker is reflected in the **Tempo Operation** window's **Position** section (the green highlighted frame). In the **Time** section (highlighted by the yellow frame), type in the timecode of the corresponding second marker, 01:00:02:15.

For Logic Pro to change the marker position to the nearest downbeat of the bar, in the **Position** section's second box, just above the yellow highlighted frame, type 2 1 1 1 as the desired destination.

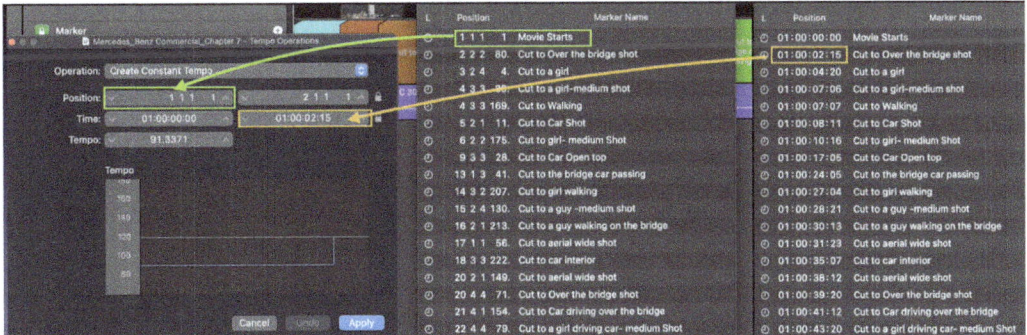

Figure 7.22: Highlighted Tempo Operations and Marker windows

After entering the numbers, Logic Pro suggests a tempo of **91.3371** bpm, displayed below the **Time** section. In the **Tempo** area at the bottom of the **Tempo Operations** window, we can see the gray line of **120** bpm and the new, suggested tempo of **91.3371** bpm as the blue line. To confirm this selection, at the bottom of the **Tempo Operations** window, click **Apply**.

Now we can see in the following screenshot that Logic Pro adjusted the second marker position in the floating **Marker** window and the tempo in the **Tempo Operations** window. The floating marker window shows the **Cut to Over the bridge shot** marker now moved to bar 2, beat 1.

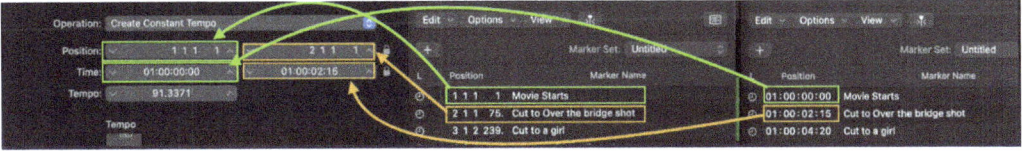

Figure 7.23: Tempo Operations Marker window detailed view

Next, we will continue to compare markers and look at the position of the second and third markers.

⊙	2 1 1 75.	Cut to Over the bridge shot	⊙	01:00:02:15	Cut to Over the bridge shot
⊙	3 1 2 239.	Cut to a girl	⊙	01:00:04:20	Cut to a girl

Figure 7.24: Marker positions and SMPTE locked markers comparison

Then, in *Figure 7.25*, we can see that the **Cut to Over the bridge shot** marker falls in the bar 2, beat 1 position and the **Cut to a girl** marker falls in the bar 3, beat 1 position. Since the **Cut to a girl** marker already falls on beat 3, beat 1, we will move on and compare the third marker **Cut to a girl** with the fourth marker **Cut to a girl-medium shot** at position **4 2 2 83**. Since the fourth marker almost falls on bar 4, beat 1, we will let Logic Pro change the fourth marker to the bar 4, beat 1 position.

To do that, type the timecode of the third marker **TC 01:00:04:20 (Cut to a girl)** into the left box in the **Time** section and type the corresponding bar location of 3 1 2 239 in the **Position** section.

For the fourth marker, type the corresponding timecode of 01:00:07:06 in the **Time** section, the second box to the right. In the **Position** section above, type 4 1 1 1 and hit *Enter*.

After entering the numbers, Logic Pro suggests a new tempo of **88.768** bpm, displayed in the **Tempo** section. Click on **Apply**. Now we can see Logic Pro adjusted the fourth marker position and adjusted the tempo.

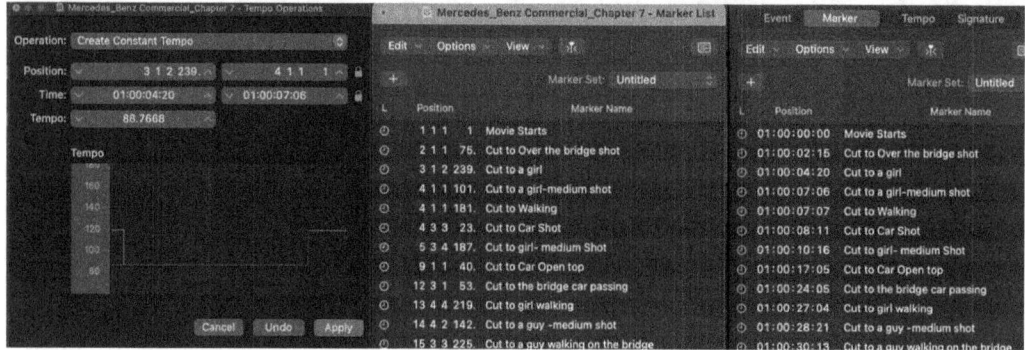

Figure 7.25: Tempo Operations window and Marker windows

We could continue with the process of letting Logic Pro adjust all the existing markers to the downbeat of a bar, but for the purpose of this exercise, what we've done so far is sufficient to start creating a tempo map.

So, to see how Logic Pro created the tempo map, right-click on any track in the Global Tracks and select **Tempo** from the drop-down menu to display the tempo track.

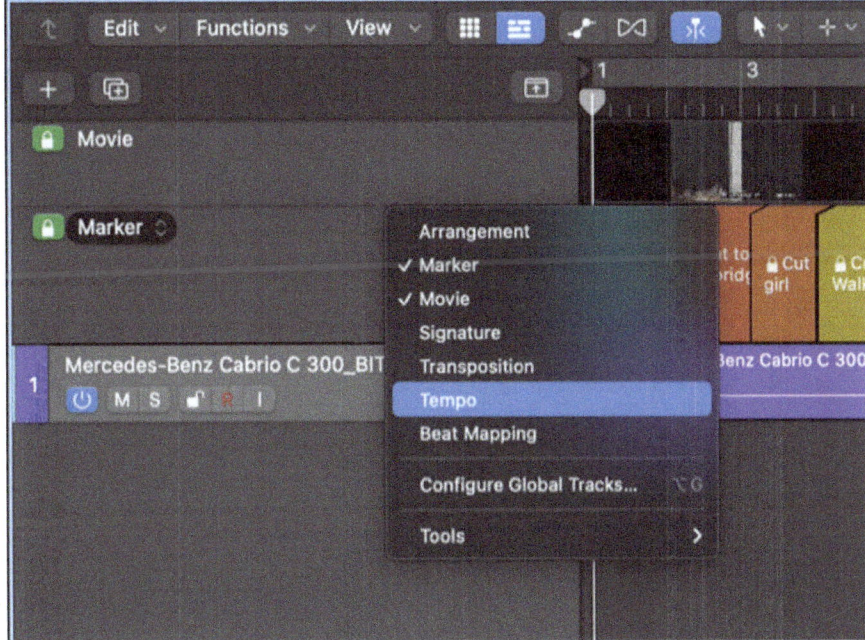

Figure 7.26: Global Tracks drop-down menu

Logic Pro now displays the tempo track with the tempo changes based on the spotting position of the markers that were entered.

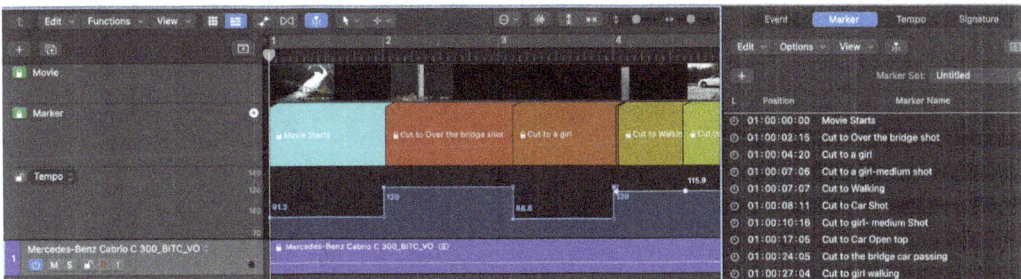

Figure 7.27: Arrange window with new tempo map

To evaluate the new changes, watch the movie from the beginning and listen to the metronome at the same time.

The general goal of creating a tempo map is to create a steady beat without drastic tempo fluctuations. The important aspect that every film composer needs to evaluate is what to do with the suggested Logic Pro tempos and whether they are useful when scoring to picture.

Next, we will explore creating a tempo map based on the specific sync points, which is another option to help with creating a tempo map.

Creating a tempo map based on hit points

In this section, we will create a tempo map working only with the hit points from the spotting list.

The first step is to view all the hit points, taken from the spotting notes list:

Position	Marker Name
01:00:00:00	Movie Starts
01:00:39:20	Cut to Over the bridge shot
01:00:54:14	Cut to couple driving car over the bridge
01:01:07:20	Cut to the couple standing outside

Figure 7.28: Spotting notes list excerpt

The next step in the same Logic Pro session that we previously used is to create a new tempo. In the **Tempo** track, create a new tempo set by selecting **New Set** from the **Tempo Sets** drop-down menu.

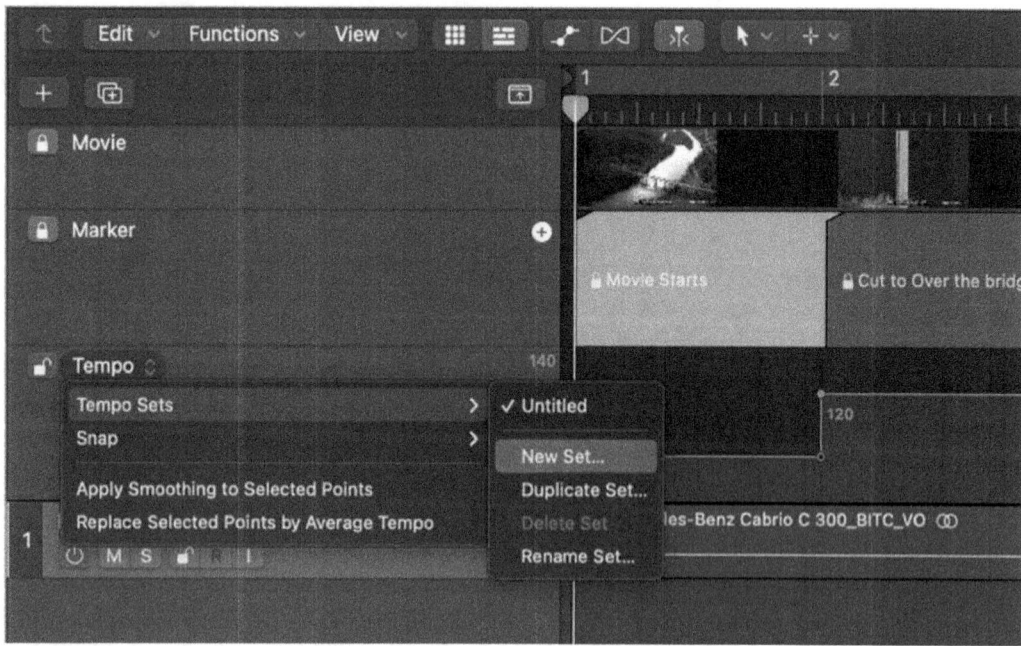

Figure 7.29: Tempo Sets drop-down menu

After creating a new tempo set on the tempo track, rename it to `Tempo II`.

Figure 7.30: Tempo track

As a result of creating a new tempo set, Logic Pro created a new default tempo of 120 bpm.

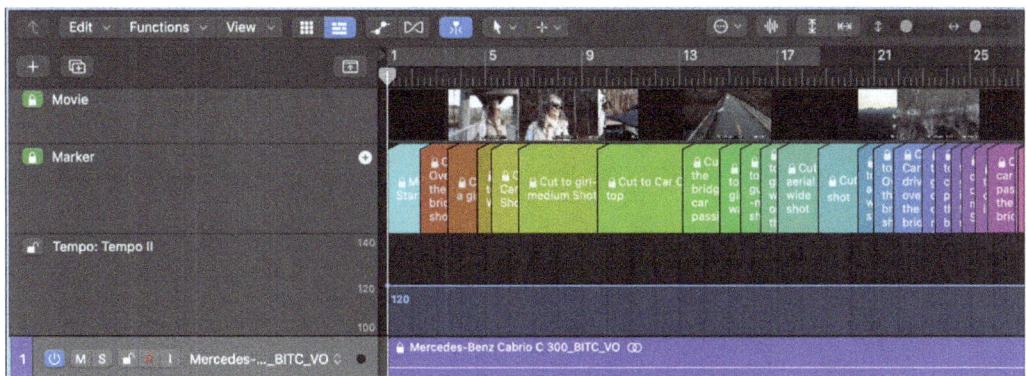

Figure 7.31: Arrange window with default tempo

Next, open the floating **Marker** window and analyze the first hit point location. Here, we can see the timecode of the first hit point, **Cut to Over the bridge shot**, is at **TC 01:00:39:20** and that this event is currently landing on bar 20, beat 4. Since the marker almost falls on bar 21, beat 1, we will let Logic Pro change the marker to the bar 21, beat 1 position.

14 3 2 207.	Cut to girl walking	01:00:27:04	Cut to girl walking
15 2 4 130.	Cut to a guy -medium shot	01:00:28:21	Cut to a guy -medium shot
16 2 1 213.	Cut to a guy walking on the bridge	01:00:30:13	Cut to a guy walking on the b
17 1 1 56.	Cut to aerial wide shot	01:00:31:23	Cut to aerial wide shot
18 3 3 222.	Cut to car interior	01:00:35:07	Cut to car interior
20 2 1 149.	Cut to aerial wide shot	01:00:38:12	Cut to aerial wide shot
20 4 4 71.	Cut to Over the bridge shot	01:00:39:20	Cut to Over the bridge shot
21 4 1 154.	Cut to Car driving over the bridge	01:00:41:12	Cut to Car driving over the bri

Figure 7.32: Floating marker with position location

To do that, type the timecode of the first marker, 01:00:00:00, into the left **Time** box and type the corresponding bar location of 1 1 1 1 in the **Position** section. Then, for the first hit point marker, type the corresponding timecode of 01:00:39:20 in the second **Time** box, and for **Position**, type 21 1 1 1. Then hit *Enter*. After entering the numbers, Logic Pro suggests a new tempo of **120.3** bpm, displayed in the **Tempo** section. Now click **Apply**.

Figure 7.33: Tempo Operations with Marker windows

Next, we will let Logic Pro calculate the tempo from the first hit point to the second hit point at **TC 01:00:54:14** and compare the first and second hit point markers' bar and beat positions.

In the floating **Marker** window, in the **Position** section, the first hit point marker is located at **bar 21 1 1 1 (Cut to over-the-bridge shot)** at **TC 01:00:39:20**, and the second hit point marker is currently falling on **bar 28 2 2 99 (Cut to a couple driving car over-the-bridge)**. Since the second marker almost falls on bar 28, beat 1, we will let Logic Pro change the second marker to the bar 28, beat 1 position.

To do that, type the timecode of the first hit point marker, 01:00:39:20, into the left box in the **Time** section and type the corresponding bar location of 21 1 1 1 in the **Position** section. For the second hit point marker, type the corresponding timecode of 01:00:54:14 in the second **Time** section and type 28 1 1 1 in the **Position** section. Then hit *Enter*.

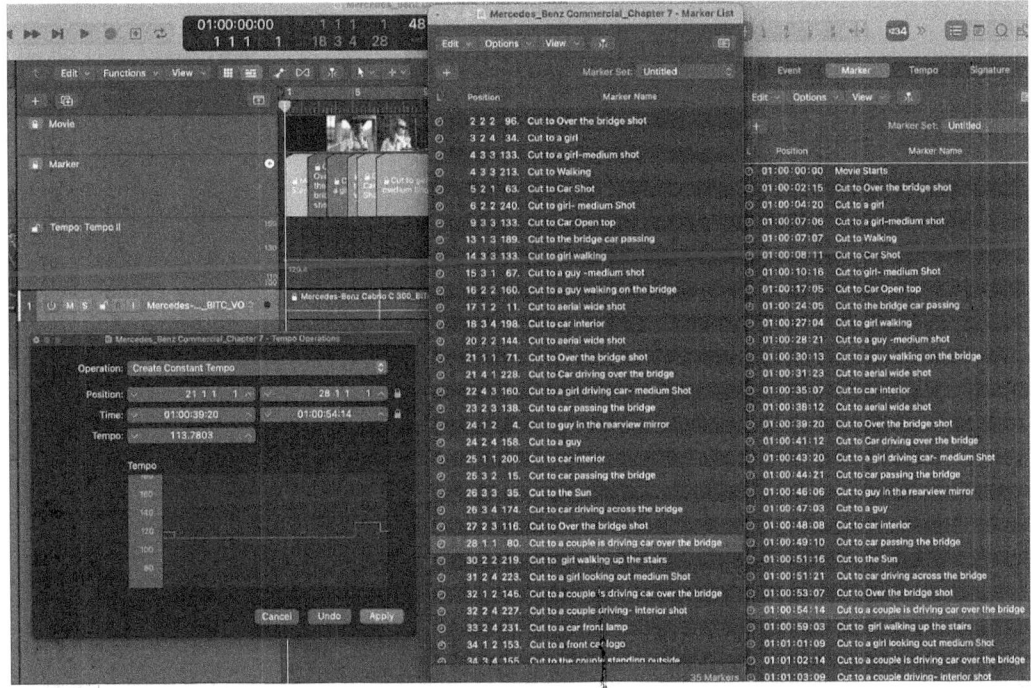

Figure 7.34: Tempo Operations with Marker windows

After entering the numbers, Logic Pro suggests a new tempo of 113.76 bpm. So, Logic Pro adjusted the tempo from 120.3 bpm to 113.76 bpm. Now click **Apply**.

Next, we will let Logic Pro calculate the tempo from the second hit point to the third hit point at **TC 01:01:07:20** and compare the second and third hit point markers' bar and beat positions.

In the floating **Marker** window, in the **Position** section, the second hit point marker is located at bar 28 1 1 1 at **TC 01:00:54:14**, and the third hit point marker is currently falling on bar 34 4 4 135. Since the third hit point marker almost falls on bar 35, beat 1, we will let Logic Pro change the third marker to the bar 35, beat 1 position.

To do that, type the timecode of the second hit point marker, 01:00:54:14, into the left box in the **Time** section and type the corresponding bar location of 28   111 in the **Position** section. For the third hit point marker, type the corresponding timecode of 01:01:07:20 in the **Time** section, the second box to the right, and in the **Position** section, type 35   111. Then hit *Enter*.

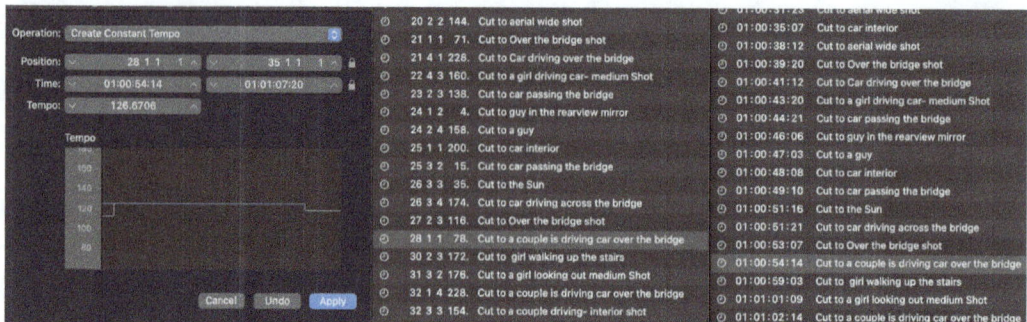

Figure 7.35: Tempo Operations with Marker windows

After entering the numbers, Logic Pro suggests a new tempo of 126.67 bpm. So, Logic Pro adjusted the tempo from 113.76 bpm to 126.67 bpm. Click **Apply**.

Now watch the movie from the beginning while listening to the metronome with the new tempo set.

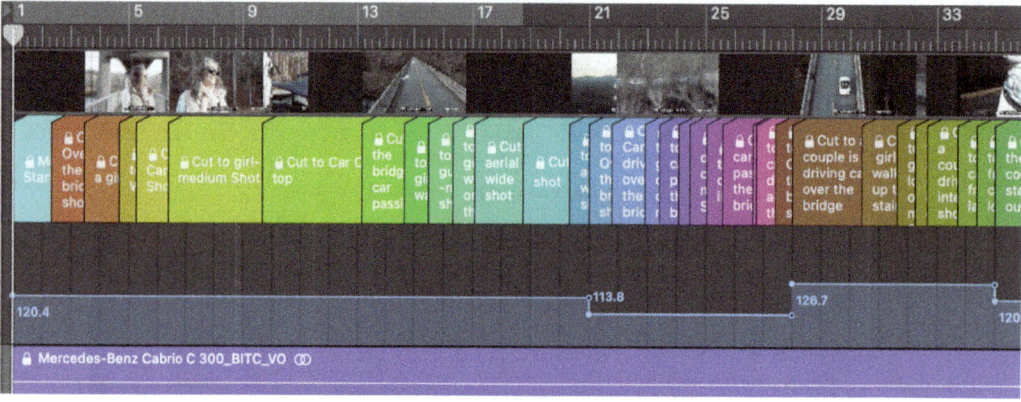

Figure 7.36: New tempo map

There are many different types of films and each one requires an individual evaluation in order to come up with the most effective tempo. This process is subjective based on the type of film and the film composer's experience.

We adjusted the markers so that they would fall on the downbeat of the bar and Logic Pro adjusted the tempo based on the selection. In the next section, we will explore adjusting the global tempo to match the hit points.

Adjusting the tempo to match the hit points

Another form of tempo mapping is the process of matching the tempo to all of the markers. In this section, we will be adjusting the global tempo and searching for the most suitable tempo that makes the markers fall on the downbeat of a bar. In this example, we will experiment with adjusting the tempo to 99 bpm, from the default bpm of 120, as the global tempo of the entire film.

To start, in the marker track, create a new marker set. Name it **Marker 3**, with the default tempo of **120** bpm. Next, change the tempo by clicking on the bpm in the LCD display and type 99, then hit *Enter*. Logic Pro will then change the tempo to 99 bpm.

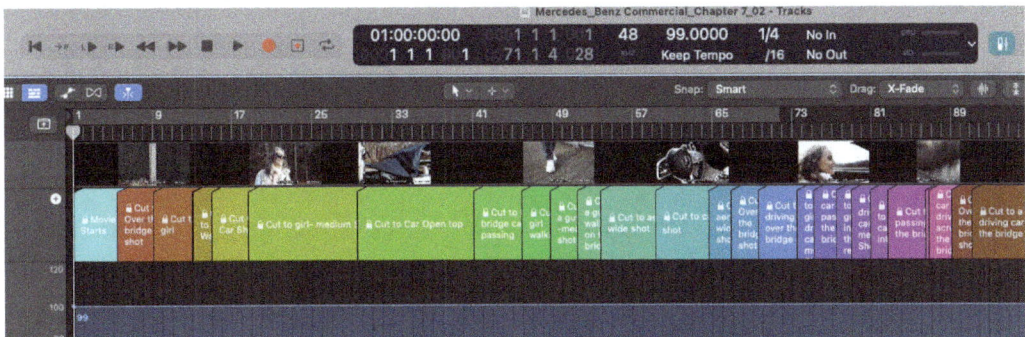

Figure 7.37: Arrange window with changed bpm

With this new tempo, watch the movie with the metronome on and observe the three different hit point locations. The objective is to see whether every hit point falls on the downbeat of a bar.

Open the **Marker** window and, while holding the *Option* key, click on the marker timecode **TC 01:00:39:20** of the first hit point. Logic Pro will move the playhead to that particular location, displaying the first hit point on bar 66, beat 1. That is a good sign because that means the current tempo makes the first hit point fall on the downbeat of a bar.

Creating Tempo Maps

Figure 7.38: Arrange window with Marker windows

Next, hold down the *Option* key and click on the location of the second hit point in the **Marker** window at **TC 01:00:54:14**.

Figure 7.39: Arrange window with Marker windows

Logic Pro then displays the second hit point falling on bar 91, beat 1. Again, that is also a good sign, because that means the current tempo makes the second hit point fall on the downbeat of a bar.

Next, hold down the *Option* key and click on the location of the third hit point at **TC 01:01:07:20**. Logic Pro displays the third hit point falling on bar 113, beat 1, and once again, the tempo is working because the third hit point falls on the downbeat of a bar.

Figure 7.40: Arrange window with Marker windows

After watching the movie and observing the three hit points, we see that the tempo of 99 bpm worked since all of the three hit points fell on the downbeat of a bar. This was done without creating a tempo map.

Finding the most suitable tempo requires a lot of experimentation and trial and error. Experimenting with different constant tempos and watching the movie while observing where the hit points fall will help you to determine the most suitable tempo. In film music though, a constant tempo may not always be what the scene needs. The film composer will use different tempo mapping methods in Logic Pro to assist in finding the most suitable tempo, along with the film director's vision and the film cuts.

Summary

In this chapter, we discussed how to deal with tempo in film music, how to evaluate a movie by watching it with a metronome, and how to use **Tap Tempo**. We also learned about marker positions and how to create a tempo map, as well as exploring different methods of how to find a suitable tempo. Additionally, we discussed how a movie can reveal to a film composer its own tempo by looking at the movie cuts or events.

Since there are different ways of finding a tempo, knowing and experimenting with the different options can be useful in many situations. This process can be time-consuming and challenging, but it is an important part of the beginning stage of scoring to picture. Music that will be written needs to create not only melodic or harmonic support but also rhythm and overall tempo. As with all areas, with more practice and repetition things will get smoother when scoring to picture.

In the next chapter, we will discuss working with beat mapping.

8
Working with Beat Mapping

In the previous chapter, we discussed how to deal with tempo in film music and create different types of tempo maps, using a spotting list and SMPTE-locked scene markers.

In this chapter, we will review how to use beat mapping in Logic Pro as another tool to help find an appropriate tempo, and we will also create a tempo map. We will also evaluate and look at markers' position numbers and their bar and beat locations, along with the overall tempo.

Additionally, we will explore different beat mapping methods to find a suitable tempo for a film, edit a **Beat Mapping** track, and discuss the overall benefit of using the Logic Pro beat mapping function.

In this chapter, we will explore beat mapping from a technical point of view in depth, which involves connecting the downbeat of a bar to a beat mapping line. Since this task takes a significant amount of time to master, we will go through multiple exercises that will help you to master the task of beat mapping.

In this chapter, we will cover the following topics:

- Understanding beat mapping
- Creating a Tap Tempo using an instrument track
- Beat mapping single MIDI notes
- Beat mapping an entire MIDI region
- Editing tempo points
- Editing a Beat Mapping track
- Using Beat Mapping scene markers
- Beat mapping the hit points

Technical requirements

To follow along with this chapter, you will need a general knowledge of using Logic-DAW, as well as a Mac computer with Logic Pro and QuickTime software installed. You will also need to be able to access the movie files provided with this book: `https://packt.link/hxCer`.

Understanding beat mapping

In general, **beat mapping** is the process of connecting the downbeat of a bar or any beat in a bar to a visible beat mapping line of a marker, a MIDI note, or an audio transient. During the process of beat mapping, Logic Pro makes the marker land on the downbeat of a bar and adjust the tempo.

Beat mapping is another method used to create a tempo map, and it is relatively faster than using the **Tempo Operations** window. There might be a project where one method is more appropriate than the other one. It's up to every user to master both methods and decide which one to choose for the project.

In *Chapter 7*, we covered how to use **Tap Tempo** by tapping on a keyboard; in the next section, we will review another option to create a **Tap Tempo** using a MIDI keyboard with an instrument track.

Creating a Tap Tempo using an instrument track

In this section, we will watch the movie and tap a MIDI keyboard, with a loaded percussion sound emulating a metronome.

Open the `Mercedes-Benz Cabrio C 300_BITC.mov` movie file that was saved in *Chapter 7*, with the SMPTE-locked scene markers. Make sure that the movie and Logic Pro are in sync, and then name and save the project (for example, I will choose `Beat mapping_01`).

In general, you can use a piano, a percussion instrument, or even a plain external MIDI track that has no instrument loaded at all. In this example, we will use a percussion instrument and tap it to create a rhythmic **Tap Tempo**.

To create an instrument in Logic Pro, use the *Option + CMD + N* shortcut. From the dialog box, click on the **Software Instrument** tab. Then, click on the **Details** downward arrow to display the **Instrument** and **Audio Output** options, if they are not already displayed.

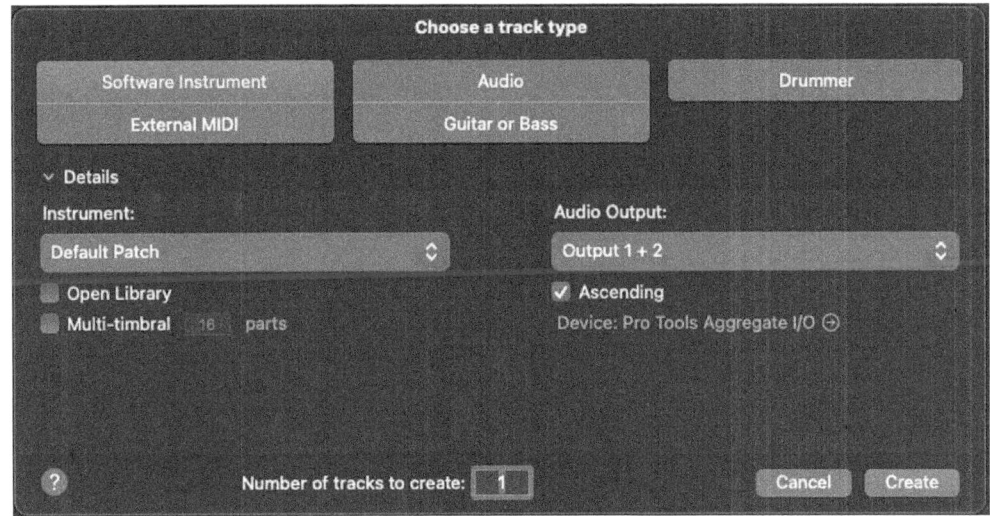

Figure 8.1: Logic Pro dialog box

In the **Instrument** section, from the drop-down menu, select **Sampler (Multi-Sample)** | **Stereo**.

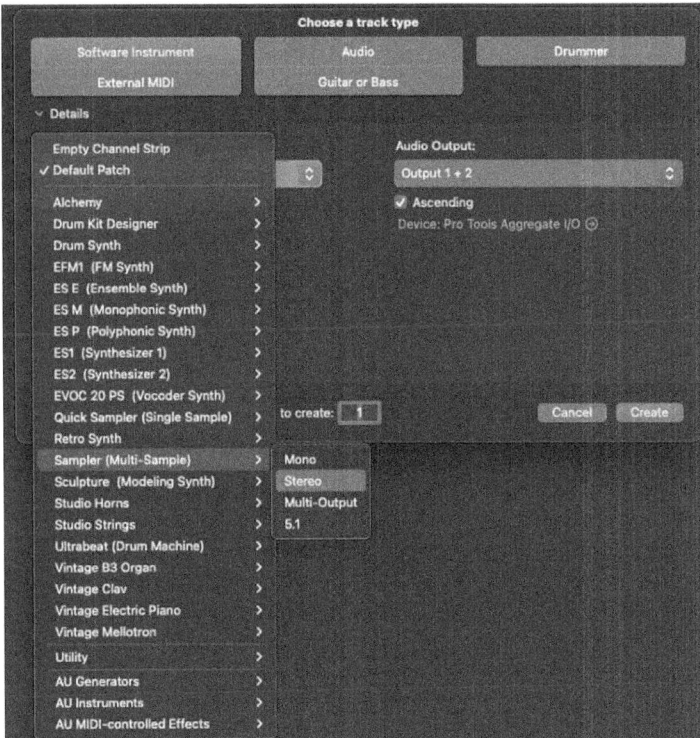

Figure 8.2: Software Instrument drop-down menu

Logic Pro will load the sampler instrument into the Logic Pro channel strip. Now, click on the blue **Sampler** button:

Figure 8.3: Channel strip

The sampler instrument window will open, as you can see here:

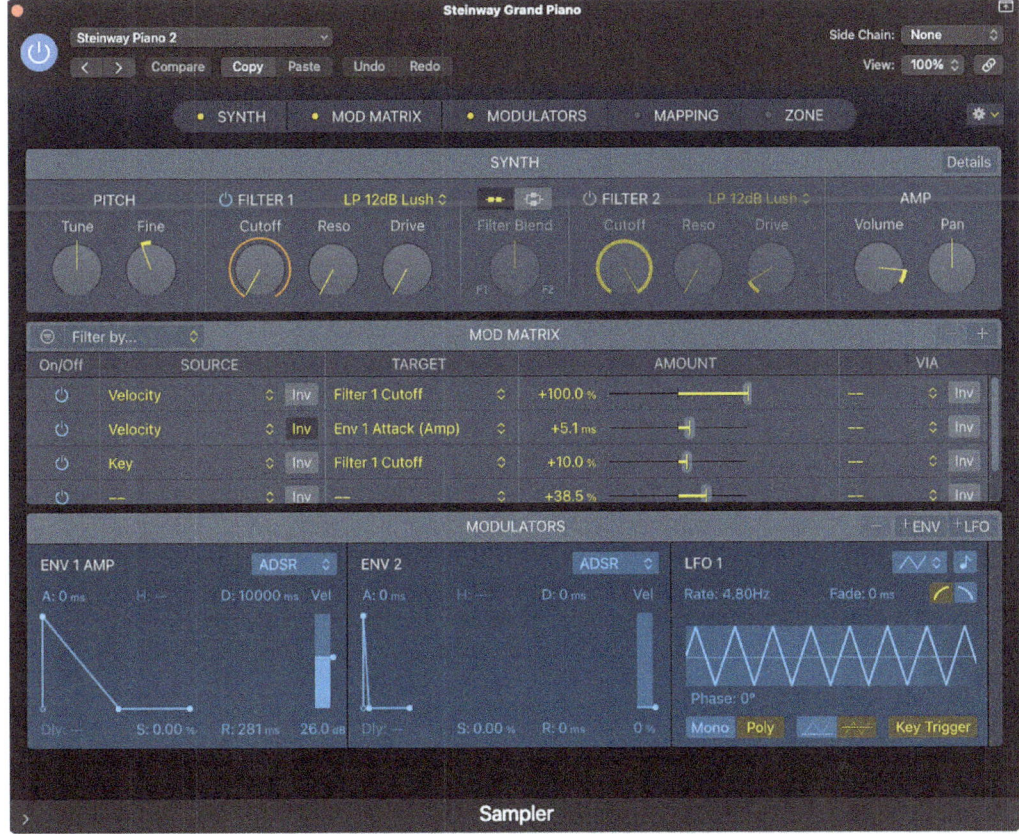

Figure 8.4: Logic Pro Sampler

To select an instrument, go to the upper-left corner, click on the search menu, and select **Factory | 03 Drums & Percussion | 05 Percussion | Single Instruments | Wood Block High**:

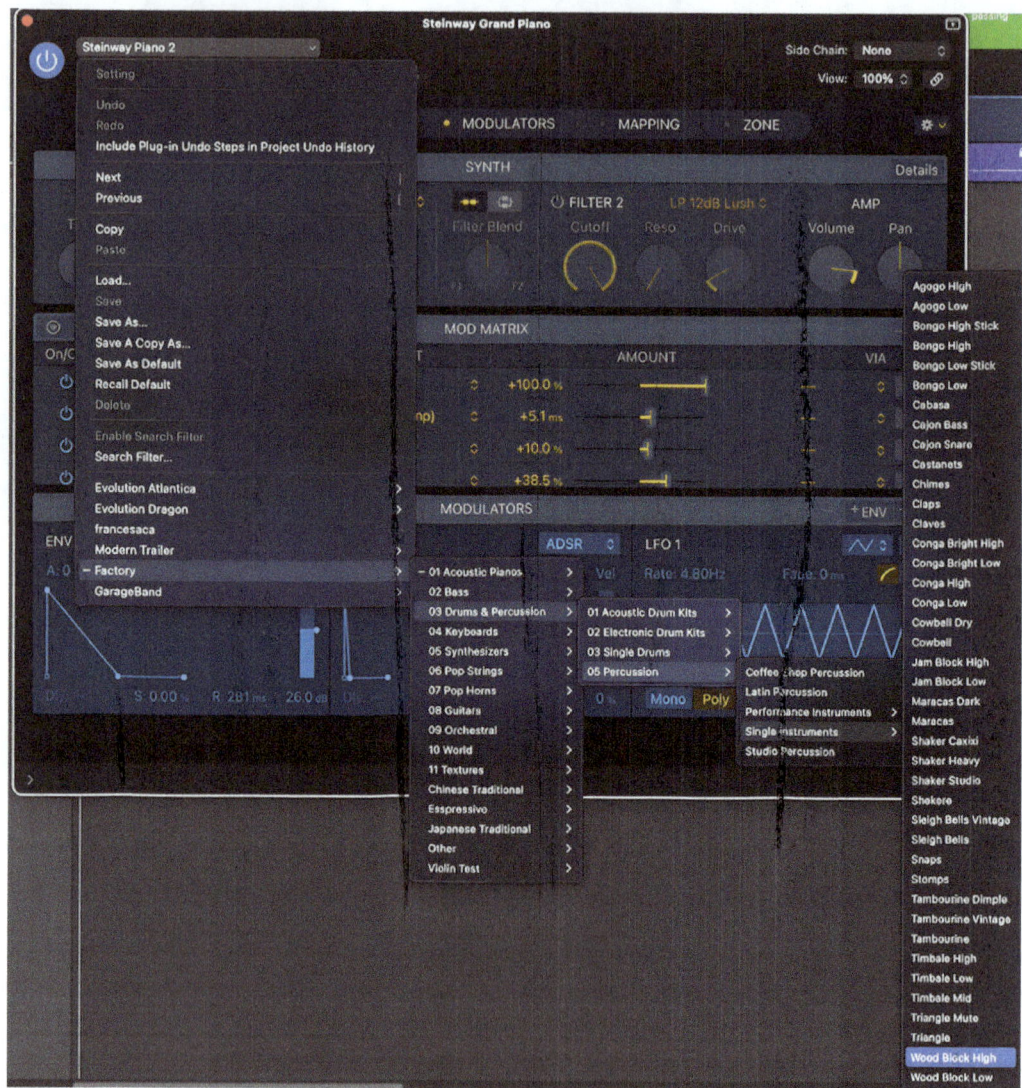

Figure 8.5: Sampler drop-down menu lists

By default, this instrument loads with other plugins on the channel strip. In order to not hear a sound with a large reverb or delay, turn off each plugin except for the **Sampler**. You can turn off the plugins by clicking on the on/off button.

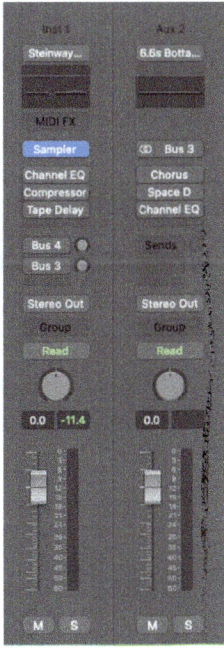

Figure 8.6: Channel strip with the effect plugins turned off

Next, turn off the Logic Pro metronome and arm your percussion track:

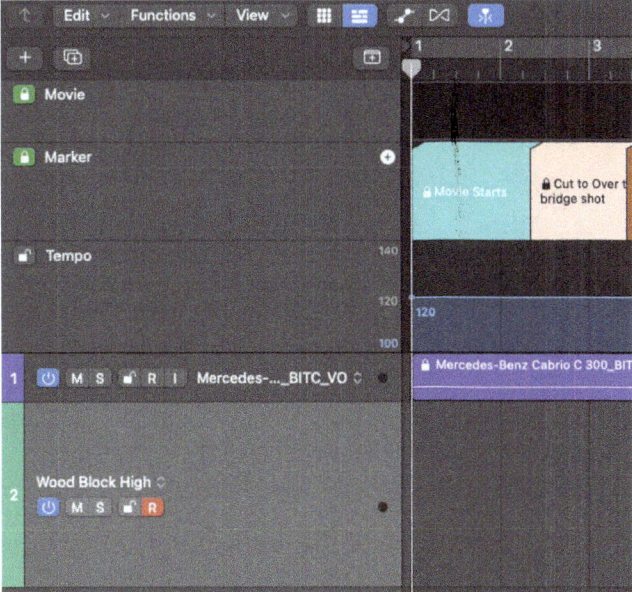

Figure 8.7: Armed percussion track

Keep the default tempo of **120** bpm and adjust the size of the movie window. The larger image will allow you to see the picture cuts and transitions better, as you follow the tempo of the visual events.

Next, watch the entire movie, and hit any key on the MIDI keyboard to follow your rhythmic tempo based on the cuts.

Figure 8.8: Arrange window with the Floating Movie window

After playing the entire movie and tapping a note on the keyboard, stop your session from playing and hit *Shift + R* (for **Capture Recording**). Logic Pro creates a MIDI region with all your MIDI note inputs recorded.

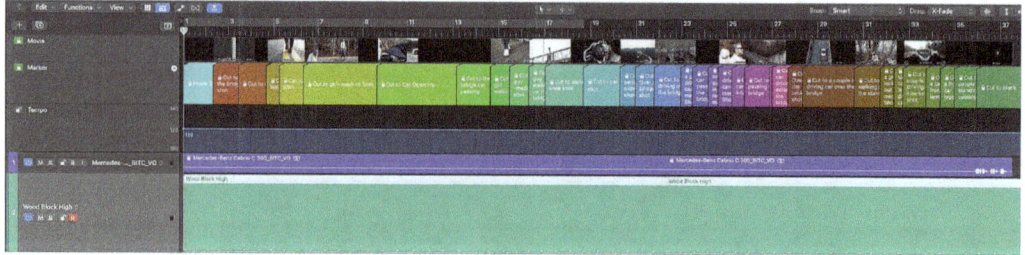

Figure 8.9: Recorded MIDI region in the Arrange window

Next, play the movie file from the beginning and listen to your recorded **Wood Block High** instrument while playing back the MIDI notes. You can adjust the individual notes and their position in the Piano Roll if needed or record a new version.

If you are not satisfied with the instrument recording results, you can use a feature that Logic Pro has called **Track Alternatives**. You can enable this function by hitting *Option + T* and selecting **Track Alternatives**.

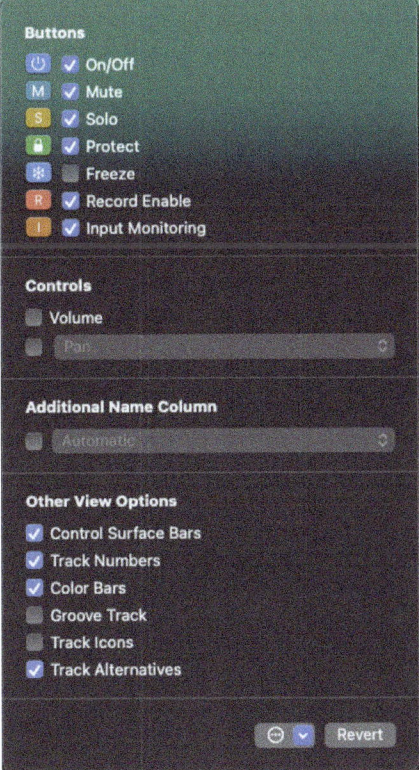

Figure 8.10: Track header options

After enabling **Track Alternatives**, the track header should display two arrows pointing in the opposite direction.

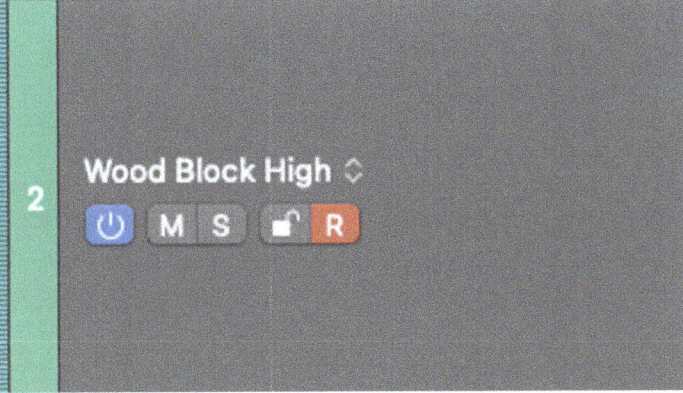

Figure 8.11: Track Alternatives enabled

Clicking on the two arrows opens a drop-down menu, allowing you to create a new track and keep the previously recorded MIDI region.

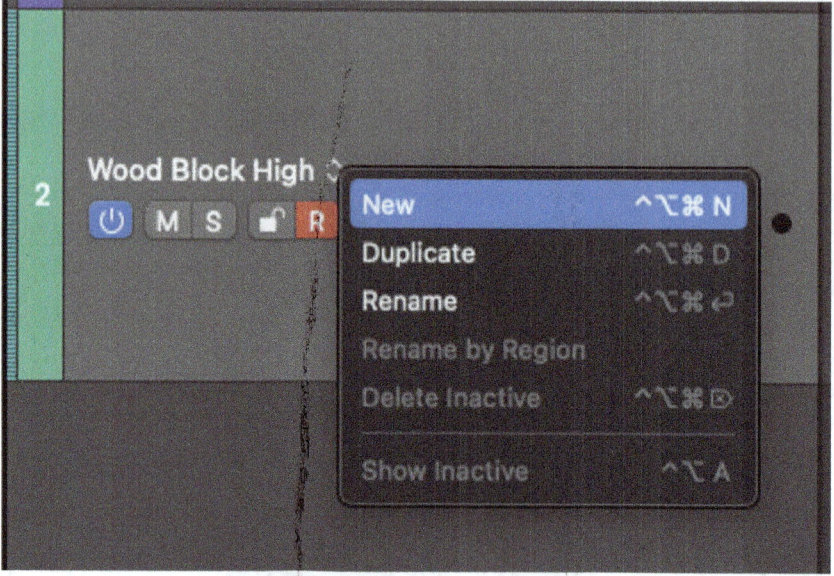

Figure 8.12: Track Alternatives drop-down menu

This is a very useful feature that allows you to use the same instrument but record different versions as layers of MIDI regions. You can then access them and switch between them for comparison.

In this section, we explored recording MIDI notes to reflect the pulse of the film. The main idea behind creating a **Tap Tempo** is to outline a temporary tempo while watching the film.

In the next section, we will explore how to connect certain MIDI notes to selected markers using the beat mapping feature.

Beat mapping single MIDI notes

Another way of directly creating a tempo map from a MIDI region is using the beats from an entire region in the **Beat Mapping** track. This process involves manually adjusting the bar and beat and moving the recorded notes one note at a time to the nearest beat of a bar. Logic Pro will then adjust the tempo.

To do this, in the global tracks, enable the **Beat Mapping** track, like so:

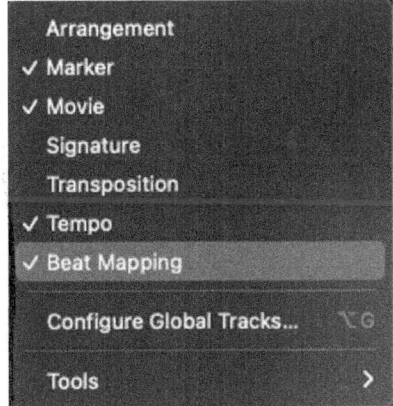

Figure 8.13: Global tracks drop-down menu

The **Beat Mapping** track should be visible in the global tracks window.

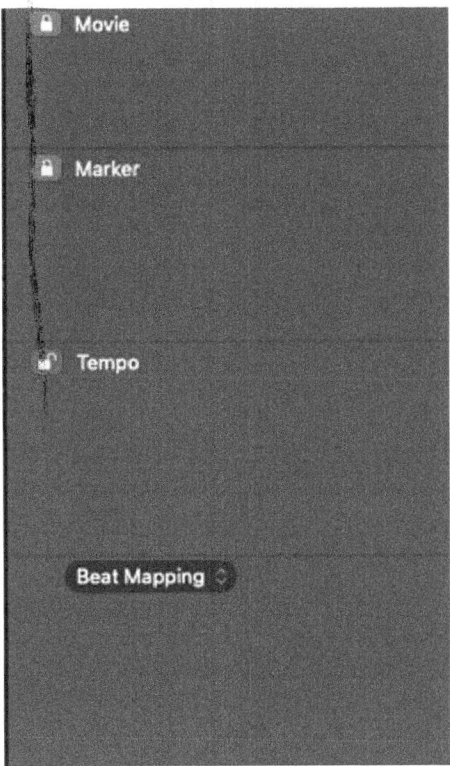

Figure 8.14: Global tracks

Next, resize the **Beat Mapping** track, as shown in *Figure 8.15*, and click on the green MIDI region. After clicking on the green MIDI region, you should be able to see a mirror reflection of the MIDI region inside of the **Beat Mapping** track.

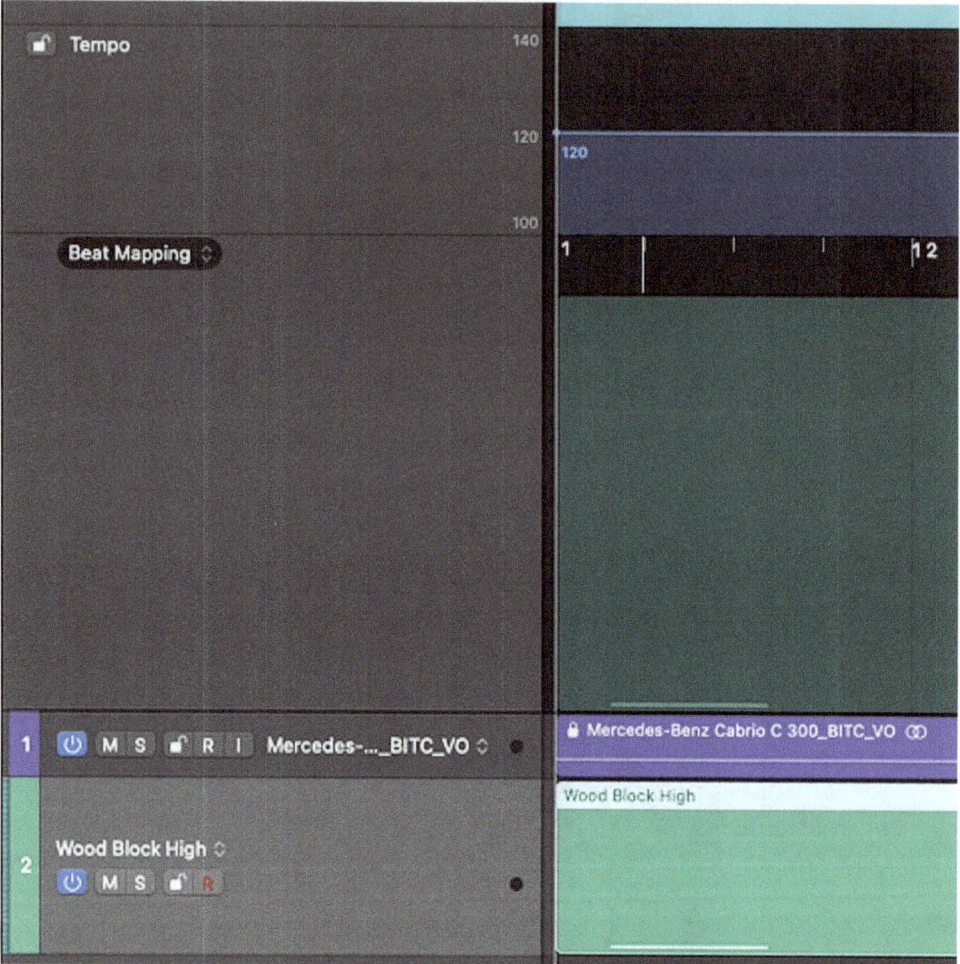

Figure 8.15: MIDI region highlighted in the Beat Mapping track

Zoom in horizontally using *CMD* + the right or left arrow on the computer keyboard to help you see the beat mapping lines more clearly. Then, move the playhead away from the bar 1, beat 1 location and place it anywhere to the side, unblocking the view of the **Beat Mapping** track.

The next task, which entails connecting the lines in the **Beat Mapping** track, takes precision and patience because it can be very tricky to complete. For this reason, it's important to follow these next steps carefully:

1. Move your pointer tool to the upper-left portion of the **Beat Mapping** track. The pointer tool will turn into a hand tool. Keep an eye on the second red arrow on the bottom of the **Beat Mapping** track representing the first recorded note on the instrument track; this is the location that you will need to connect to.

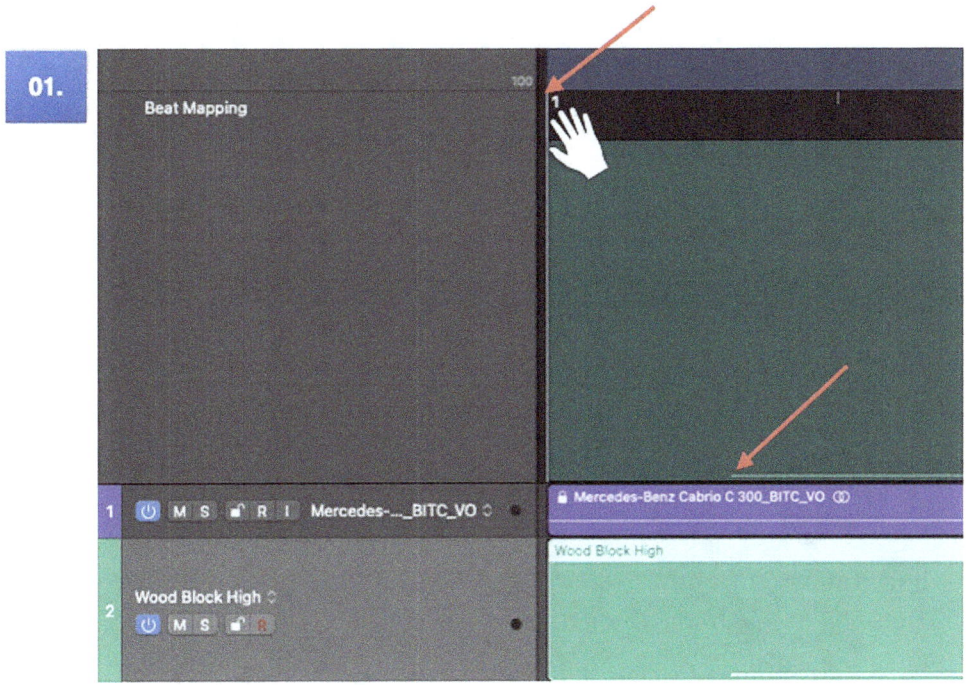

Figure 8.16: Beat Mapping track

2. Next, click and drag the hand tool from the top of the **Beat Mapping** track slightly to the right, and then down toward the green line at the bottom of the **Beat Mapping** track.

196 | Working with Beat Mapping

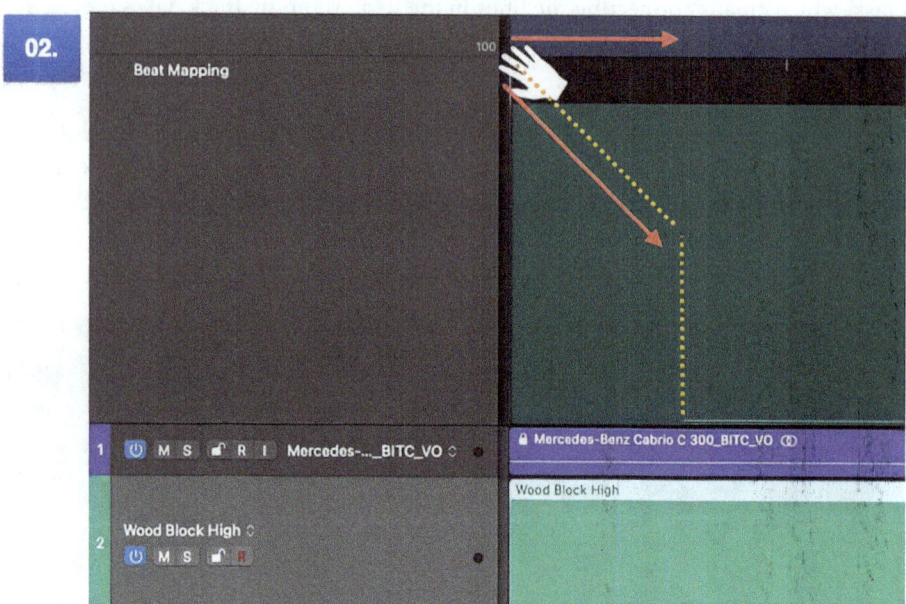

Figure 8.17: Navigating the Beat Mapping track

3. As you drag the mouse, you will see that Logic Pro connects the lines, from the top bar 1 position to the beginning of the note at the bottom of the **Beat Mapping** track.

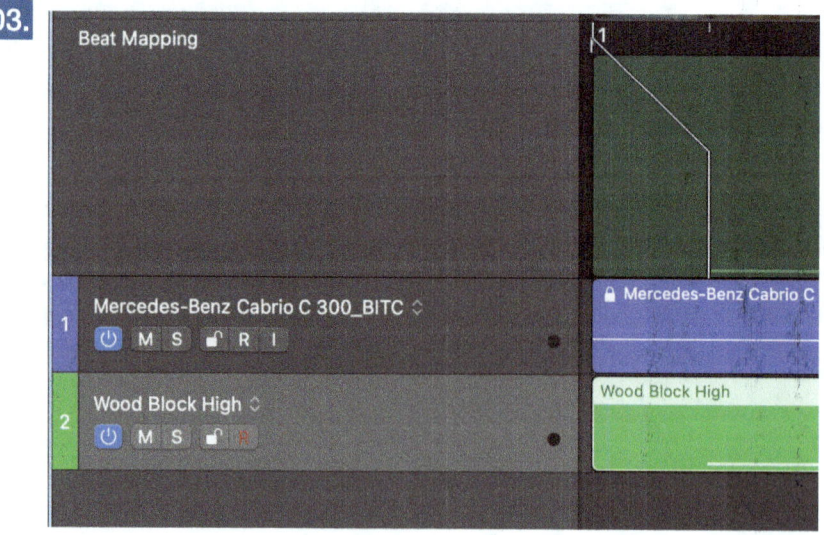

Figure 8.18: Beat mapping lines

4. As soon as you see the lines connected, let go of the mouse. The first recorded note will then move to the beginning of bar 1, beat 1.

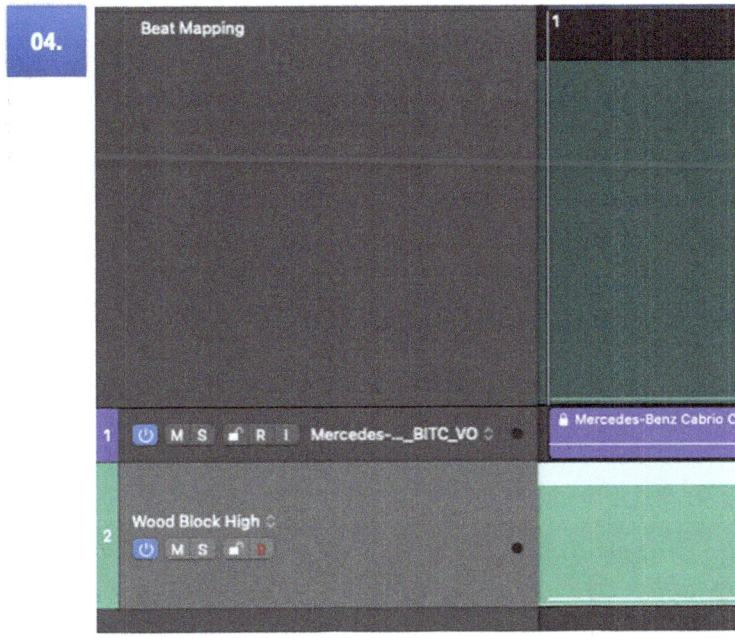

Figure 8.19: Adjusted Beat Mapping track

After the first MIDI note was beat mapped to bar 1, the second MIDI note appears to be past bar 1, beat 3, as shown in *Figure 8.20*.

Next, we will continue applying beat mapping to all the recorded notes of the MIDI region:

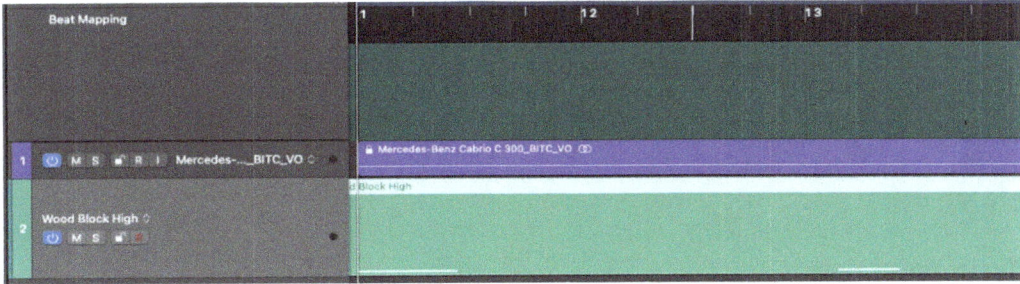

Figure 8.20: Beat mapping the MIDI region

As a result of beat mapping all of the MIDI notes, Logic Pro created new tempo changes between the bars, as you can see in *Figure 8.21*. As you continue beat mapping all the MIDI notes, Logic Pro creates a variety of tempo changes:

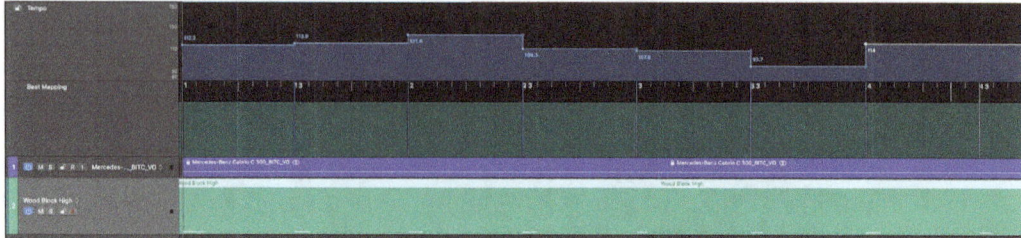

Figure 8.21: Beat mapping and the Tempo track

As you practice the task of beat mapping all the MIDI notes, you should see a variety of tempo changes, visible in the **Tempo** track. Logic Pro applies tempo changes based on the distance of the recorded notes. You can see in *Figure 8.22* that there are a lot of tempo changes based on the beat mapping process of the recorded notes.

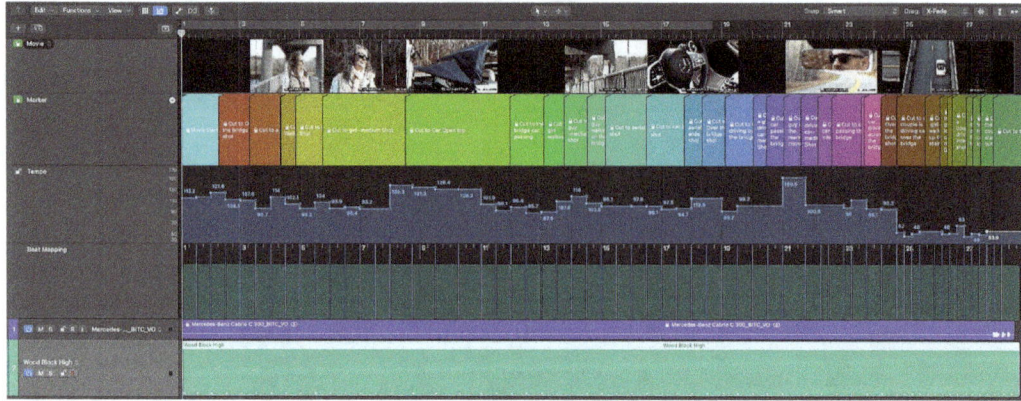

Figure 8.22: Arrange window with the final tempo map

Even though this task creates a lot of tempo changes, it's important to practice all the steps to familiarize yourself with how beat mapping works.

Once the **Tempo** track is created, you have the option to edit it by beat mapping any of the MIDI notes manually. This can be helpful when searching for the best tempo during the scoring to picture process. Since there can be multiple tempo recalculations during the beat mapping process, it's important to make sure that the final tempo benefits the picture.

Now that we've looked at beat mapping using the recorded notes of a MIDI region, we will create a tempo map using beat mapping from an entire MIDI region.

Beat mapping an entire MIDI region

In this section, we will let Logic Pro automatically create a new tempo map by analyzing an entire MIDI region, and all the notes in it, in the **Beat Mapping** track.

So, in the **Tempo** track, from the drop-down menu, create a new default Tempo of **120** bpm.

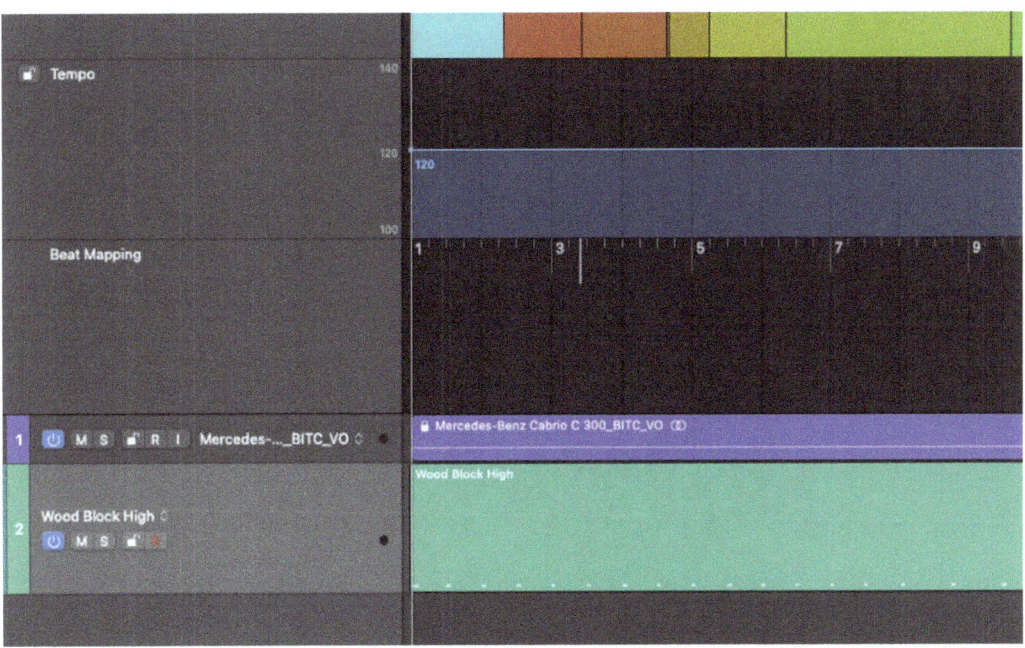

Figure 8.23: Beat mapping of the MIDI region

Then, click on the MIDI region so that it appears in the **Beat Mapping** track:

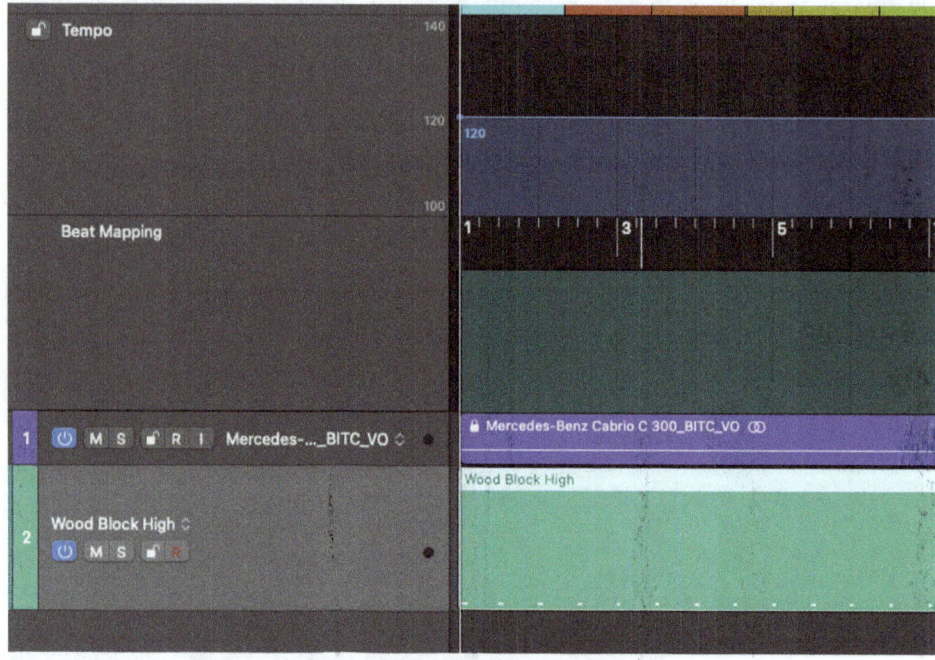

Figure 8.24: Highlighted MIDI region in the Beat Mapping track

From the **Beat Mapping** track header pop-up menu, select **Beats from Region**.

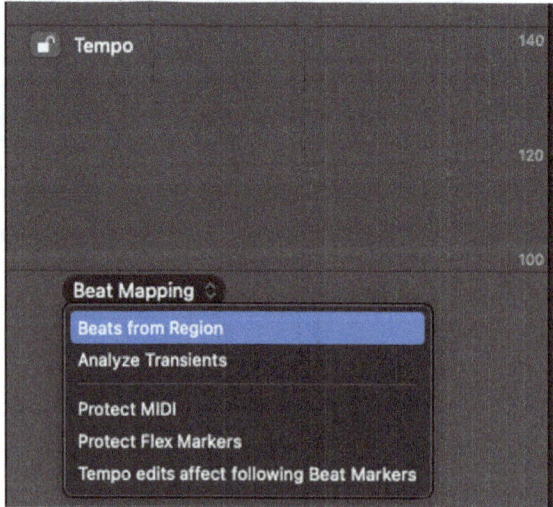

Figure 8.25: Beat Mapping track drop-down menu

The **Set Beats by Guide Region(s)** window will open, like so:

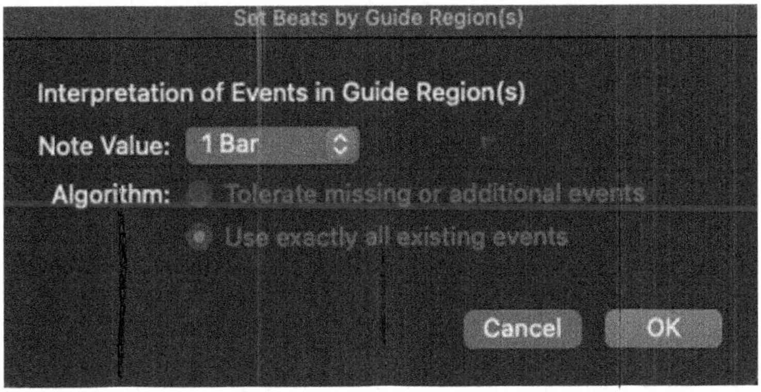

Figure 8.26: Set Beats by Guide Region(s) window

Click on the **Note Value** drop-down window and select **1/4 Note**.

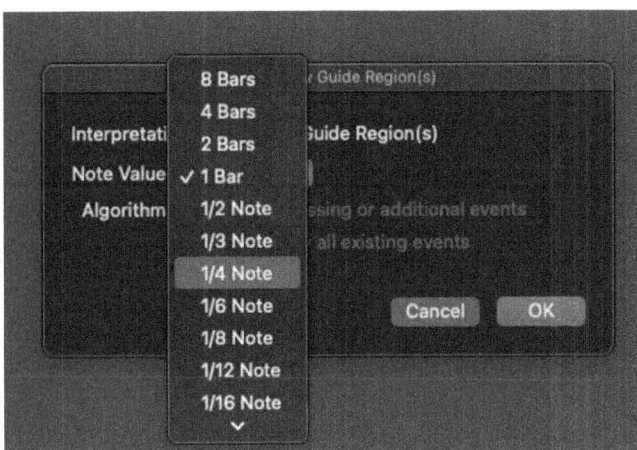

Figure 8.27: Note Value drop-down menu

Once you click **OK**, Logic Pro will automatically analyze the entire MIDI region and create a tempo map.

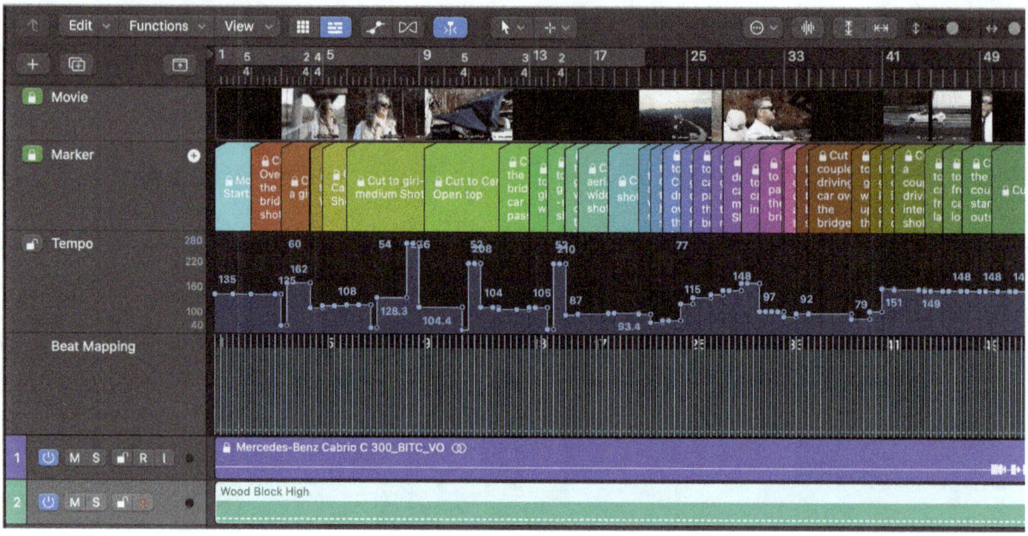

Figure 8.28: Arrange window with a final tempo map

The new tempo map outline that is created can be additionally edited as needed.

This entire process can be repeated multiple times, creating multiple tempo maps to experiment with. Whether you type rhythmically on the keyboard or play the piano while watching a film, Logic Pro has the ability to analyze your MIDI performance and create a tempo based on what you played. Experimentation is the key.

Now that we've covered beat mapping and how it's used to create a tempo map, we will go over how to edit the tempo points after finishing the beat mapping process.

Editing tempo points

Any tempo changes made inside the **Tempo** track are visible as dots and called **tempo points** (also referred to as knots). Tempo points can be edited or adjusted evenly or gradually between the selected tempo points.

The individual tempo point can be moved up or down by clicking and dragging it to the preferred bpm. If you need to adjust multiple tempo points at the same time, you can hover your mouse over the selection and Logic Pro will select all the points.

If the tempo points are white, that means they are selected; if they are shown in blue, it means they are not selected. The highlighted tempo points in the **Tempo** track can then be moved up or down to the preferred bpm:

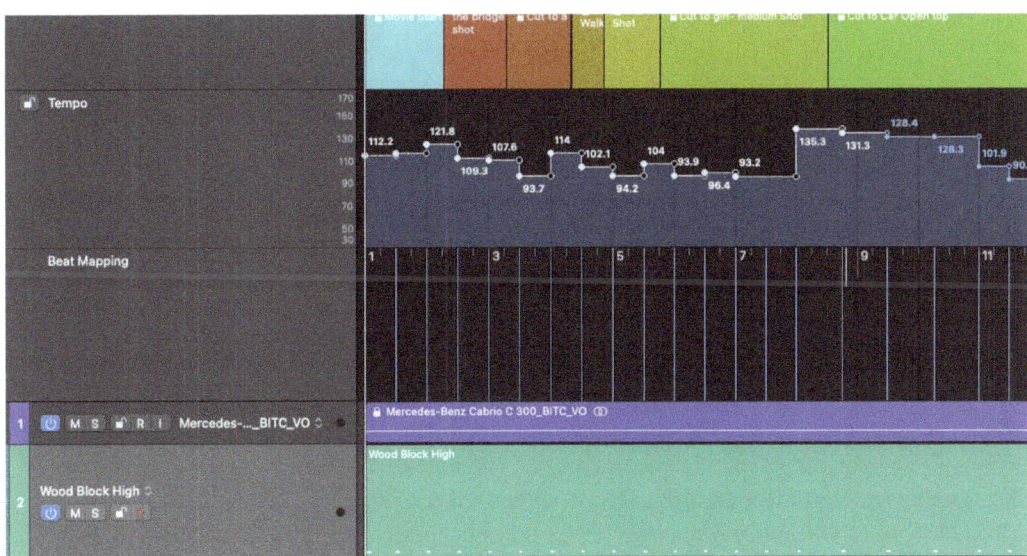

Figure 8.29: Edited tempo points in the Tempo track

There is an additional feature in Logic Pro that allows you to create a constant tempo across multiple tempo points. Once all of the tempo points are highlighted, you can click on the **Tempo** track drop-down menu and select **Replace selected Points by Average Tempo** (or *Ctrl* + click in the **Tempo** track). You can experiment with this feature by selecting fewer of the tempo points. It's recommended to start with just a few points to see whether the tempo change is suitable for what you're aiming for.

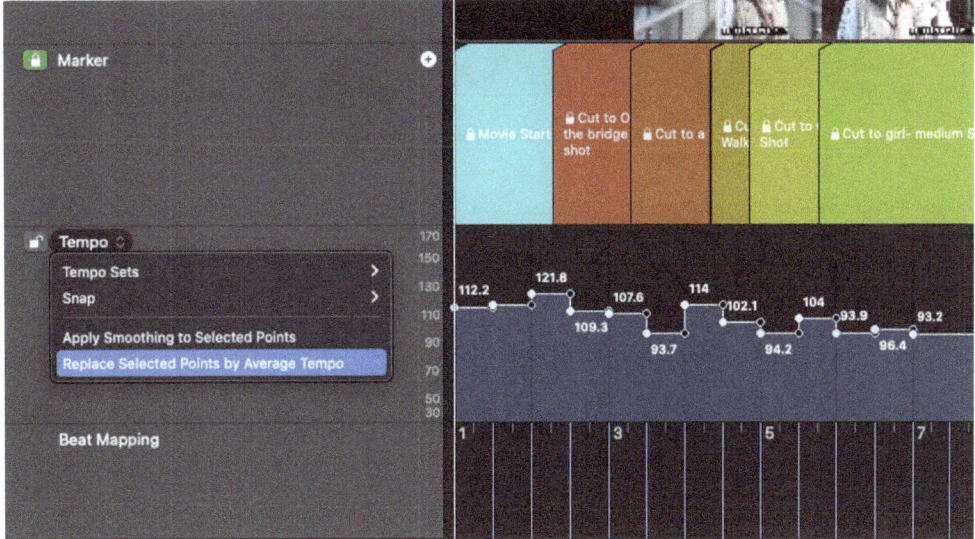

Figure 8.30: Tempo track drop-down menu

Sometimes, selecting a group of knots and tempos and letting Logic Pro adjust the tempo may not have any visible results. Since the results are unpredictable, this is more of an experimental feature that every composer can use as they see fit.

It will be up to each composer to decide whether the variety of tempo changes contributes to the film scene. It's possible that having less jarring tempo changes with a smoother tempo can be needed. Again, the choices all depend on whether the tempo contributes to the scoring of the scene. If it doesn't work, you can try to smooth the tempo changes to be less jarring. Knowing these tools and how to use them is invaluable to any film composer, and this knowledge can be used and applied when needed.

Now that we've covered how to edit tempo points, we will go over how to edit a **Beat Mapping** track.

Editing a Beat Mapping track

When working in a **Beat Mapping** track, lines can be added accidentally sometimes by just clicking in the **Beat Mapping** track. You may not even realize that it happened, and lines can accumulate quickly. In this section, we will go over how they get inserted and how you can delete them.

You can insert a single beat mapping line by double-clicking anywhere in the **Beat Mapping** track. In *Figure 8.31*, the blue and white lines show a new beat mapping line:

Figure 8.31: Individual beat mapping

To delete a single beat mapping line, double-click on the blue line with the pointer or eraser tool.

To delete all the beat mapping lines at once, click on the beat mapping track header, and Logic Pro will select all the beat mapping lines on that track:

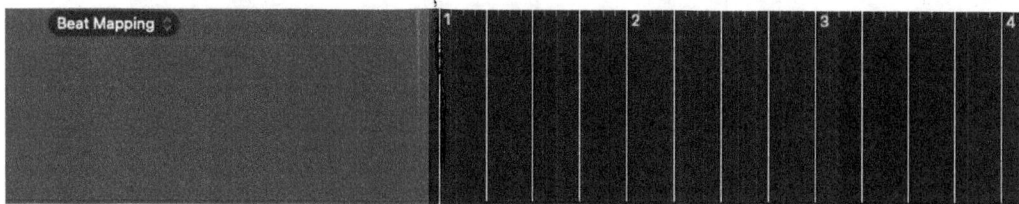

Figure 8.32: Beat Mapping track with highlighted Beat Mapping markers

Then, to delete all of them, hit the *Delete* key on the computer keyboard:

Figure 8.33: Empty Beat Mapping track

So far, we have reviewed beat mapping from a MIDI region, in the next section we will be going over **Beat Mapping** scene markers.

Using Beat Mapping scene markers

In *Chapter 7*, we discussed how to find the most suitable tempo using the **Tempo Operations** window. In this section, we will use Beat Mapping scene markers to create a tempo map, also referred to as "laying out the cue," which can be a faster way to help find an appropriate tempo.

We will use the Mercedes commercial to practice this task. However, the skill you will learn in this section can be used in any type of scoring project. You can take this skill and apply it to your own existing projects. The importance of this exercise is to become familiar with and have experience in beat mapping scene markers. Out of all the different tools available in Logic Pro, this is the most used task and, in general, the one most commonly preferred by film composers.

To do this, open the `Mercedes-Benz Cabrio C 300_BITC.mov` movie file that you saved in *Chapter 6*, with the SMPTE-locked scene markers. Make sure that the movie and Logic Pro are in sync, and then name and save the project – for example, `Beat Mapping_02`.

Next, in the global tracks, enable the **Beat Mapping** track. Then, make sure to rearrange the tracks' positions from the top to the bottom in this order – the **Movie** track, the **Marker** track, the **Beat Mapping** track, and then the **Tempo** track (this will help with the beat mapping process that we will explore later in this chapter), like so:

206 Working with Beat Mapping

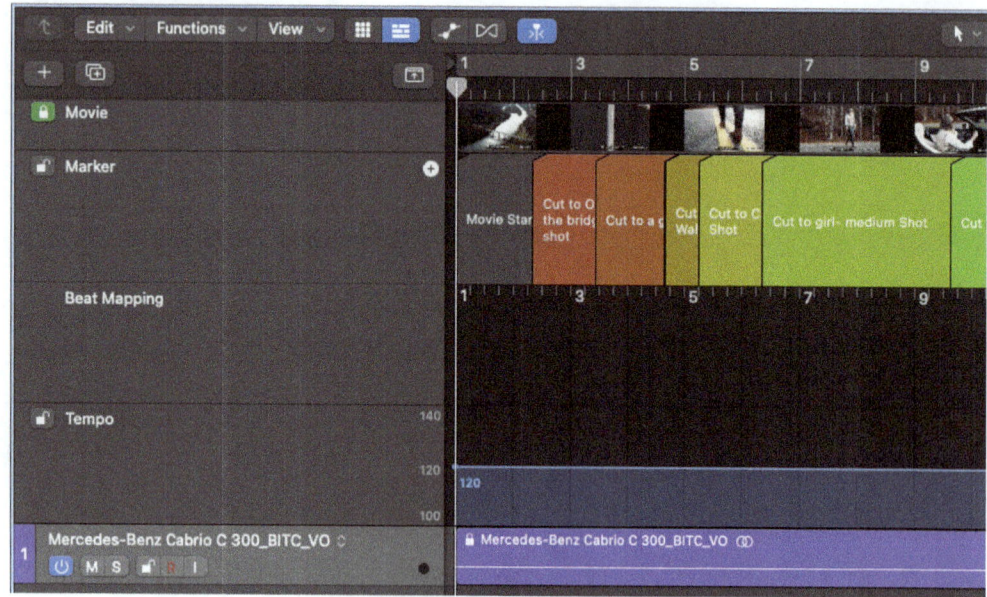

Figure 8.34: Changing the order of the global tracks

Zoom in horizontally on the marker track to make the markers and their positions more visible.

Figure 8.35: Zoomed in horizontally to the marker track

When clicking on the beat mapping track header, Logic Pro displays lines that mark the position of each of the scene markers in the **Beat Mapping** track:

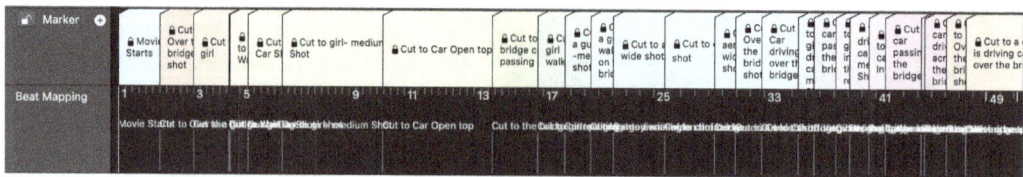

Figure 8.36: All markers highlighted in the Beat Mapping track

In this example, we'll work with individual markers, so to deselect all the markers, click on the beat mapping track header again. Then, zoom in horizontally by using *CMD* + the left or right arrows, and click on the marker labeled **Cut to Over the bridge shot**. You can then see that the marker falls almost halfway between bar 2 and 3.

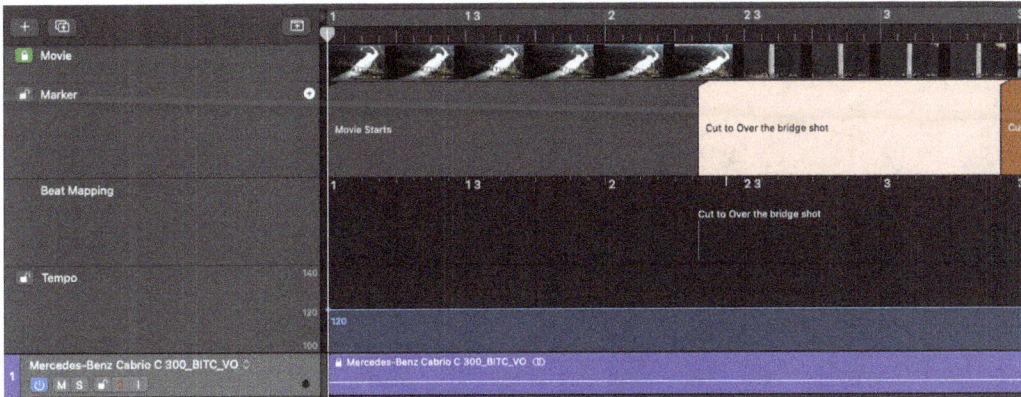

Figure 8.37: Beat Mapping track marker

Next, click on the **Cut to Over the bridge shot** marker. Logic Pro will display a line in the **Beat Mapping** track that points to the marker's position. Similar to the previous beat mapping from the MIDI region exercise, since the marker almost falls on the bar 2, beat 3 position, move the Pointer tool to the top of the location in the **Beat Mapping** track and click and hold it. It will turn into a hand tool. Then, drag the hand tool with your mouse to the left in order to connect to the visible beat mapping line, and then let go.

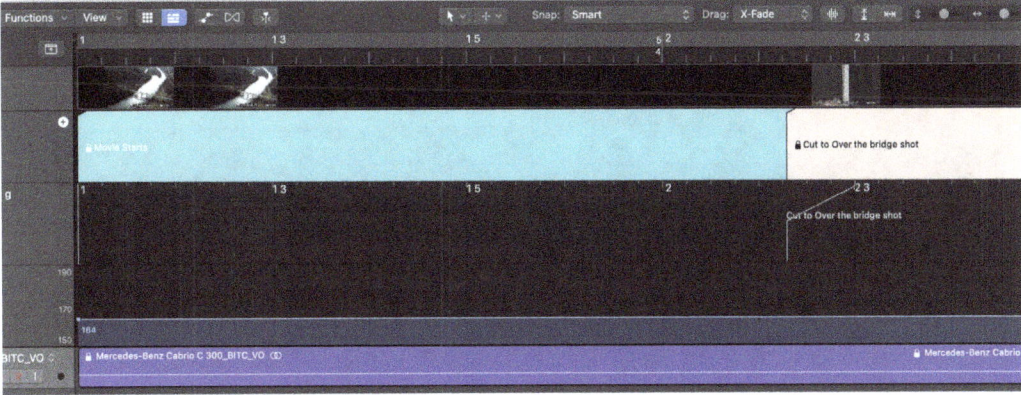

Figure 8.38: The bar 2, beat 3 position connected to a beat mapping line

Logic Pro will snap the marker position to bar 2, beat 3:

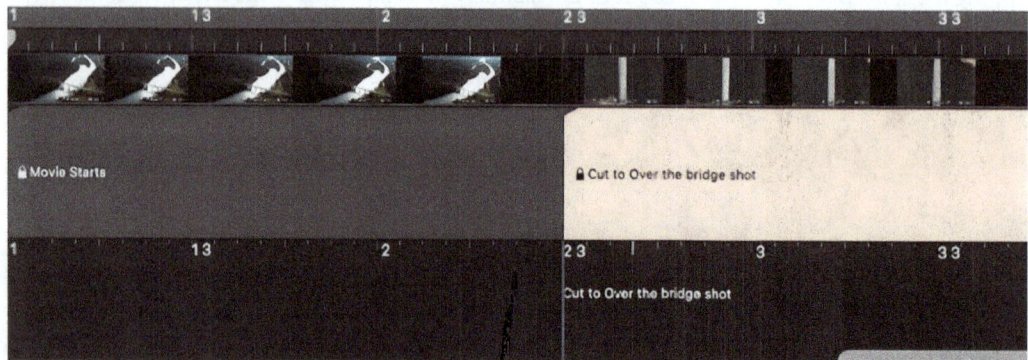

Figure 8.39: Marker position snapped to the location

Then, click on the next marker, **Cut to a girl**. We can see in the **Beat Mapping** track that the marker's location is close to bar 4, beat 1:

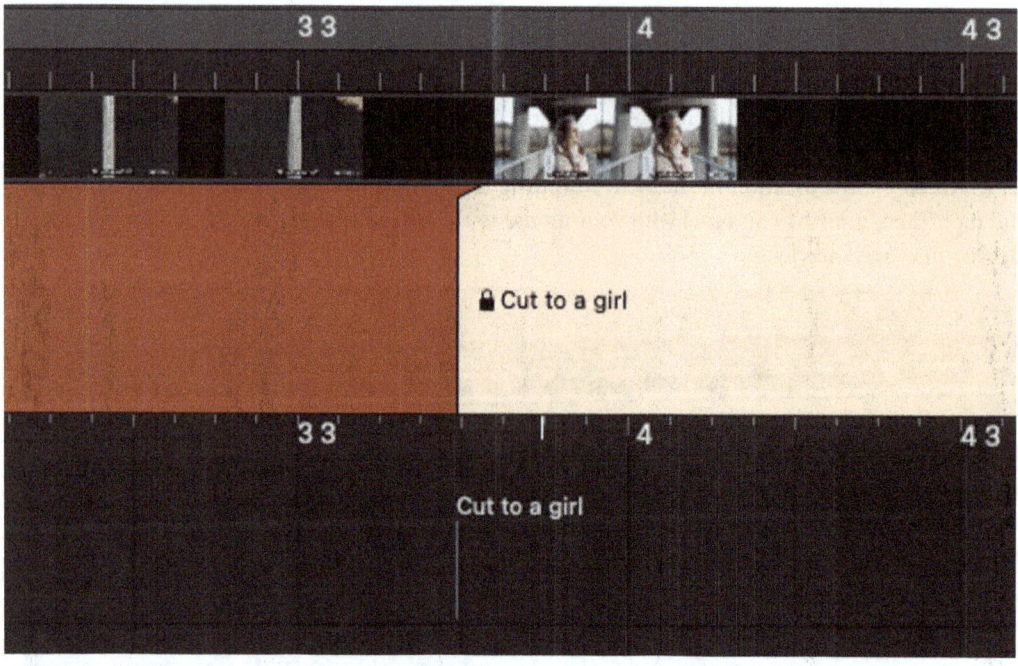

Figure 8.40: New line in the Beat Mapping track

Connect the top of bar 4 with the beat mapping line:

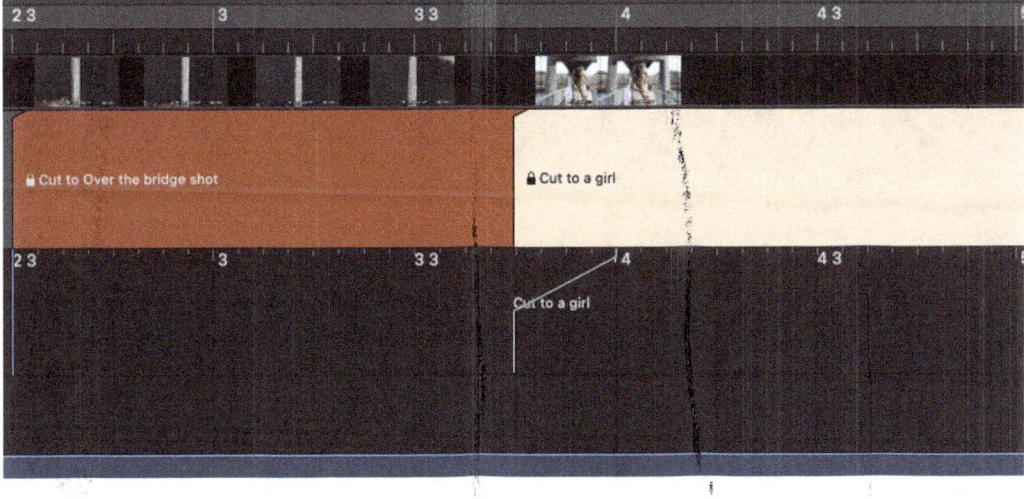

Figure 8.41: Connected downbeat of a bar to a beat mapping line

It's important to continue zooming in horizontally when dealing with many markers so that you can see clearly where a marker falls. Also, having the floating marker window visible can be very helpful to see the exact marker location, based on the position numbers.

Next, continue to the next marker, **Cut to a girl-medium shot**.

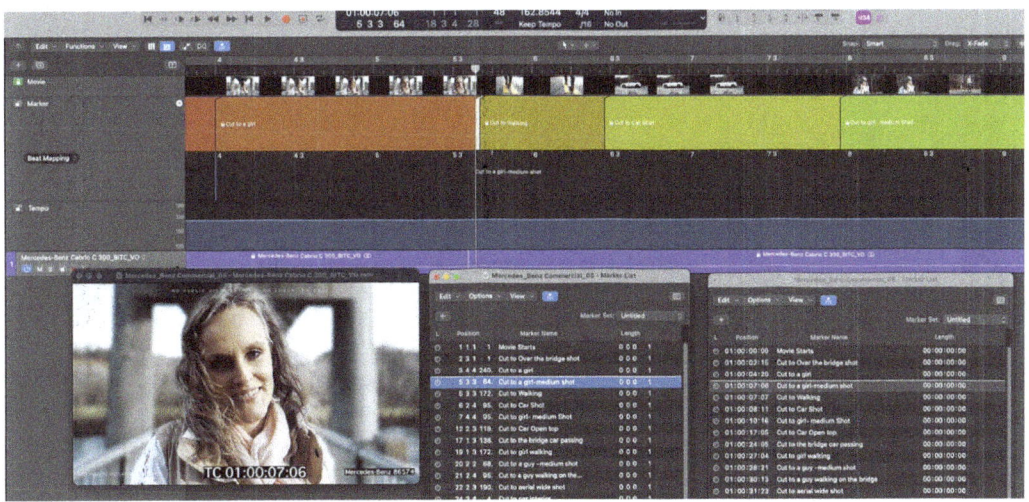

Figure 8.42: Arrange window with Floating Movie and Marker windows

Working with Beat Mapping

By zooming in horizontally, we can see that the marker falls between bar 5, beat 3 and bar 5, beat 4.

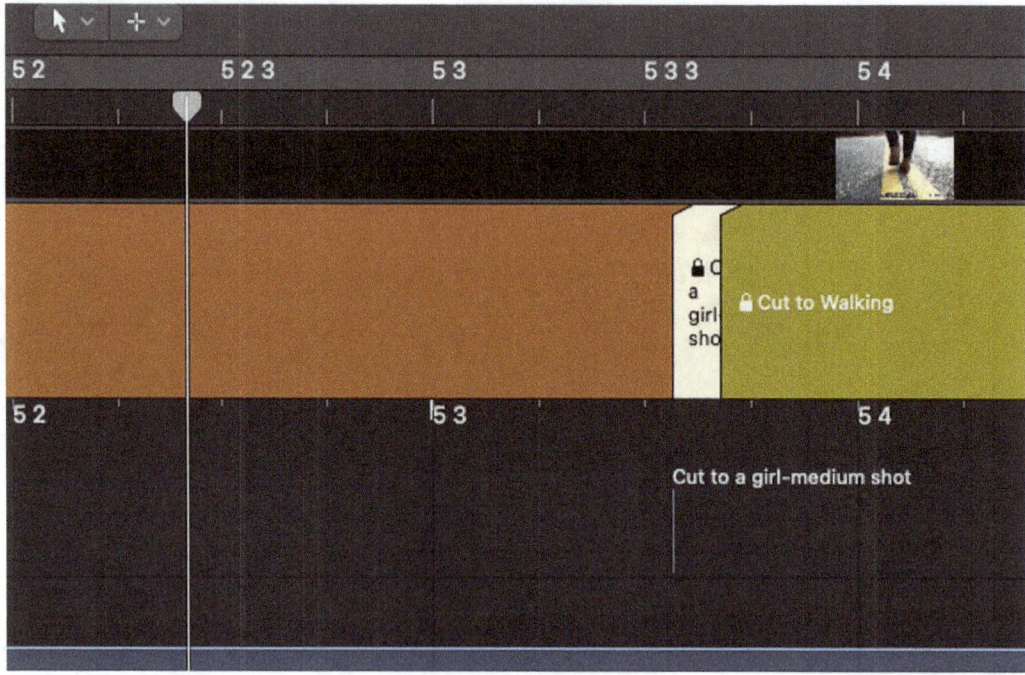

Figure 8.43: New line in the Beat Mapping track

Since the marker is closer to the middle of bar 5, connect the position of bar 5, beat 3 to the beat mapping line.

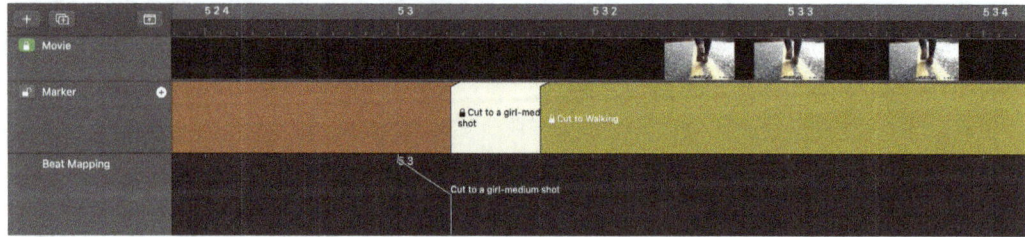

Figure 8.44: Connecting bar 5, beat 3 position to a beat mapping line

After connecting bar 5, beat 3 to the line in the **Beat Mapping** track, Logic Pro snaps **Cut to a girl-medium shot** to that location and adjusts the tempo.

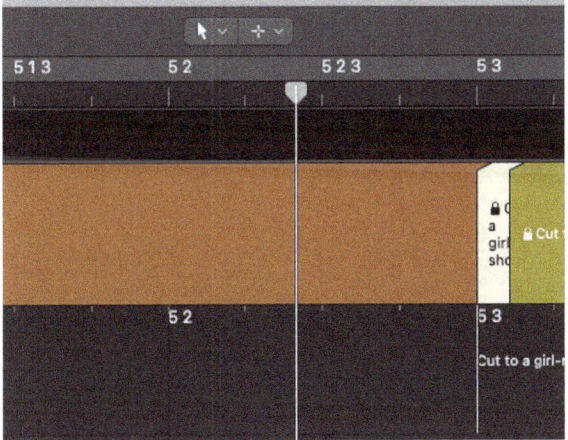

Figure 8.45: Marker position snapped to the location

Now, we will continue with the next marker, **Cut to Walking**, which we can see is close to bar 5, beat 4. Note that it can be helpful to hold down *Option* + click in the floating marker window on the **Cut to Walking** marker position to bring the playhead to that location, allowing you to view the scene in the movie window:

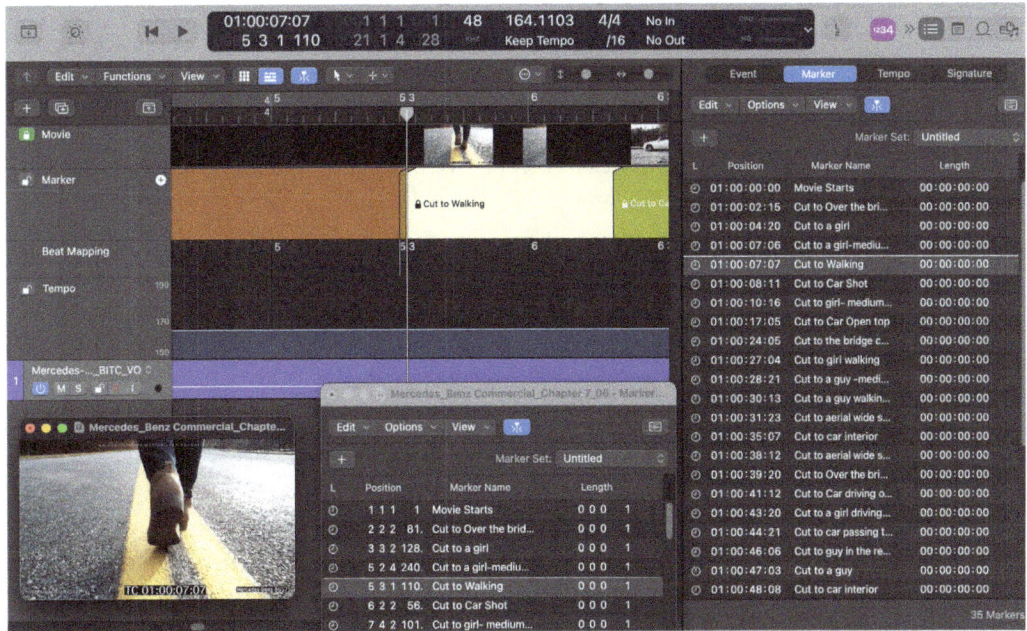

Figure 8.46: Arrange window with the Floating Movie and Marker windows

After connecting bar 5, beat 4 to the line in the **Beat Mapping** track, Logic Pro again snaps the **Cut to Walking** marker to that location and adjusts the tempo.

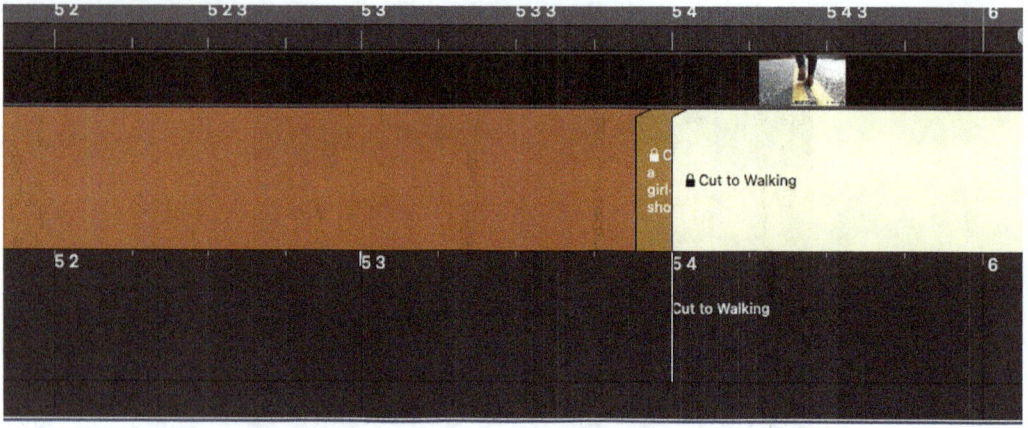

Figure 8.47: Marker position snapped to the location

Next, we will continue with the **Cut to Car Shot** marker:

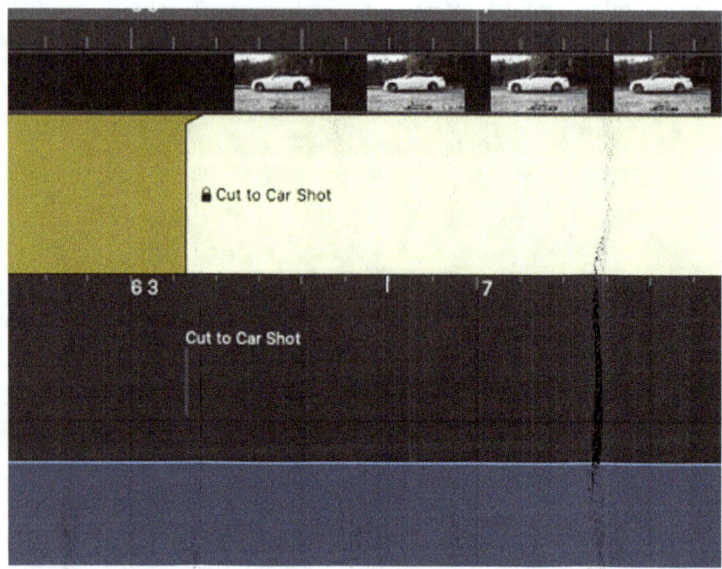

Figure 8.48: A new line in the Beat Mapping track

In the previous screenshot, we look for bar 6, beat 4, but as you can see, it's hard to determine exactly where that is. In this case, the **Giant Beats Display** can be helpful and assist you. You can click on the **Giant Beats Display**, hold any of the numbers, and drag the mouse up or down to get to the bar 6, beat 4 location:

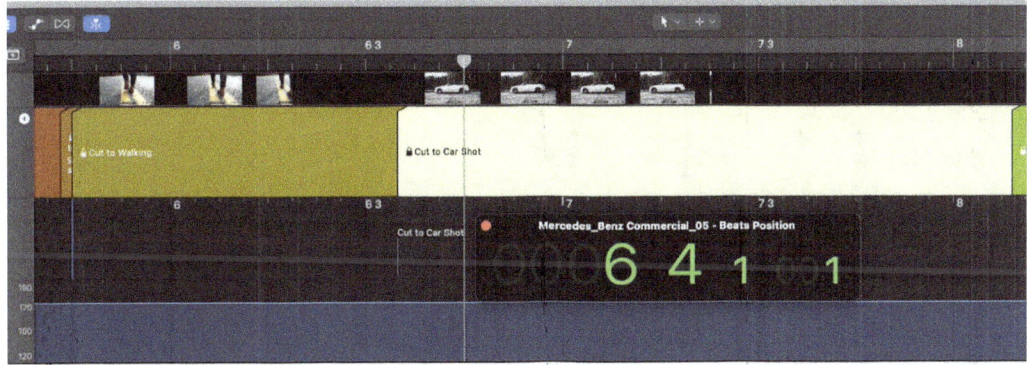

Figure 8.49: Giant Beats Display

After connecting bar 6, beat 4 to the line in the **Beat Mapping** track, Logic Pro snaps the **Cut to Car Shot** marker to that location and adjusts the tempo as a result.

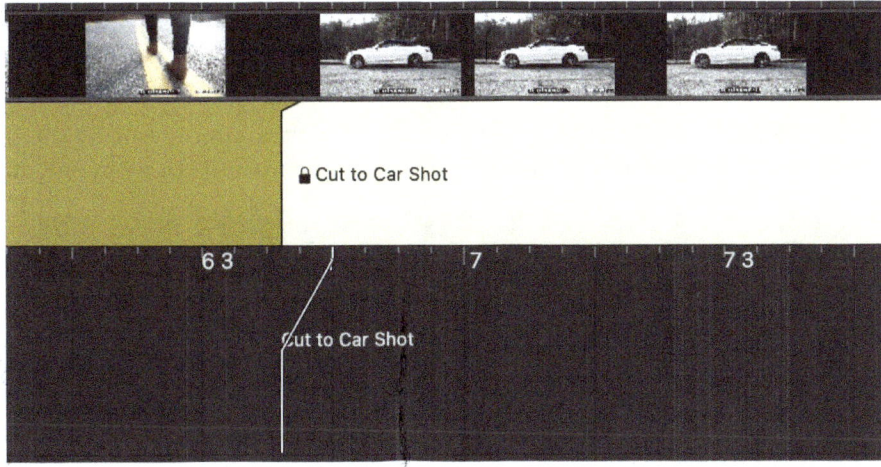

Figure 8.50: Connecting bar 6, beat 4 position to a beat mapping line

Continue to the next marker, **Cut to girl- medium shot**. When you click on the marker, you can see that the marker's name is now visible in the **Beat Mapping** track.

214   Working with Beat Mapping

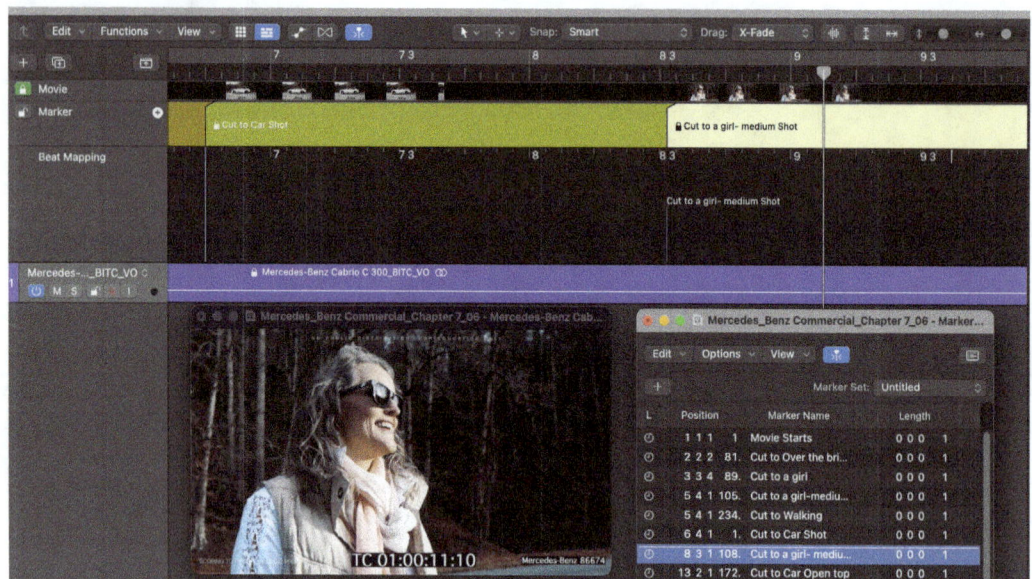

Figure 8.51: A new line in the Beat Mapping track

As you continue holding down your mouse, drag the cursor to the left in order to connect to the visible beat mapping line and let go of the mouse. The downbeat is now connected to the **Beat Mapping** marker:

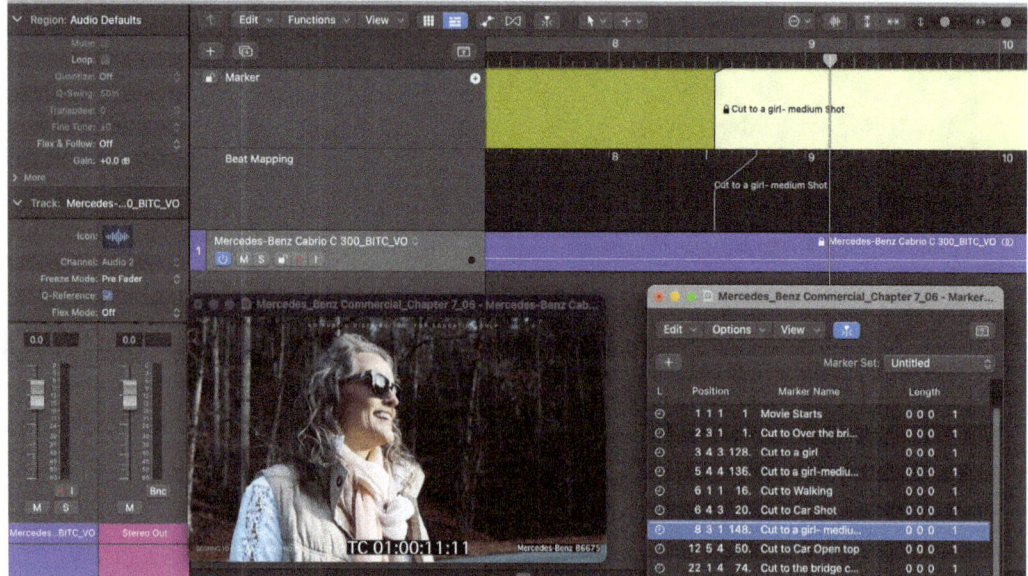

Figure 8.52: Connecting bar 8, beat 4 position to the beat mapping line

After connecting bar 8, beat 4 to the line in the **Beat Mapping** track, Logic Pro snaps the **Cut to girl-medium shot** marker to that location and adjusts the tempo.

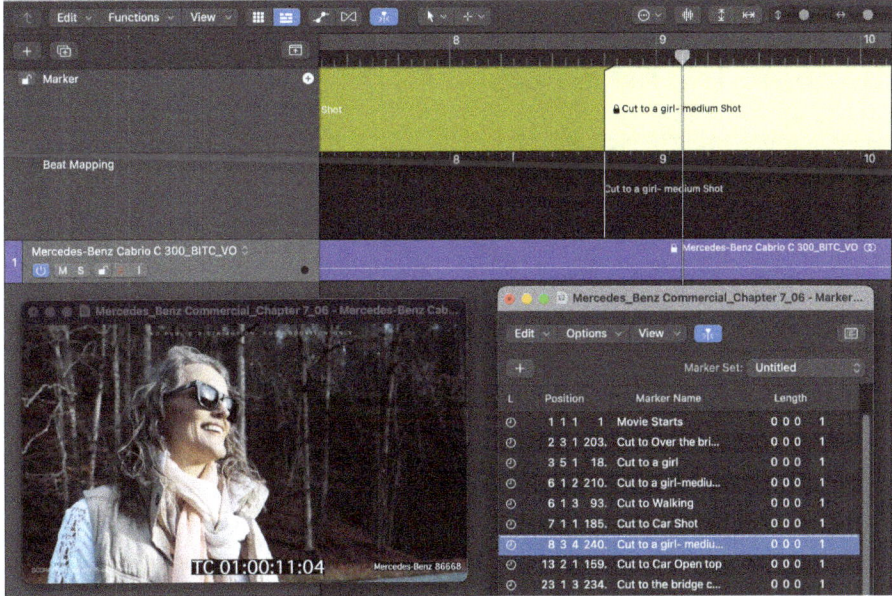

Figure 8.53: Marker position snapped to the location

After repeating the same process for all the markers, you should be able to see the entire film with the tempo map that was created, based on the beat mapping function:

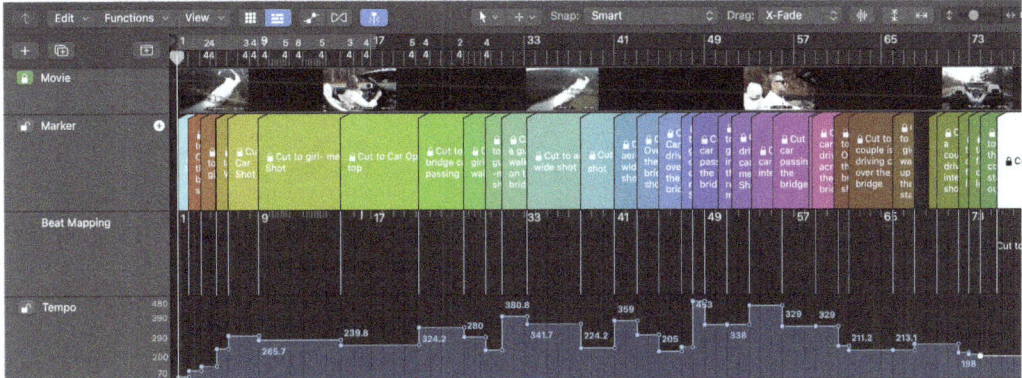

Figure 8.54: Arrange window with the final tempo map

In this section, we explored how to beat map all the markers and learned the mechanical format of connecting markers to beat mapping lines. As you can see, beat mapping every single marker will create a lot of jarring tempo variations.

216   Working with Beat Mapping

In the next section, we'll deal with a steady bpm and explore beat mapping only selected hit point markers. This will have a different outcome compared to what we explored in this section, as the goal is to try and avoid the spikes in the tempo changes.

Beat mapping the hit points

Since the hit points in scoring to picture represent the important cuts in a movie, in this section we will create a tempo map that works only with the hit points from the spotting list, using a steady bpm. This is an additional way of creating a tempo map.

The first step is to view all the hit points, taken from the spotting notes list:

Position	Marker Name
01:00:00:00	Movie Starts
01:00:39:20	Cut to Over the bridge shot
01:00:54:14	Cut to couple driving car over the bridge
01:01:07:20	Cut to the couple standing outside

Figure 8.55: Spotting notes list excerpt

Next, hold down *Option* + click on the second hit point marker, **Cut to Over the bridge shot**, at TC **01:00:39:20** in the floating marker window. The playhead then moves to that location.

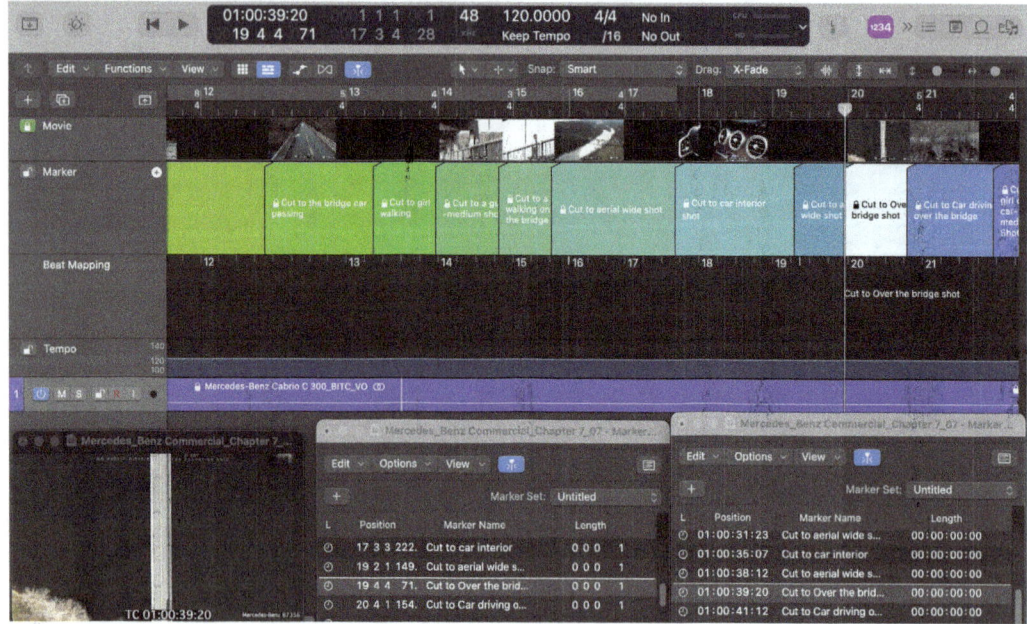

Figure 8.56: Arrange window with the hit point marker

Zoom in horizontally and move your playhead away so that you can see the marker position. It looks like the marker is very close to the bar 21, beat 1 position:

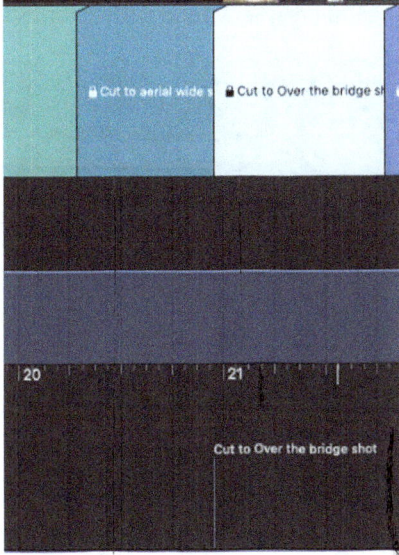

Figure 8.57: New line in the Beat Mapping track

Click on bar 21, beat 1 in the **Beat Mapping** track, and while holding down the mouse, connect it to beat mapping line.

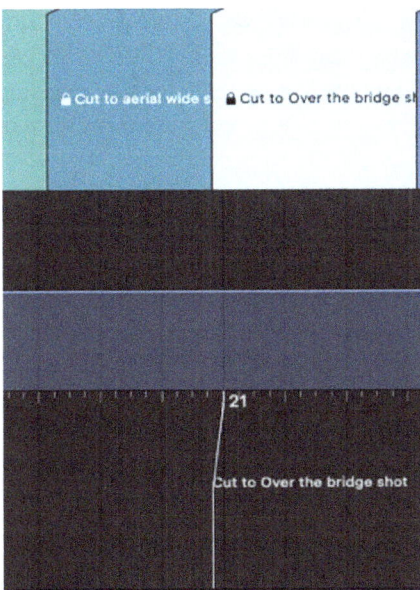

Figure 8.58: Connecting the ownbeat of a bar to a beat mapping line

After letting go of the mouse, Logic Pro moves the marker to bar 21, beat 1 and adjusts the tempo.

Next, hold down *Option* + click on the third hit point marker, **Cut to couple driving car over the bridge**, at **TC 01:00:54:14** in the floating marker window. The playhead moves to that location.

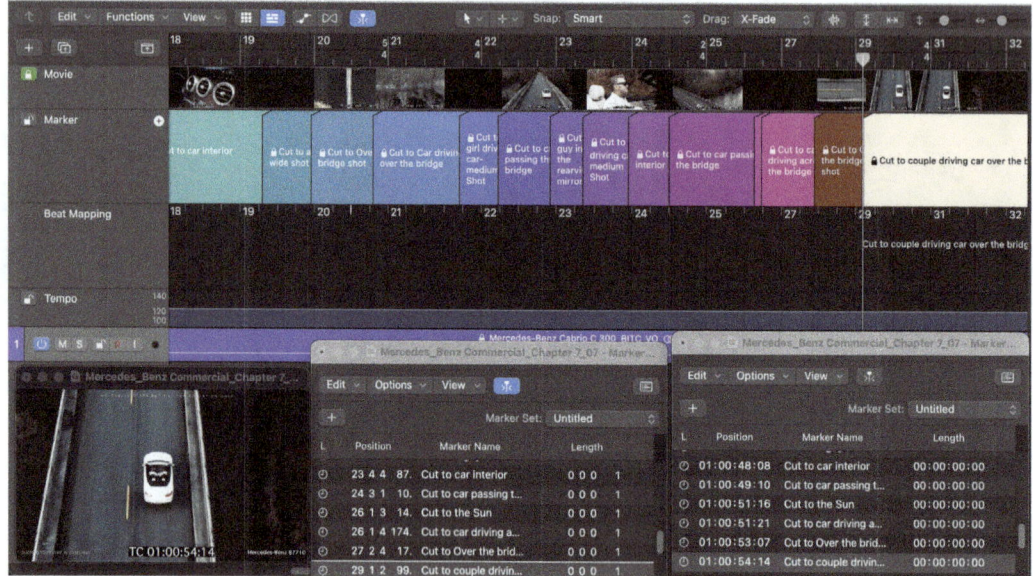

Figure 8.59: Arrange window with the new hit point marker

Zoom in horizontally and move your playhead away so that you can see the marker position. It looks like the marker is very close to the bar 28, beat 3 position. Click on bar 28, beat 3 in the **Beat Mapping** track, and while holding down the mouse, connect it to the beat mapping line. After letting go of the mouse, Logic Pro moves the marker to bar 28, beat 3 and adjusts the tempo.

Next, hold down *Option* + click on the second hit point marker, **Cut to couple standing outside**, at TC **01:01:07:20** in the floating marker window. The playhead then moves to that location.

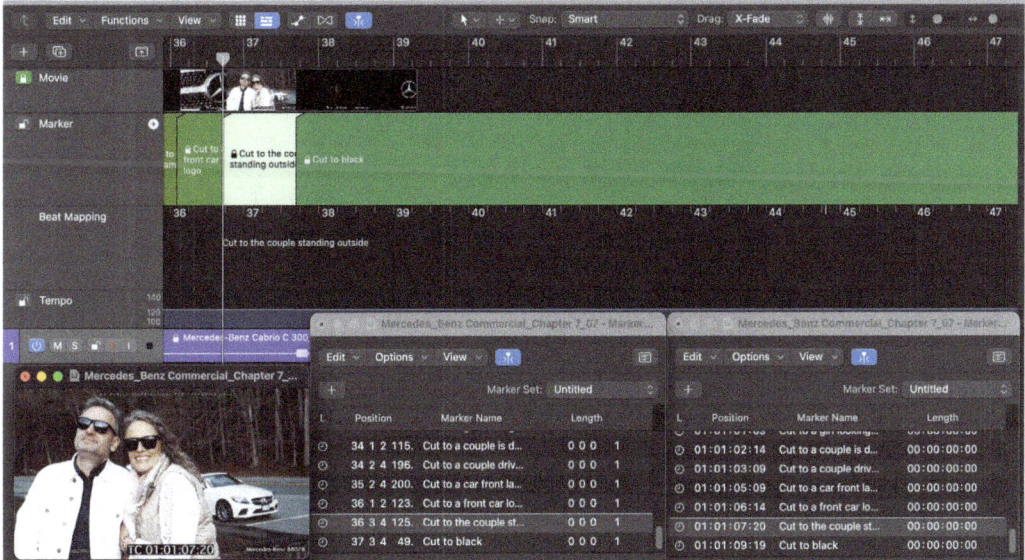

Figure 8.60: New line in the Beat Mapping track

Zoom in horizontally and move your playhead away so that you can see the marker position. It looks like the marker is very close to the bar 35, beat 1 position. Click on bar 35, beat 1 in the **Beat Mapping** track, and while holding down the mouse, connect it to the beat mapping line.

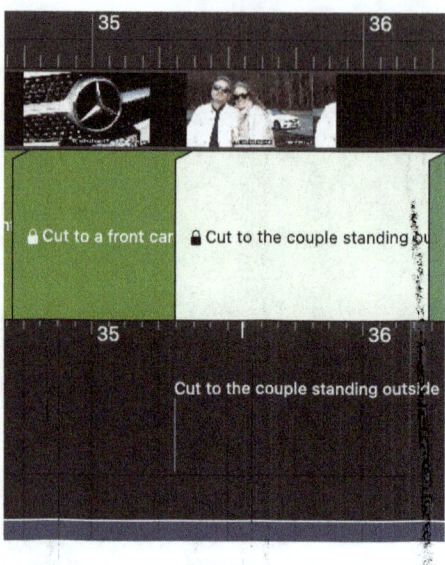

Figure 8.61: Connecting the downbeat of a bar to a beat mapping line

After letting go of the mouse, Logic Pro moves the marker to bar 35, beat 1 and adjusts the tempo.

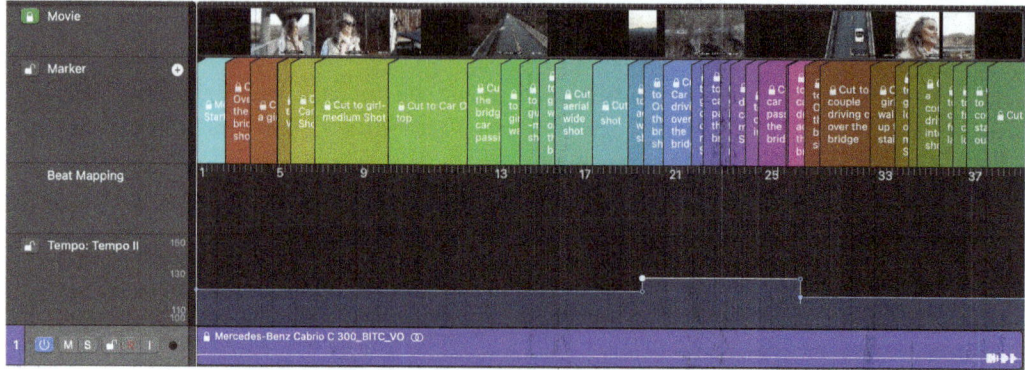

Figure 8.62: Arrange window with the final tempo map

You've now experienced a faster way to create a tempo map, for an entire film, by using certain hit points. Use this technique when you're trying to beat map only certain marker positions and let Logic Pro recalculate the tempo.

Since there are many beat mapping techniques, you can apply the one that is the most suitable for your project needs. In general, it may not be necessary to beat map every single marker, but we will talk more about this in *Chapter 9*.

Summary

In this chapter, we discussed the general concept of beat mapping, how to create a **Tap Tempo** using an instrument track, and how to beat map single MIDI notes, an entire MIDI region, scene markers, and hit points. We also discussed how to edit tempo points and a **Beat Mapping** track.

Today, film composers still heavily rely on Logic Pro's beat mapping functions. It's a valuable tool that can assist a composer in finding a suitable tempo. It's a quick way of getting any type of marker to fall on the downbeat of a bar. Additionally, it can assist a composer with finding a tempo for the project, without having any prior tempo selections. It's important to keep in mind though that it can also have irregular or drastic tempo changes as a result.

Dealing with the beat mapping process for the first time might take a little while to get used to, so practicing these steps is a great exercise. As you practice them, you can then start implementing them as needed.

In the next chapter, we will discuss time signatures and the dichotomy of music choices versus technical choices.

9
Working with a Time Signature

Previously, in *Chapters 7* and *8*, we discussed how to deal with tempo in film music and how to create different types of tempo maps using a spotting list and SMPTE-locked scene markers.

In this chapter, we will explore how to deal with multiple time signatures in Logic Pro and how they can affect the position of a marker. We will explore different ways of adding time signatures and how to deal with them when working with an existing tempo map.

Additionally, we will look at how effective technical choices, such as beat mapping, tempo operations, as well as using time signature, are versus the final musical decision that's made, and what best serves the bigger picture.

In this chapter, we will cover the following topics:

- Understanding a time signature in film music
- Reviewing a time signature in Logic Pro
- Adding time signatures to existing marker positions
- Adding time signatures to a constant tempo
- Comparing music choices versus technical choices

Technical requirements

To follow along with this chapter, you will need a general knowledge of using Logic-DAW, as well as a Mac computer with Logic Pro and QuickTime software installed. You will also need to be able to access the movie files provided with this book: `https://packt.link/hxCer`.

Understanding a time signature in film music

When it comes to music, a **time signature** is often referred to as **meter** and is used alongside the tempo, which represents the speed or pace of the music.

Working with a Time Signature

A time signature has two numbers – the upper number represents how many beats there are per bar and the bottom number indicates what value receives one beat. For example, in a 2/4 time signature, the upper number, 2, means that there are two beats in the measure, and the lower number, 4, means that a quarter note will receive one beat.

With every inserted time signature, there is an emphasis on the beginning of a downbeat, which makes a connection between where the visual event occurs, represented by the marker, and the time signature. The goal of the time signature is to reflect and support visual events throughout an entire film. Generally, in film scoring, using many or multiple types of time signatures is very common.

Before we begin working on and applying time signature changes to our Mercedes commercial, we will first review how to use a time signature and its elements in Logic Pro.

Reviewing a time signature in Logic Pro

In this section, we will review multiple ways to insert, navigate, and edit a time signature. Knowing how to work with a time signature in multiple different windows and sections can help you become more efficient as a Logic Pro user.

To change the time signature, in the LCD display, click on the default time signature of **4/4**. A drop-down menu will open, giving you additional choices to change the existing time signature.

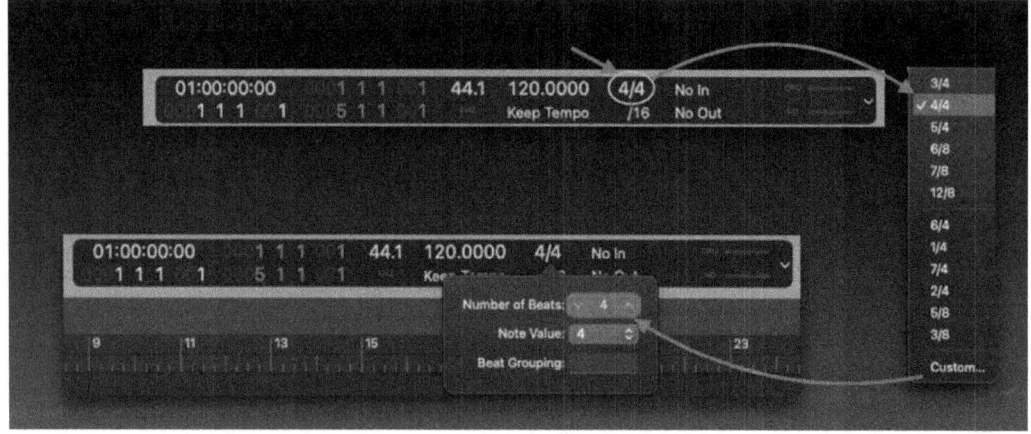

Figure 9.1: The Logic Pro LCD display

If you require a custom time signature, click on **Custom…** at the bottom of the drop-down window. A window will open where you can manually enter a custom time signature.

Another way to change the time signature is to click on the **List Editors** button (or use the *D* shortcut) and then click on the **Signature** tab. Logic Pro will then display a signature list. To add a custom time signature, place your playhead at the desired location in the **Arrange** window and hit the + button below the **Edit** button. A **Time Signature** window will open, allowing you to enter the custom time signature. Click **OK** to confirm, and Logic Pro will close this window.

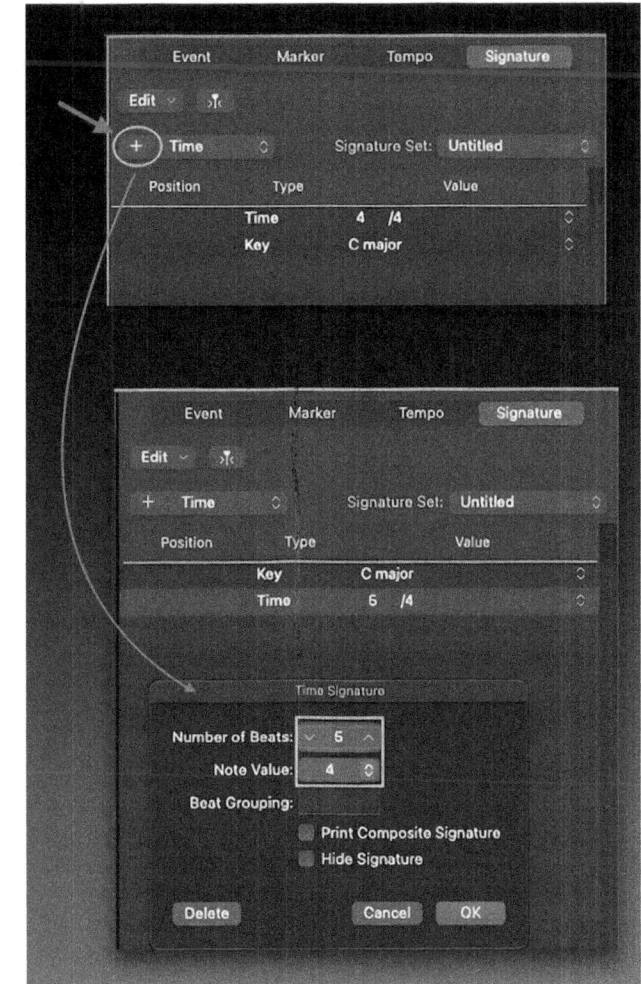

Figure 9.2: Signature list

A time signature can also be added to the signature track of the global tracks. To add a time signature, place your playhead at the desired location and click on the + button in the **Signature** track. In *Figure 9.3*, you can see that the playhead is placed at the bar 5, beat 1 position. To change the time signature value to **5/4**, for example, click on the arrows next to the numbers, select **5** or type the number 5, and then click **OK** when you're done.

226 Working with a Time Signature

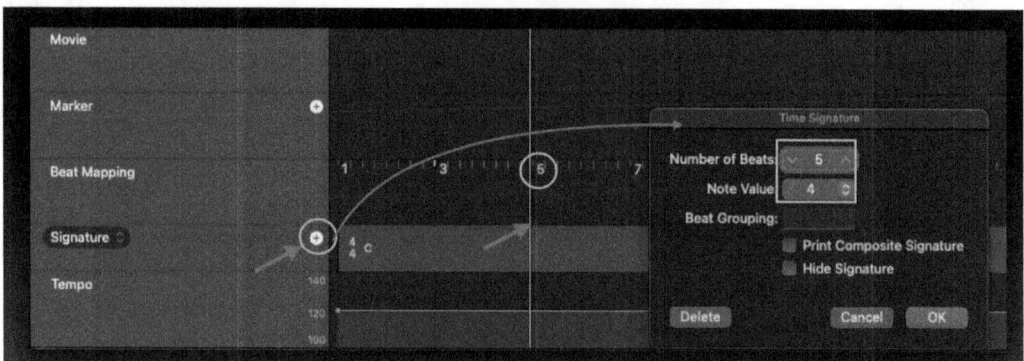

Figure 9.3: Global tracks

Logic Pro adds a new time signature at bar 5, as you can see here:

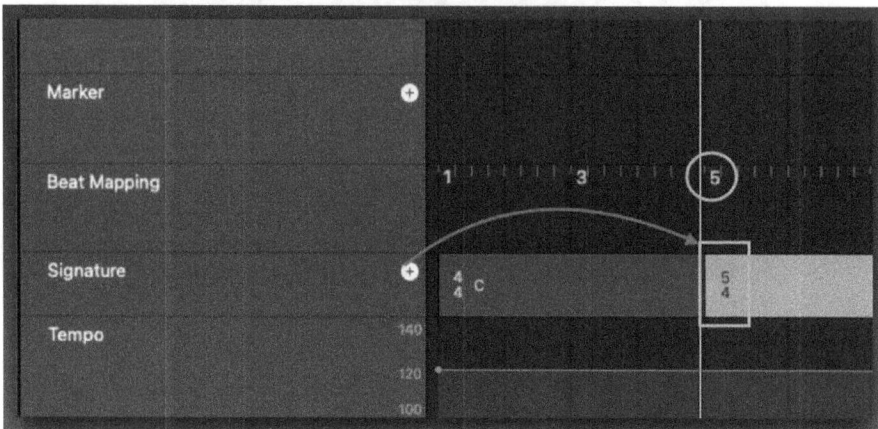

Figure 9.4: Signature track with new meter

Another way to change or add a time signature at a specified location is to use the **Pencil Tool**. To do that, hit the *T* shortcut (for tools) and select **Pencil Tool** from the drop-down menu. Then, click on the **Signature** track at a specified location. A **Time Signature** window opens. Type your desired time signature and click **OK**. Logic Pro will create a new time signature at that location.

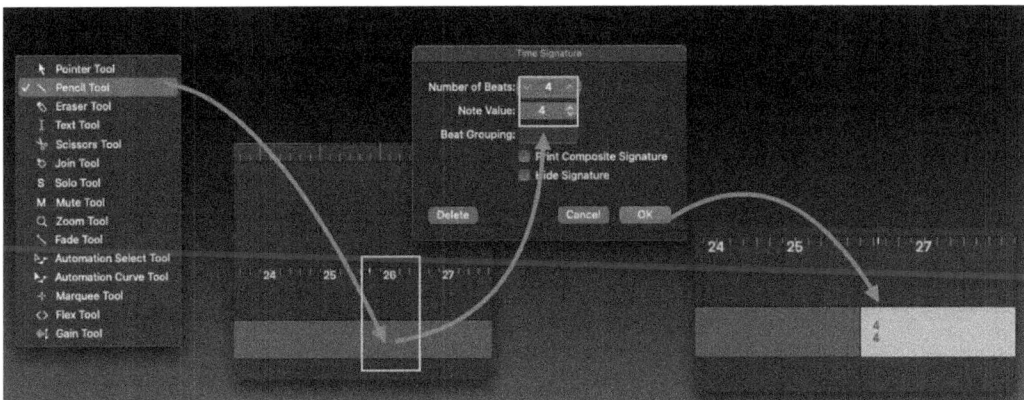

Figure 9.5: Time Signature window

To edit an existing time signature in the **Signature List** window, first, select the time signature you would like to edit, and then drag any of the numbers up or down to change their value. You can also change the length of the time signature in a similar way by altering the bar, beat, division, and tick numbers.

Figure 9.6: Signature List window

Working with a Time Signature

To further edit existing time signatures, you can use the **Scissors Tool** to split the **Time Signature** track.

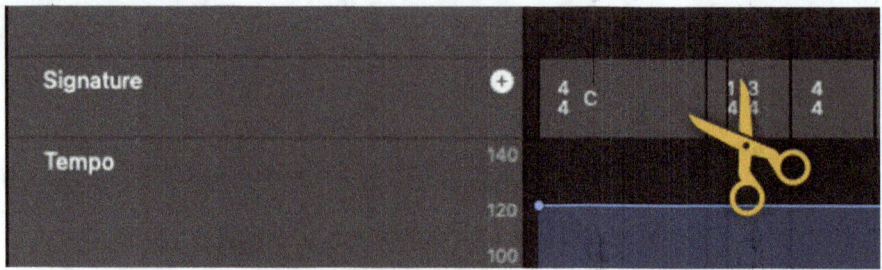

Figure 9.7: Editing a Signature track with the Scissor Tool

To delete a specific time signature, click on the **Time Signature** track. Logic Pro will highlight the time signature with a gray color. Then, you can hit the *Delete* key.

To copy a time signature, click on it and use the *CMD + C* shortcut. Then, move your playhead to the position you want to copy it to and use the *CMD + V* shortcut to paste it. Another way of copying the selected time signature is to hit *Option* and then drag it to the designated position.

To merge time signatures, hit *Shift* and click on the time signatures to highlight them:

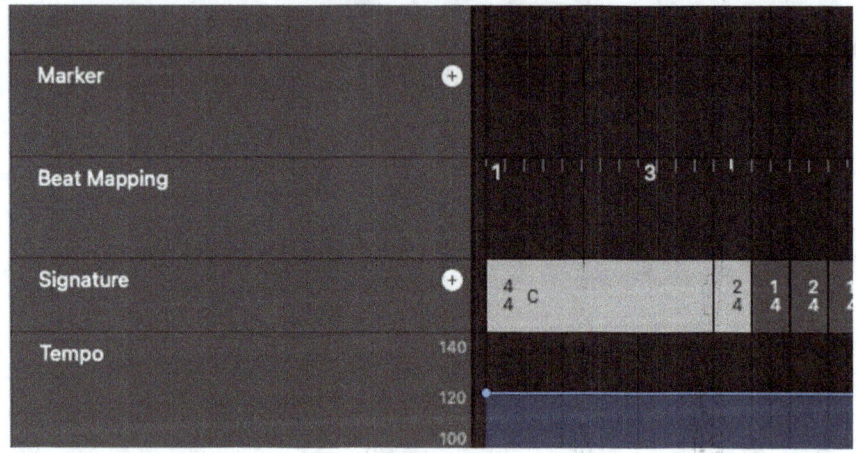

Figure 9.8: Merging time signatures

Then, use the *CMD + J* shortcut to merge them:

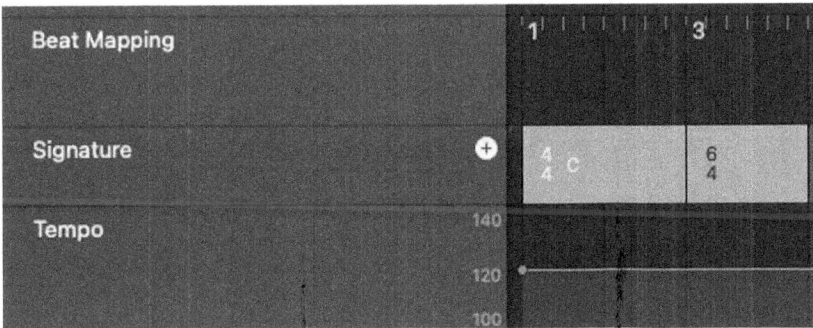

Figure 9.9: Merged time signatures

To create a new time signature set in the **Signature** track of the global tracks, hover your mouse over **Signature** on that track. The **Signature Sets** drop-down menu will open. Here, you can then create a new signature set by clicking on **New Set…**:

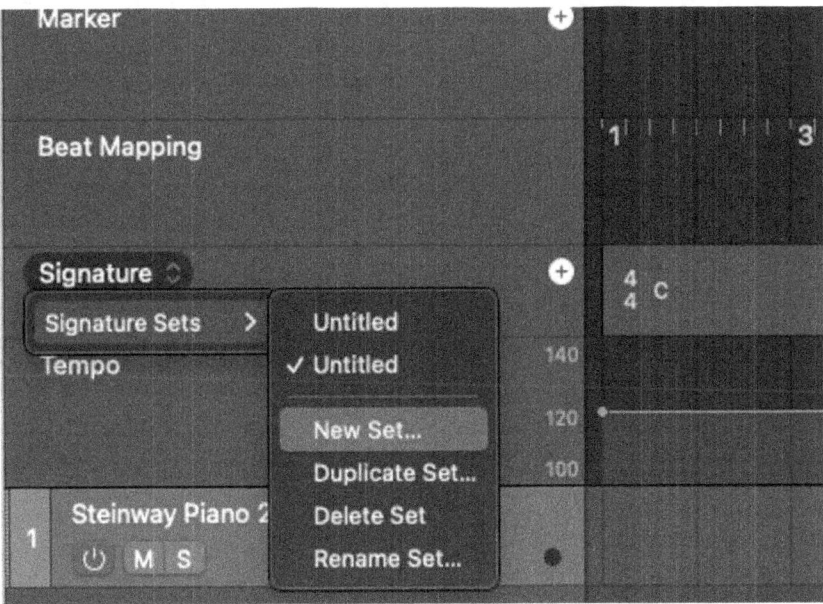

Figure 9.10: Signature track drop-down menu

Instead of hitting the + button in the **Signature** track to add the time signature, there is a quicker way to do so – creating a custom key command. To create a custom key command, use the *Option + K* shortcut to get to the **Key Command Assignment** window. Type `Signature` in the search window, and then select **Create Time Signature Change | Learn by Key Position**. Use any key you have available on your computer keyboard. In *Figure 9.11*, we're using the *F18* key:

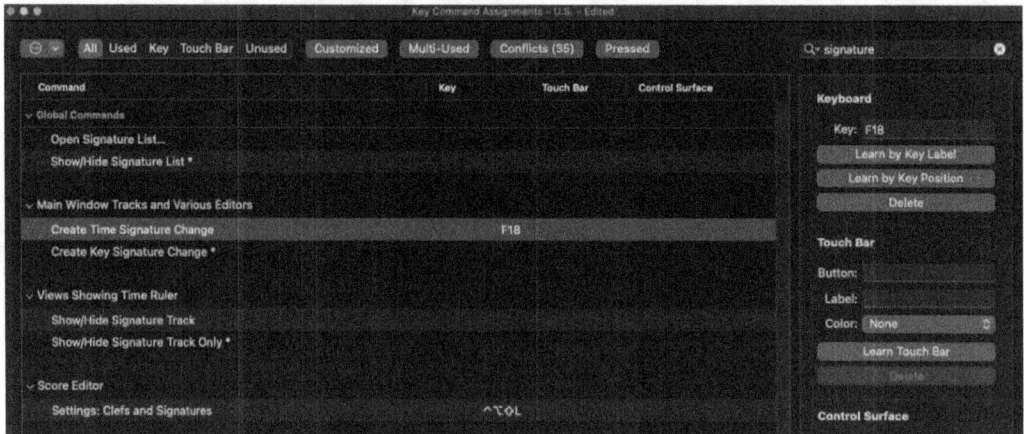

Figure 9.11: Key Command Assignments window

Now that we know how to add and edit time signatures, we will discuss how to use the time signature. We will use the Mercedes commercial with multiple tempos and beat mapping options. The goal is to adjust or add a time signature that will make the marker fall on the downbeat of a bar.

Adding time signatures to existing marker positions

In this section, we will review the technical aspect of adding a time signature. Previously, we used Beat Mapping to make the markers fall on the downbeat of a bar. As a result of this process, there were a variety of tempo changes made throughout the entire film. We will use time signature to make sure that each marker now falls on the downbeat of a bar.

This task of dealing with a time signature on its own, combined with beat mapping and tempo operations, can become challenging to deal with, so it's important to take the extra time to work through each marker in this section and the next to become familiar with them.

Open the `Mercedes-Benz Cabrio C 300_BITC.mov` movie file that was saved in *Chapter 7*, with the SMPTE-locked scene markers. Make sure that the movie and Logic Pro are in sync, and then name and save the project (for example, I will choose `Time signature_01`).

In the global tracks, right-click and select **Signature** from the drop-down menu:

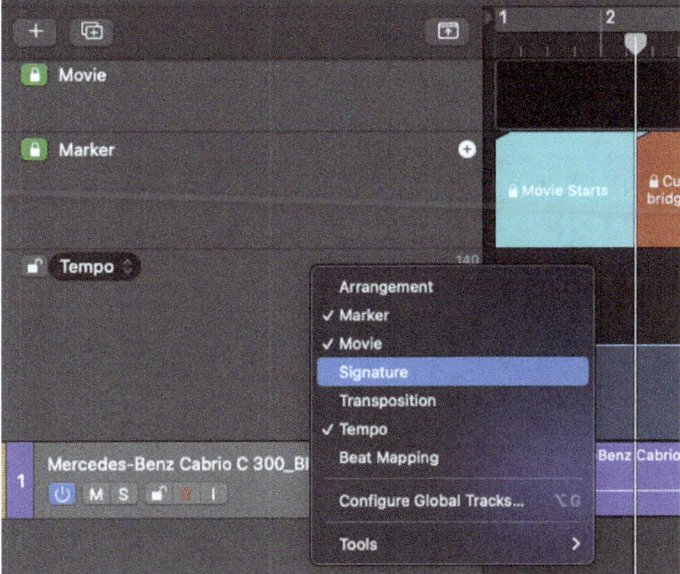

Figure 9.12: Global tracks drop-down menu with the Signature track

We can see that Logic Pro has the default time signature of **4/4**, and the position of the second marker, **Cut to Over the bridge shot**, was adjusted during the Beat Mapping process, so the marker fell between bar 2 and bar 3:

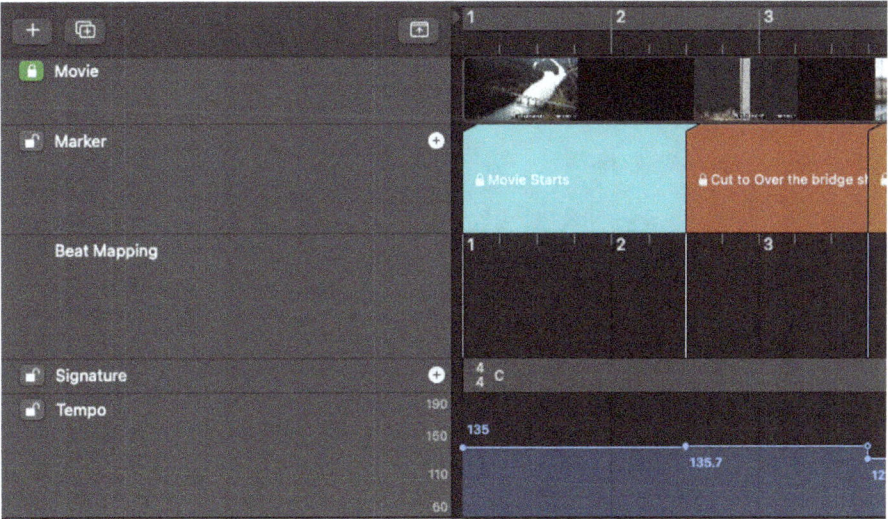

Figure 9.13: Marker comparison in the global tracks

In *Figure 9.13*, the distance from the beginning of the first marker to the beginning of the next marker is six beats. Adding the **6/4** time signature to the beginning of bar 1 will make the **Cut to Over the bridge shot** marker fall on the downbeat of bar 2.

To do that, position the playhead at the bar 1, beat 1 location and click on the + sign in the Signature track header. A **Time Signature** window will open. Change the upper number from **4** to **6**, and hit **OK**.

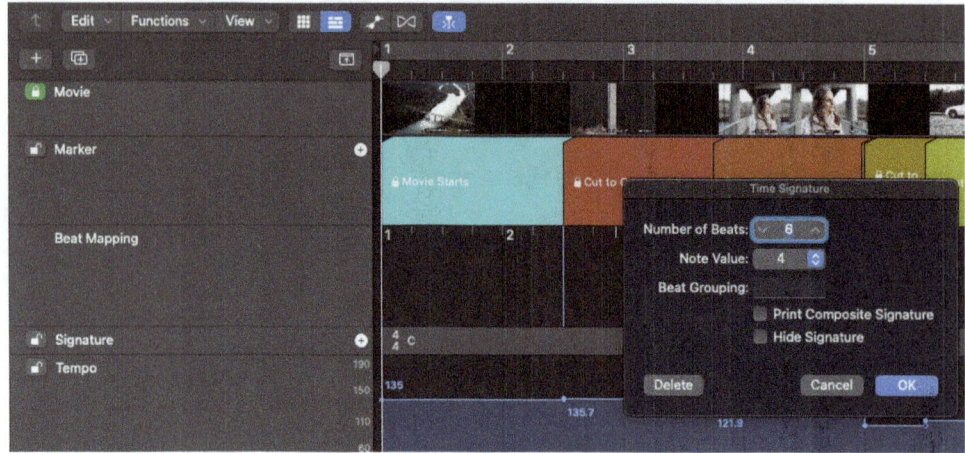

Figure 9.14: Adding a 6/4 time signature

Logic Pro creates a **6/4** time signature, and the marker is now at the beginning of bar 2, beat 1:

Figure 9.15: Marker comparison in the global tracks

Next, at the bar 2, beat 1 location, create a new time signature of **4/4**:

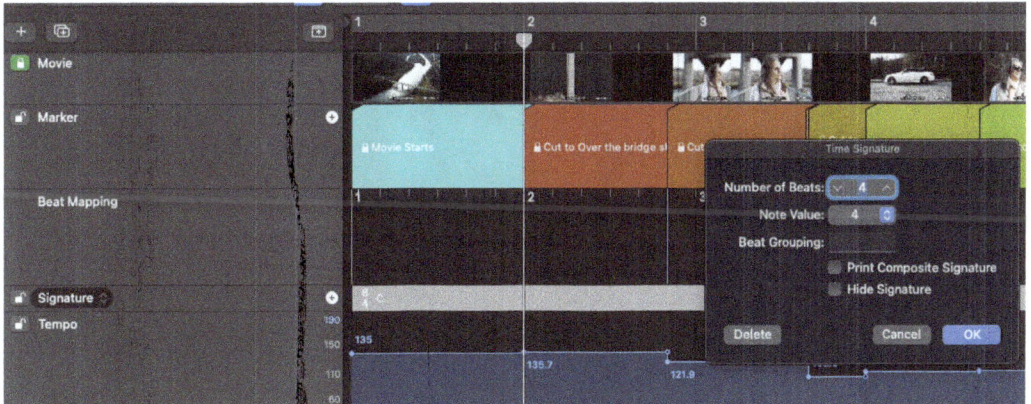

Figure 9.16: Adding a 4/4 time signature

Logic Pro will create a new time signature of **4/4** in bar 2, beat 1.

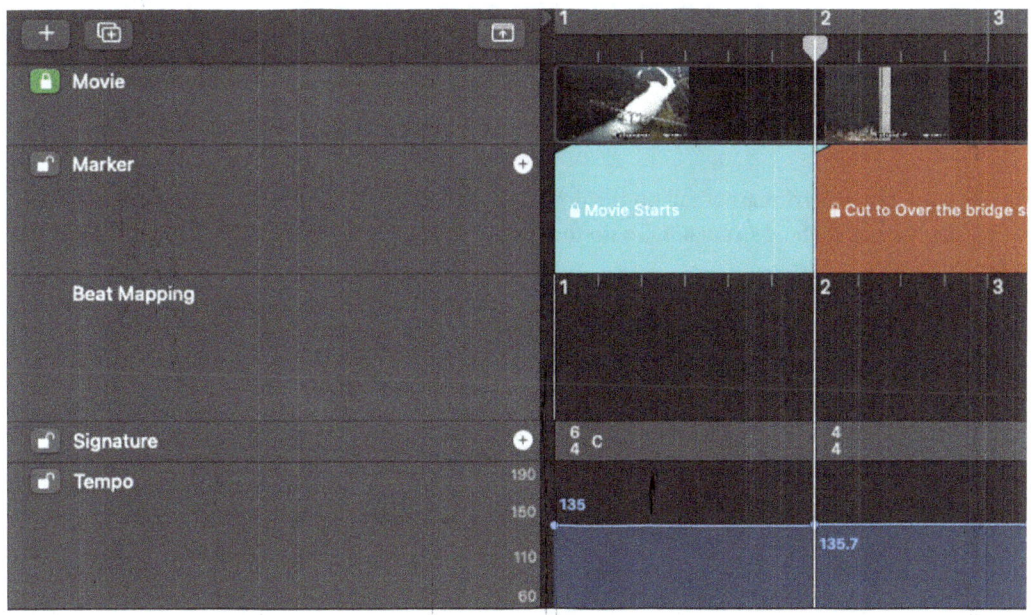

Figure 9.17: Second marker on the downbeat of bar 2

234　Working with a Time Signature

Now, let's look at the next marker, **Cut to a girl**, at bar 3, beat 2:

Figure 9.18: Marker comparison in the global tracks

To make the **Cut to a girl** marker fall on the downbeat of a bar, add the **5/4** time signature at bar 2, beat 1. This is a better choice than **4/4**. To do that, move the playhead to bar 2, beat 1 and insert the 5/4 time signature, like so:

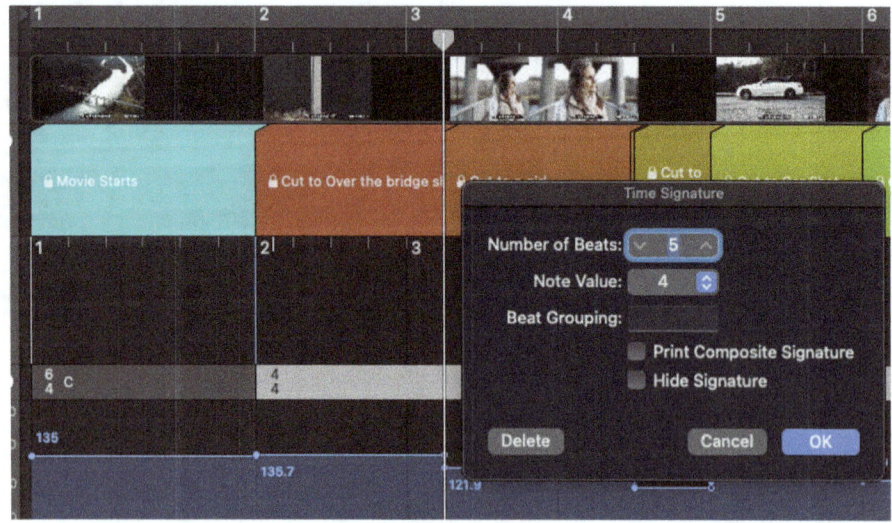

Figure 9.19: Adding the 5/4 time signature

Now we can see that by inserting the **5/4** time signature, the **Cut to a girl** marker falls on the downbeat of bar 3:

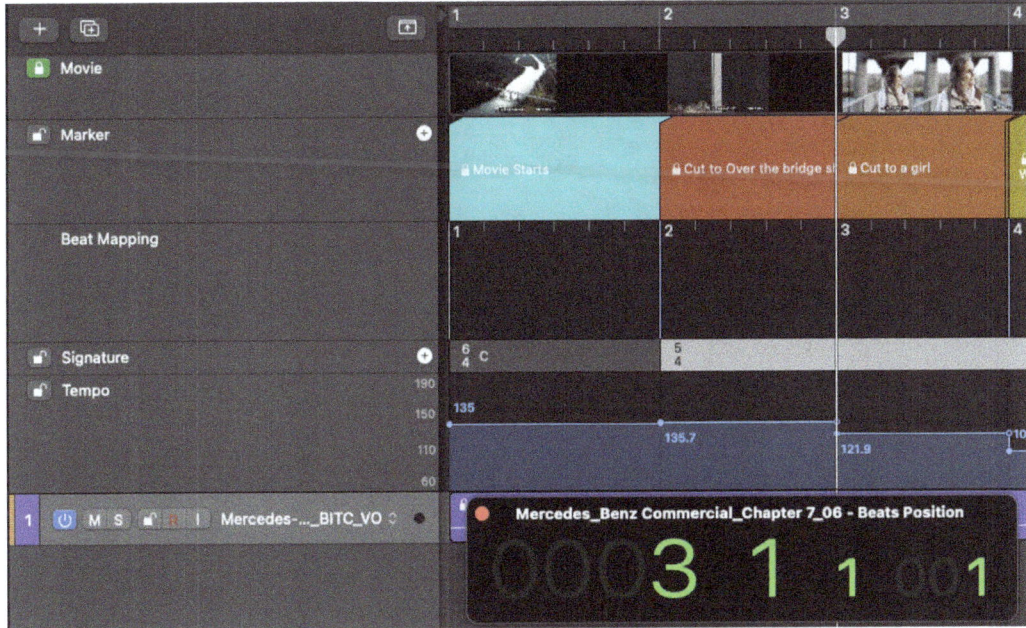

Figure 9.20: Third marker on the downbeat of bar 3

When hovering the mouse over to the next marker, **Cut to walking**, we see that it falls on bar 4, beat 1 already, so it's falling on the downbeat of bar 4. For that reason, we can move on to the next marker.

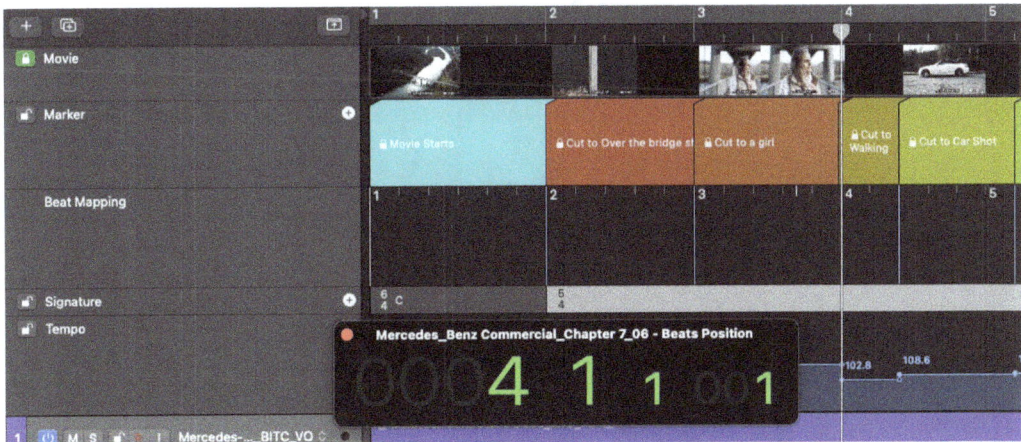

Figure 9.21: Marker comparison in the global tracks

From the bar 4, beat 1 location, insert a **2/4** time signature so that the next marker, **Cut to Car shot**, will fall on the downbeat of a bar:

Figure 9.22: Adding a 2/4 time signature

As you can see, **Cut to Car shot** now falls on the downbeat of bar 5:

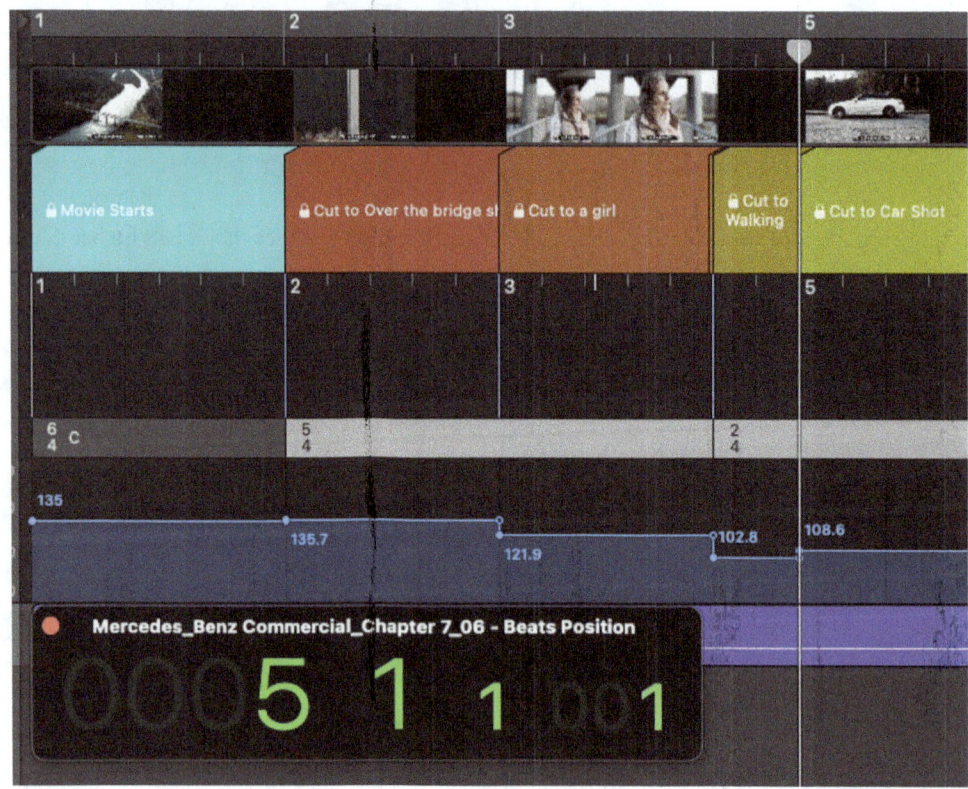

Figure 9.23: Fifth marker on the downbeat of bar 5

Next, in bar 5, beat 1, insert a **4/4** time signature:

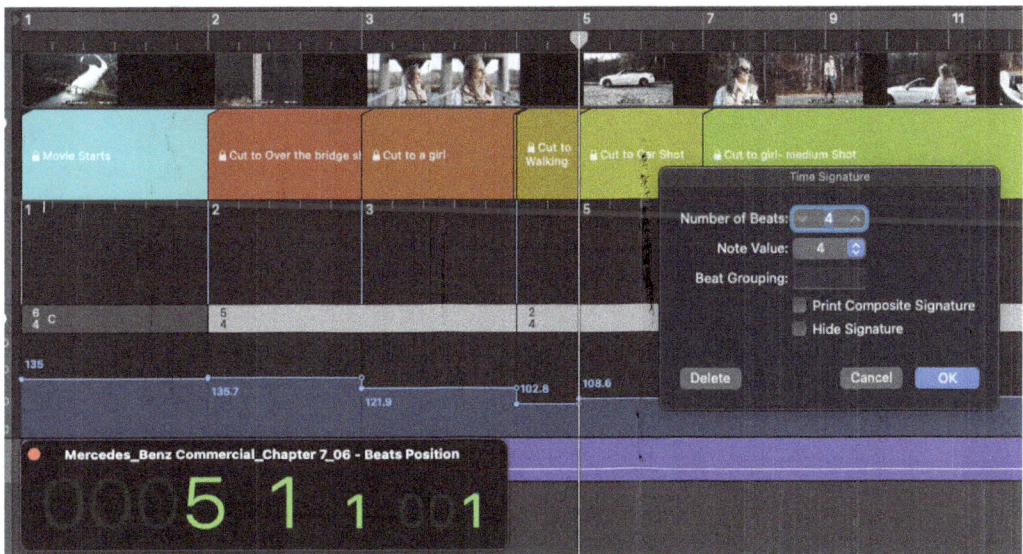

Figure 9.24: Adding a 4/4 time signature

By creating the **4/4** time signature at bar 5, the **Cut to girl- medium shot** marker falls on bar 6, beat 1:

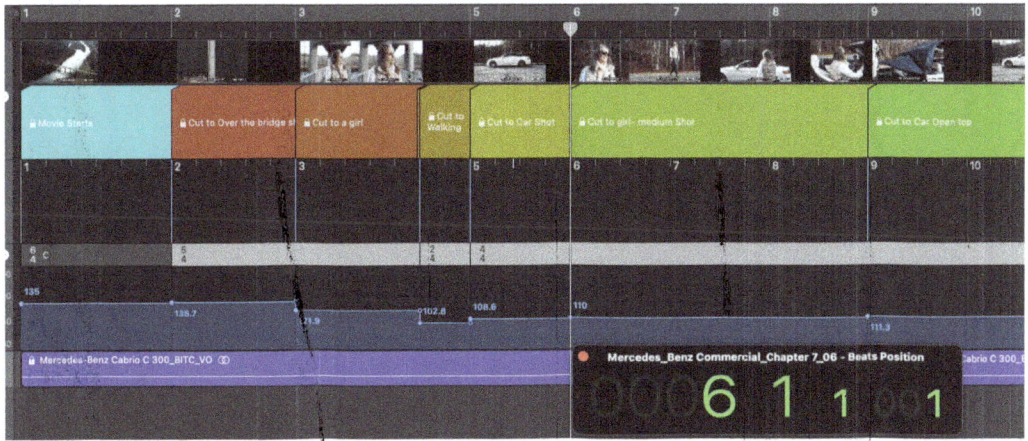

Figure 9.25: Sixth marker on the downbeat of bar 6

Luckily, the **Cut to Car Open top** marker now lands on the downbeat of bar 9, beat 1:

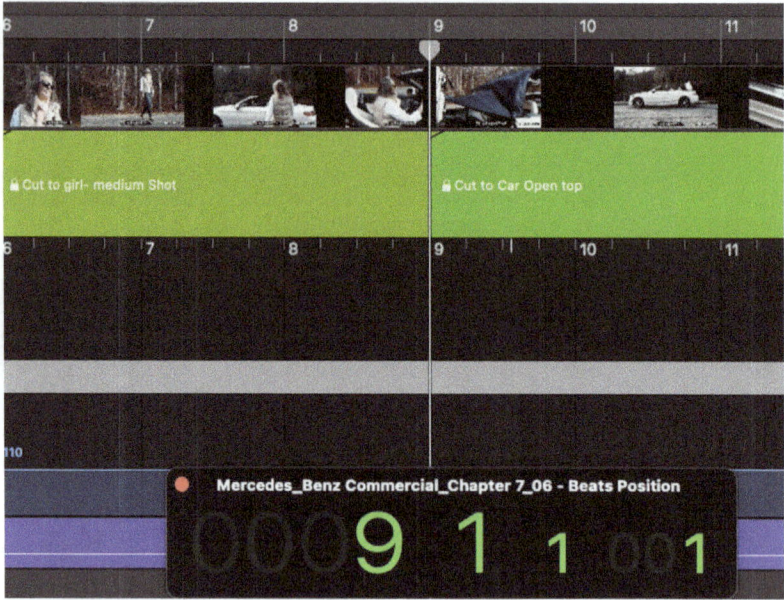

Figure 9.26: Seventh marker on the downbeat of bar 9

Since the **Cut to the bridge car passing** marker almost occurs at bar 12, beat 1, at bar 11, beat 1, insert a **5/4** time signature to make the marker fall on the downbeat.

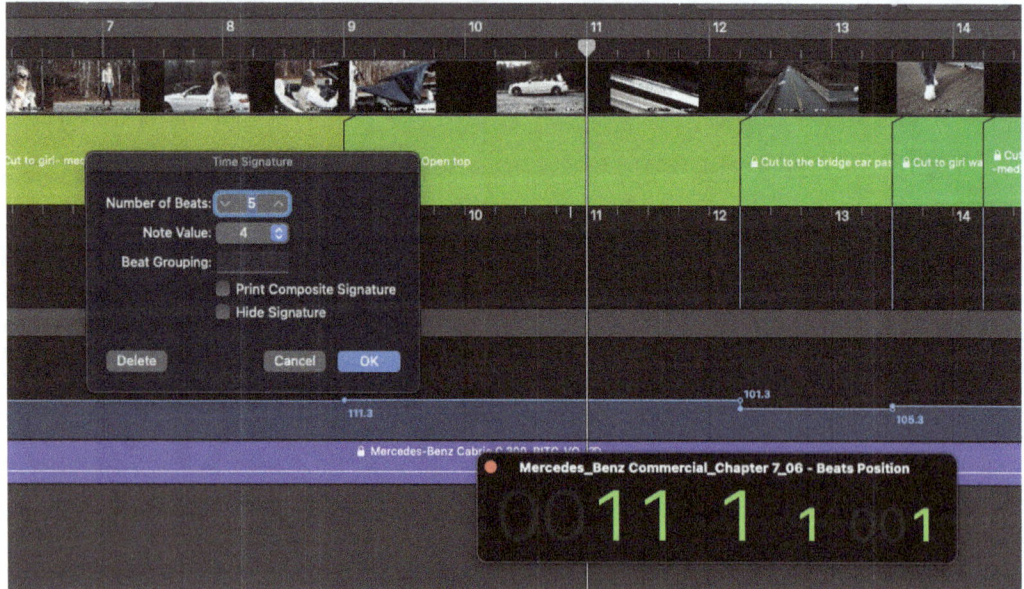

Figure 9.27: Adding a 5/4 time signature

Now the **Cut to the bridge car passing** marker falls on the downbeat of bar 12, beat 1:

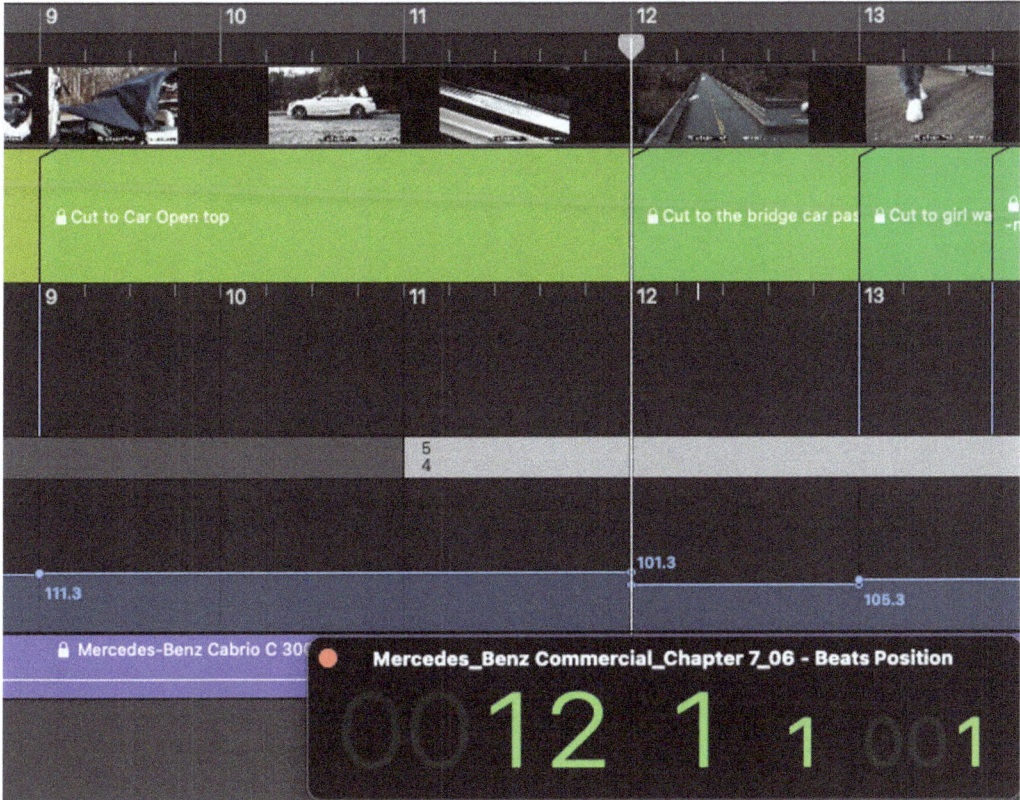

Figure 9.28: Eighth marker on the downbeat of bar 12

We can see that the next marker, **Cut to a guy -medium shot**, is three beats away from landing on the downbeat of a bar. To make the marker fall on the downbeat, insert a **3/4** time signature at bar 13, beat 1:

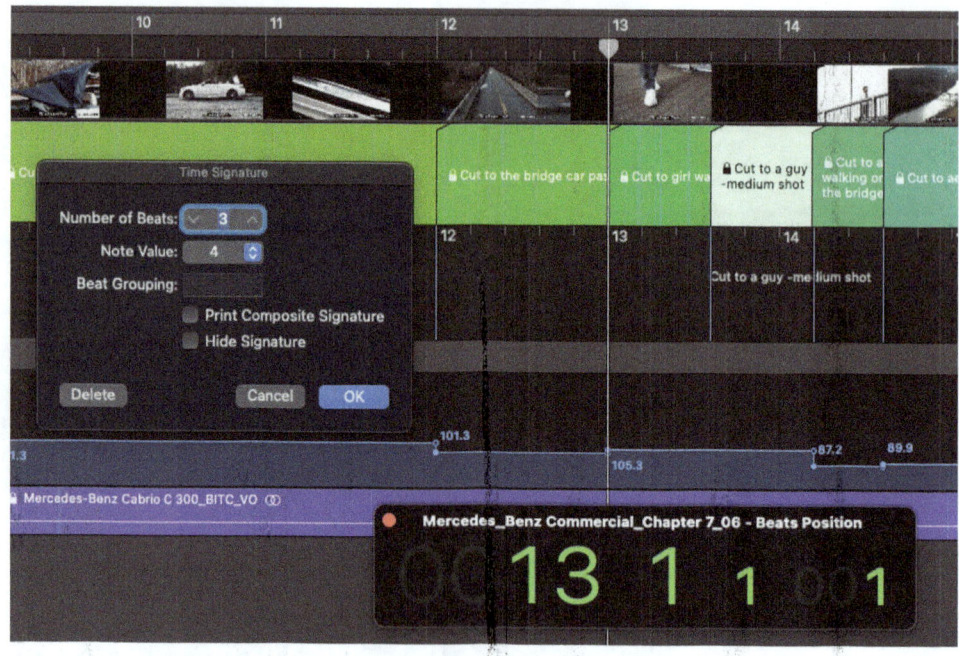

Figure 9.29: Adding a 3/4 time signature

Now, the **Cut to a guy -medium shot** marker falls on the downbeat of bar 14, beat 1:

Figure 9.30: Ninth marker on the downbeat of bar 14

The next marker, **Cut to aerial wide shot**, falls at the bar 15, beat 3 location:

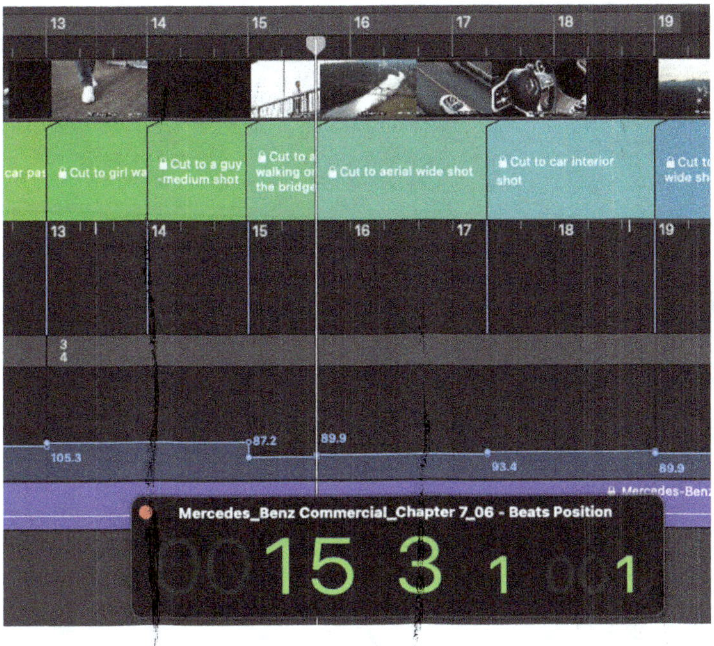

Figure 9.31: Marker comparison in the global tracks

Insert a **2/4** time signature at the downbeat of bar 15, beat 1. Logic Pro will create a **2/4** time signature at this location:

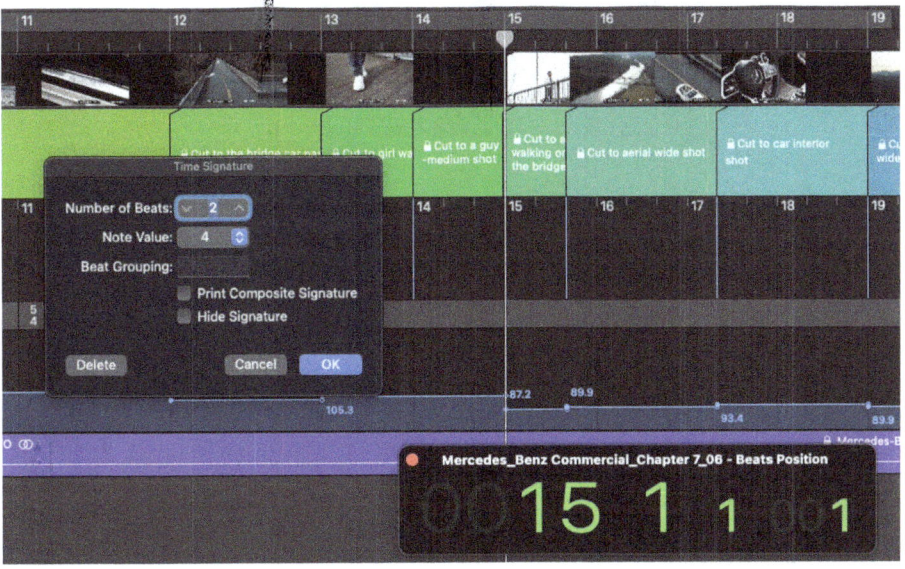

Figure 9.32: Adding a 2/4 time signature

Now, the **Cut to aerial wide shot** marker falls on the downbeat of bar 16, beat 1:

Figure 9.33: Tenth marker on the downbeat of bar 14

Make sure to continue practicing adding the time signature to the rest of the film.

> **Tip**
>
> In general, when creating time signatures during film scoring, it's important to consider the adjacent markers and evaluate their positions before determining what time signature will be the best fit, ensuring that the next marker falls on the downbeat of a bar.

Now that we've experienced how to add time signatures to existing markers, we will discuss adding time signatures to a constant tempo.

Adding time signatures to a constant tempo

In *Chapter 7*, we determined that 99 bpm was a successful tempo, making all the important hit points fall almost on the downbeat of a bar. In this section, we will review the tempo of 99 bpm and add time signatures as needed to make the markers fall on the downbeat of a bar.

Begin by reviewing the current marker positions. In *Figure 9.34* at **TC 01:00:07:06**, we can see that it would be great to have a downbeat at the location. Since that marker, **Cut to Walking**, lasts for only two beats, at bar 4, beat 1, insert a **2/4** time signature.

Figure 9.34: Adding a 2/4 time signature

Working with a Time Signature

To make the next marker, **Cut to Car Shot**, land on the downbeat, insert at bar 5, beat 1 a **4/4** time signature. This also benefits the next marker, **Cut to girl-medium shot**, because it is almost at the downbeat of bar 6, beat 1:

Figure 9.35: Adding a 4/4 time signature

When looking at bar 8, beat 1 at **TC 01:00:15:17**, we can see that this shot would benefit from a downbeat of a bar. At bar 8, beat 1, insert a **3/4** time signature so that the next marker, **Cut to Car Open top**, gets closer to the downbeat of bar 9, beat 1.

Figure 9.36: Adding a 3/4 time signature

Next, at bar 9, beat 1, insert a **4/4** time signature:

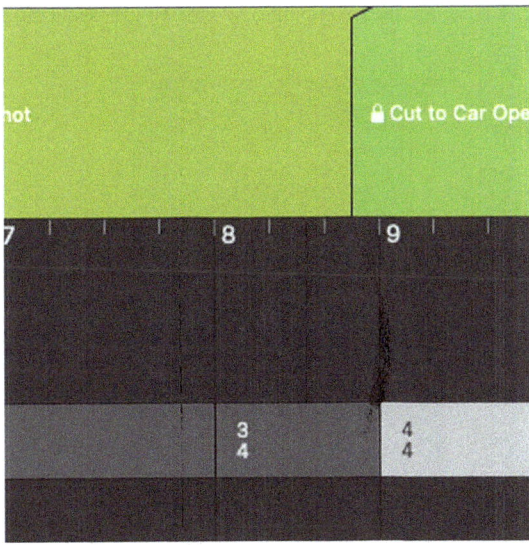

Figure 9.37: Adding a 4/4 time signature

At bar 10, beat 1, insert a **7/4** time signature so that the next marker, **Cut to the bridge passing**, falls on the downbeat of bar 11, beat 1:

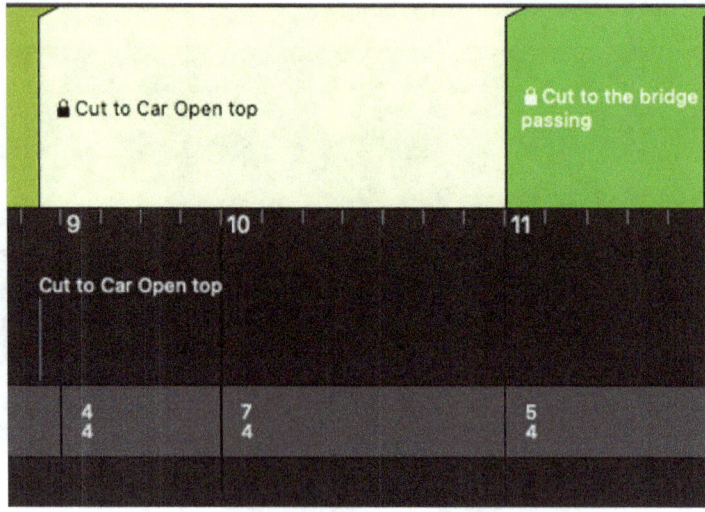

Figure 9.38: Adding a 7/4 time signature

At bar 11, beat 1, insert a **5/4** time signature so that the **Cut to girl** walking marker will fall on the downbeat of bar 12, beat 1:

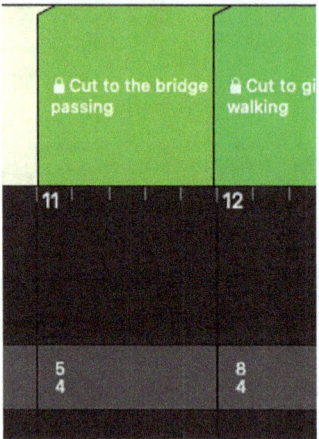

Figure 9.39: Adding a 5/4 time signature

Looking ahead to the next marker, **Cut to aerial wide shot**, it would be great to have it land on the downbeat of a bar. So, at bar 12, beat 1, insert an **8/4** time signature. In bar 12, the **Cut to a guy-medium shot** and **Cut to a guy walking on the bridge** markers are flowing nicely, even though they are slightly off-beat, so we will leave them as they are.

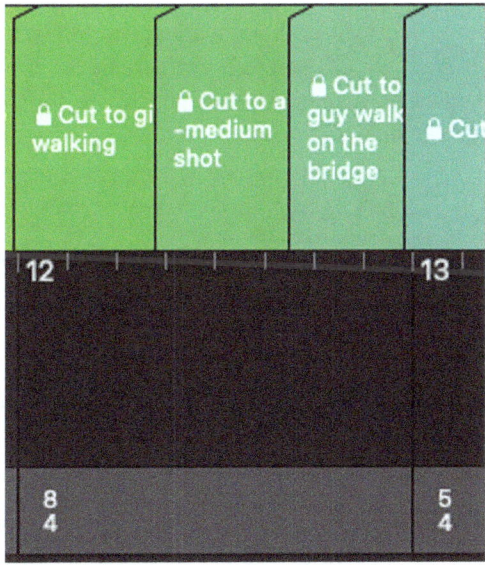

Figure 9.40: Adding an 8/4 time signature

At bar 13, beat 1, insert a **5/4** signature so that the next marker, **Cut to car interior shot**, will almost land on the downbeat of bar 14, beat 1.

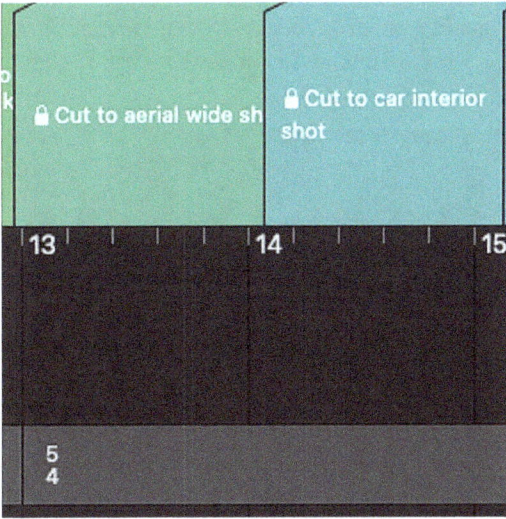

Figure 9.41: Adding a 5/4 time signature

Next, insert a **3/4** time signature so that the hit point marker, **Cut to Over the bridge shot**, falls on the downbeat of bar 16, beat 1. We could use beat mapping here so that the marker falls dead on the downbeat, but if we do that, Logic Pro will adjust the tempo, and we don't want to adjust the overall tempo. Since **Cut to Over the bridge shot** falls naturally, it is not necessary to apply Beat Mapping here.

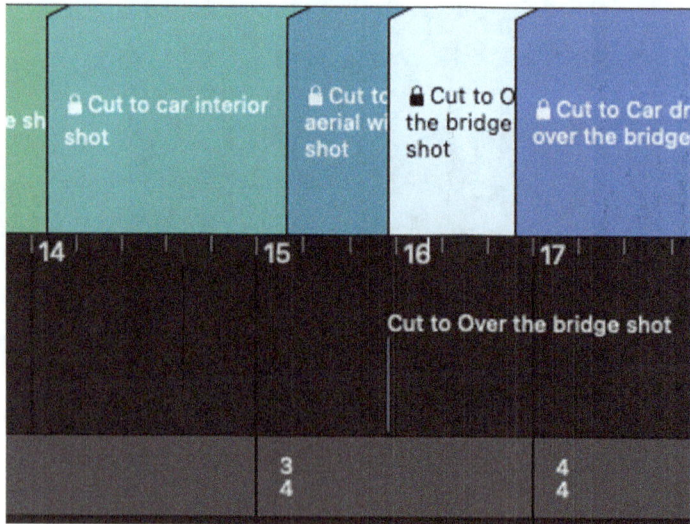

Figure 9.42: Adding a 3/4 time signature

When we insert a **4/4** time signature at bar 17, beat 1, from that point on, the film cuts fall nicely to the end of bar 20. That means when watching the movie from bar 17 to the end of bar 20, with the 4/4 meter, all the cuts in the film work smoothly.

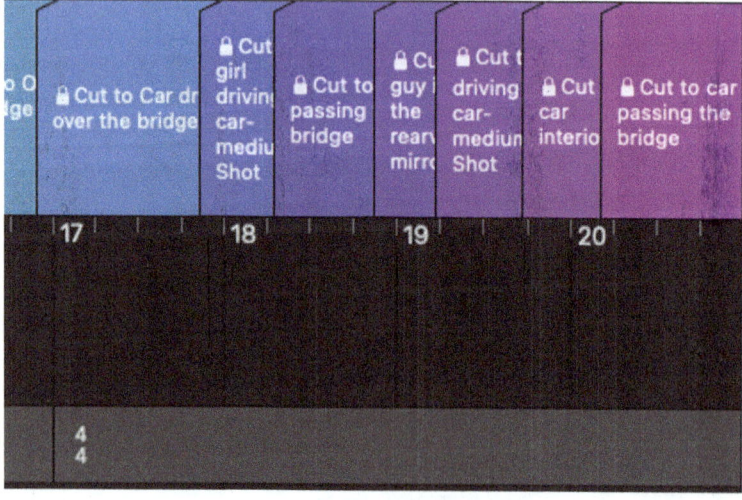

Figure 9.43: Adding a 4/4 time signature

Next, insert a **5/4** time signature at bar 21, beat 1 so that the hit point marker, **Cut to couple driving car over-the-bridge**, falls on the downbeat of bar 22, beat 1. Again, in this case, we could use Beat Mapping to precisely align the marker to fall dead on bar 22, but it is not necessary, since everything is flowing smoothly.

It's important to play the movie from time to time, through the sections, with the metronome on, to observe how the downbeats of the selected time signature line up with the important film cuts.

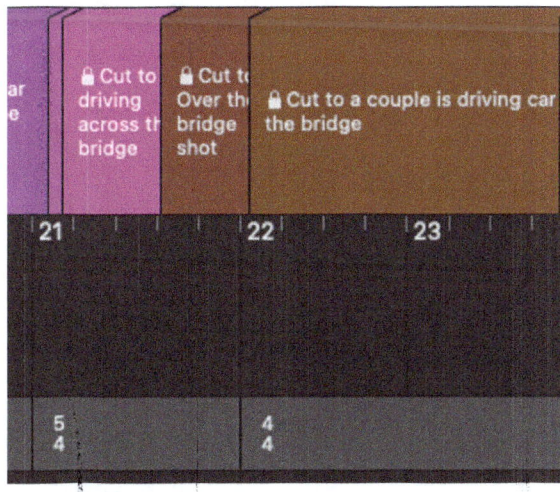

Figure 9.44: Marker on the downbeat of a bar

At bar 25, beat 1, insert a 2/4 time signature so that the hit point marker, **Cut to the couple standing outside**, falls on the downbeat of bar 30, beat 1.

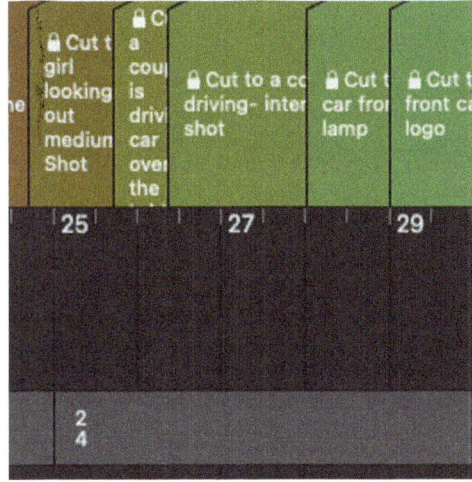

Figure 9.45: Adding a 2/4 time signature

Next, insert a **4/4** time signature at bar 30, beat 1 as the final time signature:

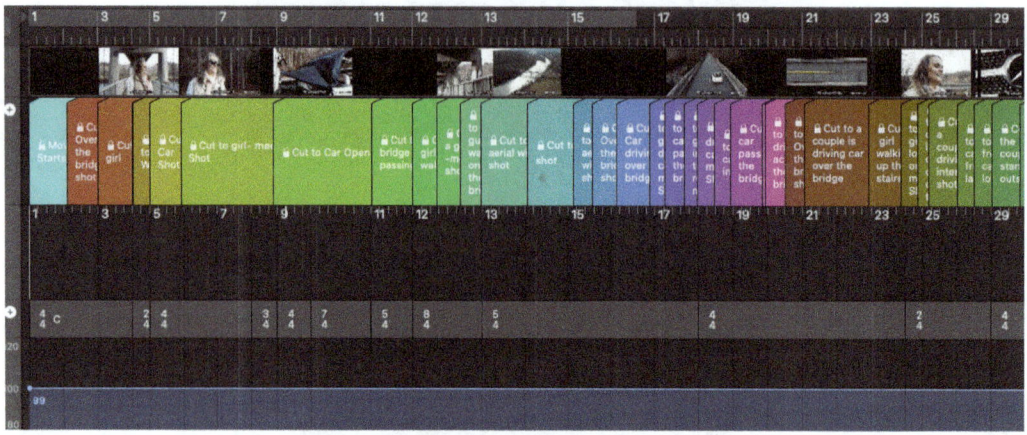

Figure 9.46: Adding a 4/4 time signature

When zooming out in the **Arrange** window, we can see the entire **Signature** track with all the time signature changes and the constant tempo:

Figure 9.47: The entire film with multiple meters

Now would be a good time to watch the entire film, from the beginning, and feel the pulse with the film cuts and the metronome on, making any additional edits as necessary.

When reviewing the selected choices, keep in mind that you can always delete or insert a time signature, adjust the tempo, or use Beat Mapping to best accommodate the film cuts. You can also experiment by creating a new **Signature** track and saving many versions to see which is the most suitable.

You'll want to consider and evaluate the specific hit points you need to deal with, and check the spotting notes from the film director to determine whether they need to fall exactly on the specific beat of a bar or can be slightly behind or before it. Sometimes, it can be difficult to make the music fall exactly on a specific moment in a scene. In general, it may be better if the music falls slightly late versus being too early.

After adding all of the time signatures to the entire piece, you may find that multiple time signature choices don't serve the music choices well, so you might want to adapt the time signatures to better serve the picture. For example, having a 4/4 time signature could have a better feel than a 3/4 time signature, which would sound like a waltz.

In some cases, multiple time signatures are needed, and in other cases, it may not be as beneficial. It is dependent on the film project's needs, and it's up to the user to decide, with the consultation of the film director.

Next, we will talk about musical versus technical choices and why it's recommended to consider one over the other at the beginning stages of scoring to picture.

Comparing musical choices versus technical choices

When you begin scoring, the technical choices you make, such as using beat mapping, tempo operations, or time signature, will likely dominate over the musical choices, such as the tempo, rhythm, moods, style, genre, instruments, and orchestration, most of the time. However, it's important to understand that the technical choices will not necessarily be the final result.

The technical choices serve as a guide to evaluate the extent to which everything that Logic Pro provides supports or doesn't support the film cuts. In film music, the goal of the musical choices is to support the story as well as the entire film. There can be many reasonable technical choices made, but in the end, they may not accommodate the final scoring process or the type of music that is needed. Therefore, the technical choices might need to be edited or changed to better serve the picture.

It's important to understand that the tools available in Logic Pro are there to be used in a smart and musical way. In TV commercials, for example, it is not always a rule to have multiple tempos with different time signatures, but it can be a good thing if it works for the picture and doesn't sound technically assembled, avoiding unnecessary "Mickey Mousing." Conversely, there are many film scenes that might require only a constant tempo, and to accommodate that, different time signature changes can be used, from the most usual of 3/4 to the less common, such as 3/16 or 2/8.

Determine visually whether the selected beat mapping and time signatures, et cetera, ultimately contribute to or benefit the musical choice. There's nothing so mesmerizing and rewarding as when the music lines up with the picture. Over time, and by practicing scoring many films, a film composer's intuition will develop.

Summary

In this chapter, we discussed time signatures in film music, navigating and using a time signature in Logic Pro, and adding time signatures to existing marker positions and a constant tempo. We also compared musical choices with technical choices.

Now that we've reviewed a variety of synchronization tools and learned how to create tempo maps and meter changes in Logic Pro, you should be greatly equipped to face and conquer the challenges when scoring to picture.

In the next chapter, we will discuss the steps of scoring a commercial.

Part 4: Synchronizing Music to Picture

In this last part, you will get an overview of a pre-composed score to analyze and emulate in your own Logic Pro session. In addition, it will cover how to shape and customize existing sounds, as well as covering advanced concepts and techniques when dealing with timings and the synchronization of music to picture.

This section contains the following chapters:

- *Chapter 10, Scoring a Commercial*
- *Chapter 11, Shaping the Score and Exporting to Video*
- *Chapter 12, Advanced Concepts of Dealing with Timing in Film Music*

10
Scoring a Commercial

In this chapter, we will explore how to score a Mercedes commercial from scratch using all the techniques that have been covered in *Chapters 1* to *9*. This chapter will give you the experience of scoring a project from beginning to end, and walk through the steps it takes to score to picture – not to simply write music for the sake of music, but to write it to support a story.

You will work through the example of scoring a commercial, using basic film scoring steps and methods. There are countless ways to score a commercial and music choices are subjective. You can certainly use any additional instruments if you find them suitable. There's no perfect number of instruments but simply what a film composer prefers and what is suitable for the project.

We will explore how to select the right sounds and instruments, looking at the form, mood, and style, as well as the tempo of the commercial. We will also go over how to find, edit, and select instruments and layer sounds, using a demo score example, and finally create an arrangement that will convey the mood and style of the commercial.

So, in this chapter, we will cover the following topics:

- Choosing a mood and style for the commercial
- Structuring the cue
- Choosing music choices over technical choices
- Reviewing the composing process and layering instruments

Technical requirements

To follow along with this chapter, you will need a Mac computer with Logic Pro and QuickTime software installed. You will also need to be able to access the movie files and should have basic knowledge of Logic Pro software and film scoring.

To start scoring to picture, the first thing to do is open the movie file. Open `Mercedes-Benz Cabrio C 300_BITC.mov`, which was saved in *Chapter 7*, with the SMPTE locked scene markers. Make sure that the movie and Logic Pro are in sync, and that the fps is set correctly. Then, name and save the project (for example, I will name it `Scoring Commercial_01`).

Choosing a mood and style for the commercial

When scoring a commercial, the first thing to consider is what music, style, or mood will benefit or be suitable for the commercial. This is where knowledge of audio branding comes in handy. **Audio branding** is a process where a brand makes a product, and then a sound or tune that's been specifically composed for the brand is merged with the product to represent the brand. It gives the brand a new, recognizable identity and connects the audience with the brand through sound on an emotional level.

When a car commercial is made, a lot of thought is given to the product that is going to be featured and also the audience that would buy the product. Knowing what the audience would be interested in, what type of sound they might like to listen to, and what would draw them into buying a car like this needs to be considered when choosing the music.

As a broader example, if you're scoring for a specific brand that you can find at a nearby mall, you might want to take the time to go to the store where the brand is being sold and listen to what sounds or music the store is using. The corporate leadership of the brand takes a lot of time studying and understanding their consumers' needs and desires and what they like and will use sounds to reach and connect with them. Watching similar commercials and doing some research on the brand will give you more insight into what an appropriate sound would be.

For the Mercedes commercial, by observation, we know that the consumer who would buy this type of car is likely sophisticated and classy, has good taste, and is more established in life. Looking at the cinematography, you can see that there are a lot of earthy colors in the commercial suggesting it's Fall. You can also see that there's an element of curiosity, mysteriousness, and intrigue as both the male and female characters are enjoying taking in the surroundings and spending quality time with one another. When it comes to the mood, it seems to have a cinematic feel with a nostalgic element.

With the popularity of lo-fi music in commercials today and its influence, it seems that this type of music will be appropriate and bring sophistication and value to the overall score. It will contribute to and create the mood that we're looking for.

When scoring to picture, beyond finding the right tempo for the music and aligning the important hit points, which are crucial elements, the other focus is to find the sonic, supportive sounds, that is, the instruments or sensors that will support the entire story.

Now that we've talked about how to identify moods and styles, next, we will go over the role of music, based on the entire structure of the commercial, and what the music should be doing in specific sections.

Structuring the cue

Structuring the cue is like creating a musical roadmap. It considers what the music should be doing during the beginning, middle, and end sections of the commercial. Before the composing process begins, it's important to know the overall story of the commercial. You will want to look at the entire commercial and come up with a structure for the cue, which will involve looking at the scene cuts and determining what type of music needs to be there and when, or you may get a rhythmic idea. This will give you a general overview of what to do musically.

In general, we are going to create one continuous piece of music, or one cue. To outline the process of structuring the cue, we will start with the lo-fi piano to set the overall mood with a few ambient sounds in the background. At bar 11, **TC 01:00:24:05** (**Cut to the bridge car passing**), we'll start to bring in more sonic elements to start building toward the middle section. At bar 16, we will use the **6/4** meter and introduce transition sound elements to better lead into the middle section, starting at bar 17, beat 1.

The middle section will now have the exciting rhythmic parts up until bar 25, beat 1, at **TC 01:00:59:09** (**Cut to girl walking up the stairs**), where then the music will soften similar to the beginning.

The music will become more lo-fi again until we hear the **voiceover** (**VO**) and the music fades out.

Now that we've learned how to structure the cue, next we will talk about using and applying music choices versus technical choices.

Choosing music choices over technical choices

Up until now, we've looked at everything from a technical point of view. In this section, we will look at how the music choices can become more important than the technical choices, with a focus on what will best serve the commercial. All the different technical skills that have been learned and acquired in the last chapters could be used and are important in any scoring, but we decided to take a simplified approach here.

In this example, even though we're using the constant tempo of 99 bpm, we are still considering the hit points to make sure they fall on the downbeat of a bar, but without the use of beat mapping. Also, instead of using many time signatures, we will only use two time signatures for the entire commercial, 4/4 and 6/4. We will use the 4/4 time signature from the beginning to bar 16 and add a 6/4 time signature at bar 16 that will continue to bar 17. The 4/4 time signature will then continue from bar 17 to the end. The entire cue then is in the 4/4 time signature except for bar 16, which will have the 6/4 time signature. Bar 16 serves as a transition between the beginning and middle sections of the commercial.

Music is very subjective, since everyone has their own take on composing music. Whatever the method is and how you're going to get there is up to each composer.

Now that we've discussed the direction of the mood and style of music and how to structure the cue and decided on the musical choices we're going to use, next we will begin writing music starting with the composition process.

Reviewing the composing process and layering instruments

In this section, we will explore and practice the creative process of layering instruments of an already existing score for the commercial. We will not discuss how and why we're using the specific chords or chord progressions because it is beyond the scope of this book. Instead, in the example, you will simply emulate the stages and the process of composition.

We will layer 37 different instruments and use them to complement one another, based on their sonic quality. We will explore creating and selecting different types of instruments and recordings from the provided notation examples. You will get an idea of how to use different preselected instruments and experience how they contribute to the specific mood of the commercial.

Since Logic Pro has countless options to assist you with selecting different sounds and instruments, finding the right one and blending it with other ones can be time consuming and challenging. Working through this example and practicing the different stages will allow you to see how to approach scoring to picture and witness how a film score is conceptualized and developed. You will then have the ability to try it on your own. It may also help to save you time, since you won't have to start from scratch each time. Also, since this is an audio-visual activity, it needs to be experienced and not simply read about.

Figure 10.1 is what the final score for the commercial will look like in the Logic Pro **Arrange** window, with all the regions, once completed. Use this figure as a visual reference and guide as you go through each step:

Figure 10.1: Logic Pro Arrange window

Additionally, *Figure 10.2* shows a list of all the tracks and instrument patches used in the commercial, for reference:

Figure 10.2: Logic Pro tracks list

After reviewing *Figures 10.1* and *10.2*, we will now begin to go step by step through how to assemble everything from the beginning.

Begin by going through all the tracks, starting from the track at the top of the list. **Track 1** is an audio track that was imported from the movie file and has the VO on it:

Figure 10.3: Track 1

Next, create an **Alchemy** instrument track as the second track. In the search window of this synth, type Garden Sanctuary. Then, double-click on the **Garden Sanctuary** patch name and Logic Pro will load this instrument and its sound settings:

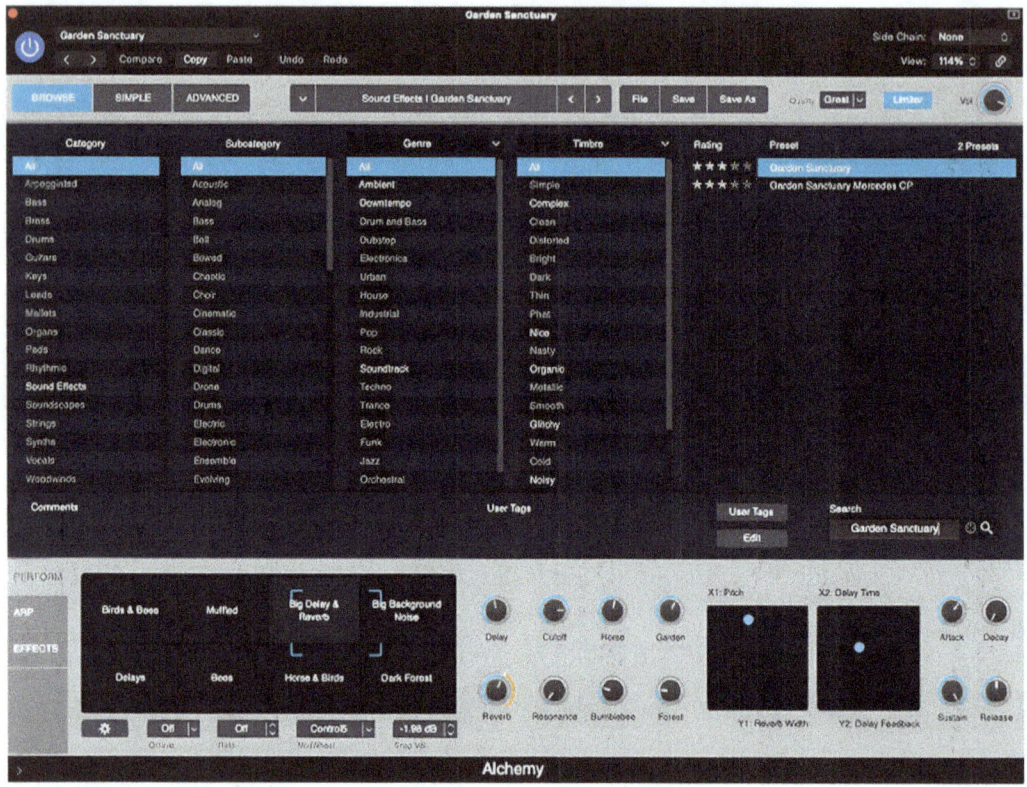

Figure 10.4: Logic Pro Alchemy instrument

Next, on this track, record a single note from **Bar 1** to **Bar 29**, as shown in *Figure 10.5*:

Figure 10.5: Track 2 notation example

Go to the Loop library (the *O* shortcut) and type `Forest` in the search window. From the listed sounds, load the **Forest** sound effect by dragging and dropping it into the **Arrange** window. Logic Pro will then create a third track. Adjust the track volume level so that you only hear a hint of a forest effect, instead of hearing the entire forest sound in the foreground.

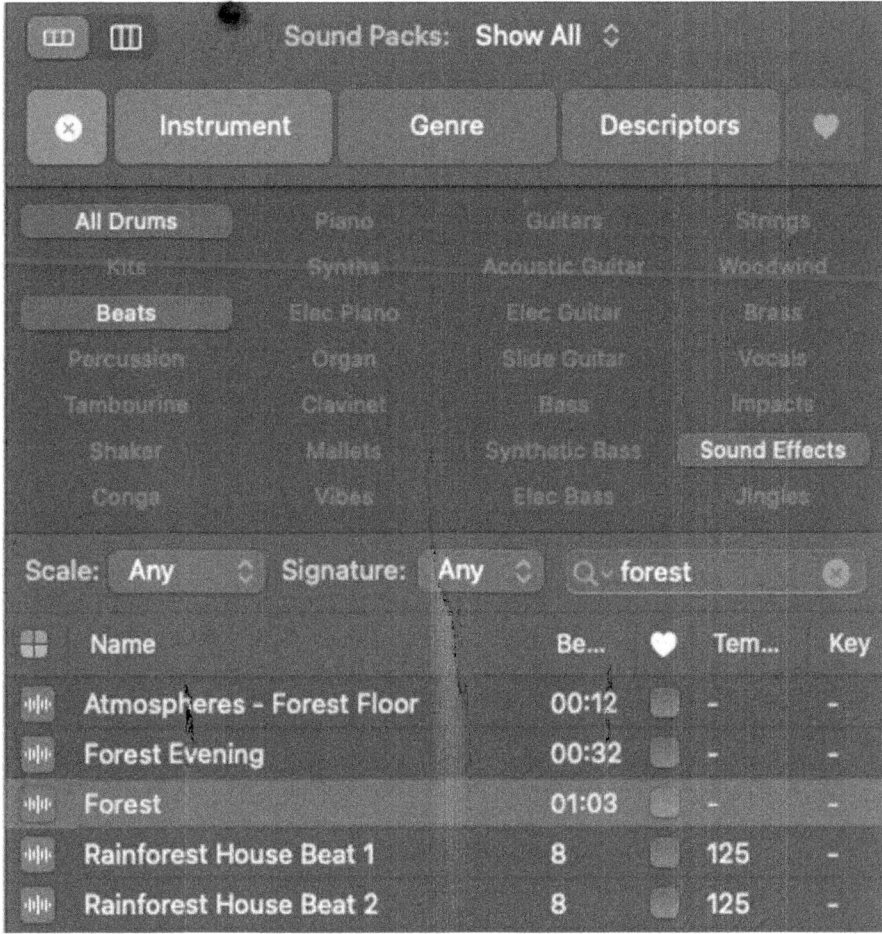

Figure 10.6: Logic Pro loop library

Next, create an instrument track and load a **Quick Sampler** as the fourth track. In the search window of the **Quick Sampler**, type `Naked Wurly`.

Figure 10.7: Logic Pro Quick Sampler

After loading the instrument, we will make a slight adjustment so that it will sound more lo-fi. To create this iconic-sounding pitch drift, click the **LFO 1** tab to view all the parameters. Then, in the **Rate** section, set the rate to **3/16**. In the **Target** section, select **Pitch** from the drop-down menu and change **Amount** to **22 cent**:

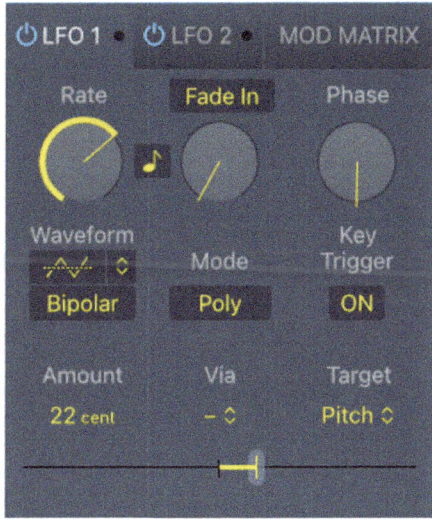

Figure 10.8: Quick Sampler LFO 1 section

Next, click on the **LFO 2** tab to view all the parameters. Using two LFOs together will emulate a tape machine effect by creating an up-and-down pitch shift drift.

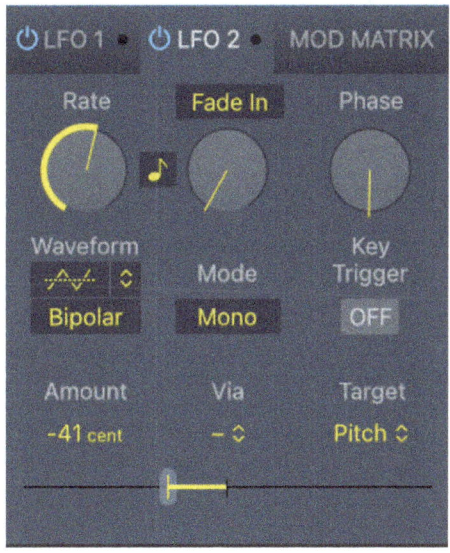

Figure 10.9: Quick Sampler LFO 2 section

After adjusting the instrument parameters to make it sound more lo-fi, make sure to save the preset and then record the notes in *Figure 10.10* on that track, starting from **Bar 2** to **Bar 16**:

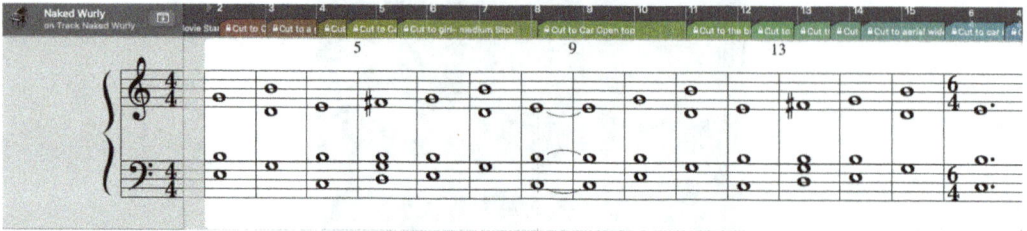

Figure 10.10: Track 4 notation example

On the same track, continue recording the notes in *Figure 10.11* from **Bar 25** to **Bar 29**.

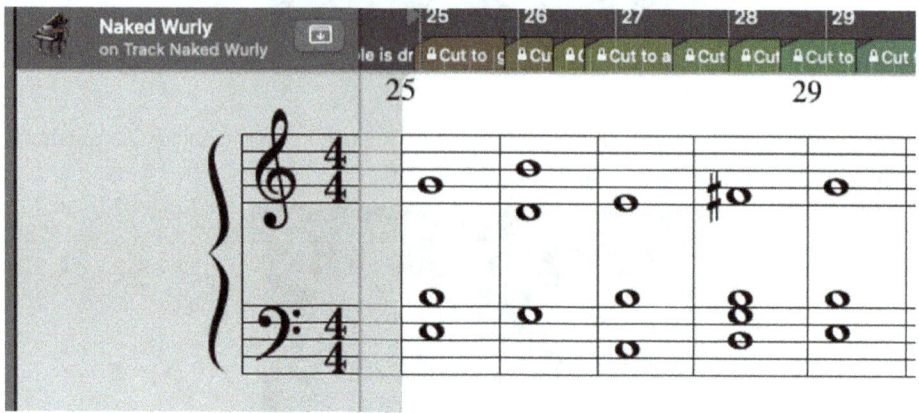

Figure 10.11: Track 4 second notation example

Next, let's create an **Alchemy** instrument track as the fifth track. In the search window of this synth, type `Choir-Female-Oh`. Then, double-click on the **Choir-Female-Oh** patch name. Logic Pro will load this instrument and its sound settings:

Reviewing the composing process and layering instruments   265

Figure 10.12: Logic Pro Alchemy instrument

Next, on this track, record the notes from **Bar 10** to **Bar 17**, as shown in *Figure 10.13*:

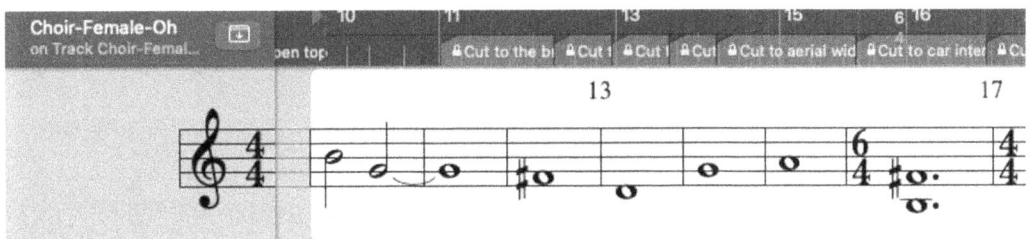

Figure 10.13: Track 5 notation example

This short melodic line will complement the harmonic content in *Figure 10.10*.

Next, create an instrument track as the sixth track. To do that, use the *Option + Cmd + N* shortcut to open the **New Tracks** dialog box. Select **Software Instrument**, then **Empty Channel Strip**, and check the box next to **Open Library**. Then, click on **Create**.

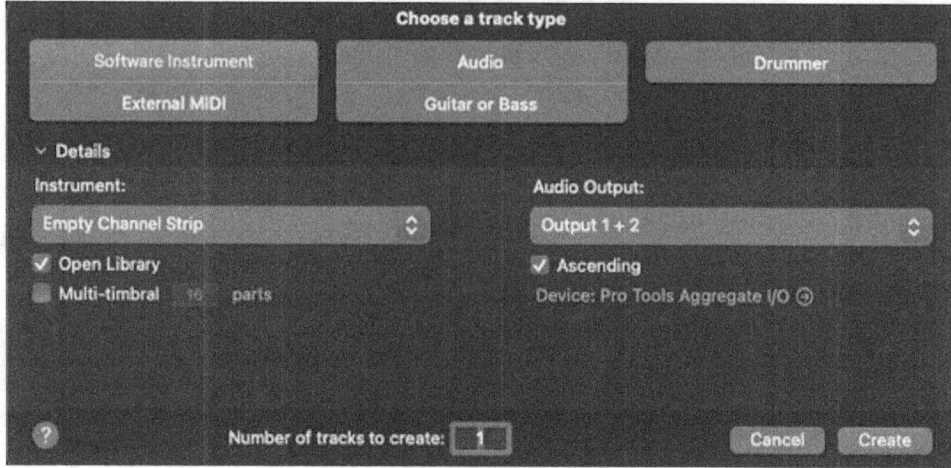

Figure 10.14: Logic Pro dialog box

The **Library** window will open (the *Y* shortcut). In the search window of this synth, type `Modwheel Sizzler`, then click on the synth's name. Logic Pro will then load this instrument and its sound settings:

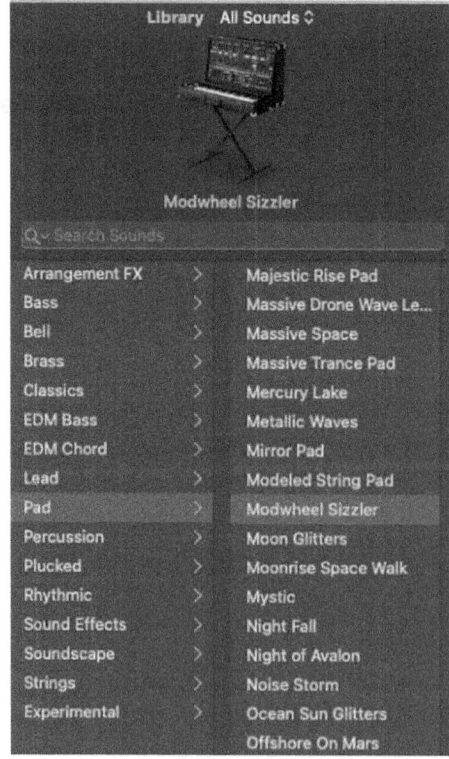

Figure 10.15: Logic Pro library

To open the instrument, double-click on the **ES2** instrument tab in the channel strip:

Figure 10.16: Logic Pro channel strip

The instrument window will open, and you can then make additional adjustments to the original sound, if needed:

Figure 10.17: Logic Pro ES2 instrument

Next, on this track, record the notes from **Bar 10** to **Bar 17**, as shown in *Figure 10.18*:

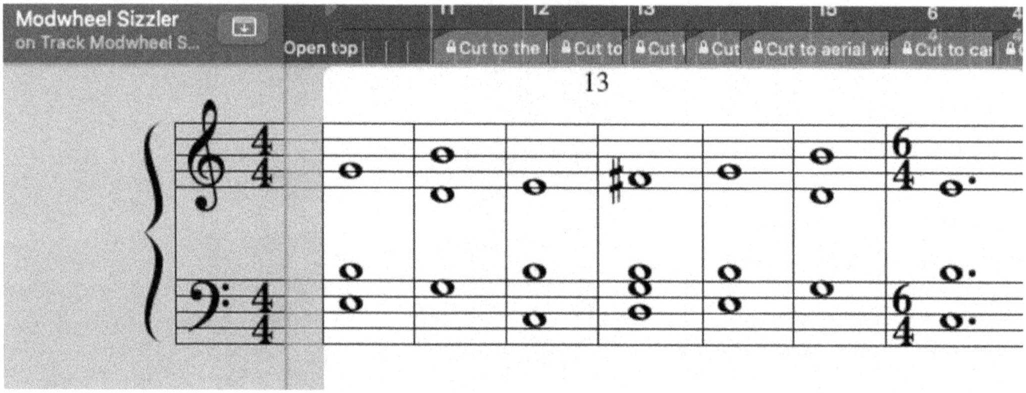

Figure 10.18: Track 6 notation example

Next, create an instrument track as the seventh track. Use the *Option + Cmd + N* shortcut to open the **New Tracks** dialog box. Select **Software Instrument**, then **Empty Channel Strip**, and check the box next to **Open Library**. Then, click on **Create**.

The Logic Pro library opens. In the search window of this synth, type `Fireflies`, then click on the synth's patch name. Logic Pro will load this instrument and its sound settings.

Figure 10.19: Logic Pro library

To open the instrument, double-click on the **Sculpture** instrument tab in the channel strip:

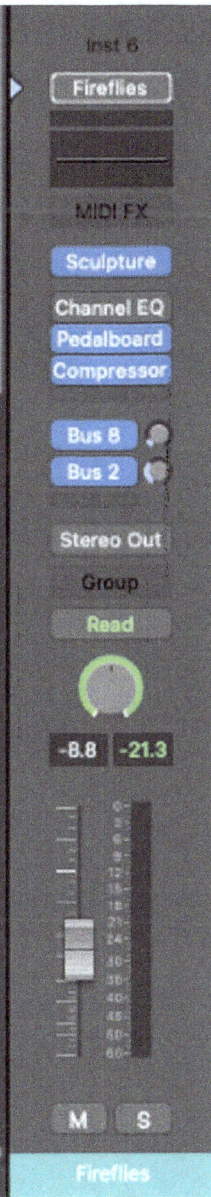

Figure 10.20: Logic Pro channel strip

The instrument window will open, and you can then make additional adjustments to the original sound, if needed:

Figure 10.21: Logic Pro Sculpture instrument

On this track, record the notes from **Bar 10** to **Bar 17**, as shown in *Figure 10.22*:

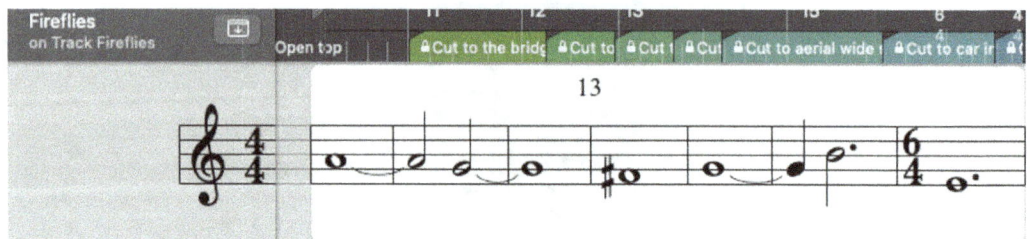

Figure 10.22: Track 7 notation example

Using the **New Tracks** dialog box, create an instrument track as the eighth track. Select **Software Instrument**, then **Empty Channel Strip**, and check the box next to **Open Library**. Then, click on **Create**.

The Logic Pro library opens. In the search window of this synth, type `Outer Lands Synth`, then click on the synth's patch name. Logic Pro will load this instrument and its sound settings.

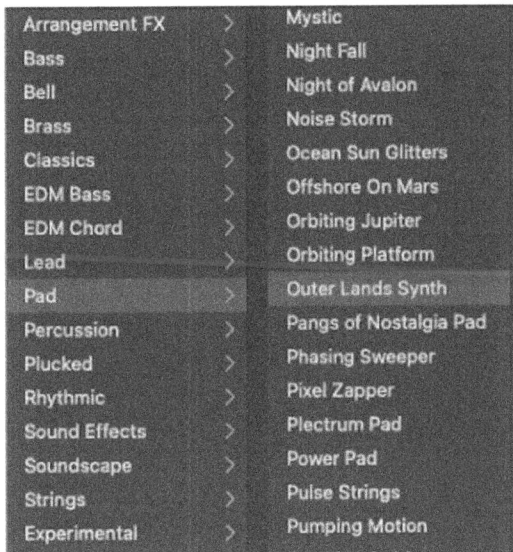

Figure 10.23: Logic Pro library

On this track, record the notes from **Bar 7** to **Bar 17**, as shown in *Figure 10.24*:

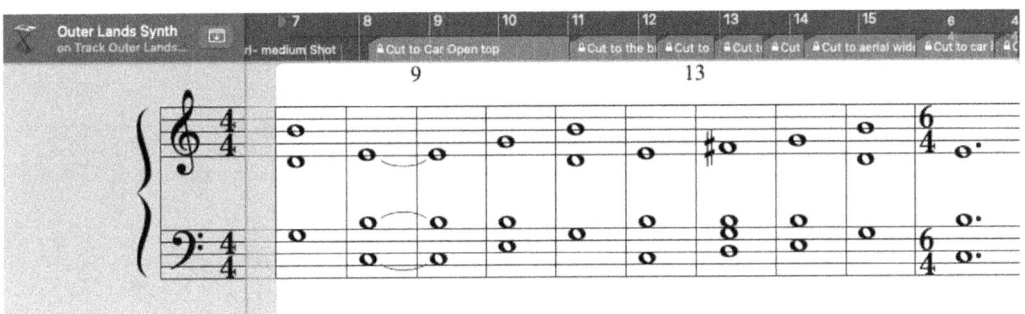

Figure 10.24: Track 8 notation example

Using the **New Tracks** dialog box, create an instrument track as the ninth track. Select **Software Instrument**, then **Empty Channel Strip**, and check the box next to **Open Library**. Then, click on **Create**.

The Logic Pro library opens. In the search window of this synth, type `Slow Breaths`, then click on the synth's patch name. Logic Pro will load this instrument and its sound settings.

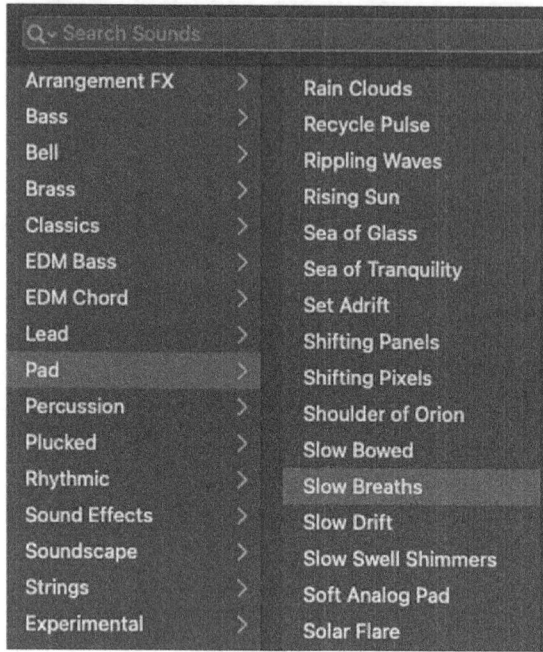

Figure 10.25: Logic Pro library

On this track, record the notes from **Bar 7** to **Bar 17**, as shown in *Figure 10.26*.

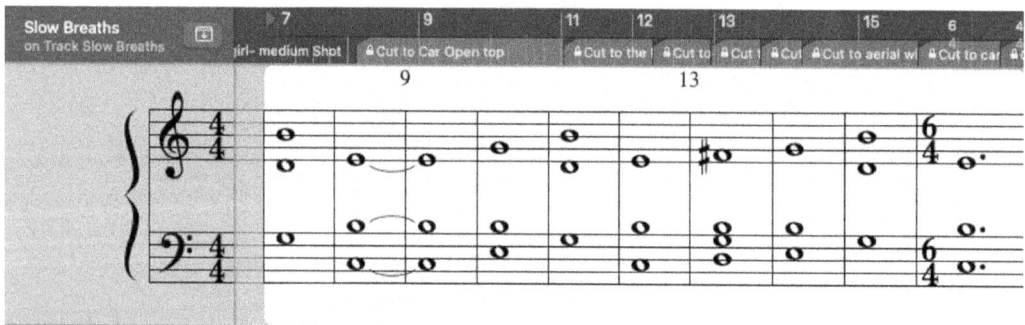

Figure 10.26: Track 9 notation example

Using the **New Tracks** dialog box, create an instrument track as the tenth track. Select **Software Instrument**, then **Empty Channel Strip**, and check the box next to **Open Library**. Then, click on **Create**.

The Logic Pro library opens. In the search window of this synth, type `Carbon Particles`, then click on the synth's patch name. Logic Pro will load this instrument and its sound settings.

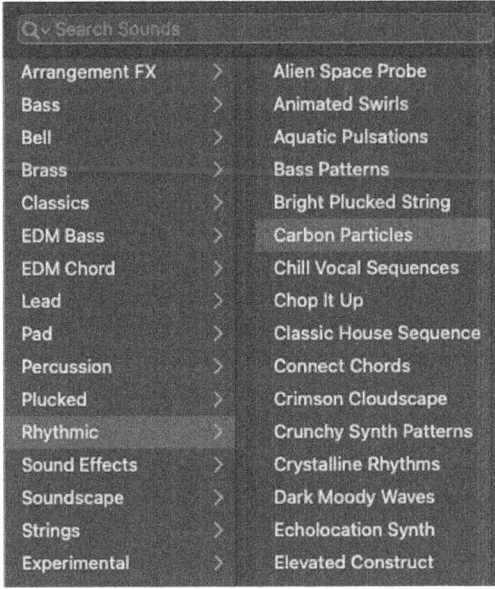

Figure 10.27: Logic Pro library

On this track, record the notes from **Bar 10** to **Bar 17**, as shown in *Figure 10.28*:

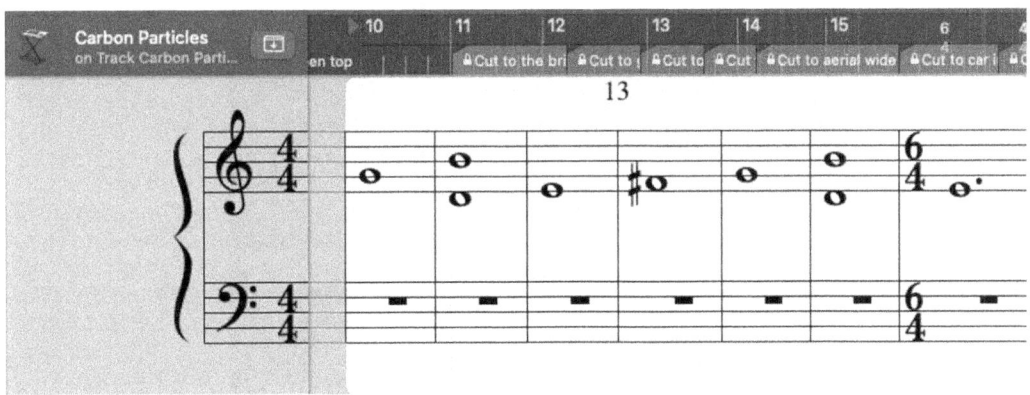

Figure 10.28: Track 10 notation example

Then, on the same track, continue recording the notes from **Bar 25** to **Bar 29**, as shown in *Figure 10.29*:

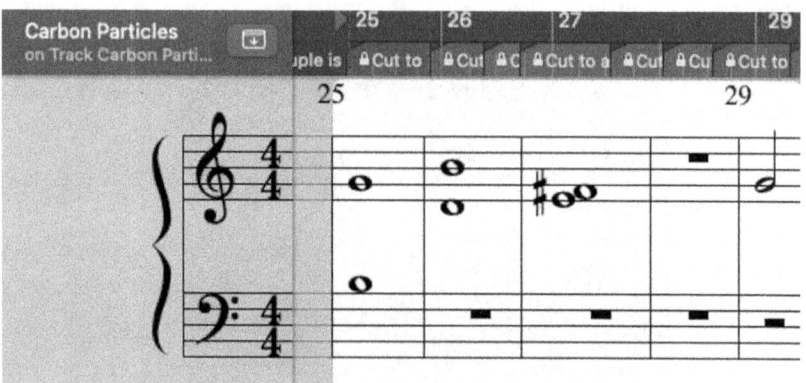

Figure 10.29: Track 10 second notation example

Using the **New Tracks** dialog box, create an instrument track as the eleventh track. Select **Software Instrument**, then **Empty Channel Strip**, and check the box next to **Open Library**. Then, click on **Create**.

The Logic Pro library opens. In the search window of this synth, type `Pulsed Pad`, then click on the synth's patch name. Logic Pro will load this instrument and its sound settings:

Figure 10.30: Logic Pro library

On this track, record the notes from **Bar 11** to **Bar 17**, as shown in *Figure 10.31*:

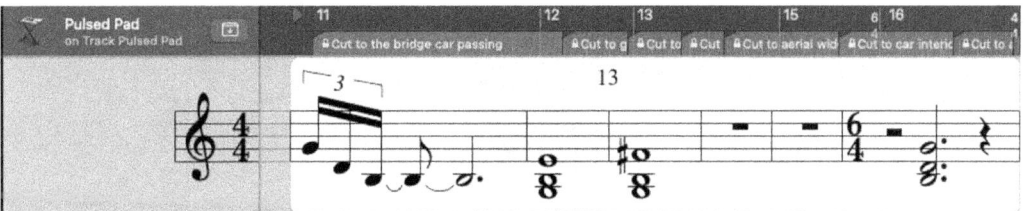

Figure 10.31: Track 11 notation example

Using the **New Tracks** dialog box, create an instrument track as the twelfth track. Select **Software Instrument**, then **Empty Channel Strip**, and check the box next to **Open Library**. Then, click on **Create**.

The Logic Pro library opens. In the search window of this synth, type `Ghostly Reversed Organ`, then click on the synth's patch name. Logic Pro will load this instrument and its sound settings.

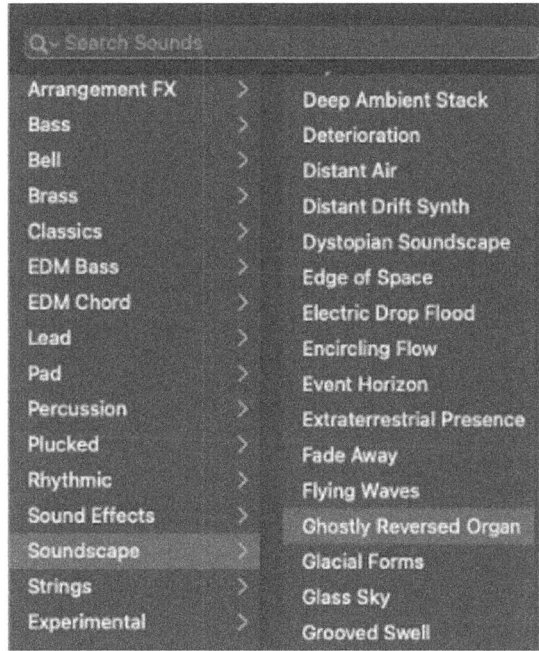

Figure 10.32: Logic Pro library

To open the instrument, double-click on the **Vintage B3** instrument tab in the channel strip:

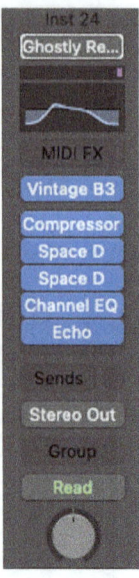

Figure 10.33: Logic Pro channel strip

The instrument window will open, and you can then make additional adjustments to the original sound, if needed.

Figure 10.34: Logic Pro Vintage B3 instrument

On this track, record the notes from **Bar 1** to **Bar 17**, as shown in *Figure 10.35*:

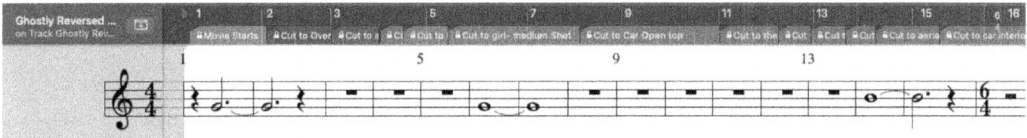

Figure 10.35: Track 12 notation example

Using the **New Tracks** dialog box, create an instrument track as the thirteenth track. Select **Software Instrument**, then **Empty Channel Strip**, and check the box next to **Open Library**. Then, click on **Create**.

The Logic Pro library opens. In the search window of this synth, type `Lost Reverse`, then click on the synth's patch name. Logic Pro will load this instrument and its sound settings.

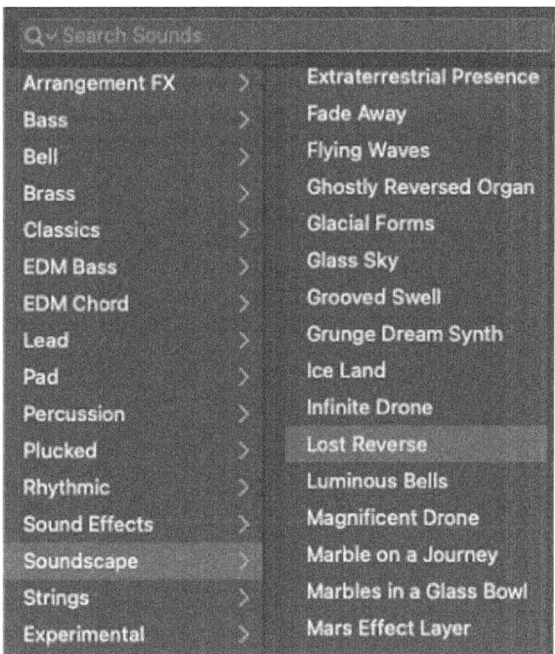

Figure 10.36: Logic Pro library

On this track, record the notes from **Bar 4** to **Bar 17**, as shown in *Figure 10.37*:

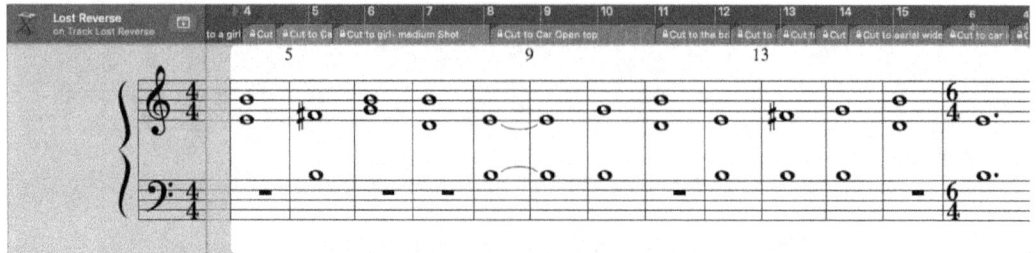

Figure 10.37: Track 13 notation example

Using the **New Tracks** dialog box, create an instrument track as the fourteenth track. Select **Software Instrument**, then **Empty Channel Strip**, and check the box next to **Open Library**. Then, click on **Create**.

The Logic Pro library opens. In the search window of this synth, type `Floating Plasma`, then click on the synth's patch name. Logic Pro will load this instrument and its sound settings.

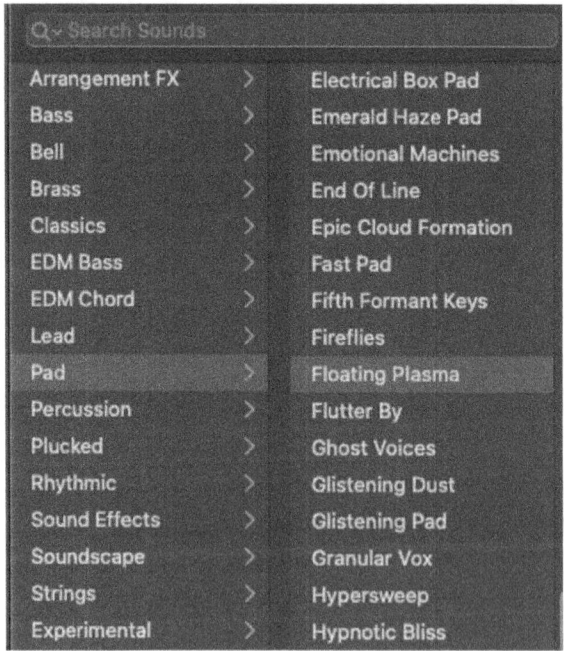

Figure 10.38: Logic Pro library

On this track, record the notes from **Bar 6** to **Bar 10**, as shown in *Figure 10.39*:

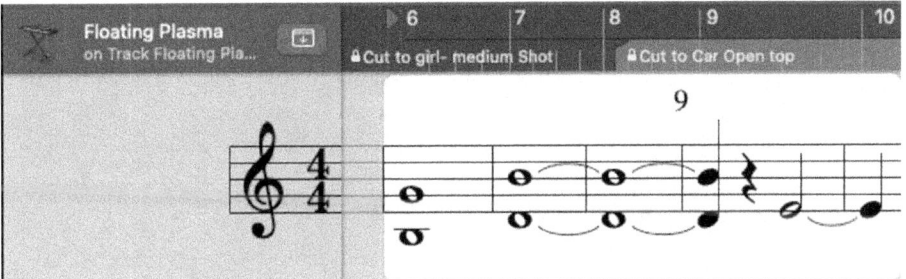

Figure 10.39: Track 14 notation example

Using the **New Tracks** dialog box, create an instrument track as the fifteenth track. Select **Software Instrument**, then **Empty Channel Strip**, and check the box next to **Open Library**. Then, click on **Create**.

The Logic Pro library opens. In the search window of this synth, type `Lost Reverse`, then click on the synth's patch name. Logic Pro will load this instrument and its sound settings.

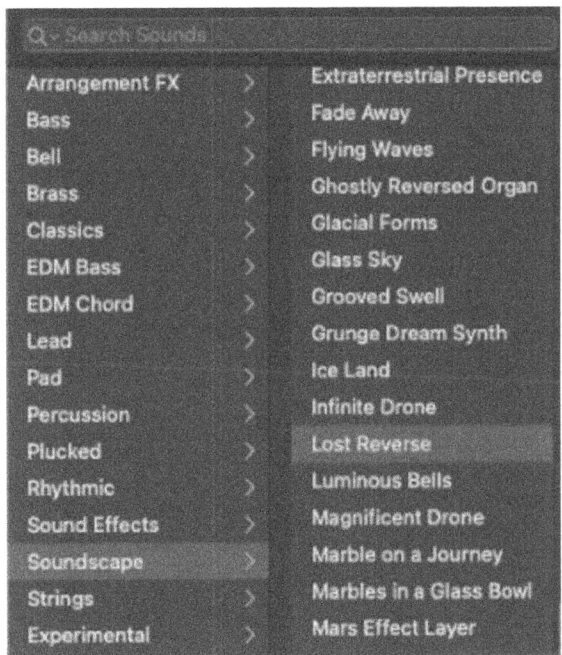

Figure 10.40: Logic Pro library

On this track, record the notes from **Bar 25** to **Bar 29**, as shown in *Figure 10.41*:

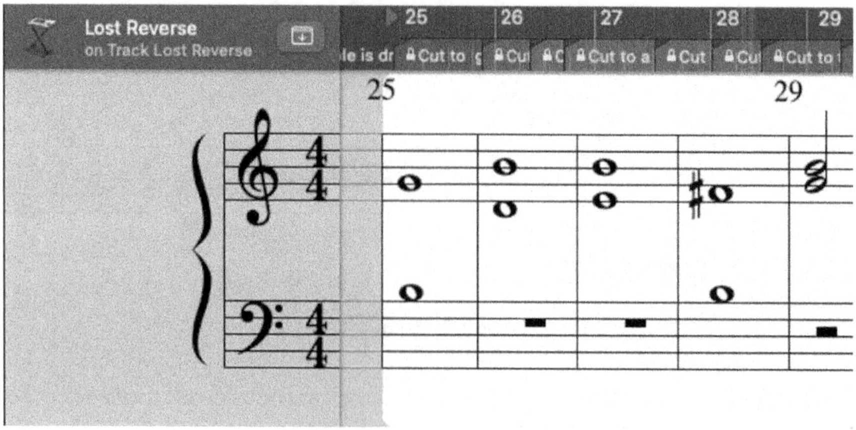

Figure 10.41: Track 15 notation example

Using the **New Tracks** dialog box, create an instrument track as the sixteenth track. Select **Software Instrument**, then **Empty Channel Strip**, and check the box next to **Open Library**. Then, click on **Create**.

The Logic Pro library opens. In the search window of this synth, type `Metallic Memories Bowl`, then click on the synth's patch name. Logic Pro will load this instrument and its sound settings.

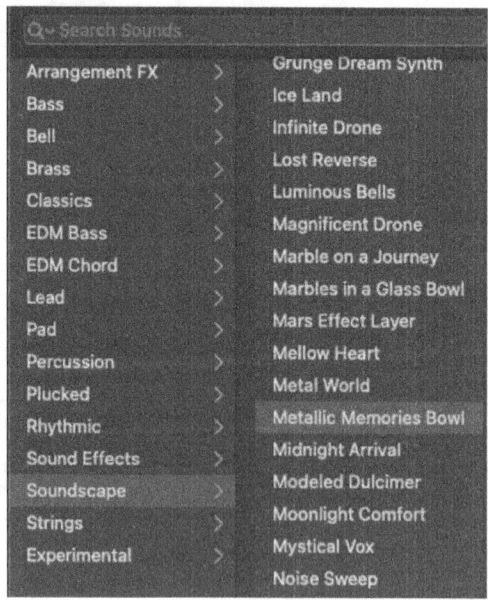

Figure 10.42: Logic Pro library

On this track, record the notes from **Bar 1** to **Bar 9**, as shown in *Figure 10.43*:

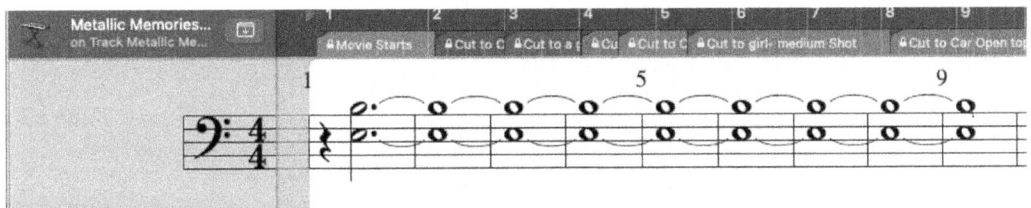

Figure 10.43: Track 16 notation example

Then, on the same track, continue recording the notes from **Bar 25** to **Bar 29**, as shown in *Figure 10.44*:

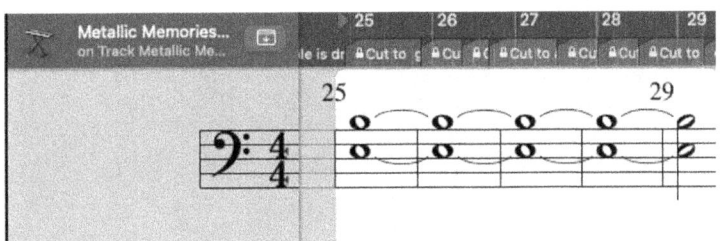

Figure 10.44: Track 16 second notation example

Using the **New Tracks** dialog box, create an instrument track as the seventeenth track. Select **Software Instrument**, then **Empty Channel Strip**, and check the box next to **Open Library**. Then, click on **Create**.

The Logic Pro library opens. In the search window of this synth, type Stratosphere, then click on the synth's patch name. Logic Pro will load this instrument and its sound settings.

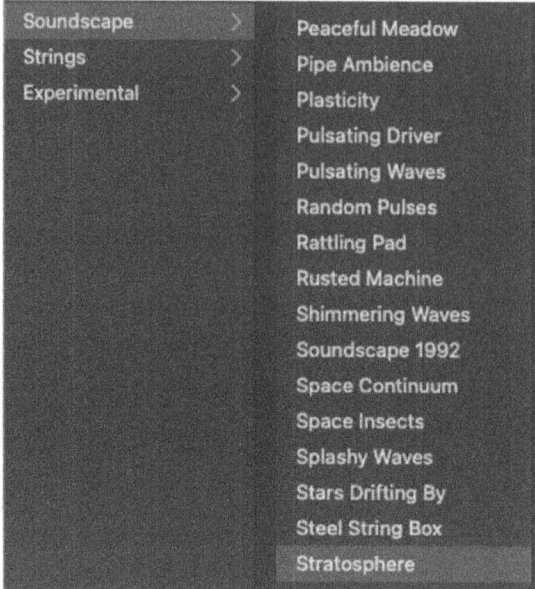

Figure 10.45: Logic Pro library

To open the instrument, double-click on the **Retro Synth** instrument tab in the channel strip:

Figure 10.46: Logic Pro channel strip

The instrument window will open, and you can then make additional adjustments to the original sound, if needed.

Figure 10.47: Logic Pro Retro Synth instrument

On this track, record the notes from **Bar 1** to **Bar 17**, as shown in *Figure 10.48*:

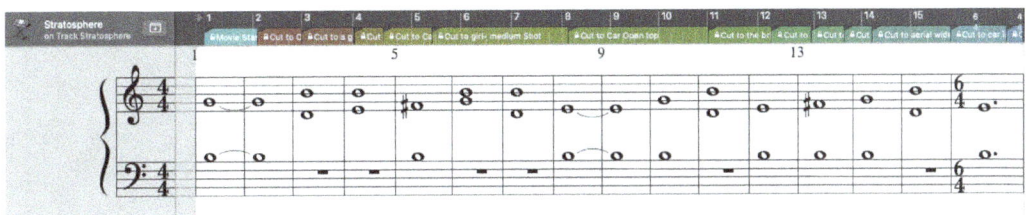

Figure 10.48: Track 17 notation example

Then, on the same track, continue recording the notes from **Bar 25** to **Bar 29**, as shown in *Figure 10.49*:

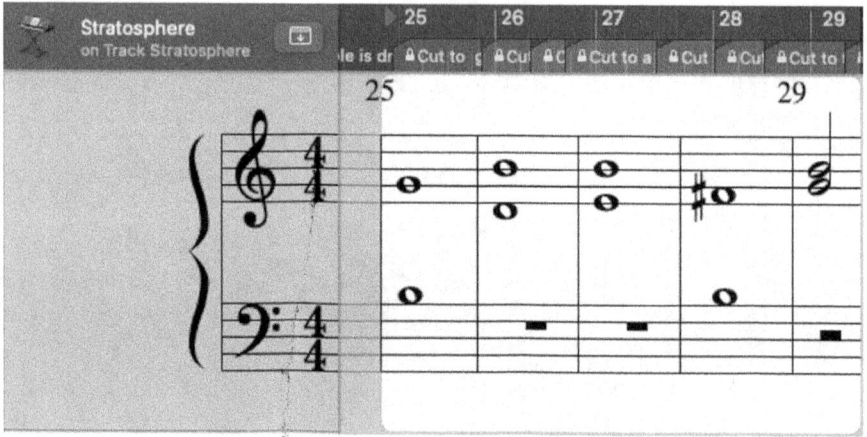

Figure 10.49: Track 17 second notation example

Using the **New Tracks** dialog box, create an instrument track as the eighteenth track. Select **Software Instrument**, then **Empty Channel Strip**, and check the box next to **Open Library**. Then, click on **Create**.

The Logic Pro library opens. In the search window of this synth, type `Light Harmonics`, then click on the synth's patch name. Logic Pro will load this instrument and its sound settings.

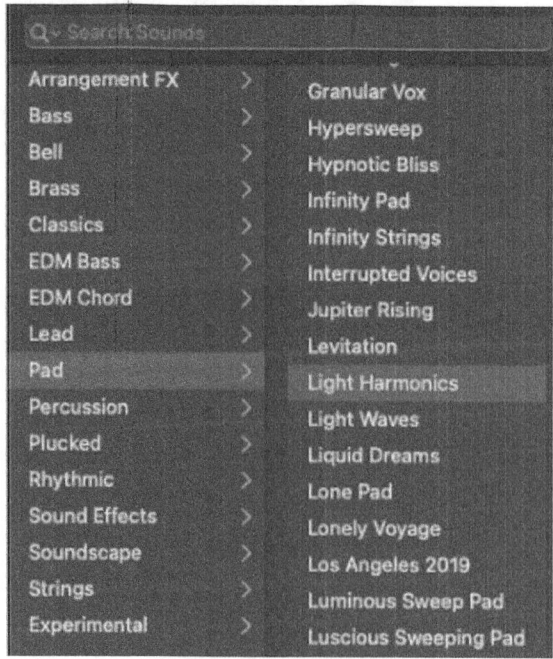

Figure 10.50: Logic Pro library

On this track, record the notes from **Bar 17** to **Bar 25**, as shown in *Figure 10.51*:

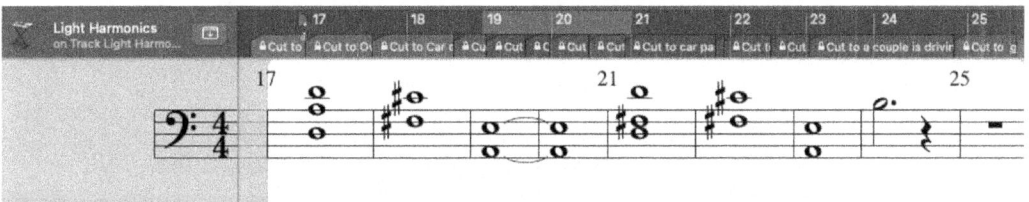

Figure 10.51: Track 18 notation example

Using the **New Tracks** dialog box, create an instrument track as the nineteenth track. Select **Software Instrument**, then **Empty Channel Strip**, and check the box next to **Open Library**. Then, click on **Create**.

The Logic Pro library opens. In the search window of this synth, type `Lonely Voyage`, then click on the synth's patch name. Logic Pro will load this instrument and its sound settings.

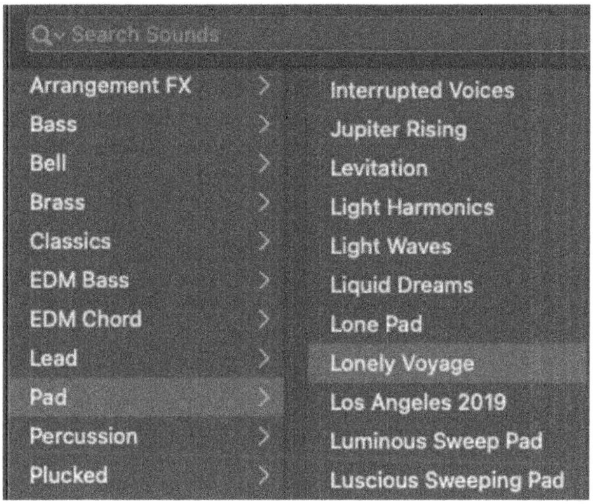

Figure 10.52: Logic Pro library

On this track, record the notes from **Bar 17** to **Bar 25**, as shown in *Figure 10.53*:

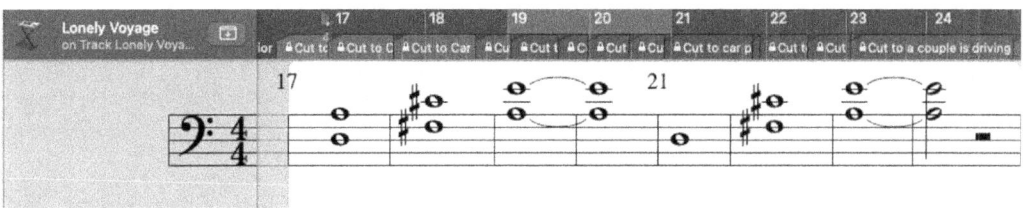

Figure 10.53: Track 19 notation example

Using the **New Tracks** dialog box, create an instrument track as the twentieth track. Select **Software Instrument**, then **Empty Channel Strip**, and check the box next to **Open Library**. Then, click on **Create**.

In the search window of this synth, type Orbiting Jupiter, then click on the synth's patch name. Logic Pro will load this instrument and its sound settings.

Figure 10.54: Logic Pro library

On this track, record the notes from **Bar 17** to **Bar 25**, as shown in *Figure 10.55*:

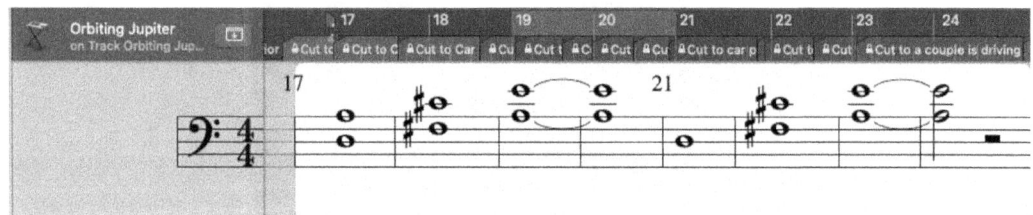

Figure 10.55: Track 20 notation example

Using the **New Tracks** dialog box, create an instrument track as the twenty-first track. Select **Software Instrument**, then **Empty Channel Strip**, and check the box next to **Open Library**. Then, click on **Create**.

The Logic Pro library opens. In the search window of this synth, type Infinity Strings, then click on the synth's patch name. Logic Pro will load this instrument and its sound settings.

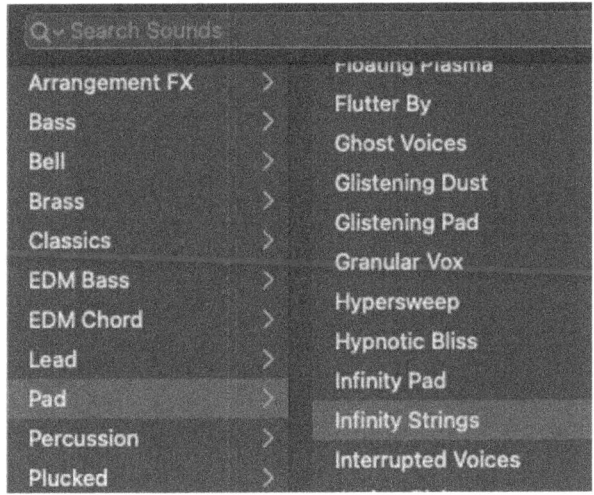

Figure 10.56: Logic Pro library

On this track, record the notes from **Bar 17** to **Bar 25**, as shown in *Figure 10.57*:

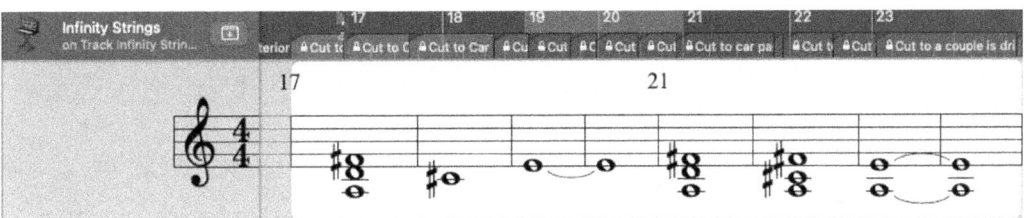

Figure 10.57: Track 21 notation example

Using the **New Tracks** dialog box, create an instrument track as the twenty-second track. Select **Software Instrument**, then **Empty Channel Strip**, and check the box next to **Open Library**. Then, click on **Create**.

The Logic Pro library opens. In the search window of this synth, type `Bass Patterns`, then click on the synth's patch name. Logic Pro will load this instrument and its sound settings.

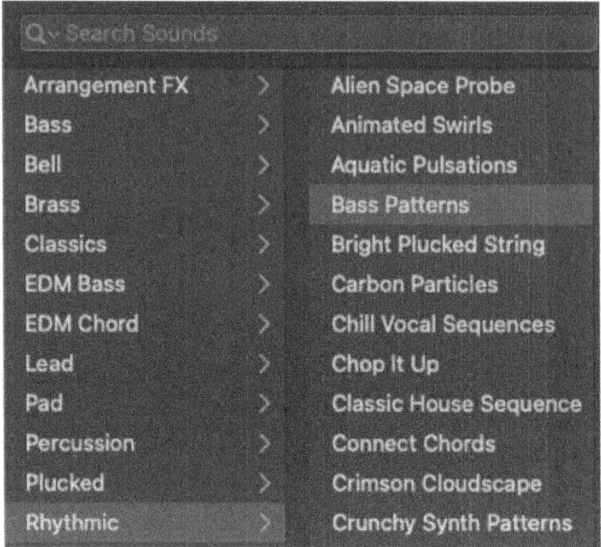

Figure 10.58: Logic Pro library

On this track, record the notes from **Bar 17** to **Bar 25**, as shown in *Figure 10.59*:

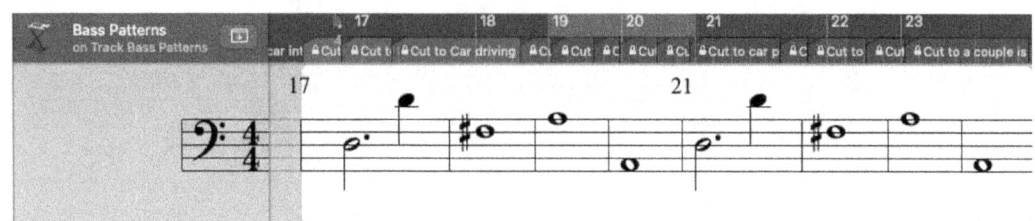

Figure 10.59: Track 22 notation example

Using the **New Tracks** dialog box, create an instrument track as the twenty-third track. Select **Software Instrument**, then **Empty Channel Strip**, and check the box next to **Open Library**. Then, click on **Create**.

The Logic Pro library opens. In the search window of this synth, type `Slow Drift`, then click on the synth's patch name. Logic Pro will load this instrument and its sound settings.

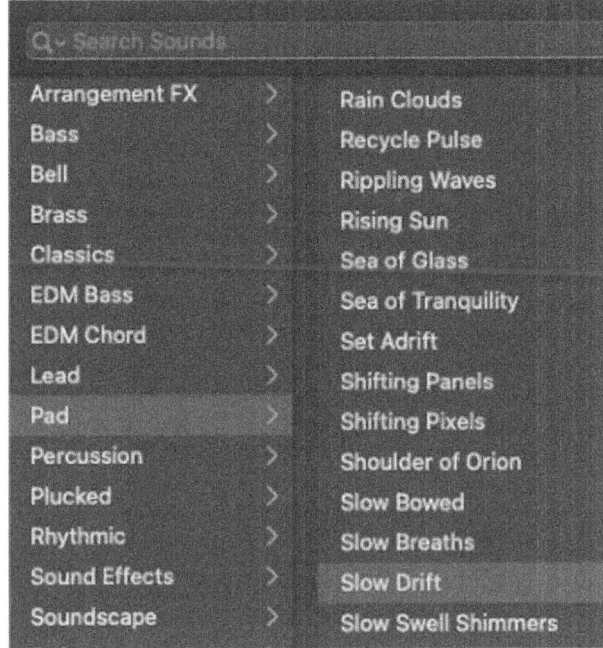

Figure 10.60: Logic Pro library

On this track, record the notes from **Bar 17** to **Bar 25**, as shown in *Figure 10.61*:

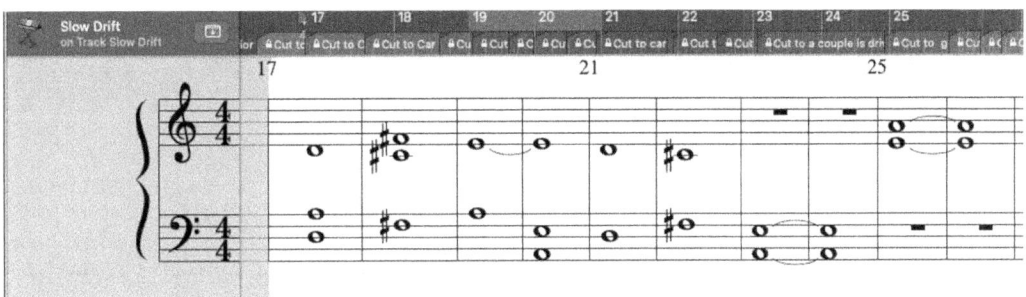

Figure 10.61: Track 23 notation example

Using the **New Tracks** dialog box, create an instrument track as the twenty-fourth track. Select **Software Instrument**, then **Empty Channel Strip**, and check the box next to **Open Library**. Then, click on **Create**.

The Logic Pro library opens. In the search window of this synth, type `Chill Vocal Sequences`, then click on the synth's patch name. Logic Pro will load this instrument and its sound settings.

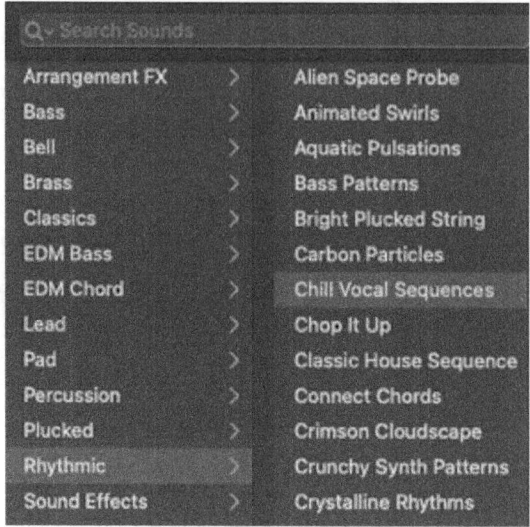

Figure 10.62: Logic Pro library

On this track, record the notes from **Bar 17** to **Bar 24**, as shown in *Figure 10.63*:

Figure 10.63: Track 24 notation example

Using the **New Tracks** dialog box, create an instrument track as the twenty-fifth track. Select **Software Instrument**, then **Empty Channel Strip**, and check the box next to **Open Library**. Then, click on **Create**.

The Logic Pro library opens. In the search window of this synth, type `Tektonic Grooves`, then click on the synth's patch name. Logic Pro will load this instrument and its sound settings.

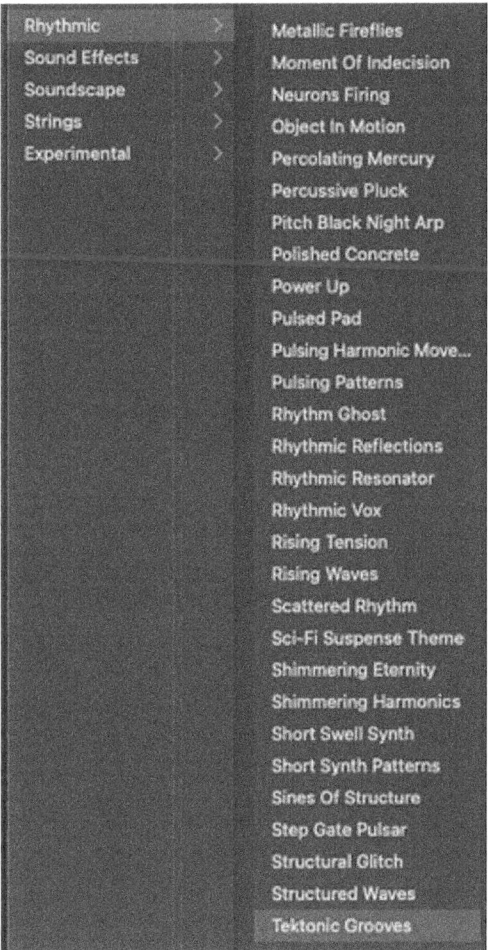

Figure 10.64: Logic Pro library

On this track, record the notes from **Bar 19** to **Bar 25**, as shown in *Figure 10.65*:

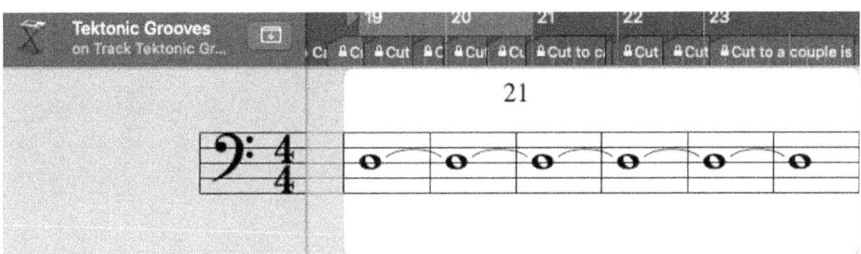

Figure 10.65: Track 25 notation example

Using the **New Tracks** dialog box, create an instrument track as the twenty-sixth track. Select **Software Instrument**, then **Empty Channel Strip**, and check the box next to **Open Library**. Then, click on **Create**.

The Logic Pro library opens. In the search window of this synth, type `Structural Glitch`, then click on the synth's patch name. Logic Pro will load this instrument and its sound settings.

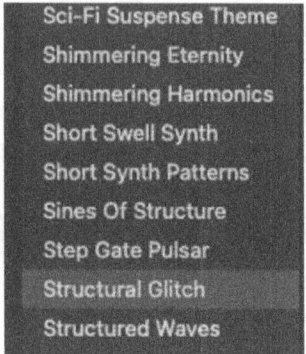

Figure 10.66: Logic Pro library

On this track, record the notes from **Bar 17** to **Bar 25**, as shown in *Figure 10.67*:

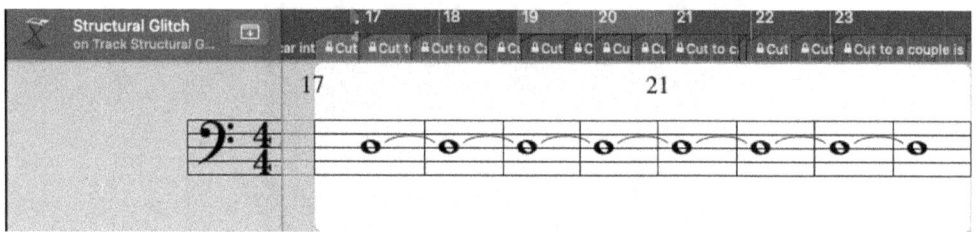

Figure 10.67: Track 26 notation example

Using the **New Tracks** dialog box, create an instrument track as the twenty-seventh track. Select **Software Instrument**, then **Empty Channel Strip**, and check the box next to **Open Library**. Then, click on **Create**.

The Logic Pro library opens. In the search window of this synth, type `Evolving Currents`, then click on the synth's patch name. Logic Pro will load this instrument and its sound settings.

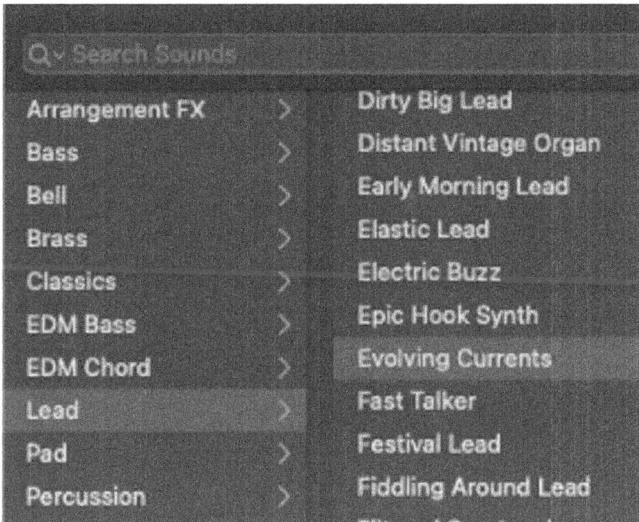

Figure 10.68: Logic Pro library

On this track, record the notes from **Bar 17** to **Bar 25**, as shown in *Figure 10.69*:

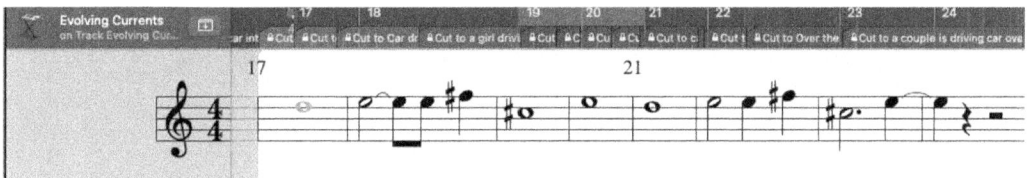

Figure 10.69: Track 27 notation example

Using the **New Tracks** dialog box, create an instrument track as the twenty-eighth track. Select **Software Instrument**, then **Empty Channel Strip**, and check the box next to **Open Library**. Then, click on **Create**.

In the search window of this synth, type `Lyrical Synth`, then click on the synth's patch name. Logic Pro will load this instrument and its sound settings.

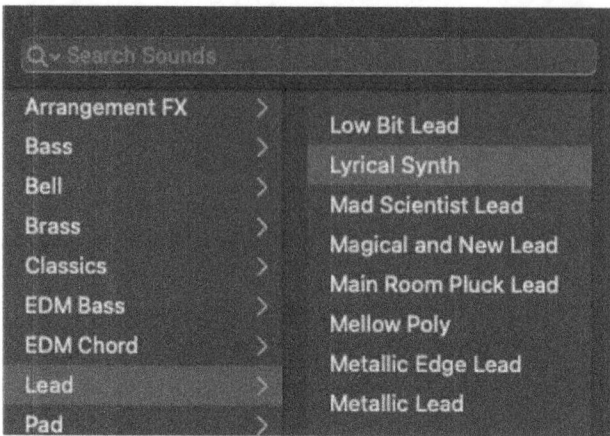

Figure 10.70: Logic Pro library

On this track, record the notes from **Bar 17** to **Bar 25**, as shown in *Figure 10.71*:

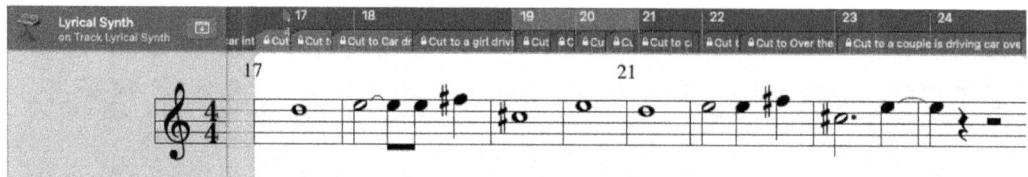

Figure 10.71: Track 28 notation example

Next, create an instrument track as the twenty-ninth track. This is going to be the same sound as the twenty-eighth track, so we will duplicate the **Lyrical Synth** instrument by using the *Cmd + D* shortcut. Then, on this track, record the notes from **Bar 19** to **Bar 24**, as shown in *Figure 10.72*:

Figure 10.72: Track 29 notation example

Using the **New Tracks** dialog box, create an instrument track as the thirtieth track. Select **Software Instrument**, then **Empty Channel Strip**, and check the box next to **Open Library**. Then, click on **Create**.

The Logic Pro library opens. In the search window of this synth, type Dream Dancer, then click on the synth's patch name. Logic Pro will load this instrument and its sound settings.

Figure 10.73: Logic Pro library

On this track, record the notes from **Bar 19** to **Bar 24**, as shown in *Figure 10.74*:

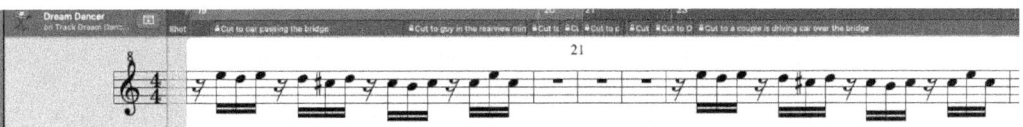

Figure 10.74: Track 30 notation example

Using the **New Tracks** dialog box, create an instrument track as the thirty-first track. Select **Software Instrument**, then **Empty Channel Strip**, and check the box next to **Open Library**. Then, click on **Create**.

The Logic Pro library opens. In the search window of this synth, type Old Fragile Vinyl Keys, then click on the synth's patch name. Logic Pro will load this instrument and its sound settings.

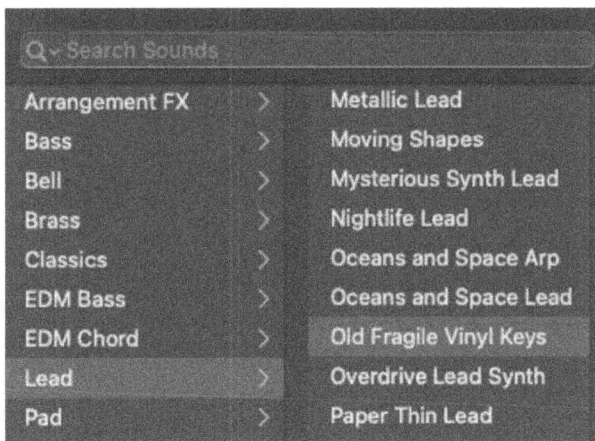

Figure 10.75: Logic Pro library

On this track, record the notes from **Bar 19** to **Bar 24**, as shown in *Figure 10.76*:

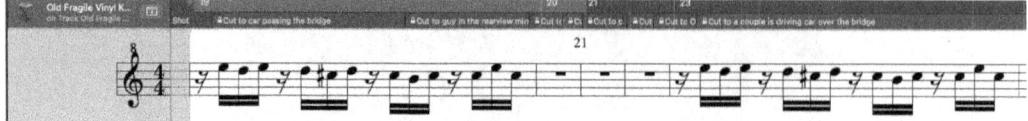

Figure 10.76: Track 31 notation example

Using the **New Tracks** dialog box, create an instrument track as the thirty-second track. Select **Software Instrument**, then **Empty Channel Strip**, and check the box next to **Open Library**. Then, click on **Create**.

The Logic Pro library opens. In the search window of this synth, type `Fog Machine`, then click on the synth's patch name. Logic Pro will load this instrument and its sound settings.

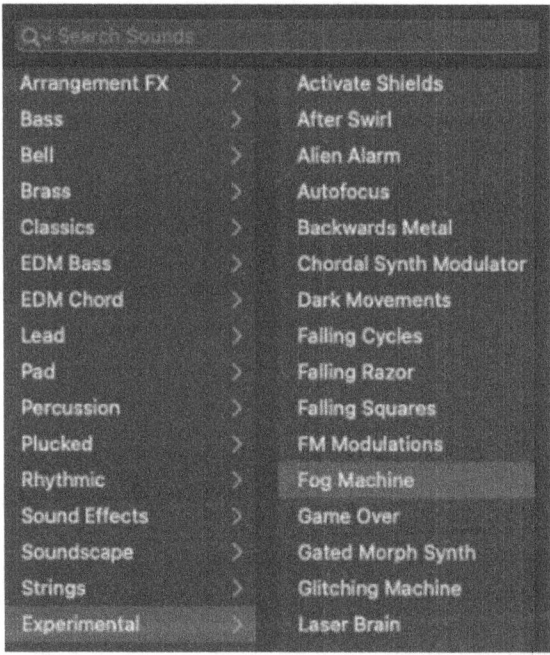

Figure 10.77: Logic Pro library

On this track, record the notes from **Bar 16** to **Bar 18**, as shown in *Figure 10.78*:

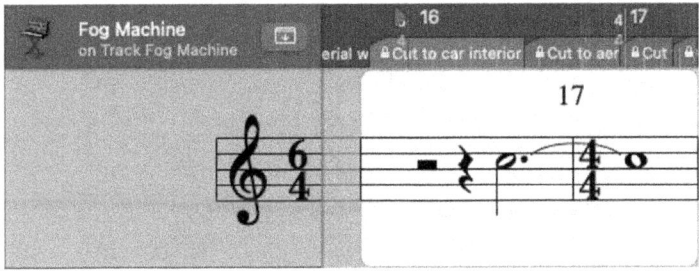

Figure 10.78: Track 32 notation example

Then, on the same track, continue recording the notes from **Bar 25** to **Bar 26**, as shown in *Figure 10.79*:

Figure 10.79: Track 32 second notation example

Using the **New Tracks** dialog box, create an instrument track as the thirty-third track. Select **Software Instrument**, then **Empty Channel Strip**, and check the box next to **Open Library**. Then, click on **Create**.

The Logic Pro library opens. In the search window of this synth, type `Cymbal Swell`, then click on the synth's patch name. Logic Pro will load this instrument and its sound settings.

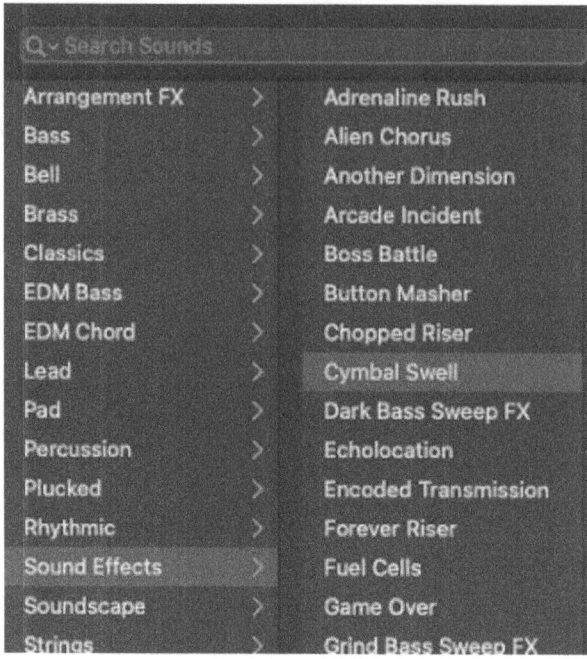

Figure 10.80: Logic Pro library

On this track, record the notes from **Bar 16** to **Bar 18**, as shown in *Figure 10.81*:

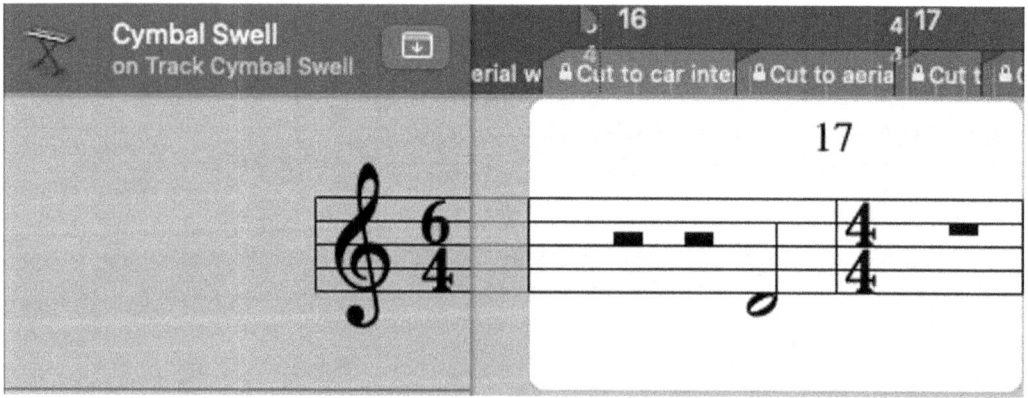

Figure 10.81: Track 33 notation example

Then, on the same track, continue recording the notes from **Bar 24** to **Bar 25**, as shown in *Figure 10.82*:

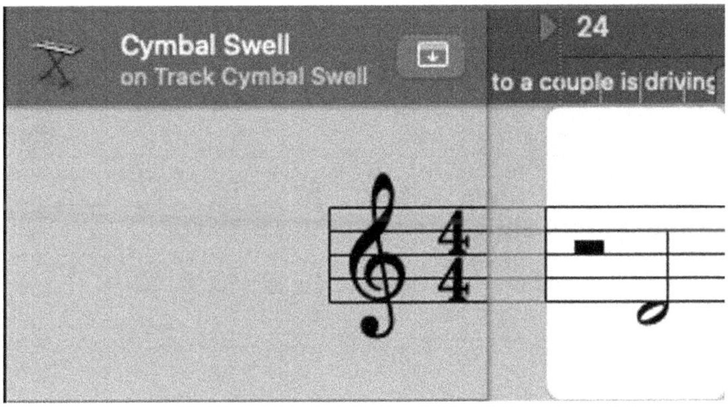

Figure 10.82: Track 33 second notation example

Using the **New Tracks** dialog box, create an instrument track as the thirty-forth track. Select **Software Instrument**, then **Empty Channel Strip**, and check the box next to **Open Library**. Then, click on **Create**.

The Logic Pro library opens. In the search window of this synth, type `Ocean Waves Modular`, then click on the synth's patch name. Logic Pro will load this instrument and its sound settings.

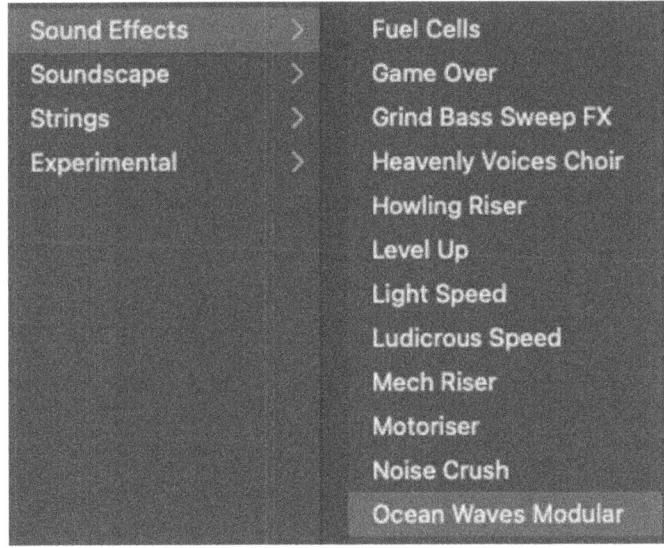

Figure 10.83: Logic Pro library

On this track, record the notes from **Bar 16** to **Bar 17**, as shown in *Figure 10.84*:

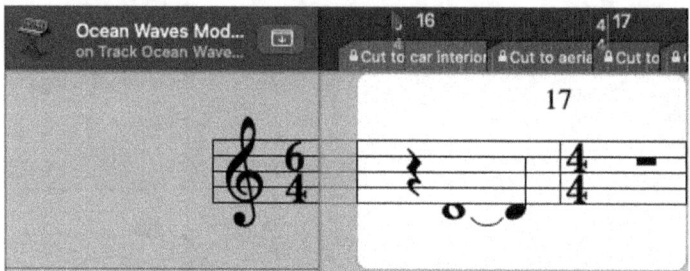

Figure 10.84: Track 34 notation example

Then, on the same track, continue recording the notes from **Bar 24** to **Bar 25**, as shown in *Figure 10.85*:

Figure 10.85: Track 34 second notation example

Using the **New Tracks** dialog box, create an instrument track as the thirty-fifth track. Select **Software Instrument**, then **Empty Channel Strip**, and check the box next to **Open Library**. Then, click on **Create**.

The Logic Pro library opens. In the search window of this synth, type `Warped Pluck`, then click on the synth's patch name. Logic Pro will load this instrument and its sound settings.

Reviewing the composing process and layering instruments 301

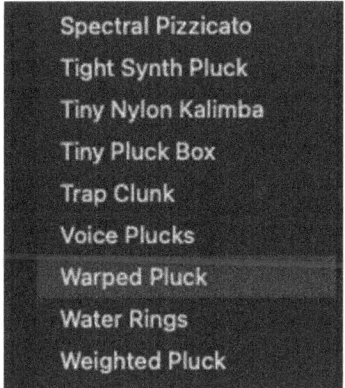

Figure 10.86: Logic Pro library

On this track, record the notes from **Bar 17** to **Bar 29**, as shown in *Figure 10.87*:

Figure 10.87: Track 35 notation example

Using the **New Tracks** dialog box, create an instrument track as the thirty-sixth track. Select **Software Instrument**, then **Empty Channel Strip**, and check the box next to **Open Library**. Then, click on **Create**.

The Logic Pro library opens. In the search window of this synth, type `Warped Pluck`, then click on the synth's patch name. Logic Pro will load this instrument and its sound settings.

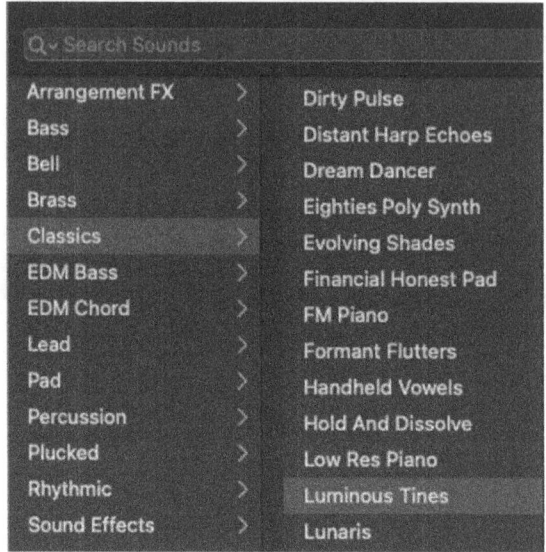

Figure 10.88: Logic Pro library

On this track, record the notes from **Bar 16** to **Bar 18**, as shown in *Figure 10.89*:

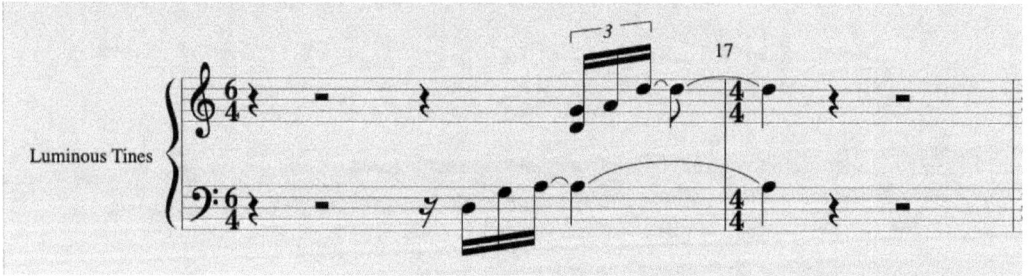

Figure 10.89: Track 36 notation example

Using the **New Tracks** dialog box, create an instrument track as the thirty-seventh track. Select **Software Instrument**, then **Empty Channel Strip**, and check the box next to **Open Library**. Then, click on **Create**.

The Logic Pro library opens. In the search window of this synth, type `Noise Sweep`, then click on the synth's patch name. Logic Pro will load this instrument and its sound settings.

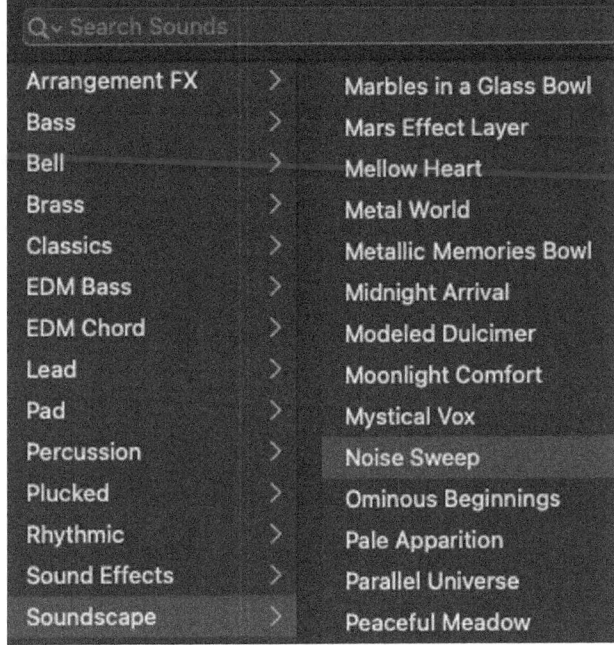

Figure 10.90: Logic Pro library

On this track, record the notes from **Bar 16** to **Bar 17**, as shown in *Figure 10.91*:

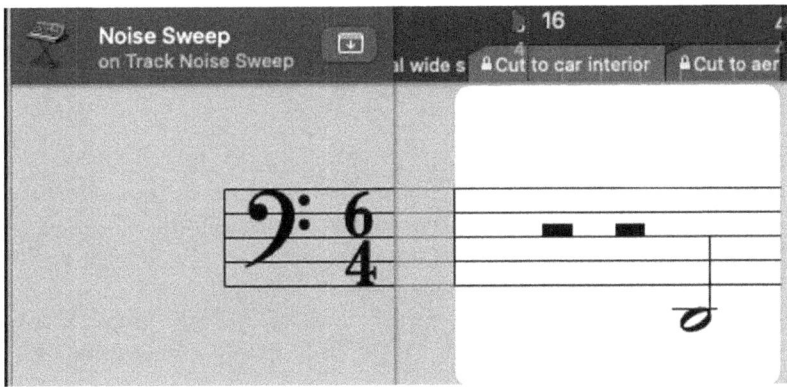

Figure 10.91: Track 37 notation example

Now you should have sequenced all the tracks and your session should look similar to *Figure 10.92*:

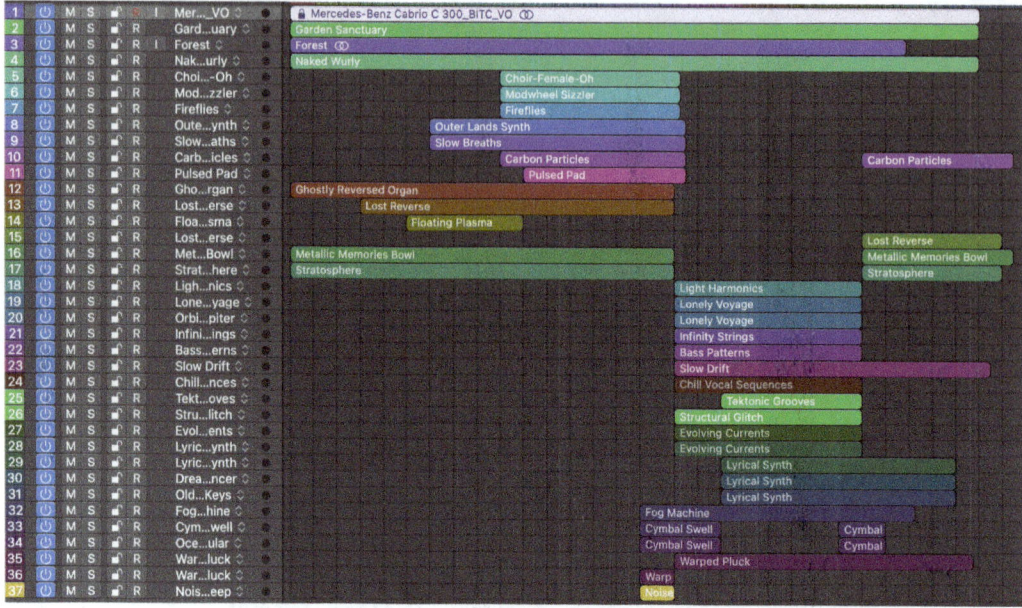

Figure 10.92: Logic Pro Arrange window

In this section, we have reviewed how to select, create, and edit MIDI regions, as well as layer instruments and record them. You can now edit or add instruments as needed to make sure the music contributes to the overall mood and story of the commercial.

After reviewing all the suggested steps, you can now try to score this commercial as an example and implement all of the learned techniques right away in your other projects.

Summary

In this chapter, we explored how to choose the right mood and style for the commercial. We also looked at how to structure a cue before scoring begins and how to use musical choices versus technical choices. Finally, we reviewed the entire process of layering instruments and recording music from existing sheet music and created an entire arrangement.

In the next chapter, we will discuss the steps of shaping the sound and finalizing and exporting the entire score to a movie.

11
Shaping the Score and Exporting to Video

Previously, in *Chapter 10*, we discussed and presented an example of how to score a Mercedes commercial from scratch. We discussed how to find and select appropriate sounds, moods, and styles; structure the cue; choose music choices over technical choices; and layer instruments to create an entire arrangement.

Now, using the instruments previously recorded in *Chapter 10*, we will explore how to set up volume and panning, as well as how to blend the sounds by adding some of the Logic Pro plugins. We will exclusively use Logic Pro plugins for audio processing instead of using any existing third-party plugins.

Additionally, we will go over how to change, shape, and customize the existing instruments so that the final mix contributes to the overall mood of the commercial. Since mixing and mastering can be a very elaborate task, for the sake of the exercise in this chapter, we will cover just the basic mixing elements to get you started.

Finally, we will also review different ways of exporting the entire score to video.

This chapter should serve as an exercise, and by completing it, you will familiarize yourself with the steps of scoring a commercial and shaping the sound to the final stage of exporting.

So, in this chapter, we will cover the following topics:

- Evaluating the mix
- Setting the volume level of tracks
- Setting panning for each track
- Shaping the sound and finalizing the basic mix
- Exporting the score to video

Technical requirements

To follow along with this chapter, you will need a Mac computer with Logic Pro and QuickTime software installed and basic audio engineering skills. You will also need to be able to access the movie files (through `https://packt.link/hxCer`) and should have basic knowledge of Logic Pro software and film scoring.

To begin, open `Mercedes-Benz Cabrio C 300_BITC.mov`, which was saved in *Chapter 10*. Make sure that the movie and Logic Pro are in sync, and that the fps is set correctly. Then, name and save the project (for example, I will name it `Exporting Score to Video_01`).

Evaluating the mix

In general, before we can customize sounds, it is important to listen to each track separately, in the context of the entire mix or similar sounds. By listening to each track separately and in context, you can evaluate it and then determine what to do with each sound and how when you work on your projects. Mixing sounds, like composing music, can be very subjective, but we will go over a couple of examples of how sounds can be customized a little more.

Similar to *Chapter 10*, you will be guided step by step through examples of how sounds and instruments can be customized. Keep in mind that everything in this chapter is related to the score composed in *Chapter 10*, based on my preferences and choices. Since we're going to review and cover the basic steps of editing and mixing instruments, it is important to follow and emulate each step in your DAW.

Professional audio engineering tasks are beyond the scope of this book and will not be discussed here, but basic Logic Pro knowledge should give you sufficient skills to understand the editing and mixing of instruments. However, the more skilled you are in audio engineering, the more it will help you achieve better sonic results.

Setting the volume level of tracks

In this section, we will go through all the tracks in the commercial and set approximate volume levels to help them blend better together so that the sound will support the commercial.

Setting the volume level of each track involves considering the mood and the mixture of sounds in the arrangement – some may need to be louder and some softer. Also, prioritizing each track volume level, based on the role of the sound, is crucial during the mixing process. When mixing, you need to consider whether the sound should be placed in the foreground, middle ground, or background. In all of the examples in this section, we will explore sound placement by using busses.

After reviewing why we should set the volume level, we will now go through all of the tracks and explore how to set the volume levels. As you're working through each step of the examples, make sure to save your session.

To begin, we will start with track 1. Since it is a pre-recorded voiceover, we will keep the default volume level at **0 dB**.

Next, select track 2, **Garden Sanctuary**, and set the channel fader to **0 dB**. You can use a shortcut by holding down *Option* and clicking on the channel fader to automatically set the channel fader to **0 dB**:

Figure 11.1: Logic Pro channel strip

Next, select track 3, **Forest**, and set the **Region** gain to **-23 dB**.

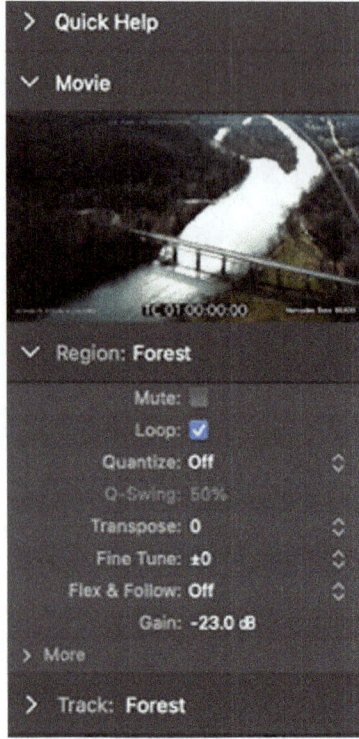

Figure 11.2: Logic Pro Region inspector

Additionally, set the channel fader to **–25 dB**.

Now, use the following list to set the rest of the track volumes:

- Select track 4, **Naked Wurly**, and set the channel fader to **0 dB**
- Select track 5, **Choir-Female-Oh**, and set the channel fader to **-10.4 dB**
- Select track 6, **Modwheel Sizzler**, and set the channel fader to **-11.6 dB**
- Select track 7, **Fireflies**, and set the channel fader to **-8.8 dB**
- Select track 8, **Outer Lands Synth**, and set the channel fader to **-9.6 dB**
- Select track 9, **Slow Breaths**, and set the channel fader to **-12 dB**
- Select track 10, **Carbon Particles**, and set the channel fader to **-16.6 dB**
- Select track 11, **Pulsed Pad**, and set the channel fader to **-12.2 dB**
- Select track 12, **Ghostly Reversed Organ**, and set the channel fader to **-3.9 dB**

- Select track 13, **Lost Reverse**, and set the channel fader to **-13.8 dB**
- Select track 14, **Floating Plasma**, and set the channel fader to **-7.6 dB**
- Select track 15, **Lost Reverse**, and set the channel fader to **-13 dB**
- Select track 16, **Metallic Memories Bowl**, and set the channel fader to **-9.8 dB**
- Select track 17, **Stratosphere**, and set the channel fader to **-9.8 dB**
- Select track 18, **Light Harmonics**, and set the channel fader to **-8.8 dB**
- Select track 19, **Lonely Voyage**, and set the channel fader to **-2.5 dB**
- Select track 20, **Orbiting Jupiter**, and set the channel fader to **-9.6 dB**
- Select track 21, **Infinity Strings**, and set the channel fader to **-4.1 dB**
- Select track 22, **Bass Patterns**, and set the channel fader to **-9 dB**
- Select track 23, **Slow Drift**, and set the channel fader to **-10.4 dB**
- Select track 24, **Chill Vocal Sequences**, and set the channel fader to **-2.6 dB**
- Select track 25, **Tektonic Grooves**, and set the channel fader to **-5.1 dB**
- Select track 26, **Structural Glitch**, and set the channel fader to **-6.0 dB**
- Select track 27, **Evolving Currents**, and set the channel fader to **-1.5 dB**
- Select track 28, **Lyrical Synth**, and set the channel fader to **0.0 dB**
- Select track 29, **Lyrical Synth**, and set the channel fader to **-2.9 dB**
- Select track 30, **Dream Dancer**, and set the channel fader to **-11.6 dB**
- Select track 31, **Old Fragile Vinyl Keys**, and set the channel fader to **-10.4 dB**
- Select track 32, **Fog Machine**, and set the channel fader to **-2.6 dB**
- Select track 33, **Cymbal Swell**, and set the channel fader to **-5.7 dB**
- Select track 34, **Ocean Waves Modular**, and set the channel fader to **-7.2 dB**
- Select track 35, **Warped Pluck**, and set the channel fader to **-3.6 dB**
- Select track 36, **Luminous Tines**, and set the channel fader to **-1.1 dB**
- Select track 37, **Noise Sweep**, and set the channel fader to **-14.4 dB**

After setting the appropriate volume levels for each track, next, we will review how to set panning for each track.

Setting panning for each track

Next, we will go over all the tracks and set up an approximate panning level, to better place each sound in the stereo field.

By default, the pan knob on the channel strip is set to **Balance**. We will change the pan knob settings to **Stereo Pan**. To do that, right-click (or press *Ctrl* and click) on the pan knob and select **Stereo Pan** from the pop-up window:

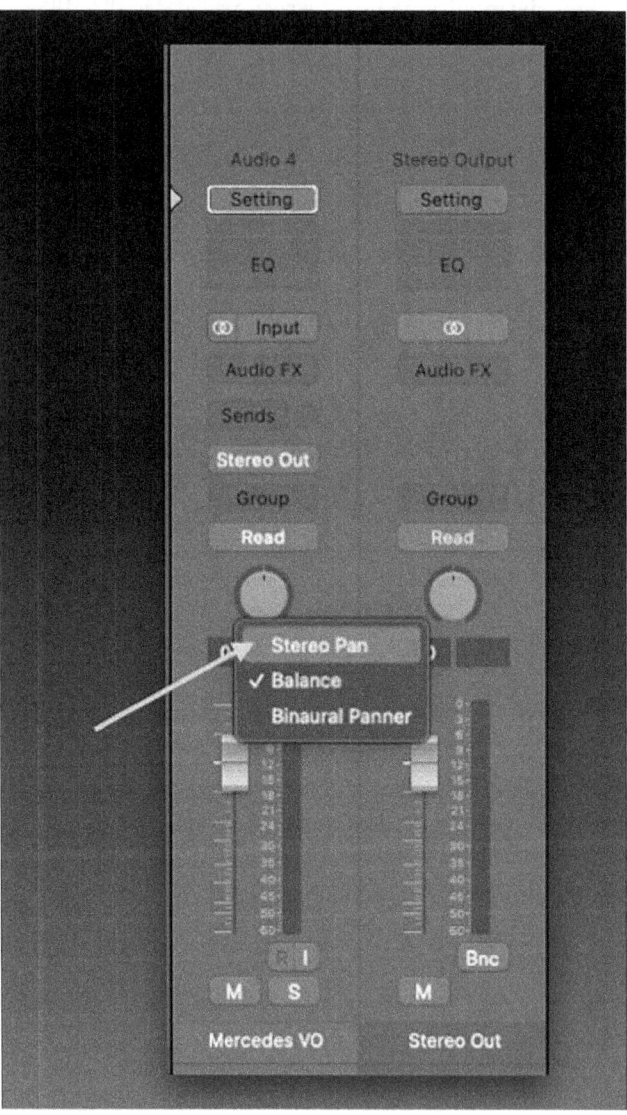

Figure 11.3: Logic Pro pan knob pop-up window

Logic Pro now displays a **Stereo Pan**, indicated by a green ring around the pan knob:

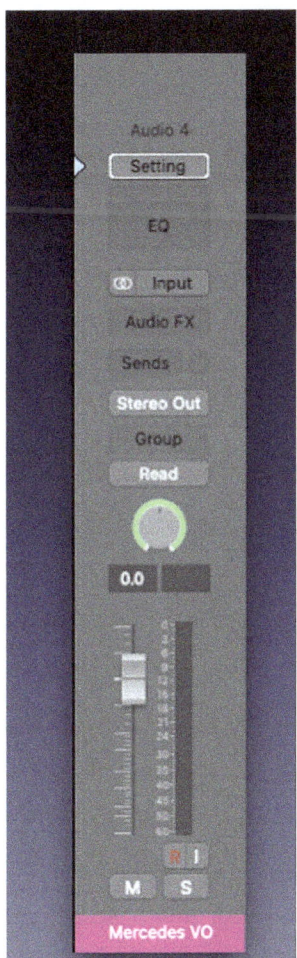

Figure 11.4: Logic Pro channel strip with Stereo Pan visible

Next, go through all the channel strips and set each track's panning setting accordingly:

- Select track 1, **Mercedes VO**, change it to **Stereo Pan**, and set it at the center
- Select track 2, **Garden Sanctuary**, change it to **Stereo Pan**, and set it at the center
- Select track 3, **Forest**, change it to **Stereo Pan**, and set it at the center
- Select track 4, **Naked Wurly**, change it to **Stereo Pan**, and set it at the center
- Select track 5, **Choir-Female-Oh**, change it to **Stereo Pan**, and set it to **-18**

- Select track 6, **Modwheel Sizzler**, change it to **Stereo Pan**, and set it to **+15**
- Select track 7, **Fireflies**, change it to **Stereo Pan**, and set it at the center
- Select track 8, **Outer Lands Synth**, change it to **Stereo Pan**, and set it at the center
- Select track 9, **Slow Breaths**, change it to **Stereo Pan**, and set it to **-13**
- Select track 10, **Carbon Particles**, change it to **Stereo Pan**, and set it to **+16**
- Select track 11, **Pulsed Pad**, change it to **Stereo Pan**, and set it to **-18**
- Select track 12, **Ghostly Reversed Organ**, change it to **Stereo Pan**, and set it at the center
- Select track 13, **Lost Reverse**, change it to **Stereo Pan**, and set it to **-19**
- Select track 14, **Floating Plasma**, change it to **Stereo Pan**, and set it to **+13**
- Select track 15, **Lost Reverse**, change it to **Stereo Pan**, and set it to **-13dB**
- Select track 16, **Metallic Memories Bowl**, change it to **Stereo Pan**, and set it to **-19**
- Select track 17, **Stratosphere**, change it to **Stereo Pan**, and set it at the center
- Select track 18, **Light Harmonics**, change it to **Stereo Pan**, and set it to **-18**
- Select track 19, **Lonely Voyage**, change it to **Stereo Pan**, and set it to **+12**
- Select track 20, **Orbiting Jupiter**, change it to **Stereo Pan**, and set it to **-19**
- Select track 21, **Infinity Strings**, change it to **Stereo Pan**, and set it at the center
- Select track 22, **Bass Patterns**, change it to **Stereo Pan**, and set it at the center
- Select track 23, **Slow Drift**, change it to **Stereo Pan**, and set it to **-19**
- Select track 24, **Chill Vocal Sequences**, change it to **Stereo Pan**, and set it at the center
- Select track 25, **Tektonic Grooves**, change it to **Stereo Pan**, and set it at the center
- Select track 26, **Structural Glitch**, change it to **Stereo Pan**, and set it at the center
- Select track 27, **Evolving Currents**, change it to **Stereo Pan**, and set it to **-22**
- Select track 28, **Lyrical Synth**, change it to **Stereo Pan**, and set it to **-14**
- Select track 29, **Lyrical Synth**, change it to **Stereo Pan**, and set it to **+22**
- Select track 30, **Dream Dancer**, change it to **Stereo Pan**, and set it to **-4**
- Select track 31, **Old Fragile Vinyl Keys**, change it to **Stereo Pan**, and set it to **+15**
- Select track 32, **Fog Machine**, change it to **Stereo Pan**, and set it at the center
- Select track 33, **Cymbal Swell**, change it to **Stereo Pan**, and set it at the center
- Select track 34, **Ocean Waves Modular**, change it to **Stereo Pan**, and set it to **-19**

- Select track 35, **Warped Pluck**, change it to **Stereo Pan**, and set it at the center
- Select track 36, **Luminous Tines**, change it to **Stereo Pan**, and set it to **-21**
- Select track 37, **Noise Sweep**, change it to **Stereo Pan**, and set it to **+12**

Now that we've set up where the sound needs to be in the stereo field, next, we will review how to further work on the sound by shaping it and then finalizing the basic mix.

Shaping the sound and finalizing the basic mix

In this section, we will focus on how to shape or customize each instrument one at a time and also make them sound better in a group of instruments. In general, it's good practice to listen to sounds with other sounds together, to make them blend with one another. We will apply this technique here to make sure the final sound mix supports the commercial.

We will explore how to modify and enhance each sound, as we go track by track, applying basic EQ, compression, reverb, and additional volume automation as needed.

So, on track 2, **Garden Sanctuary**, turn off **Channel EQ**. Then, open the second **Compressor** plugin and change the **Makeup** gain to **4.0 dB**:

Figure 11.5: Logic Pro Compressor

314   Shaping the Score and Exporting to Video

You will see that currently, **Bus 4** is not sending any of the channel strip signal to the AUX track:

Figure 11.6: Logic Pro channel strip

Now, we will insert a reverb effect on the AUX bus. To start, open the **Mix** window (the *X* shortcut), then scroll over to the AUX of track 10 and insert a reverb effect. As you can see on the **Mix** window, the corresponding **Bus 4** is not affected.

Next, to insert an effect, hover your mouse over the AUX of track 10 and select the first slot. Then, hover over the slot and select **Reverb** | **Space Designer** | **Stereo** from the drop-down menu:

Figure 11.7: Logic Pro channel strip drop-down menu

Then, open the **Reverb** plugin on the AUX of track 10 and change **Wet Signal** to **-6.4 dB**:

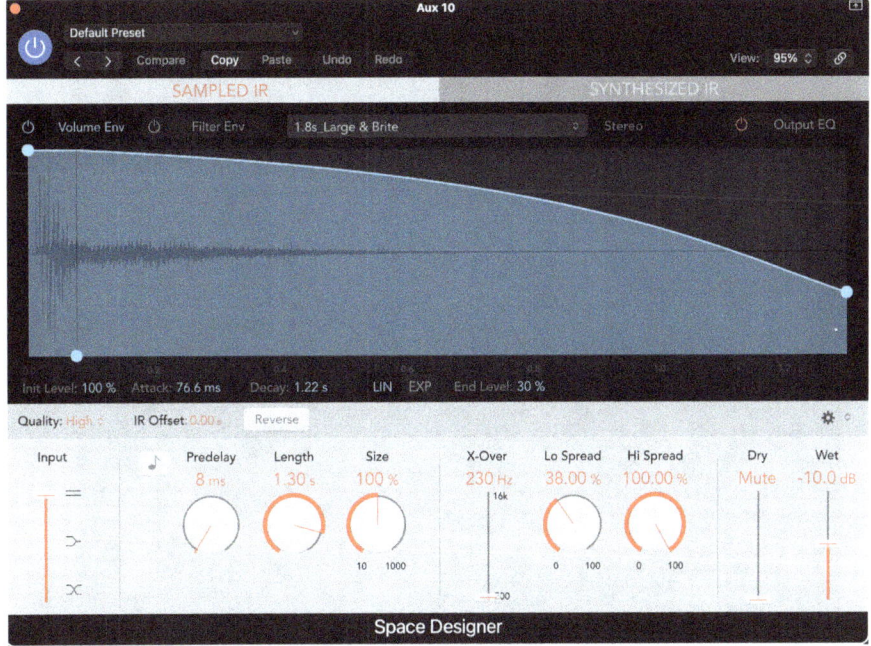

Figure 11.8: Logic Pro Reverb plugin

Next, on track 2, increase the **Send** level to **-9.3 dB** (that's all we will do on this track).

On track 3, **Forest**, click on the **EQ** slot to open the **EQ** plugin. Since the **Forest** effect doesn't need much of the low-end, we'll use the **High-Pass Filter (HPF)** and cut until about **1380 Hz**, like so:

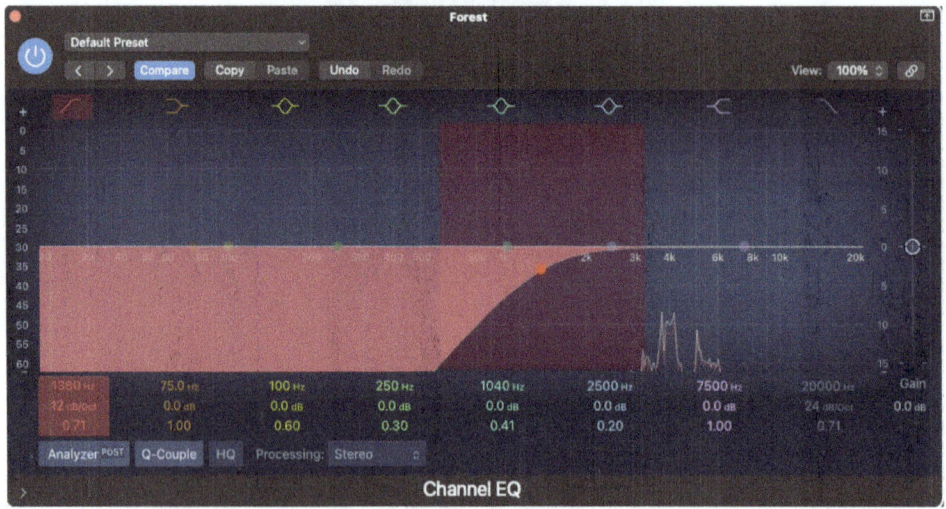

Figure 11.9: Logic Pro EQ plugin

On track 4, **Naked Wurly**, click on the **Compressor** plugin and change the **Makeup** gain to **5.0 dB**:

Figure 11.10: Logic Pro Compressor

Additionally, we will add an **EQ** plugin using **HPF** by cutting at **116 Hz**, like so:

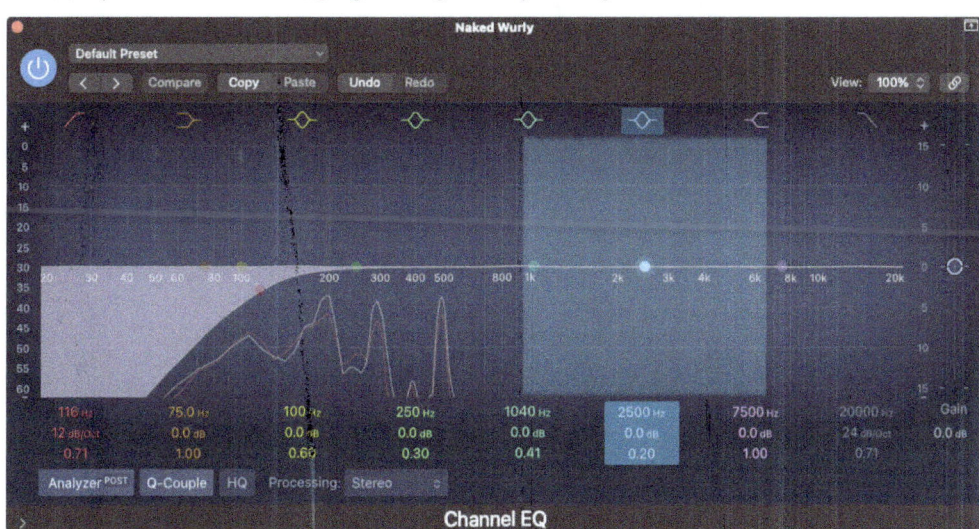

Figure 11.11: Logic Pro EQ plugin

Next, insert **Bus 4** on this channel strip and send **-13.5 dB** to the **Reverb** bus. Then, turn on the **Tape Delay** plugin and keep the default settings on:

Figure 11.12: Logic Pro Tape Delay

On track 5, **Choir Female-Oh**, insert an **EQ** plugin with the **HPF** setting by cutting **312 Hz**:

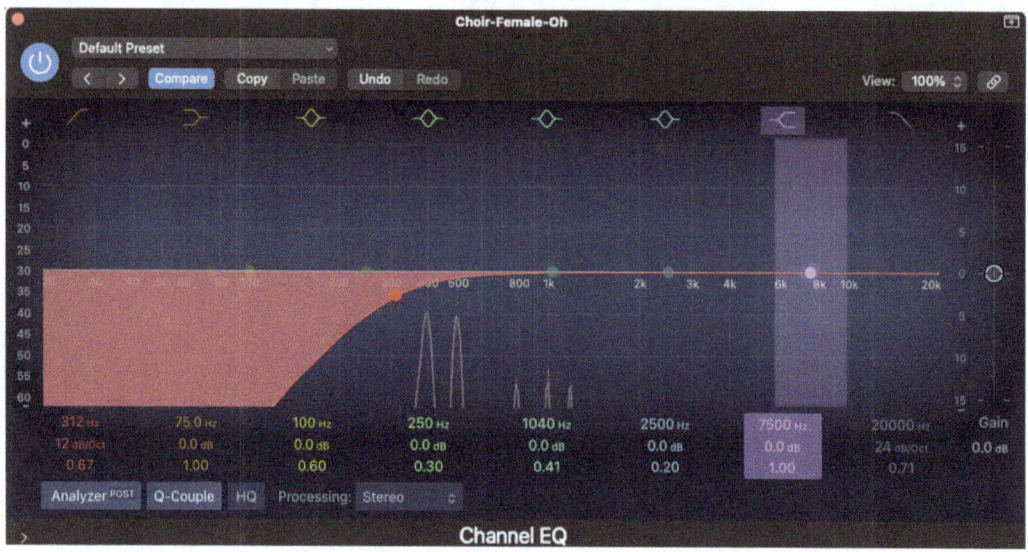

Figure 11.13: Logic Pro EQ plugin

Insert **Bus 4** on this channel strip and send **-8.2 dB** on that bus. Then, change the **Makeup** gain to **5 dB**:

Figure 11.14: Logic Pro Compressor

On track 6, **Modwheel Sizzler**, insert an **EQ** plugin and use **HPF** with a **125 Hz** cut:

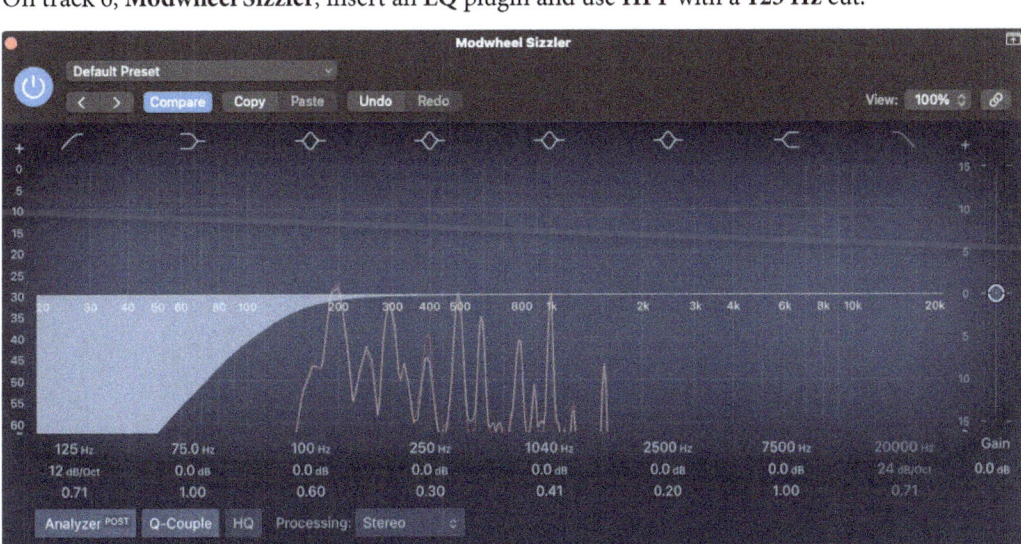

Figure 11.15: Logic Pro EQ plugin

On track 7, **Fireflies**, turn off the **Pedalboard** plugin and insert an **EQ** plugin. Then, use **HPF** with a **262 Hz** cut:

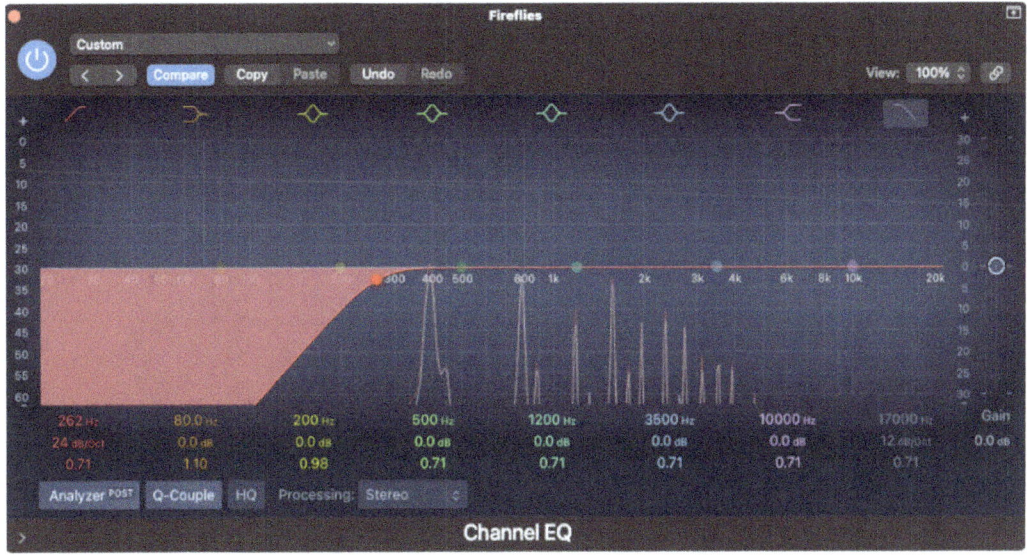

Figure 11.16: Logic Pro EQ plugin

On track 8, **Outer Lands Synth**, double-click on the **Alchemy** synth, go to the **Advanced** section, and turn off source **B**:

Figure 11.17: Logic Pro Alchemy

Next, insert **Bus 4** to send a portion of the signal channel to the **Reverb** bus and set it to **-6.8 dB**.

On the AUX of track 11, insert the **Classic VCA Compressor** plugin with its default settings:

Figure 11.18: Logic Pro Compressor

Add **Bus 3** to send a portion of the channel strip's signal and set the bus volume level to **-10.1 dB**. Then, insert an **EQ** plugin, and use **HPF** with a **137 Hz** cut:

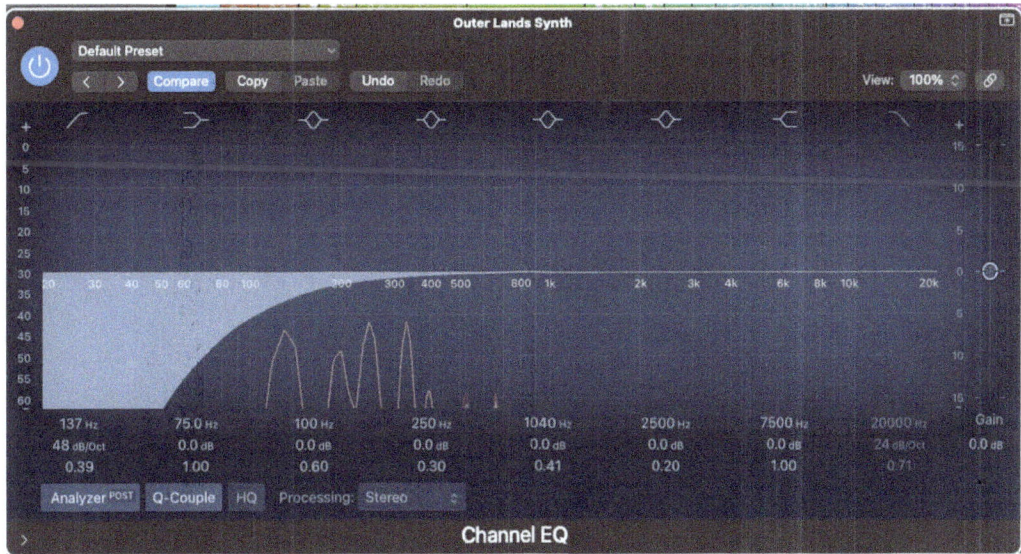

Figure 11.19: Logic Pro EQ plugin

On track 9, **Slow Breaths**, insert an **EQ** plugin and use **HPF** with a **280 Hz** cut:

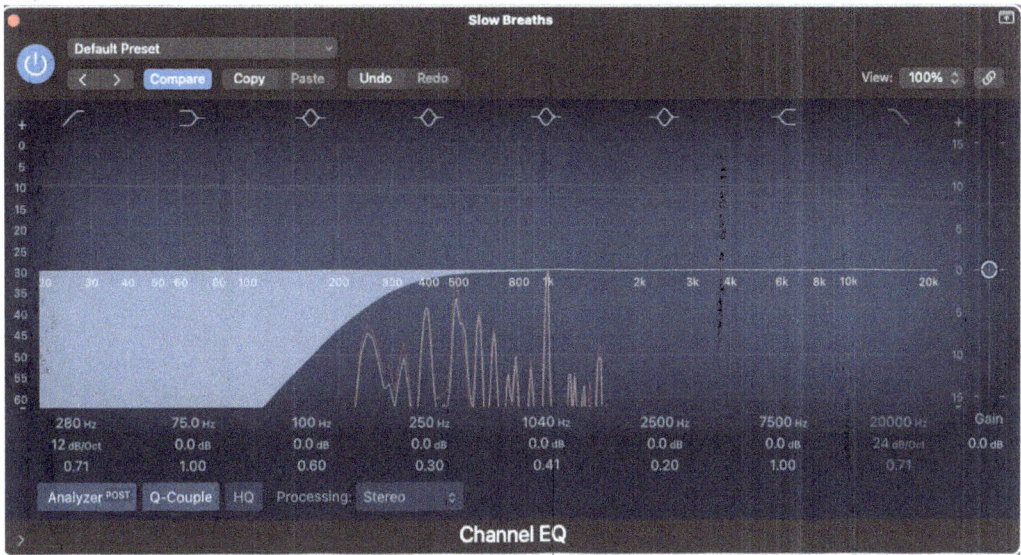

Figure 11.20: Logic Pro EQ plugin

Next, insert **Bus 3** with a volume level of **-9.9 dB**, and then add **Bus 4**, setting it to **-11.1 dB**.

On track 10, **Carbon Particles**, open the **Alchemy** synth, click on the **Advanced** settings, and turn off source **A**:

Figure 11.21: Logic Pro Alchemy

Next, insert **Bus 3** and set it to **-8.7 dB**. Then, click on the **EQ** plugin and make additional changes in the **Low-Pass Filter (LPF)** by cutting at **2020 Hz** and adding an **HPF** by cutting at **306 Hz**, like so:

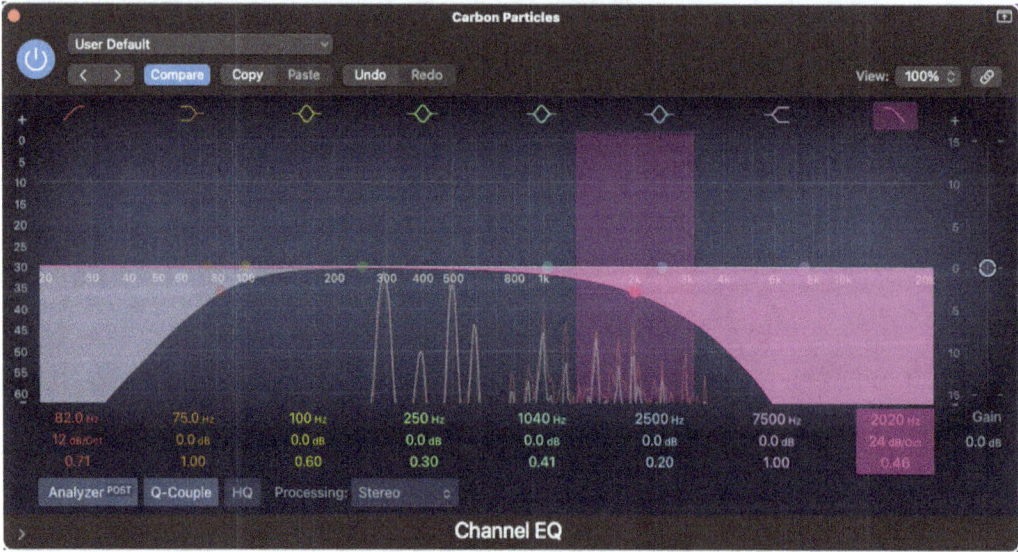

Figure 11.22: Logic Pro EQ plugin

On track 11, **Pulsed Pad**, use the *A* shortcut to open **Automation**. Change **Track Automation** to **Region Automation**. Then, add a volume point starting at the bottom of the MIDI region and another volume point of **-9.8 dB** at **Bar 11 4 2 92**:

Figure 11.23: Logic Pro Region Automation

Next, click on the **EQ** plugin and make additional changes in the **HPF** by cutting at **306 Hz** and in the **LPF** by cutting at **5400 Hz**, like so:

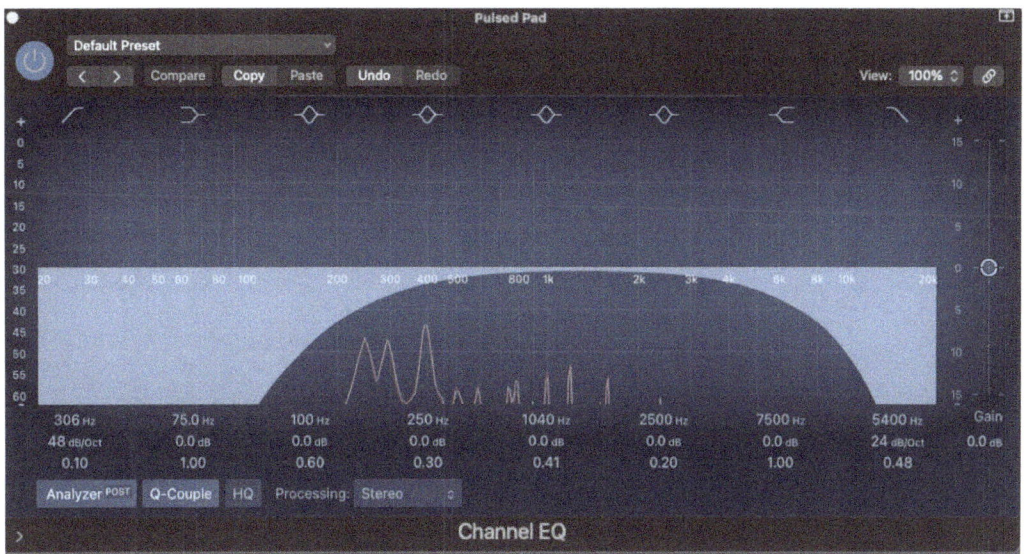

Figure 11.24: Logic Pro EQ plugin

Then, insert **Bus 3** and set it to **-11.7 dB**.

On track 12, **Ghostly Reversed Organ**, click on the **EQ** plugin and make an additional change in the **HPF** by cutting at **130 Hz**, like so:

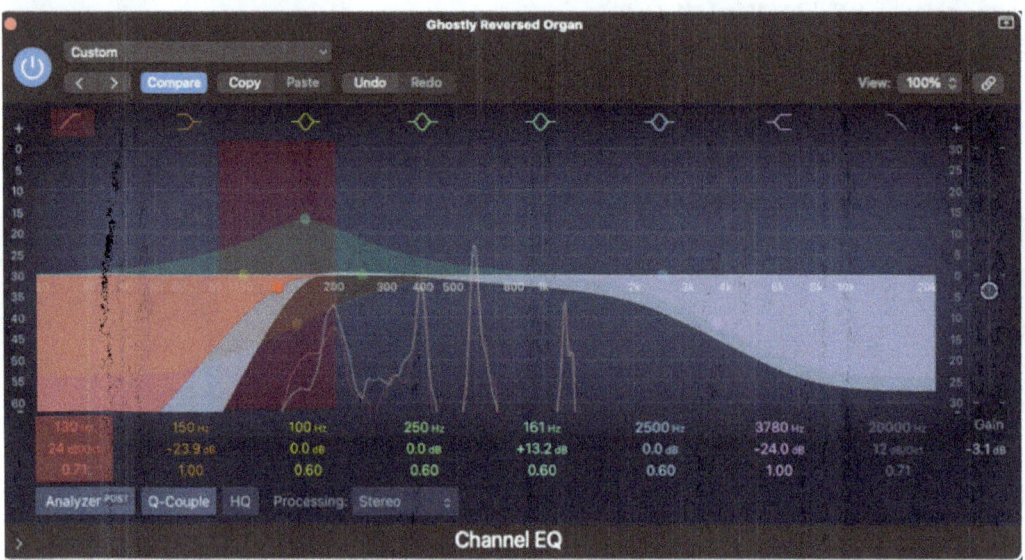

Figure 11.25: Logic Pro EQ plugin

Next, on this track, add a **Tremolo** plugin. Then, change **Rate** to **1/8**, the **Smoothing** setting to **59%**, **Depth** to **83%**, and **Phase** to **0** degrees:

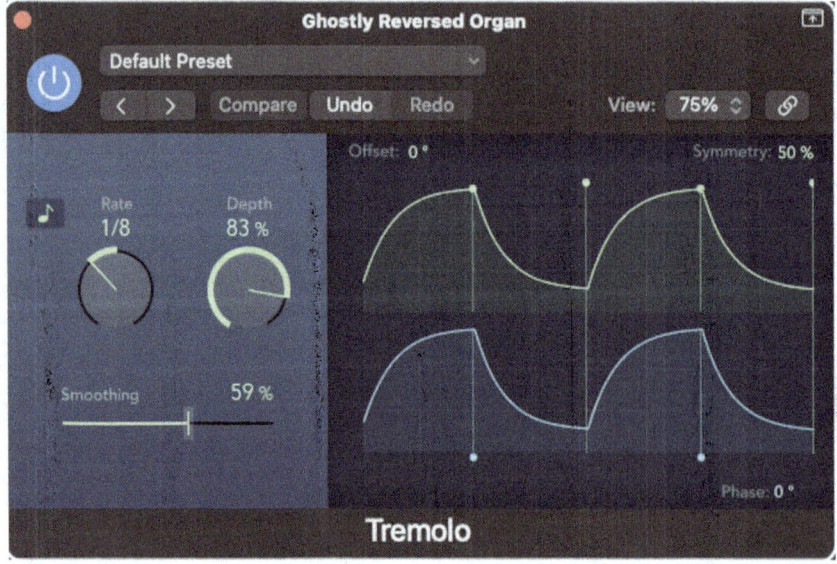

Figure 11.26: Logic Pro Tremolo plugin

On track 13, **Lost Reverse**, click on the **EQ** plugin and add an **HPF** by cutting at **172 Hz**, like so:

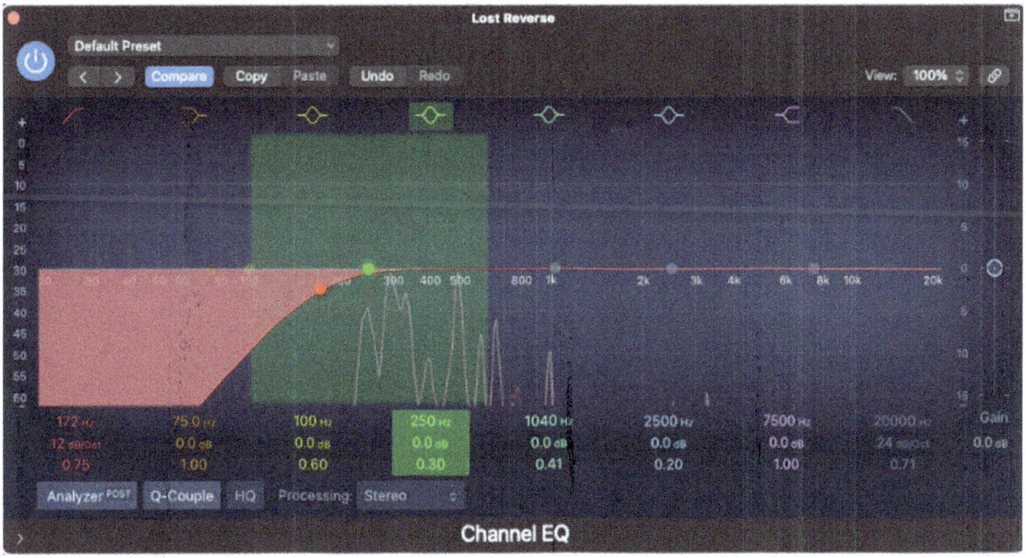

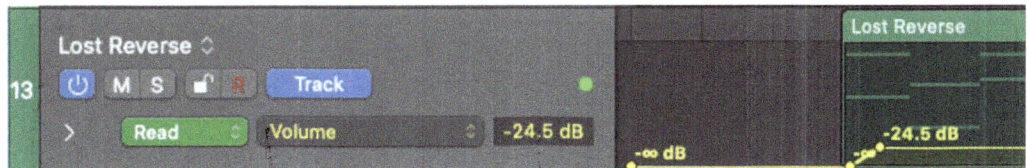

Figure 11.27: Logic Pro EQ plugin

Insert **Bus 3** with a volume level of **-13.4 dB**, then add **Bus 4** and set it to **-9.8 dB**. Then, inset a gradual volume automation at the beginning of the region.

Figure 11.28: Logic Pro Track Automation

On track 14, **Floating Plasma**, click on the **EQ** plugin and add an **HPF** by cutting at **214 Hz**, like so:

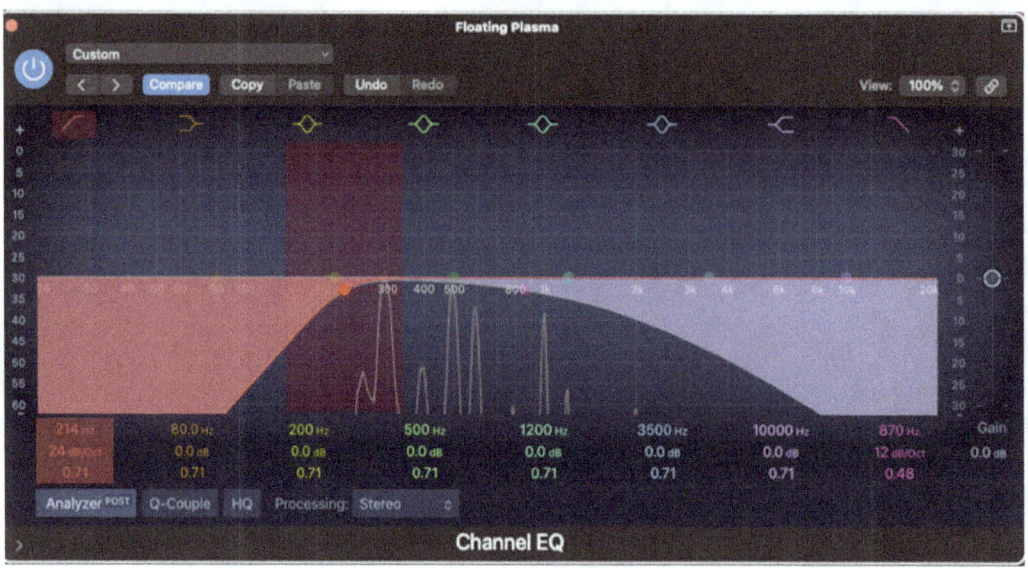

Figure 11.29: Logic Pro EQ plugin

Next, add **Bus 4** and set it to **-6.6 dB**.

On track 15, **Lost Reverse**, click on the **EQ** plugin and add an **HPF** by cutting at **236 Hz**, like so:

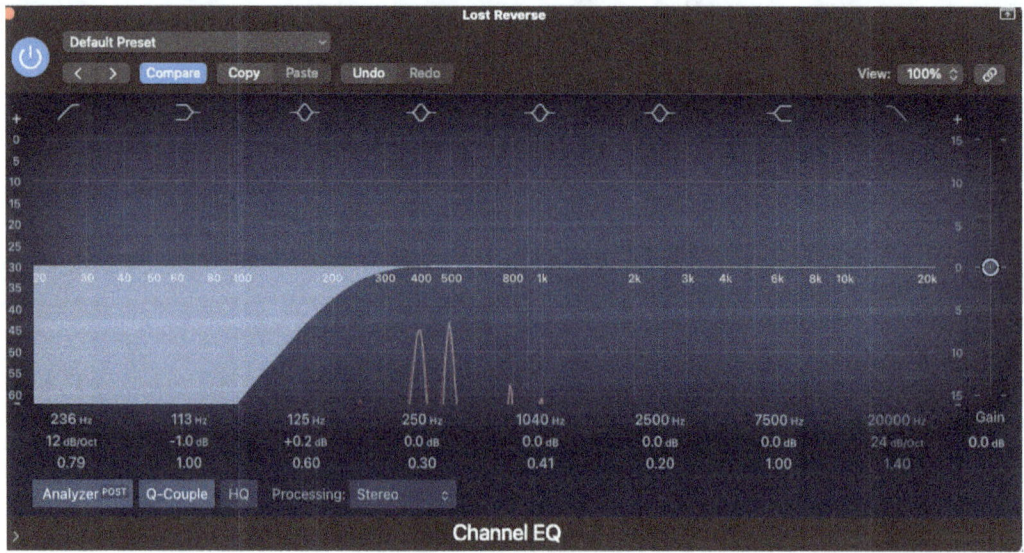

Figure 11.30: Logic Pro EQ plugin

On track 16, **Metallic Memories Bowl**, click on the **EQ** plugin and add an **HPF** by cutting at **248 Hz**, and an **LPF** by cutting at **1090 Hz**, like so:

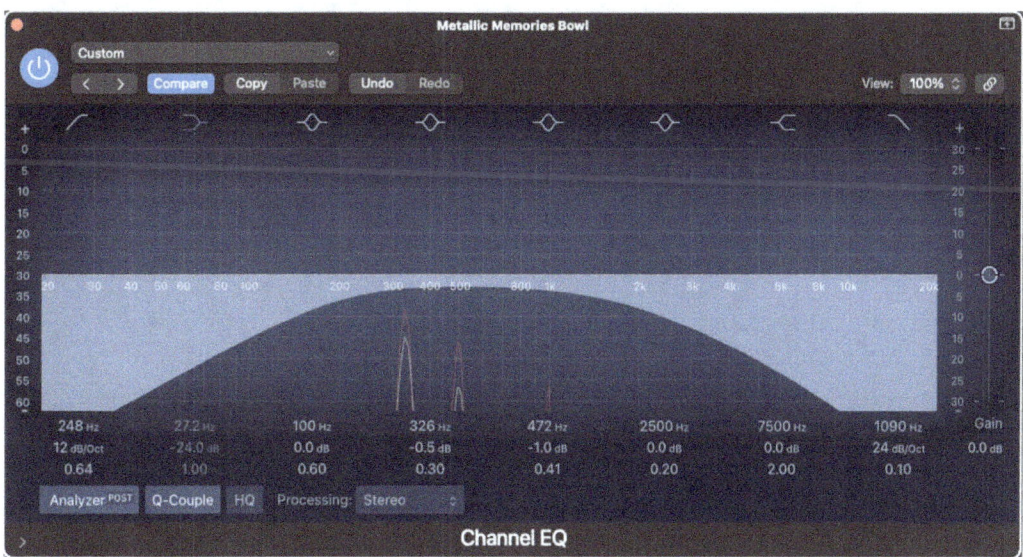

Figure 11.31: Logic Pro EQ plugin

Then, set **Bus 6** to **-6.3 dB**.

On track 17, **Stratosphere**, click on the **EQ** plugin and add an **HPF** by cutting at **244 Hz**, like so:

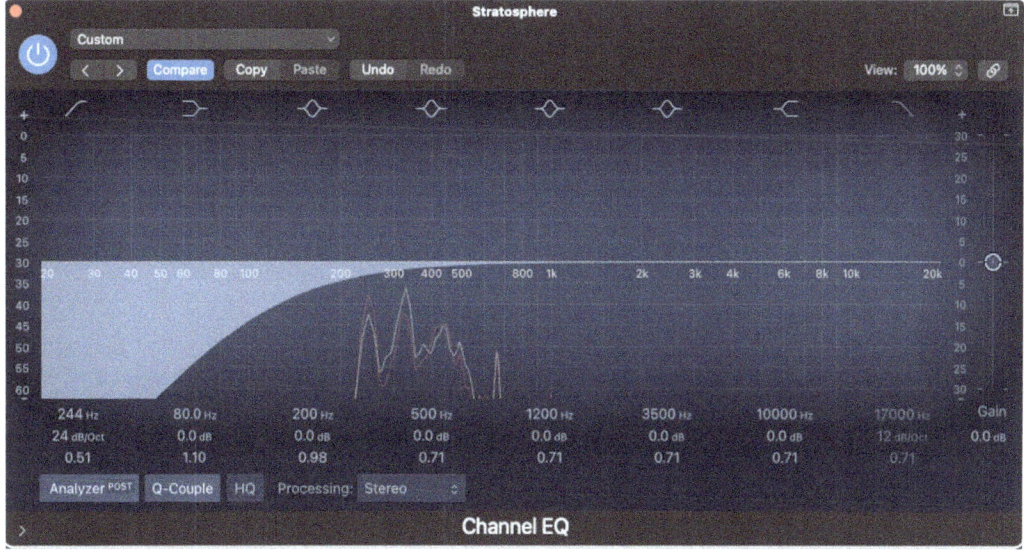

Figure 11.32: Logic Pro EQ plugin

On track 18, **Light Harmonics**, click on the **EQ** plugin and add an **HPF** by cutting at **161 Hz**, like so:

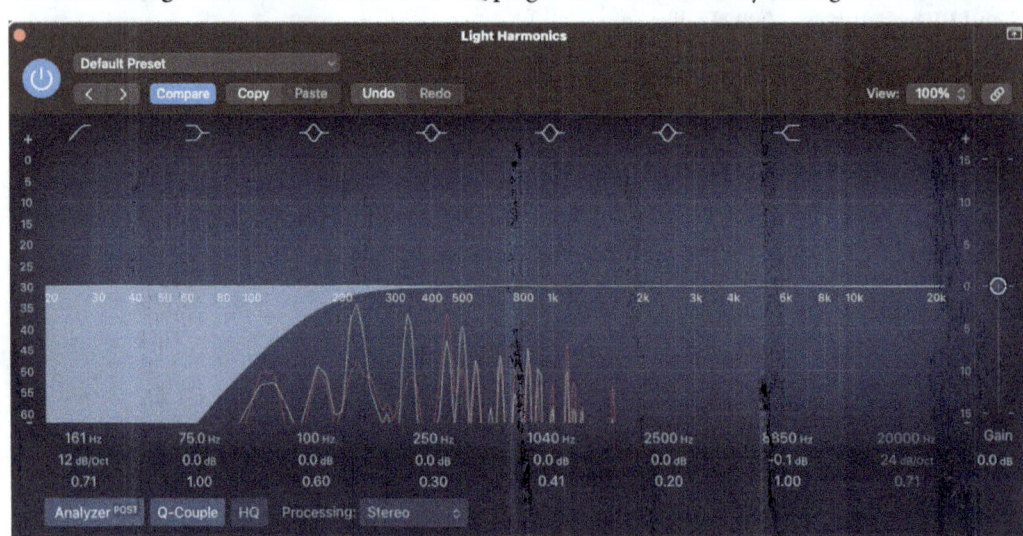

Figure 11.33: Logic Pro EQ plugin

Then, insert **Bus 3** and set it to **-16.8 dB**. Also, add **Bus 4** and set it to **-18.8 dB**.

On track 19, **Lonely Voyage**, click on the **EQ** plugin and add an **HPF** by cutting at **324 Hz** and an **LPF** by cutting at **1520 Hz**, like so:

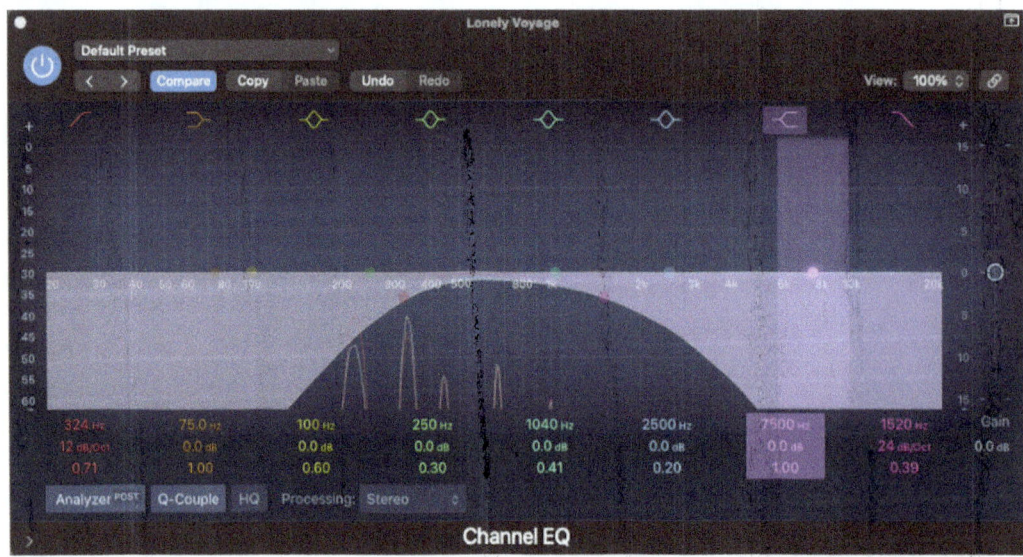

Figure 11.34: Logic Pro EQ plugin

Then, insert **Bus 3** and set it to **-9.5 dB**.

On track 20, **Orbiting Jupiter**, click on the **EQ** plugin and add an **HPF** by cutting at **164 Hz**, like so:

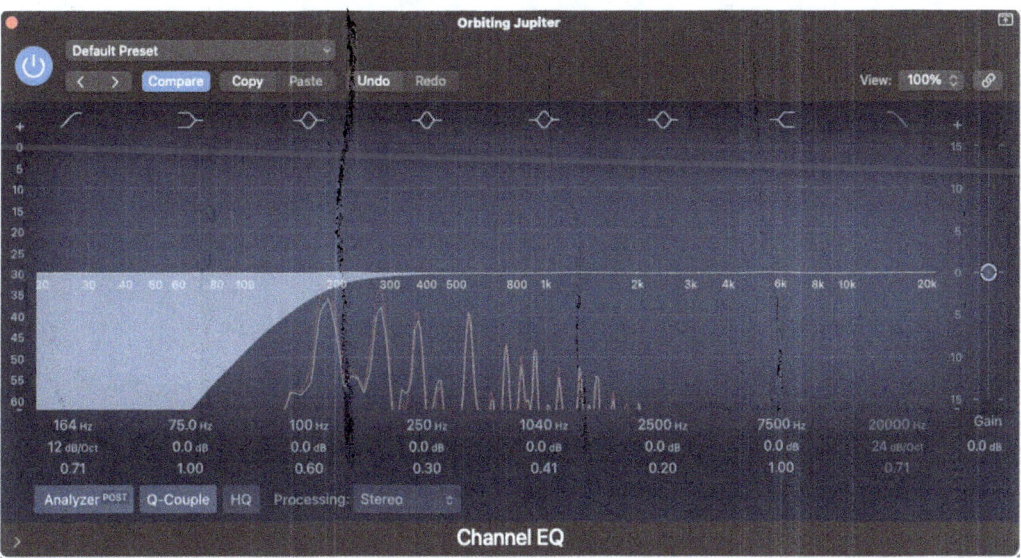

Figure 11.35: Logic Pro EQ plugin

Then, insert **Bus 3** and set it to **-21.4 dB**. Also, add **Bus 4** and set it to **-21.1 dB**.

On track 21, **Infinity Strings**, click on the **EQ** plugin and add an **HPF** by cutting at **300 Hz**, like so:

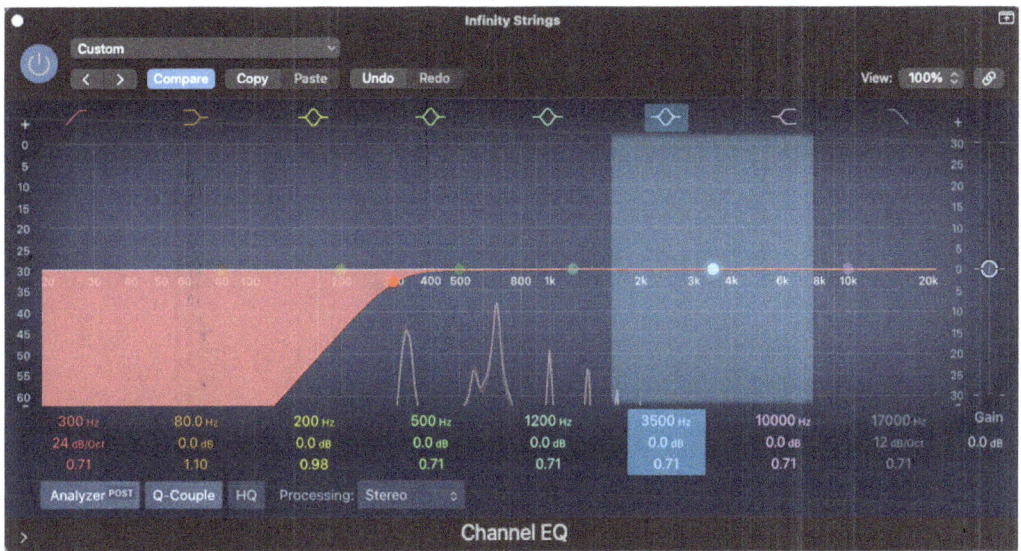

Figure 11.36: Logic Pro EQ plugin

On track 22, **Bass Patterns**, click on the **EQ** plugin and add an **HPF** by cutting at **75.5 Hz**, like so:

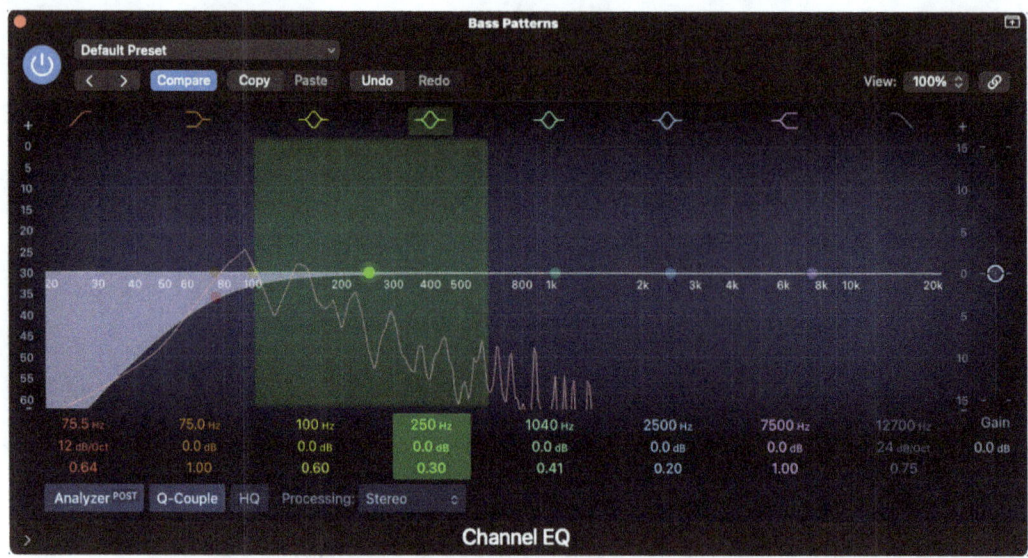

Figure 11.37: Logic Pro EQ plugin

Then, insert a **Compressor** and, from the **Preset** menu, select **03 Guitars | Direct Bass**:

Figure 11.38: Logic Pro Compressor

On track 23, **Slow Drift**, click on the **EQ** plugin and add an **HPF** by cutting at **75.5 Hz**, like so:

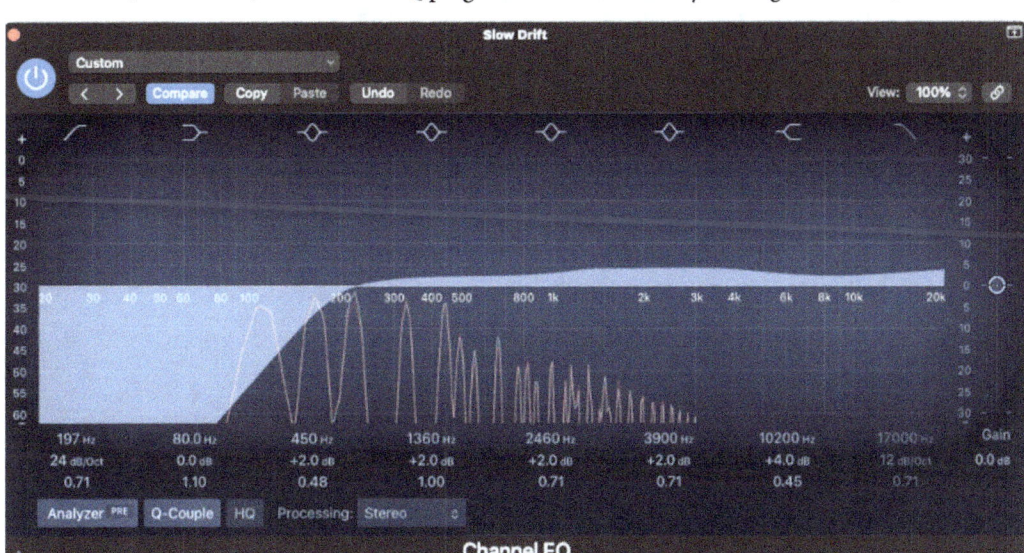

Figure 11.39: Logic Pro EQ plugin

Then, set **Bus 8** to **-9.8 dB**, then add **Bus 2**, and set it to **-5.7 dB**.

On track 24, **Chill Vocal Sequences**, click on the **EQ** plugin, then add an **HPF** by cutting at **480 Hz** and an **LPF** by cutting at **9200 Hz**, like so:

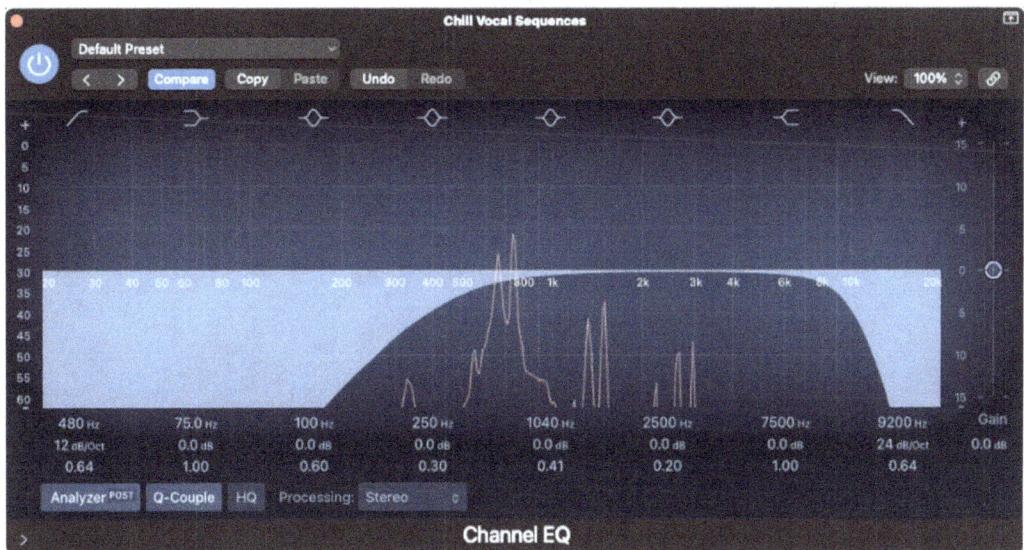

Figure 11.40: Logic Pro EQ plugin

On track 25, **Tektonic Grooves**, click on the **EQ** plugin and select **01 Drums | Clean Up Kick** from the **Preset** drop-down menu, like so:

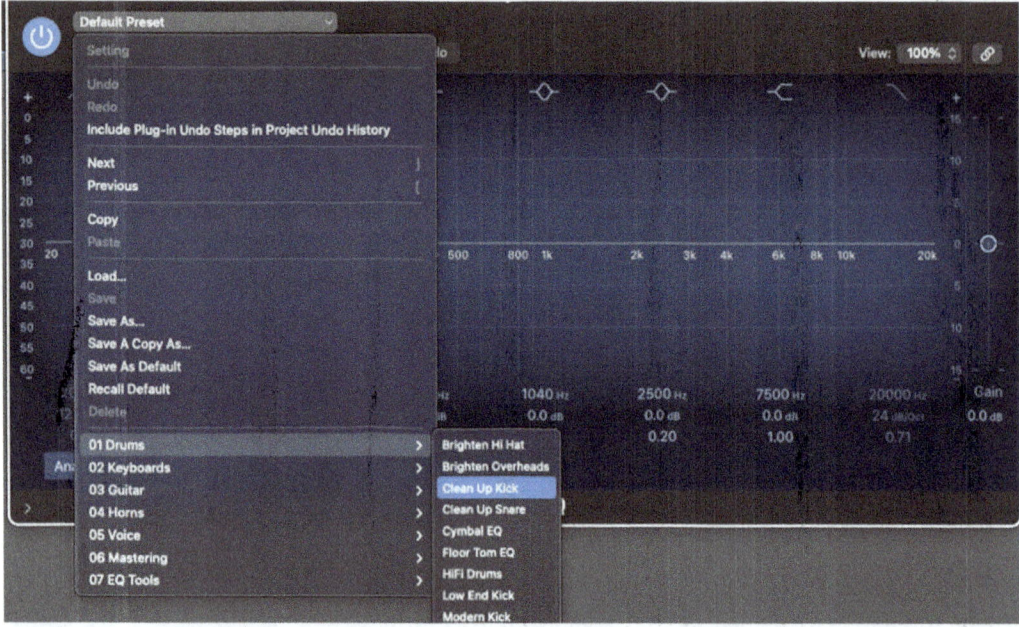

Figure 11.41: Logic Pro EQ preset menu

Logic Pro will then load the EQ preset, **Clean Up Kick**:

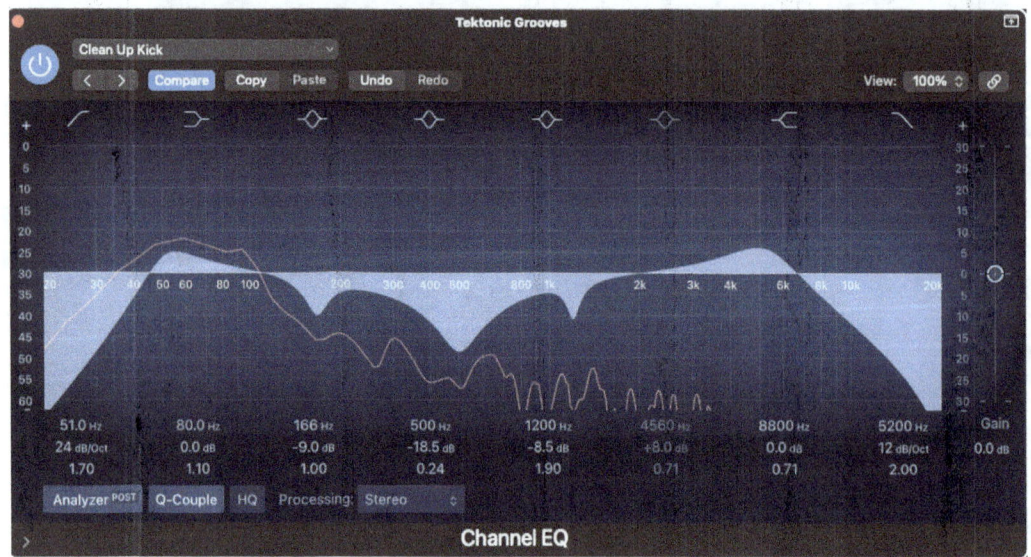

Figure 11.42: Logic Pro EQ plugin

Next, add a **Compressor** and, from the **Preset** menu, select **01 Drums | Rock Kick**:

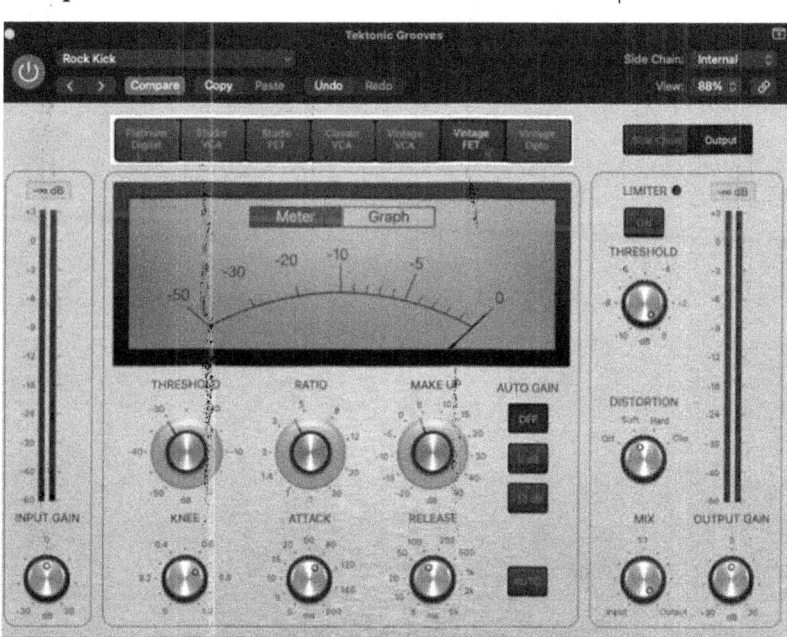

Figure 11.43: Logic Pro Compressor

Then, open the **Alchemy** synth, click on the **ADVANCED** tab, and just keep source **A** on:

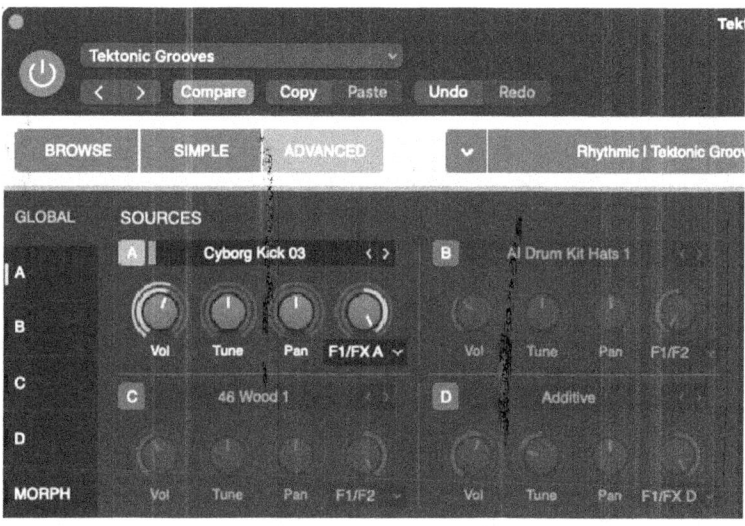

Figure 11.44: Logic Pro Alchemy

On track 26, **Structural Glitch**, click on the **EQ** plugin and select **01 Drums | Rock Kick Drum** from the **Preset** menu. Also, add an **HPF** by cutting at **54.0 Hz**, like so:

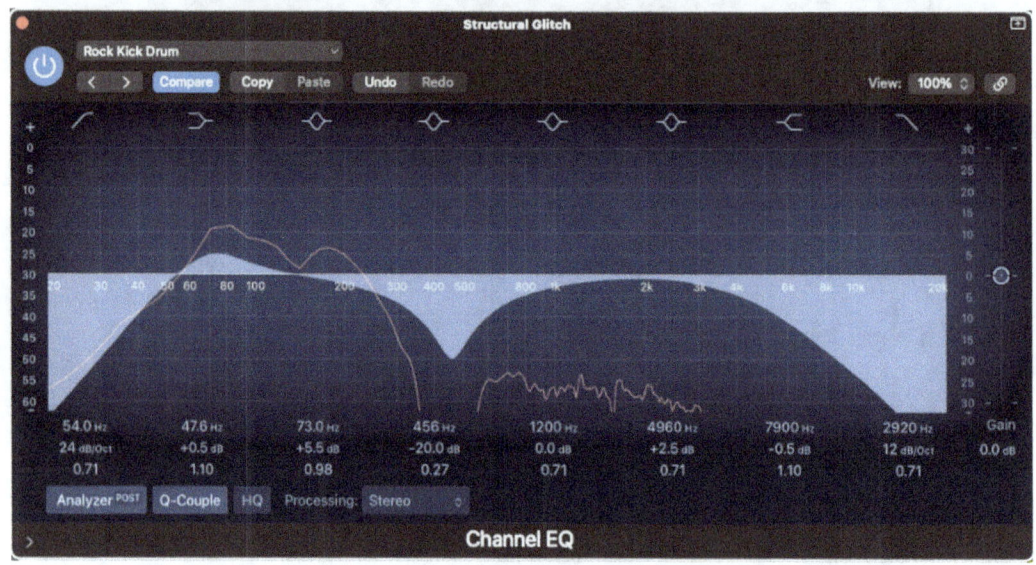

Figure 11.45: Logic Pro EQ plugin

Then, open the **Alchemy** synth, click on the **Advanced** tab, and just keep source **D** on:

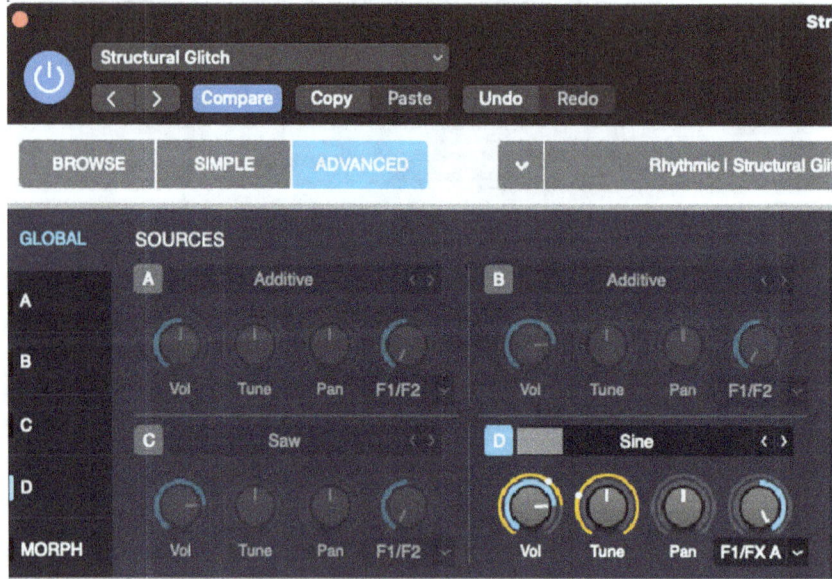

Figure 11.46: Logic Pro Alchemy

On track 27, **Evolving Currents**, click on the **EQ** plugin and select **02 Keyboards | Synth Lead Presence** from the **Preset** menu. Also, add an **HPF** by cutting at **232 Hz**, like so:

Figure 11.47: Logic Pro EQ plugin

Then, add **Bus 3** and set it to **-14.5 dB**.

On track 28, **Lyrical Synth**, click on the **EQ** plugin and select **02 Keyboards | Synth Lead** from the **Preset** menu. Also, add an **HPF** by cutting at **645 Hz**, like so:

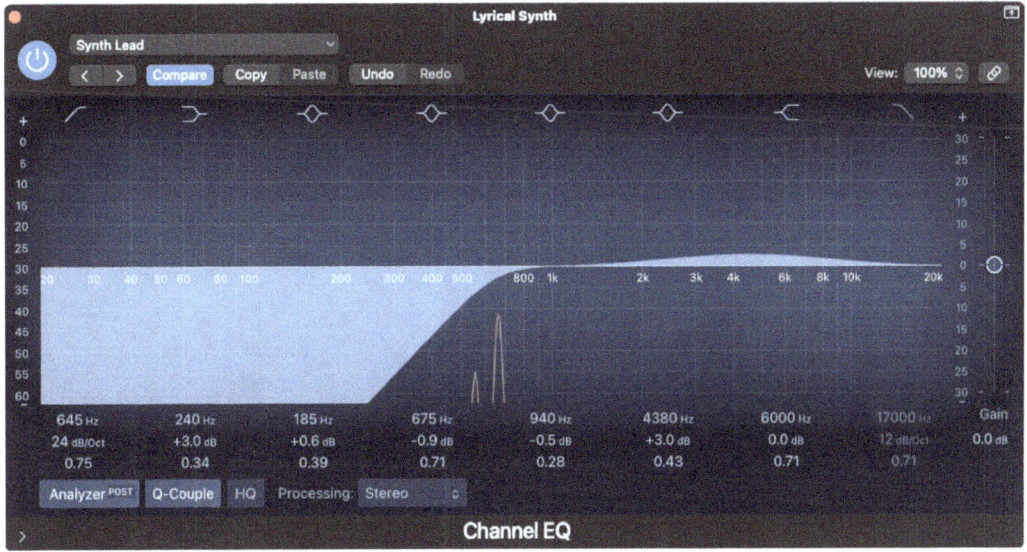

Figure 11.48: Logic Pro EQ plugin

Then, set **Bus 2** to **-15.1 dB**.

On track 29, **Lyrical Synth**, click on the **EQ** plugin and select **02 Keyboards | Synth Lead Presence** from the **Preset** menu, like so:

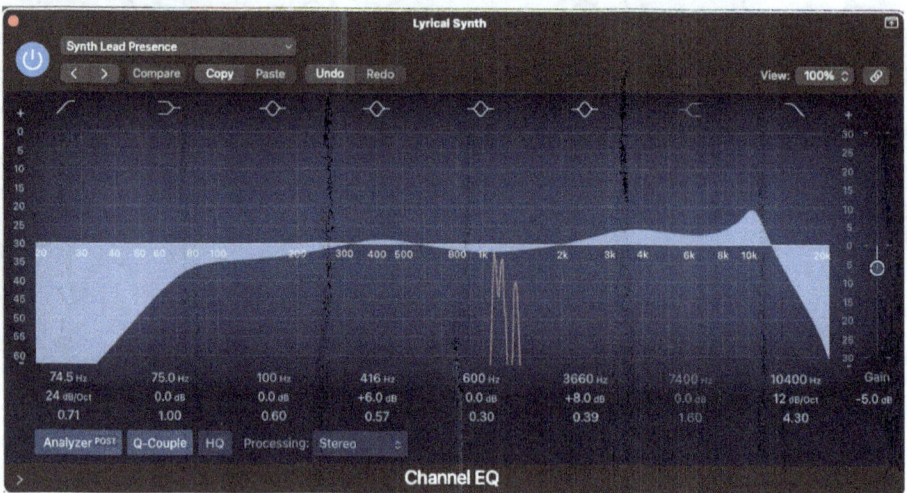

Figure 11.49: Logic Pro EQ plugin

Then, add **Bus 4** and set it to **-15.1 dB**.

On track 30, **Dream Dancer**, add **Bus 4** and set it to **-11.7 dB**.

On track 31, **Old Fragile Vinyl Keys**, click on the **EQ** plugin and select **02 Keyboards | Synth Lead Presence** from the **Preset** menu, like so:

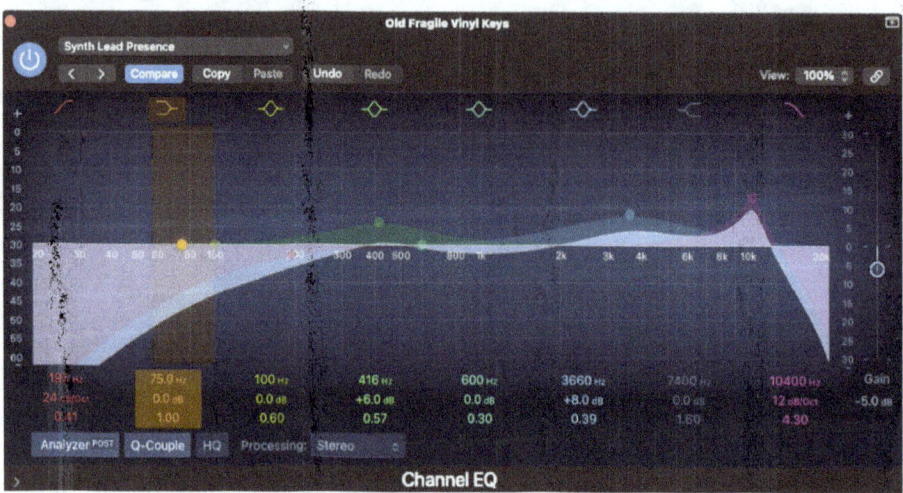

Figure 11.50: Logic Pro EQ plugin

Then, open the **Alchemy** synth, click on the **Advanced** tab, and just keep sources **A** and **B** open:

Figure 11.51: Logic Pro Alchemy

On track 32, **Fog Machine**, add **Bus 3** and set it to **-6.3 dB**.

On track 33, **Cymbal Swell**, click on the **EQ** plugin and select **01 Drums | Cymbal EQ** from the **Preset** menu. Also, add an **HPF** by cutting at **630 Hz** and an **LPF** by cutting at **3900 Hz**, like so:

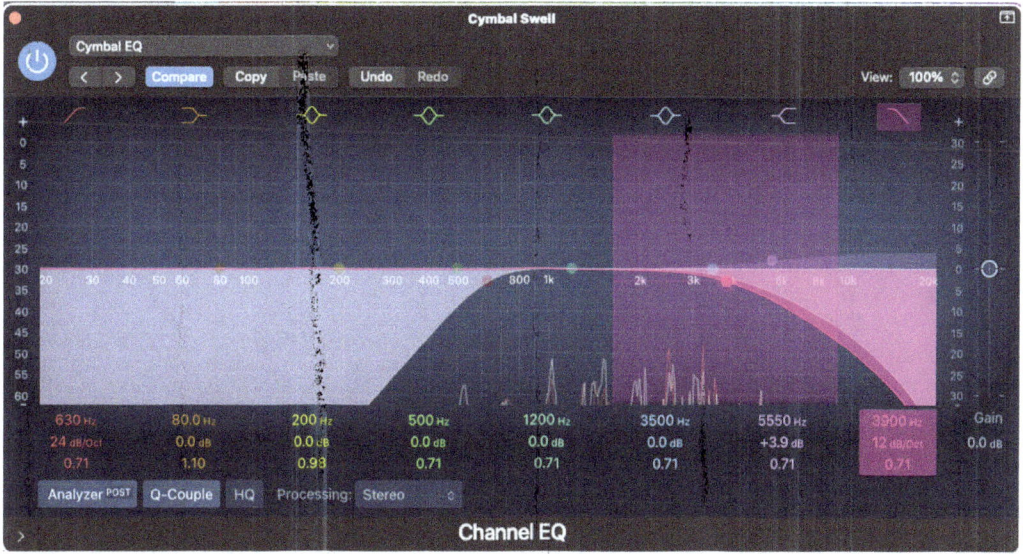

Figure 11.52: Logic Pro EQ plugin

On track 34, **Ocean Waves Modular**, click on the **EQ** plugin and add an **HPF** by cutting at **635 Hz** and a **High-Shelf Filter (HSF)** by boosting at **9900 Hz**, like so:

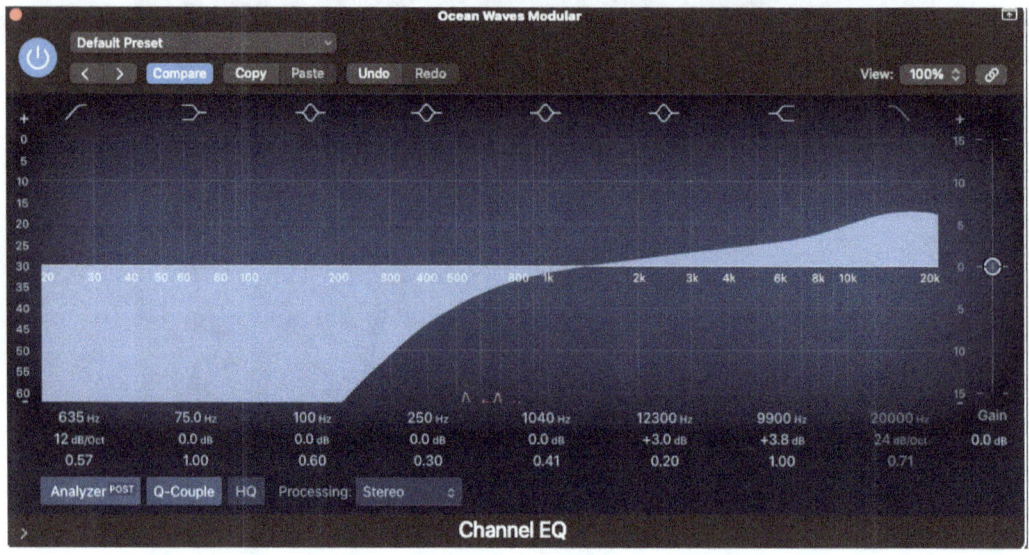

Figure 11.53: Logic Pro EQ plugin

Then, add **Bus 3** and set it to **-4.4 dB**.

On track 35, **Warped Pluck**, click on the **EQ** plugin and select **03 Guitars | Acoustic Rhythm Guitar** from the **Preset** menu:

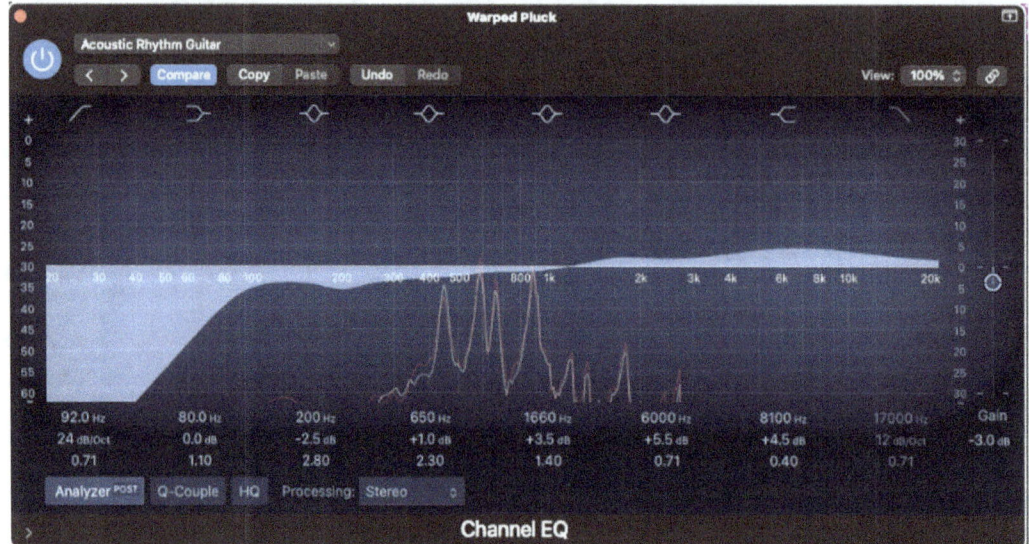

Figure 11.54: Logic Pro EQ plugin

Then, add **Bus 4** and set it to **-14.5 dB**.

On track 36, **Luminous Tines**, click on the **EQ** plugin and select **02 Keyboards | Clean Up Organ** from the **Preset** menu. Also, add an **HPF** by cutting at **140 Hz**, like so:

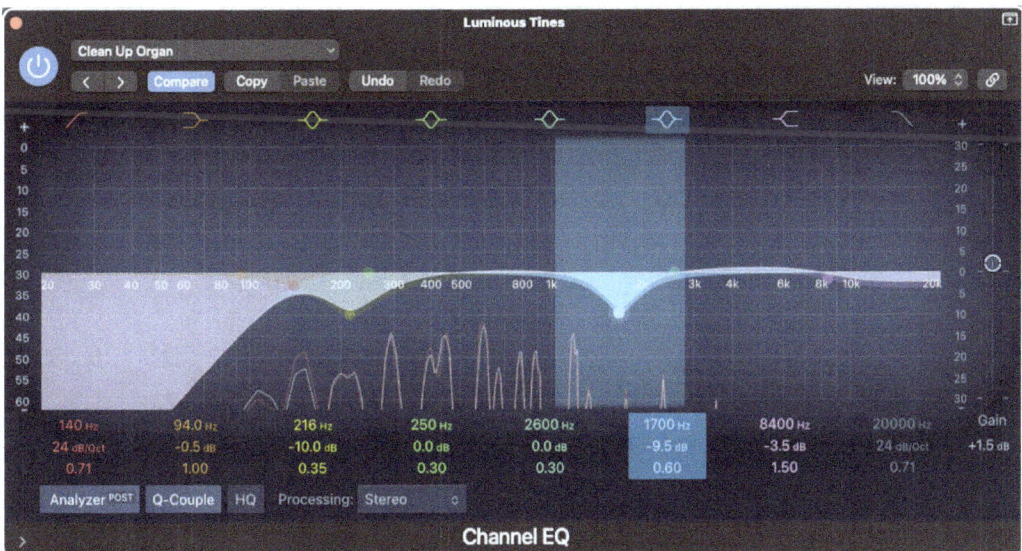

Figure 11.55: Logic Pro EQ plugin

On track 37, **Noise Sweep**, add an **HPF** by cutting at **640 Hz** and an **LPF** by cutting at **12200 Hz**, like so:

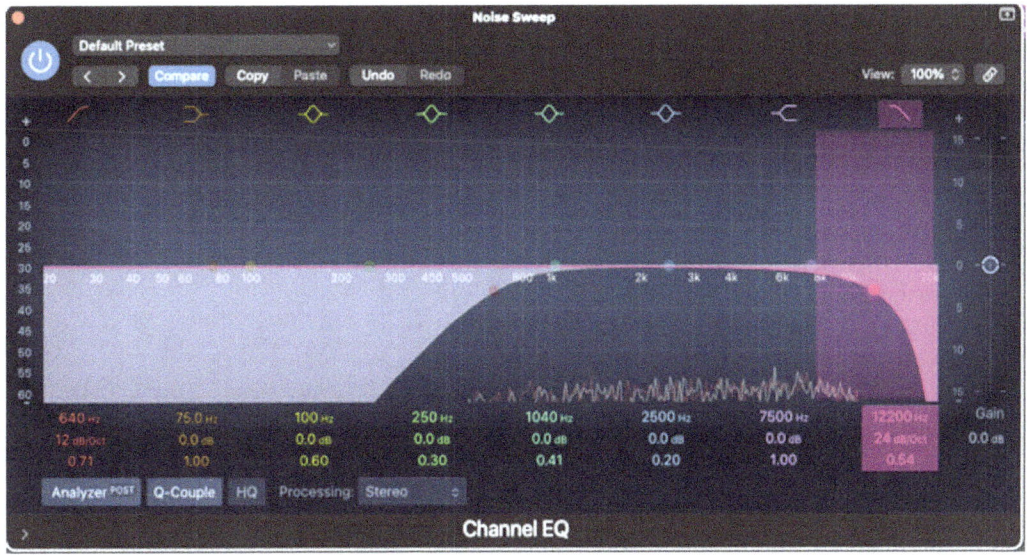

Figure 11.56: Logic Pro EQ plugin

Then, add **Bus 3** and set it to **-9.5 dB**.

After completing all of the customization steps that were covered here, make sure you copy these settings to your system. Then, review the mix that you created in your DAW and listen to it a couple of times:

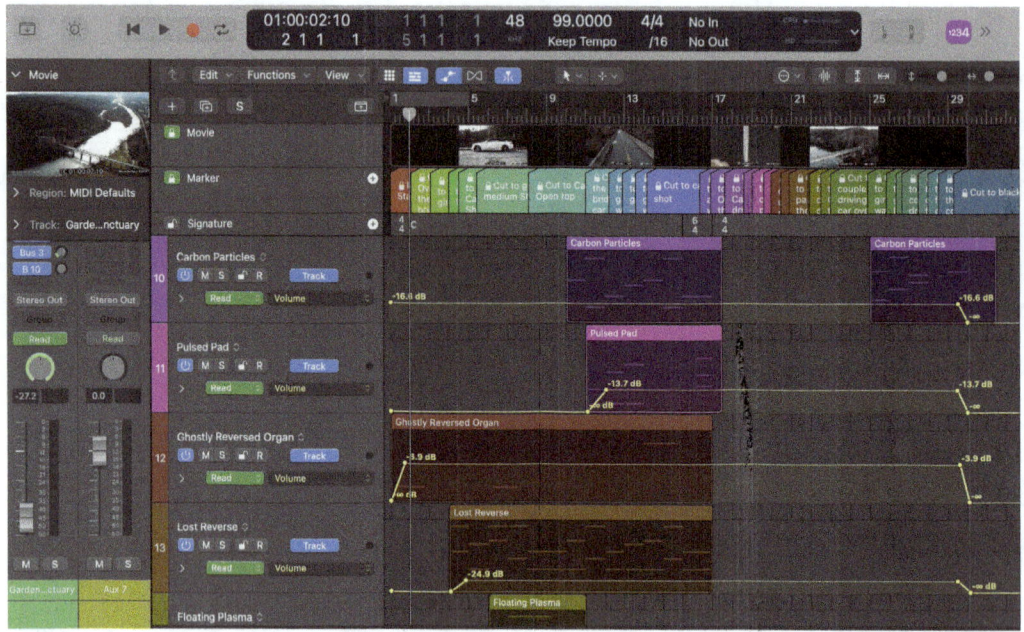

Figure 11.57: Logic Pro Arrange window

Make adjustments as needed to any of the channels' volume automation to smooth the start and end of all the regions, and to make them blend well with one another on your computer system. Always keep in mind that the overall sound you're creating should support the commercial.

To polish the mix, we will add final audio processing plugins to the main stereo output channel. Hover your mouse over the upper section of the **Stereo Output** channel strip and select **App Presets | Top 40**:

Figure 11.58: Logic Pro channel strip drop-down menu

Logic Pro will add a channel preset with different plugins loaded:

Figure 11.59: Logic Pro channel strip

Next, we will make a couple of custom adjustments to some of the plugins. Click on the **Exciter** plugin and select **Edge Addition** from the **Preset** menu. Then, adjust the **Harmonics** setting to **+69.6%**:

Figure 11.60: Logic Pro Exciter

Next, click on the **Multipressor** plugin and select **Final Pop Compressor** from the **Preset** menu:

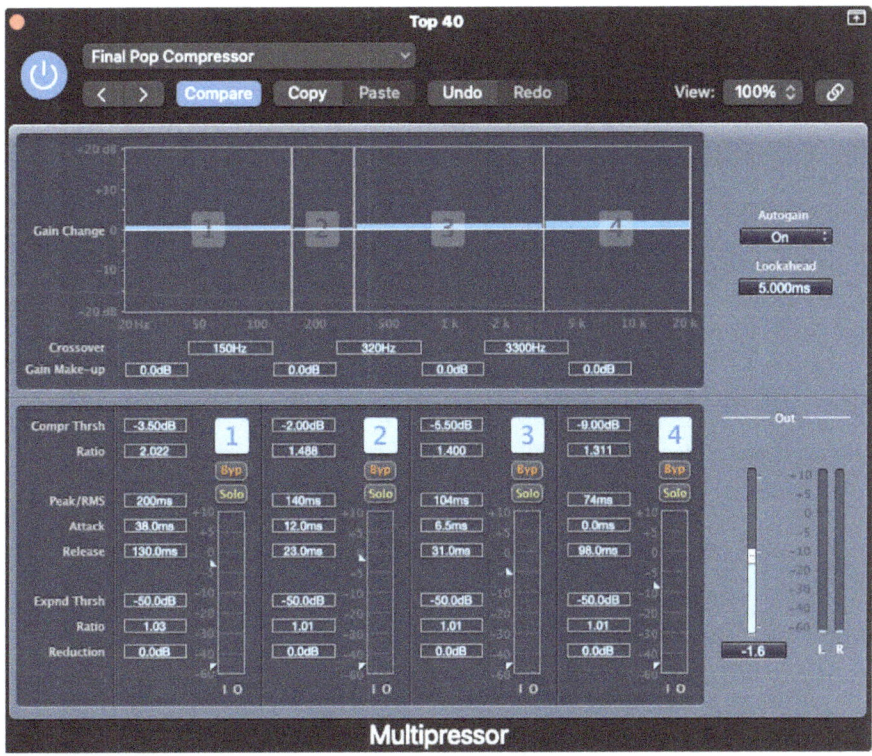

Figure 11.61: Logic Pro Multipressor

Then, open the **Limiter** plugin and set the output level to **-0.3 dB**:

Figure 11.62: Logic Pro Limiter

Now that we are at the final customization stage of the audio mix, listen to the mix as many times as needed and make additional adjustments until you are satisfied, in preparation for exporting the entire score. I highly recommend that you listen to your mix on good studio monitors and avoid mixing on headphones if possible.

When it comes to mixing, it's important to understand that it is an art form that takes specific skill sets. In the world of film music, depending on the project, commonly, a film composer's task is to do a basic mix.

After the final score is approved by the film director or a producer, all the individual tracks, called multi-tracks, or grouped instrument sections, called stems, are sent over to the mixing and mastering engineer as the final stage. How you deliver the final score depends on the client's preference.

Now that the score is finalized, next, we will go over how to export the score to a movie.

Exporting the score to video

To export the entire score to video, enable a cycle selection from the beginning to the end of the commercial, like so:

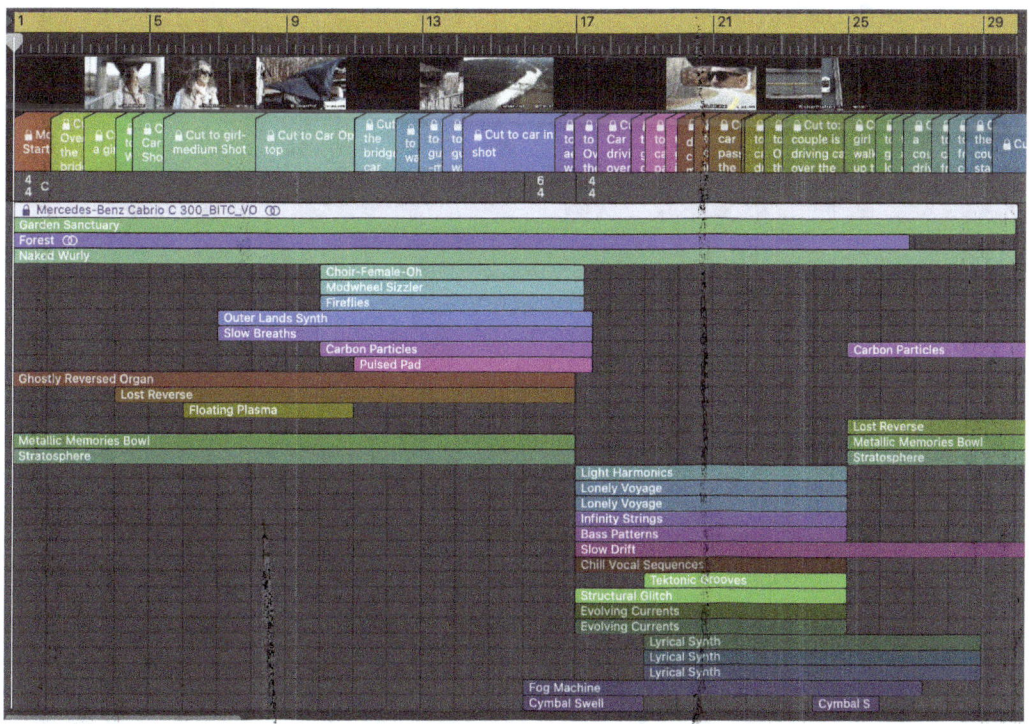

Figure 11.63: Logic Pro Arrange window

Next, go to **File | Movie | Export Audio to Movie…**:

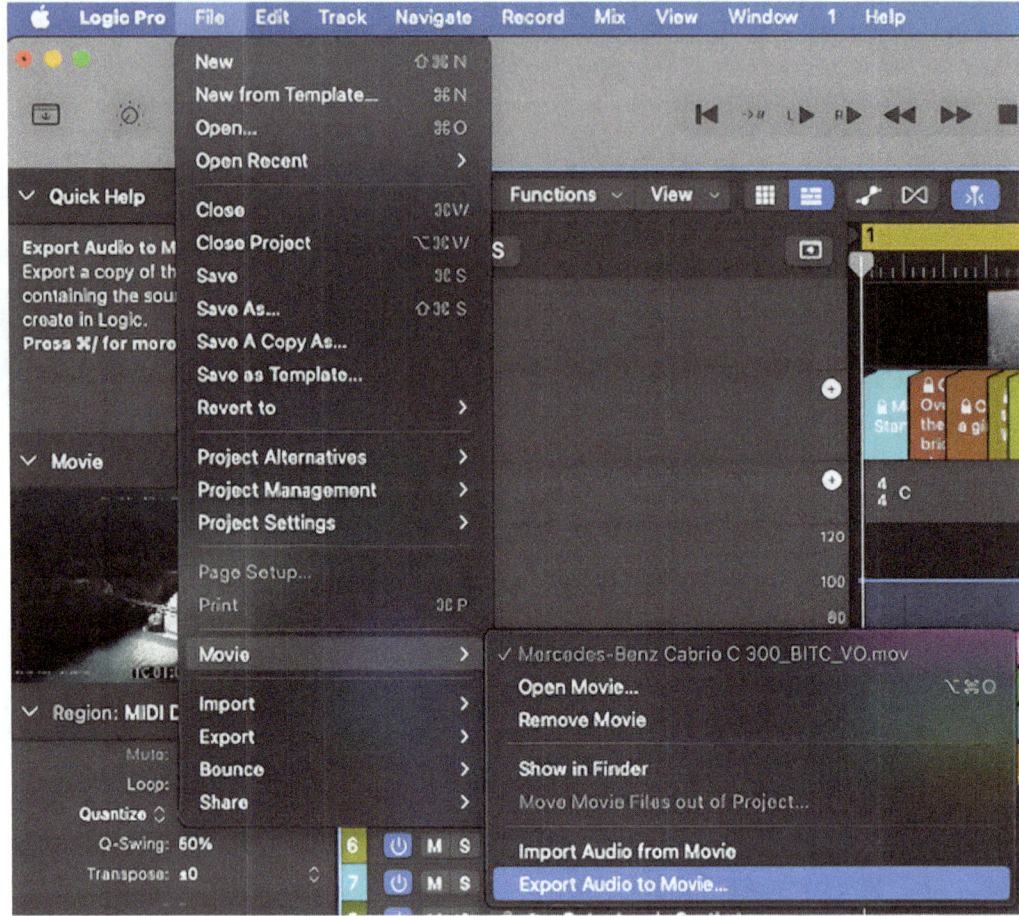

Figure 11.64: Logic Pro File drop-down menu

In the new window that opens, name the file `Mercedes-Benz Cabrio C300_Scored_BITC_VO`. Then, determine where you would like to save your final movie file – I chose the `Desktop` folder. Finally, select **24** from the **Bit Depth** drop-down menu and click **Save**:

Exporting the score to video   347

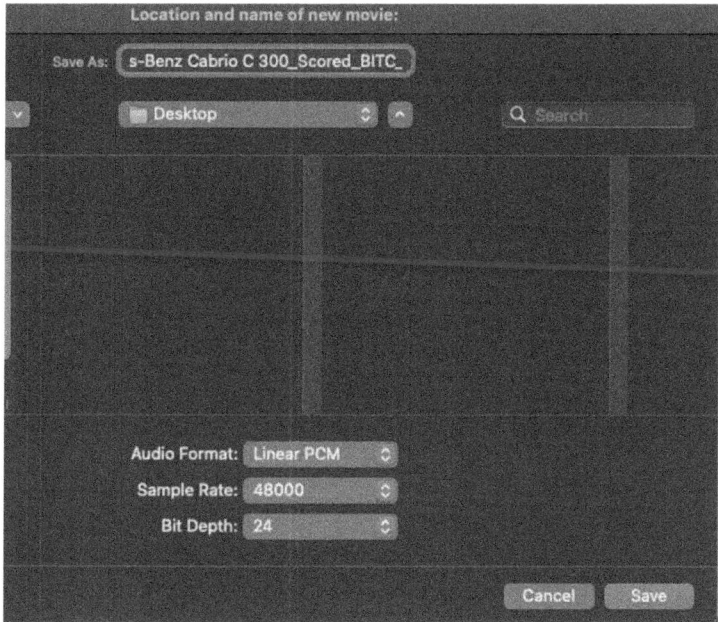

Figure 11.65: Logic Pro file save window

After clicking on the **Save** button, another window will open. Since the dialogue VO track was imported into the Logic Pro session, and we want to export the entire score and the VO to the movie, the **Enabled** box does not need to be checked. If the original audio is enabled and included in the export, it will end up with two VO tracks, which will create an unwanted chorusing effect. Click **OK** when done.

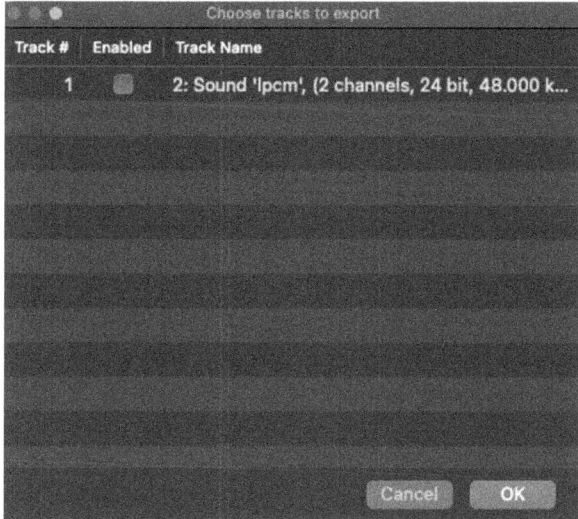

Figure 11.66: Logic Pro track export window

Logic Pro will now export the score and the VO track to the movie. Now open the `Mercedes-Benz Cabrio C 300_Scored_BITC_VO.mov` file, then watch and listen to the final version.

Figure 11.67: Final movie

You can additionally import the provided exported score as an MP3 and a WAV file into your session for comparison. Since the final result of the mix is subjective, there are many customizations that can be done to each of the channels to shape and transform the sound, but for the sake of this chapter, this will give you a good starting point. At this stage, if you're not satisfied with your mix, you could also send your score to an audio mixing engineer or audio mastering engineer to further mix and finalize your version of the score.

Summary

In this chapter, we explored how to customize existing sounds and set up the volume levels and panning. We also looked at how to blend all the tracks and create a basic mix to achieve a sound that supports the commercial. Finally, we reviewed how to finalize the project and export the entire score to movie.

It is recommended that you review and become familiar with the steps so that you can then implement all of the material in your own project.

This now completes the journey of scoring to picture. In the next and final chapter, we will discuss advanced concepts of dealing with timings in film music.

12
Advanced Concepts for Dealing with Timing in Film Music

In *Chapter 11*, we discussed how to enhance and shape blended sounds together and export the final score to video. Since we've explored synchronization aspects and dealing with timings specific to film scoring in Logic Pro, we are now going to look at some advanced concepts in general, and how to deal with timing in film music.

It's not an easy task to get film and music synchronized and if you're working with a complex music cue, it may require more elaborate timing calculations. The more complex the timings of the film, the more challenging it will be to synchronize the music to the picture.

In this chapter, we will look at how to manually calculate bars and beats based on the length of the film and find the most suitable tempo with the most compelling form and structure. We will compare the old methods of synchronization to picture and what's applicable today. We will also look at additional visual synchronization methods that can enhance the working environment of Logic Pro users. The methods and concepts covered in this chapter will help Logic Pro users deal with advanced timing challenges and give them deeper insight and a broader perspective on how to find the needed solution based on their project needs.

So, in this chapter, we will cover the following topics:

- Outlining structure and timings
- Calculating timings using a DAW
- Synchronizing music to picture during the Golden Age of Hollywood
- Exploring visual synchronization methods used today

Technical requirements

To follow along with this chapter, you will need a Mac computer with Logic Pro and QuickTime software installed.

Outlining structure and timings

Film composers score countless projects during their career journeys, including short films, documentaries, infomercials, commercials, feature films, et cetera. Often, they will first sit at the piano with a blank sheet of music and a pencil, trying to figure out timings, meter, tempo, bars, melodies, and harmonies. Others may go straight to Logic Pro and use the software to do this. The main objective in film music is to figure out the appropriate tempo so that the specific events (hit points) fall on the downbeat of a bar and complement the scene.

If a film composer has to write a short piece of music, let's say, if a film director requests 30 seconds of music for a commercial, the question now becomes: how can I fit and format music in those 30 seconds? Calculating the music timing can be challenging because most want to get straight to writing the music. But to know what to write, and in what format to write it, you have to go through some calculation procedures.

Figure 12.1 is an example of an empty sheet of music that a film composer commonly uses when they start sketching ideas at the piano:

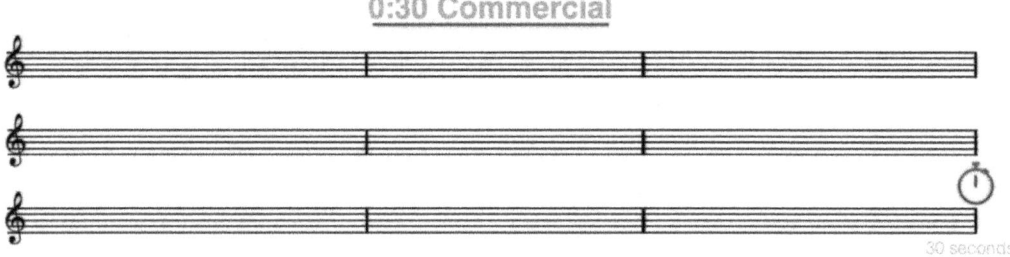

Figure 12.1: Empty sheet music

Before scoring the 30-second commercial, the elements of tempo, time signature, and number of bars the final score will be for the 30 seconds of the commercial's duration need to be considered. Additionally, we need to think about the direction we're heading in this commercial. Does it need to have a traditional melodic theme? Or does it need more electronic-sounding elements that give more flexibility without being bound to specific bars and beats, as are commonly used in regular songwriting?

Let's evaluate and explore how to score a 30-second commercial and evaluate structure and timing settings. To begin, create a new Logic Pro session, then create a default instrument track and save the session (for example, here we will name the session `Advanced Timing_01`).

Next, right-click in the **Arrange** window to create an empty MIDI region. Expand the region so that it starts at bar 1, beat 1, and ends at bar 16, beat 1:

Figure 12.2: Logic Pro MIDI region

Then, in the **Arrange** window, go to **View** and select **Secondary Ruler** from the drop-down menu:

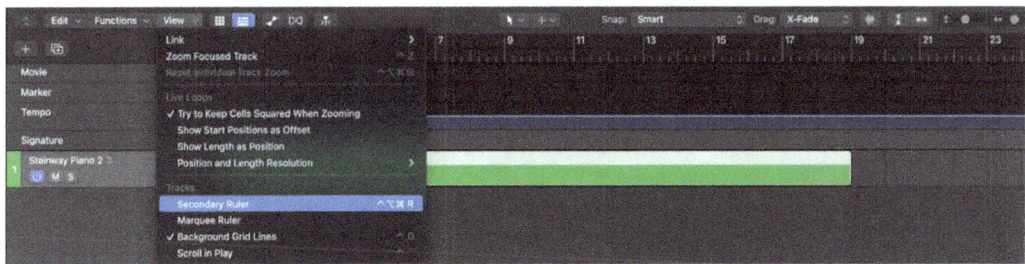

Figure 12.3: Logic Pro Secondary Ruler

Next, go to **File** and select **Project Settings | Synchronization...**:

Figure 12.4: Logic Pro File drop-down menu

In the **Synchronization** window, check **Enable separate SMPTE view offset**, and in the **Displayed as SMPTE** section, type 00 : 00 : 00 : 00:

Outlining structure and timings 353

Figure 12.5: Logic Pro Synchronization window

Now that the secondary ruler and separate SMPTE view offset are enabled, Logic Pro displays the seconds above the bar numbers. It shows the relationship between the length of the piece and the number of bars, so you can see how many bars are within the 30-second timeframe.

In *Figure 12.6*, you can see, at the 30-second mark, that Logic Pro displays 16 available bars:

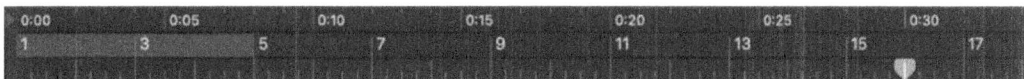

Figure 12.6: Logic Pro Secondary Ruler

Now, use the keyboard shortcut *N* to display the **Notation** window and the bar numbers. The **Arrange** window and the **Score** window will together display the number of bars and the time signature:

354　Advanced Concepts for Dealing with Timing in Film Music

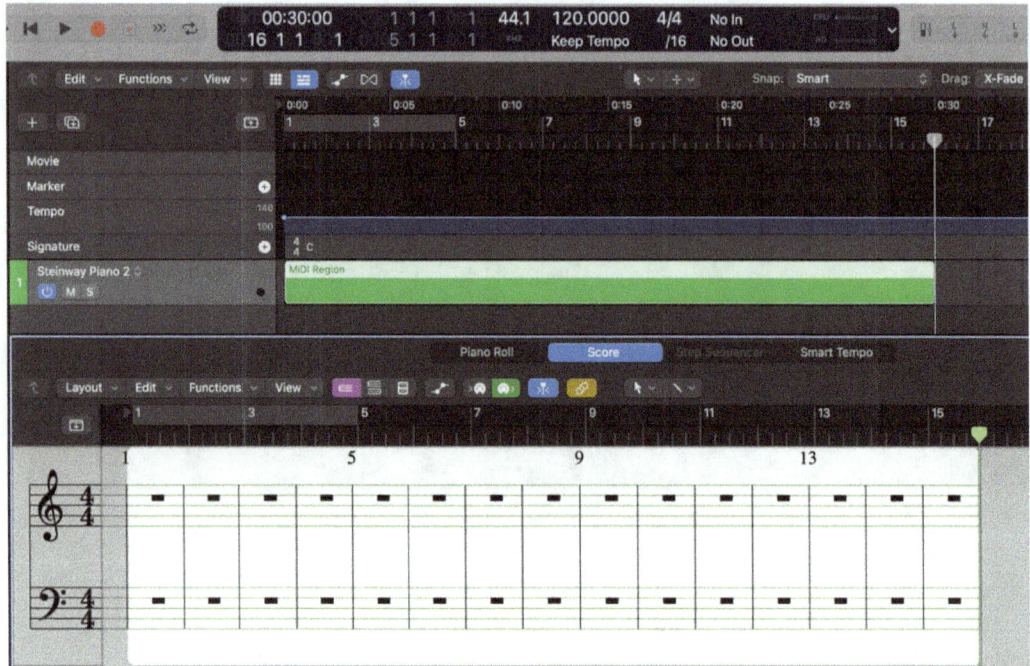

Figure 12.7: Logic Pro Notation window

Now, we will look at a couple of scenarios using different time signatures and tempos to see how they work within the 30-second timeframe. When structuring a commercial, there may need to be a musical introduction and a theme, depending on the type of commercial. The picture will dictate the musical and rhythmical choices that will be made.

Scenario 1 – using 120 bpm and the 3/4 time signature

In this example, the tempo is 120 bpm and we will choose the **3/4** time signature. If we change the default time signature of **4/4** to **3/4** at 120 bpm from the beginning of the session, bar 21 lands exactly at the 30-second mark. That means we have 20 bars of 3/4 to be used:

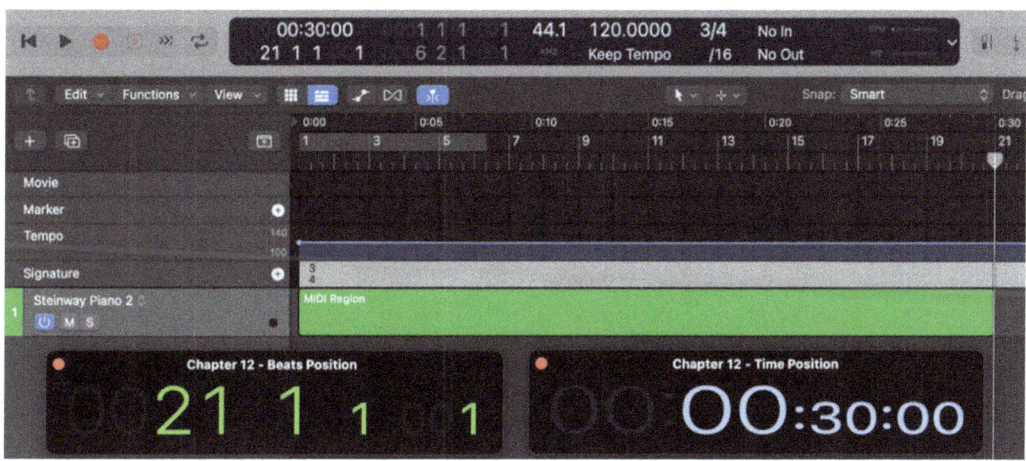

Figure 12.8: Logic Pro Arrange window

Now that we know there are 20 bars available, based on the selection, we can sketch an idea of what that could look like. The sketching can happen either in Logic Pro or on a sheet of music at the piano.

In the following example, if we decide to use four bars for an introduction, eight bars for Theme A, and another eight bars for Theme B, there won't be space left over for an ending section. This is the process of starting to sketch and outline what that piece of music might look like before we make our final decision:

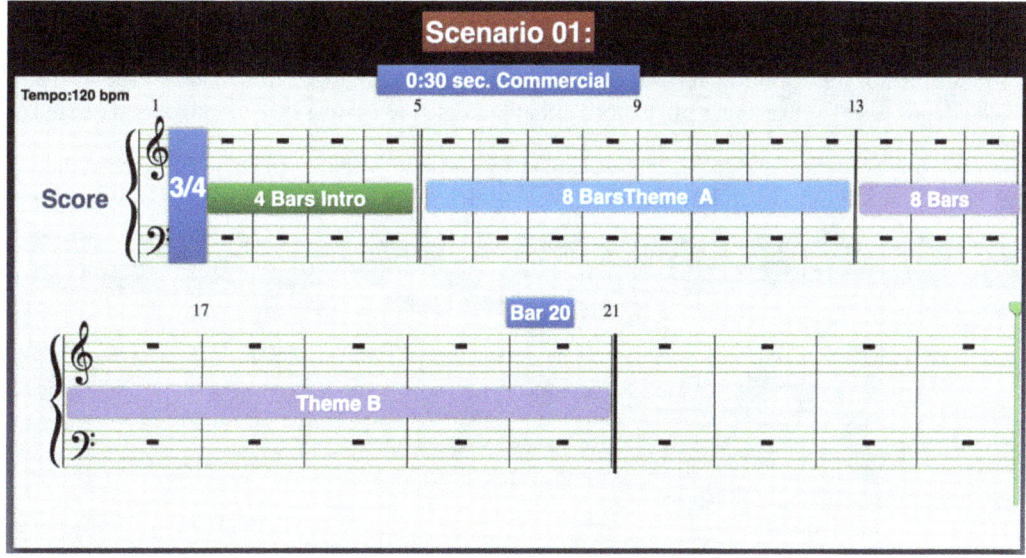

Figure 12.9: Logic Pro Notation view

The most important thing to consider, as mentioned earlier, is how the music in the end affects and supports the commercial.

Scenario 2 – using 120 bpm and the 4/4 time signature

In this example, we will keep the tempo at 120 bpm and we will choose the **4/4** time signature. If we change back to the default time signature of **4/4** at 120 bpm from the beginning of the session, bar 16 lands exactly at the 30-second mark. That means we have 15 bars of 4/4 to be used:

Figure 12.10: Logic Pro Arrange window

Now that we know there are 15 bars available, based on the selection, we can sketch an idea of what that could look like. The sketching can happen either in Logic Pro or on a sheet of music at the piano.

In the following example, if we decide to use eight bars for Theme A and seven bars for Theme B, there won't be space for an intro or ending section, unless we create it by choosing a different bar structure:

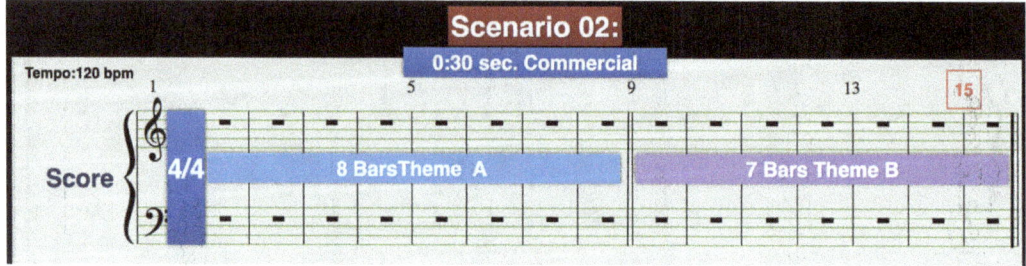

Figure 12.11: Logic Pro Notation view

Scenario 3 – using 192 bpm and the 4/4 time signature

In this example, we will change the tempo to 192 bpm and we will choose the **4/4** time signature. By keeping the time signature of **4/4** at 192 bpm from the beginning of the session, bar 25 lands exactly at the 30-second mark. That means we have 24 bars of 4/4 to be used:

Figure 12.12: Logic Pro Arrange window

Now that we know there are 24 bars available, based on the selection, we can sketch an idea of what that could look like. The sketching can happen either in Logic Pro or on a sheet of music at the piano.

In the following example, if we decide to use eight bars for Theme A and eight bars for Theme B, then we will have another eight bars left to repeat the first eight bars if needed:

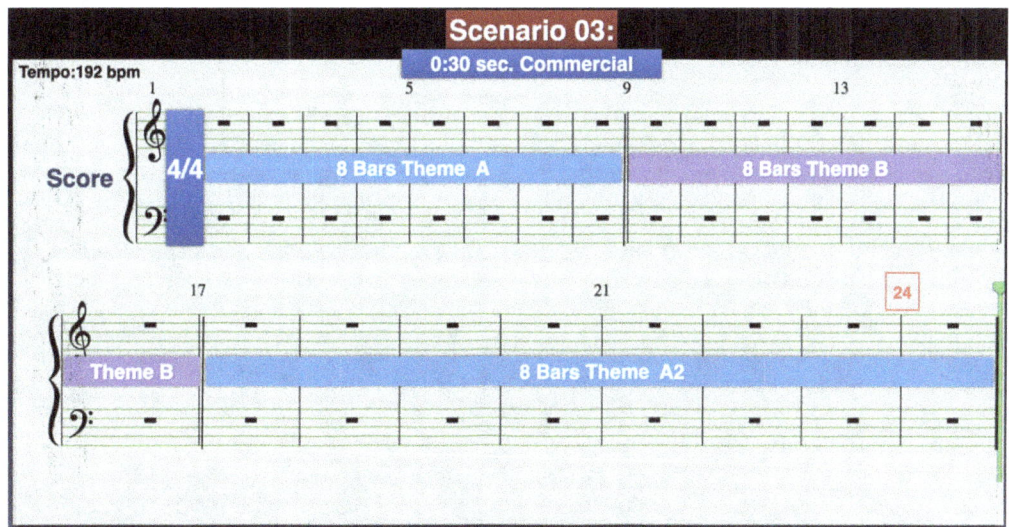

Figure 12.13: Logic Pro Notation window

Now that we've reviewed the different scenarios on how to start sketching and planning, in the next section, we will look at how to calculate timings in DAW. We will go over how to figure out the calculations inside or outside Logic Pro.

Calculating timings using a DAW

As mentioned earlier, in general, many film composers sketch their ideas on sheet music at a piano before scoring in Logic Pro. The main challenge is to outline the length of music needed that will fit the timing desired. So, before deciding what the music needs to be doing, the goal is to figure out how many bars and what meter the length of the project can fit.

In this section, we will continue working with a 30-second commercial, exploring new ways of calculating timings in Logic Pro. Since we're dealing with calculating timings, keep in mind that a beat is the steady pulse, a tempo is the rate per second of that pulse, and the time signature is the meter of the pulse.

Suppose you have a cue (music for a scene) that lasts exactly 30 seconds. If you know you want the tempo to be approximately 192 bpm, you could use different methods and formulas to calculate the length of the cue. In the following examples, we will review these different methods and formulas.

Method 1 – calculating timings inside Logic Pro

The first method would be to open Logic Pro and create a new session and instrument track. Next, set the main tempo to 192 bpm and change the time signature from **4/4** to **1/4**. After that, enable **Secondary Ruler** from the **View** drop-down menu. Then, in the **Synchronization** window, select **Enable separate SMPTE view offset** and type 00 : 00 : 00 : 00 in the **Displayed as SMPTE** section. Place the playhead at the 30-second location and open **Giant Time and Beats Displays**.

In *Figure 12.14*, you can see there are now 97 beats from the beginning of the session to where the 30-second mark passes. Selecting the tempo of 192 bpm will make the 30-second mark land exactly on beat 97 (keep in mind that the time signature is set to **1/4**):

Figure 12.14: Logic Pro Arrange window

Knowing the total number of beats allows you to begin forming bars and adding time signatures.

Next, we need to figure out how many bars can fit into the 97 beats. Let's look at an example using the **4/4** time signature to see how many will fit into 97 beats. If we change the time signature from **1/4** to **4/4**, we can see there are now 24 bars to work with:

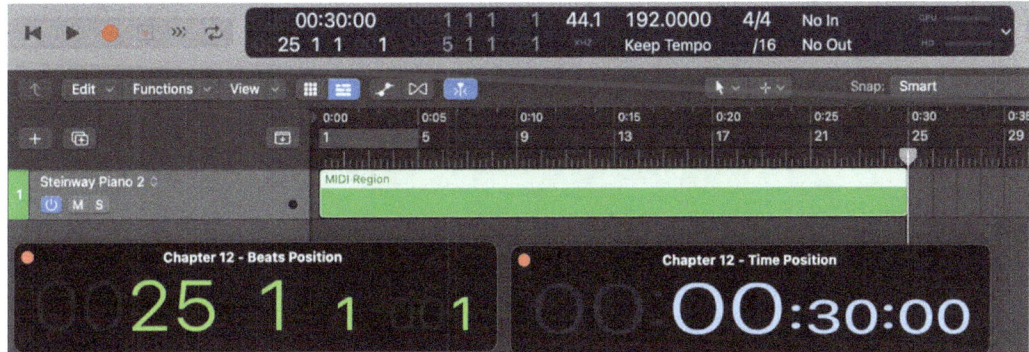

Figure 12.15: Logic Pro Arrange window

There are only 96 beats to work with, since 97 total beats – 1 beat = 96 beats. Then, we divide 96 beats by 4 to get 24 bars. So, there are 24 bars using the **4/4** time signature at 192 bpm.

To see how many bars of a **3/4** time signature would work in 30 seconds, go to the time signature in the LCD display and change it to **3/4**. Now, you can see that Logic Pro displays 32 full bars of 3/4:

Figure 12.16: Logic Pro Arrange window

Since we now know how to use Logic Pro to find the appropriate tempo with the suitable number of bars, next, we will look at formulas that will help calculate the timings. This can be done with or without Logic Pro.

Method 2 – calculating timings using formulas

This second method, using formulas, is helpful when you're sketching your ideas on a sheet of music at the piano. The first formula we're going to look at will help you to find the beat that the marker falls on if you know the bpm and the length of the music. To do this calculation, you take your selected bpm and multiply it by the number of seconds in the commercial, then divide that by 60 and add 1:

$$\frac{(BPM) \times Seconds}{60} + 1 = Beats$$

Figure 12.17: Beats calculation formula

For example, using 192 bpm and the 30-second length of the commercial, we would insert the numbers as shown in *Figure 12.18* and the result is 97 beats. So, there are 97 beats using 192 bpm in a 30-second timeframe:

$$\frac{192\ BPM \times 30\ sec}{60} + 1 = 97\ Beats$$

Figure 12.18: Beats calculation example

The next formula we will look at will help you find out the number of bars based on the number of beats and the time signature selection:

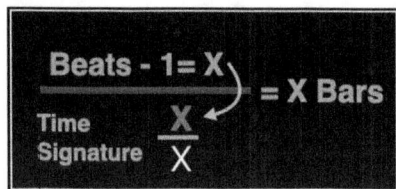

Figure 12.19: Bars calculation formula

To calculate how many 4/4 bars will be in 97 beats of 30 seconds, first, take 97 and subtract 1, which gives us 96 full bars. Then, divide 96 by 4 and that gives us the number of bars. So, there are 24 bars of the 4/4 time signature in the 30-second timeframe:

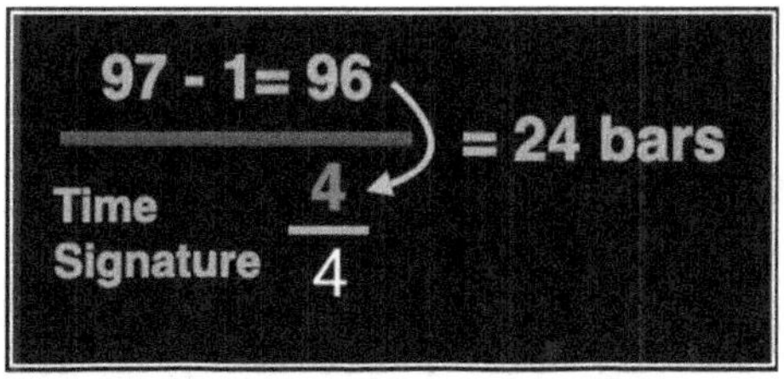

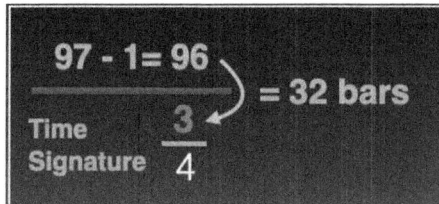

Figure 12.20: Bars calculation example

To calculate how many 3/4 bars will be in 97 beats of 30 seconds, similar to the previous formula, subtract 1 from 97 to get 96. Then, divide 96 by 3 to get the number of bars. There are 32 bars of the 3/4 time signature in the 30-second timeframe:

$$\frac{97 - 1 = 96}{\text{Time Signature } \frac{3}{4}} = 32 \text{ bars}$$

Figure 12.21: Bars calculation example

To calculate how many 2/4 bars will be in 97 beats of 30 seconds, start again by subtracting 1 from 97 to get 96. Then, divide 96 by 2 to get the number of bars. There are 48 bars of the 2/4 time signature in the 30-second timeframe:

$$\frac{97 - 1 = 96}{\text{Time Signature } \frac{2}{4}} = 48 \text{ bars}$$

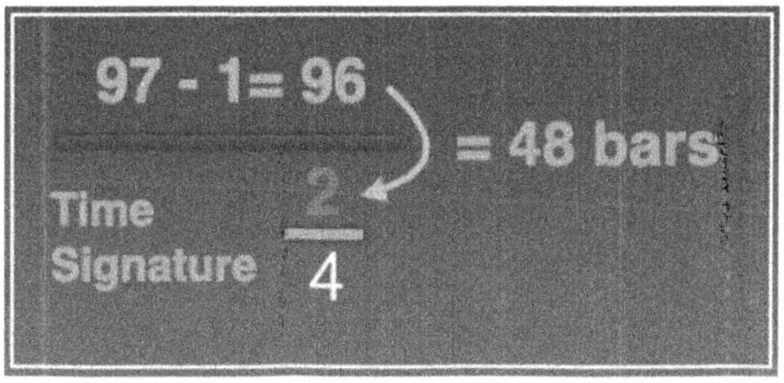

Figure 12.22: Bars calculation example

The next formula we're going to look at will help you to find the bpm based on the number of beats and the length of the score:

Formula

$$\frac{(\text{Beat} - 1) \times 60 \text{ seconds}}{\text{Seconds}} = \text{BPM}$$

Figure 12.23: The bpm calculation formula

For example, using 35 beats and the 30 seconds of the commercial, we would insert the numbers as shown in *Figure 12.24*. Since beat 35 occurred at the 30-second mark, we have to subtract 1, which gives us 34 full bars. Multiply 34 by 60, which gives us 2,040, and then divide 2,040 by 30 to get 68 bpm. So, there are 68 bpm occurring in a 30-second timeframe:

Example:

$$\frac{(35 \text{ Beat} - 1) \times 60 \text{ sec}}{30 \text{ sec.}} = 68 \text{ BPM}$$

Figure 12.24: A bpm calculation example

The next formula will help you to calculate how many seconds you have using the number of beats and the bpm:

Formula

$$\frac{(60 \text{ sec}) \times (\text{Beat} - 1)}{\text{BPM}} = \text{Seconds}$$

Figure 12.25: Seconds calculation formula

For example, using 68 beats and 134 bpm, we would insert the numbers as shown in *Figure 12.26*. So, multiply 60 by 68, then minus 1 to get 4,020. Then, divide 4,020 by 134 bpm, and we get 30 seconds. This means the length of time is 30 seconds:

$$\frac{(60 \text{ sec}) \times (\text{Beat } 68-1)}{134 \text{ BPM}} = 30 \text{ sec.}$$

Figure 12.26: Seconds calculation example

Keep these formulas with you and use them when you need to calculate the bpm, number of beats, or number of seconds.

Additionally, here we can see the formulas with a corresponding example:

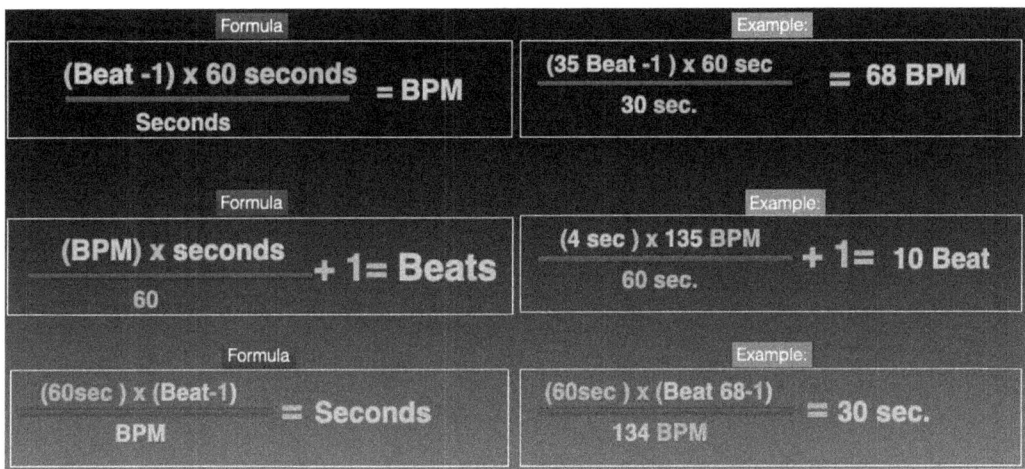

Figure 12.27: The bpm, beats, and seconds calculation formulas and examples

Now that we've looked at useful formulas on how to calculate different timings, next, we will review and explore how timings and the methods of synchronizing music to picture were accomplished during the early days of cinema. We will also explore which of those methods are applicable today.

Synchronizing music to picture during the Golden Age of Hollywood

In the 1930s, one of the main challenges for a film composer was the process of synchronizing music to picture. A film is made of still photos that occur at a steady rate of 24 **frames per second** (**fps**), no matter how fast any of the events happen. Since the images per second appeared at a fast pace, it gave the eyes the sensation of images being blended together while watching, hence films were referred to as "moving pictures."

Before a film composer began working on a film, the film editor created the cue sheet to list the important events (hit points) that would need to be acknowledged by the music. Music is different from film in that it is adaptable and flexible when it comes to timing and tempo, and when music merged with film, the important question was how to find the best, most suitable tempo for the important events so that the music and the picture were effectively synchronized.

The solution was to use a metronome (**click track**) that was set to **frames per beat** (**fpb**) instead of **beats per minute** (**bpm**). This helped to determine what beat the event fell on and became the way to synchronize the music with the film.

In this section, we will explore the synchronization methods of music to picture during the early days of cinema, including looking at a single frame of a 35 mm film, the click book, and events calculation. We will also look at methods that are relevant to film composers today, including the Logic Pro display options of viewing frame click instead of bpm and film footage instead of SMPTE.

A single frame of a 35mm film

In this section, we will take a look at what a frame in 35 mm celluloid film might have looked like during the Golden Age of Hollywood. *Figure 12.28* shows two frames, A and B. You can see each frame is surrounded by four film sprockets on each side, and on the left side, you can see where the optical soundtrack was added:

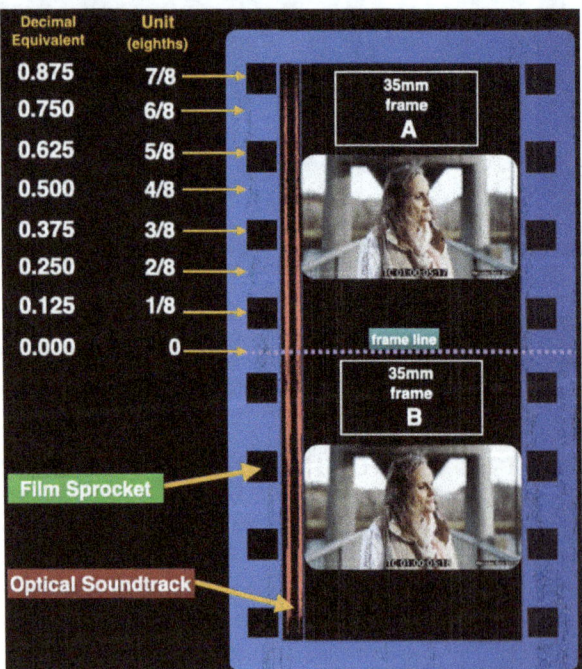

Figure 12.28: 35 mm film frame

Music editors recognized that the four sprockets of a frame made the projector create audible clicks. They decided to subdivide the film frame into eight equal parts that gave additional tempo possibilities. They also punched holes in the optical track on the celluloid film or recorded a click onto a film, so that it would produce a sound referred to as a click track.

The click track was created to allow music and film to be synchronized in a recording session. During the recording session, the conductor of the orchestra was then able to hear the click track in their headphones while watching the film on the big screen and conducting the orchestra. It was a clever way of synchronizing music.

If the film composer wanted to convert, for example, 80 bpm to fpb, they used the method of 1,440 divided by 80, which equals 18 frame clicks or 18 fpb. That also means that the editors created perforation of the film every 18 frames to deliver a steady click track representing 80 bpm. If the composer needed the click track to be faster, they could change the location of the holes, using the eight possible division increments of the frame to change the click track speed.

Click book

A **click book** was used along with a cue sheet to assist a film composer in synchronizing music and film and finding the best tempos for a film's events. The click book was mapped out in fpb to assist a film composer in determining whether the selected steady tempo worked with multiple hit points. If the tempo wasn't working, another attempt was made to find a working tempo by searching in the list of tempos.

The process involved the music editor and the film composer opening the click book and looking at the table of frame clicks to see what beat was the closest to the selected bpm. If the event fell between two beats, instead of directly on the beat, they would continue to search for another suitable tempo. The goal of using the click book was to find a constant tempo that would acknowledge the specific events from the cue sheet.

BPM versus FPB

In this section, we will examine the speed of the frames in a Logic Pro environment and the relationship between fpb and bpm. We will also look at frames per bar in a Logic Pro **Arrange** window, where they fall within the bar and beat relationship, and how that relates to the occurring frames.

Let's take the example shown in *Figure 12.29*. The Logic Pro session is set to 24 fps and the tempo is set at 60 bpm, which means every beat will equal 1 second. It also means that at the time the first second occurs, there are already 24 frames of film:

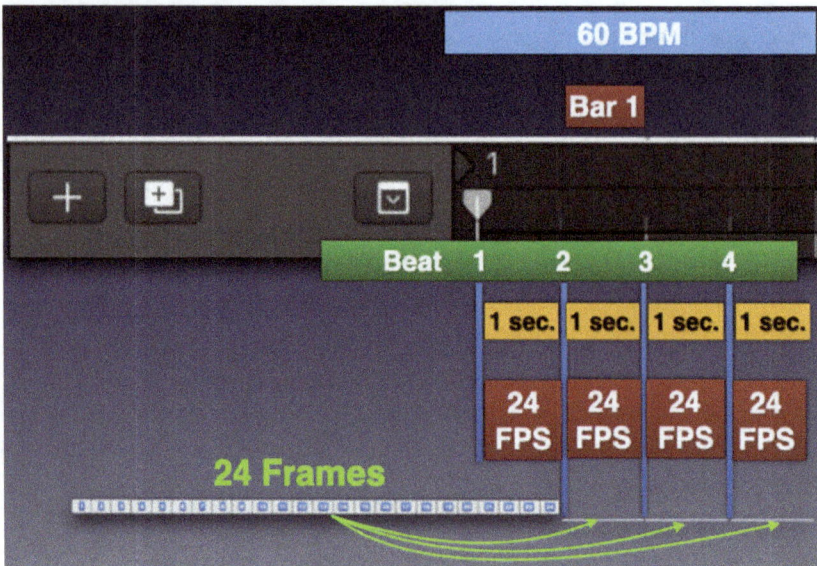

Figure 12.29: Fragment of a Logic Pro Arrange window

When we look closer at a single bar at 60 bpm and a 4/4 time signature in Logic Pro, we can clearly see that there are four beats in this bar and every beat is worth a quarter note. We can also see that at 60 bpm, each quarter note beat lasts a second.

When looking at the single frame of a film, the total number of frames that occur in the entire bar is 96. We multiply the 24 fps by 4 beats, which gives us 96 total frames. That means 1 bar of 60 bpm at 24 fps has a total of 96 frames or is 4 seconds long.

So, for example, when keeping the tempo of 60 bpm and extending the duration to 1 minute in length, the total number of frames in 60 seconds will be 1,440 fpm. This number of 1,440 will help to calculate the frame clicks, which is discussed later in this section.

It is also important to note that the duration of each frame lasts 0.04166667 seconds (1 second divided by 24 frames = 0.04166667 of a second or 41.667 milliseconds). Since it's not an even number, it will be difficult to work with, but it's good to know what the frame length is at this time.

Calculating timings using fpb formulas

As an overview, the following are some useful film scoring abbreviations we will be using in this section:

```
BPM= Beats Per Minute
BPS=Beats Per Second
FPS=Frames Per Second
FPM=Frames Per Minute
FPB= Frames Per Beat
```

Figure 12.30: Film scoring abbreviations

In summary, 24 fpb equals 1 bps, 1 bps equals 60 bpm, and so 60 bpm equals 24 fpb:

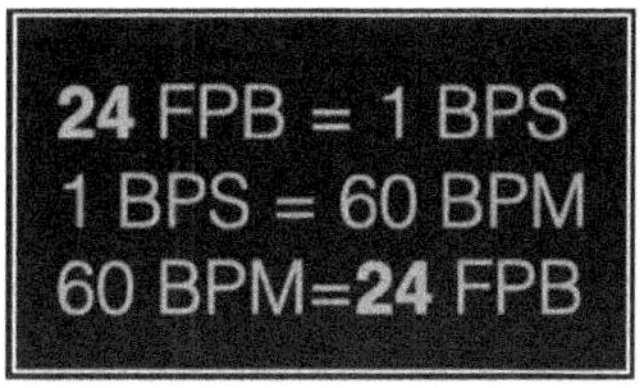

```
24 FPB = 1 BPS
1 BPS = 60 BPM
60 BPM=24 FPB
```

Figure 12.31: The bps, bpm, and fpb conversion

For example, since 12 fpb equals 2 bps and 2 bps equals 120 bpm, then 120 bpm equals 12 fpb:

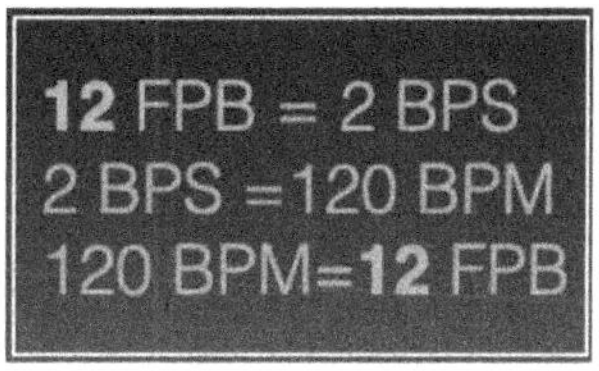

```
12 FPB = 2 BPS
2 BPS =120 BPM
120 BPM=12 FPB
```

Figure 12.32: The bps, bpm, and fpb conversion

Using these abbreviations and conversions, let's look at a couple more formulas that film composers use mostly to calculate a specific tempo, based on the event that occurs on the screen, using bpm and fpm.

In *Figure 12.33*, we can see that 1,440 fpm divided by the bpm will give us the frame click amount. 1,440 is the total number of frames in 60 seconds:

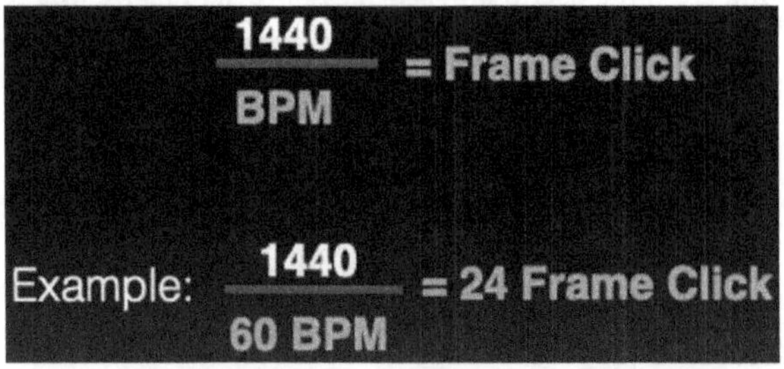

$$\frac{1440}{BPM} = \text{Frame Click}$$

$$\text{Example: } \frac{1440}{60 \text{ BPM}} = 24 \text{ Frame Click}$$

Figure 12.33: The bpm to frame click calculation formula

Then, in *Figure 12.34*, we can see that 1,440 fpm divided by the frame click will give us the bpm amount:

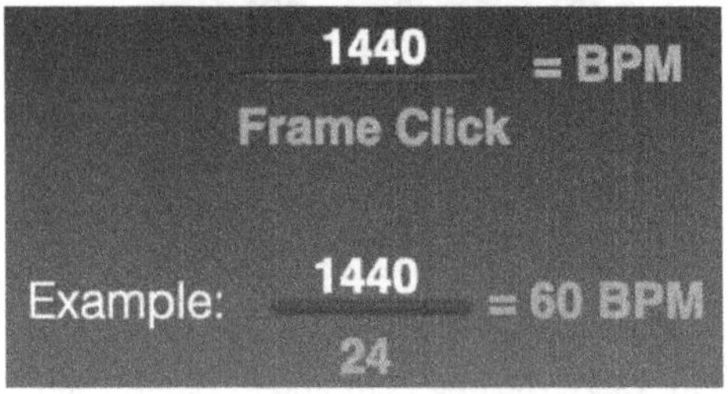

$$\frac{1440}{\text{Frame Click}} = BPM$$

$$\text{Example: } \frac{1440}{24} = 60 \text{ BPM}$$

Figure 12.34: Frame click to bpm calculation formula

Figure 12.35 shows the formulas used to calculate the beats, fpb, and seconds when dealing with frames per beat:

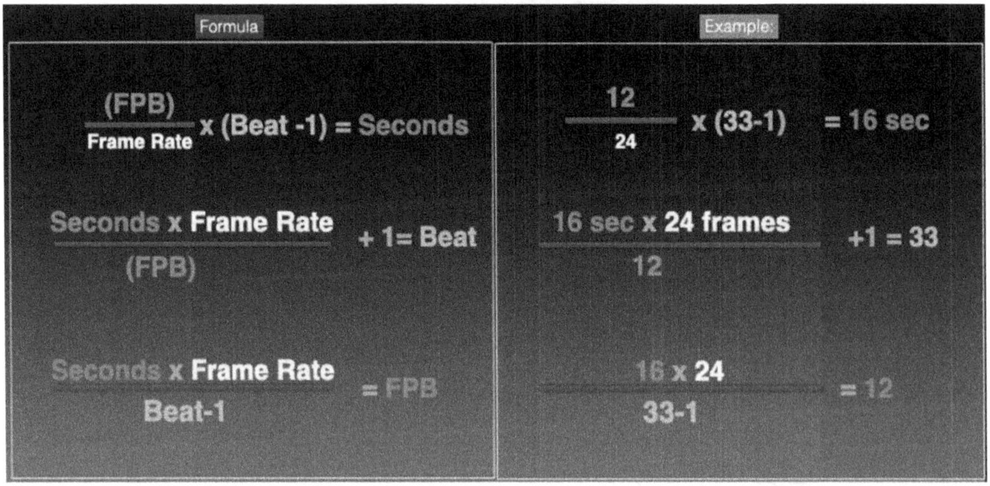

Formula	Example:
$\frac{(FPB)}{\text{Frame Rate}} \times (\text{Beat} -1) = \text{Seconds}$	$\frac{12}{24} \times (33-1) = 16 \text{ sec}$
$\frac{\text{Seconds} \times \text{Frame Rate}}{(FPB)} + 1 = \text{Beat}$	$\frac{16 \text{ sec} \times 24 \text{ frames}}{12} + 1 = 33$
$\frac{\text{Seconds} \times \text{Frame Rate}}{\text{Beat}-1} = FPB$	$\frac{16 \times 24}{33-1} = 12$

Figure 12.35: Seconds, beats, and fpb calculation formulas and examples

For example, to calculate an event that occurred after 16 seconds at 120 bpm, divide 1,440 by 120 bpm, which equals 12 frame clicks or 12 fpb. Now that we have the fpb, we'll take the 16 seconds and multiply that by 24 fps, and this will equal 384 frames. Next, divide 384 frames by the 12 frame clicks to get 32. Then, add 1 to 32 to get 33. So, the event that happened at 16 seconds at 120 bpm will fall on beat 33.

Based on the previous graphic, these formulas will now allow you to calculate FPB, beats, or seconds for a specific event when away from the computer.

Logic Pro is still equipped today to display film lengths in feet. In the next section, we will take a closer look at this.

Displaying time as feet and frames in Logic Pro

In this section, we will look at how Logic Pro can change the SMPTE view to a feet and frames view.

To begin, open a new Logic Pro session and keep the default tempo of **120** bpm and the **1/4** time signature. After that, create an instrument track and then open **Giant Time Display** and **Giant Beats Display**. From the **View** drop-down menu, enable **Secondary Ruler**.

Next, in the **Synchronization** window, do the following:

- Set **Frame Rate** to **24** fps.
- Select **Enable separate SMPTE view offset** and place your playhead at bar 33, beat 1. This will also display the position of **16** seconds.

Figure 12.36 shows the playhead position at bar 33, beat 1, and a **SMPTE view** of **01:00:16:00**:

Figure 12.36: Logic Pro Arrange window

Now, unselect **Enable separate SMPTE view offset** and click on **File**, then **Display**. In the **Displays** section, click on the drop-down list next to **Display Time As** and select **Feet and Frames, 35 mm Film**:

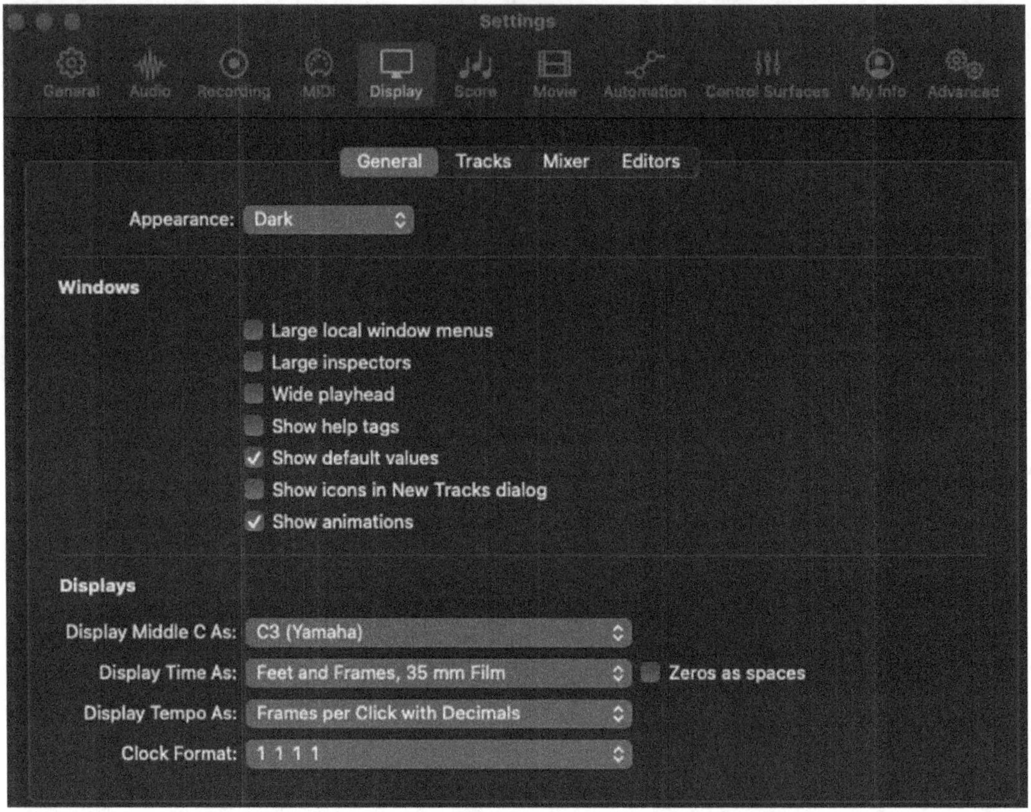

Figure 12.37: Logic Pro Display window

When switching **Display Time As** from the **SMPTE view** to the **Feet and Frames, 35 mm Film** view, Logic Pro displays **5424** feet at bar 33, which is equal to 86,784 frames of film:

Figure 12.38: Logic Pro Display window

In general, when switching the **SMPTE view** from **TC 01:00:00:00** to display as feet and frames of 35 mm film, Logic Pro will display the **SMPTE timecode** as **5400. 0/0** feet and frames:

Figure 12.39: Logic Pro Arrange window

In order to understand the **5400** number, you have to understand how film speed is calculated. A 35 mm film at 24 fps has a projection speed of 90 feet per minute and 16 frames per foot. When you switch the **SMPTE view** to 35 mm film, Logic Pro will display **5400** by default, since 90 feet per minute multiplied by 60 minutes equals 5,400 feet.

In *Figure 12.40*, the playhead is at the **34 1 2 2** position. The SMPTE timecode position view will display **TC 01:00:16:15** and, since we changed **Display Time As** to feet and frames, Logic Pro now displays this **SMPTE timecode** as **5424. 15/0** feet and frames:

Figure 12.40: Logic Pro Arrange window

Additionally, when manually dragging the frame numbers from 0 to 15, the next frame will add a foot number to the left number. As you can see in *Figure 12.41*, the 16th frame changed the clock to **5425** feet in total length:

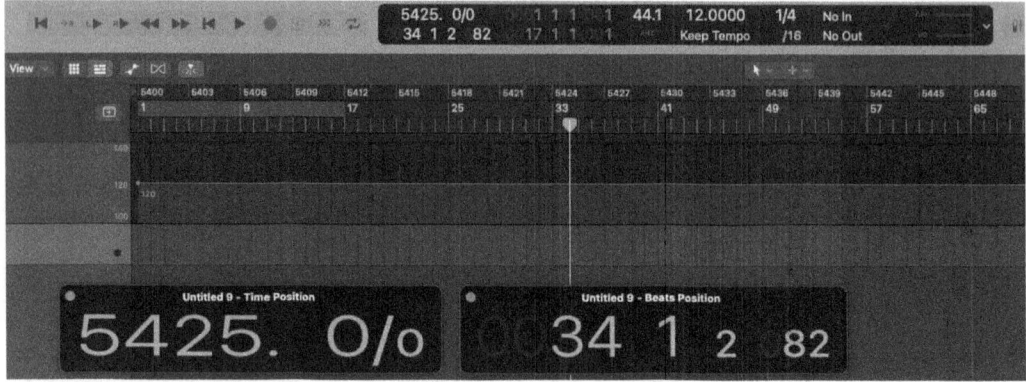

Figure 12.41: Logic Pro Arrange window

You can use this format by changing the numbers to move frame by frame as needed. Make sure to keep an eye on the bar and beats display.

Logic Pro today is still equipped to also display frame click instead of BPM. In the next section, we will take a closer look at that.

Displaying tempo as frame click in Logic Pro

In this section, we will look at how Logic Pro can change the BPM view to FPB.

Click on **File** and **Display**, then in the **Displays** section, change **Display Tempo As** to **Frames per Click with Decimals**. In *Figure 12.42*, you can see that Logic Pro changed the number of 120 bpm in the LCD display to the decimal number of **12.000**, which is 12 fpb (frame click):

Figure 12.42: Logic Pro Arrange window

Although these methods of converting bpm to fpb may not be as used or as useful today, some film composers may still use the calculations when away from the computer and when trying to figure out timings by hand. From the historic perspective of synchronizing music to picture, it is important to know these methods and to know how they function to have an overall perspective on film music.

Instead, you can use Logic Pro, which can assist with all kinds of tempo calculations when it comes to synchronizing music to picture. Logic Pro DAW generates the click track and replaces the cumbersome tempo and events calculations of the olden days. It also makes synchronization tasks easier since we're dealing with BITC and SMPTE.

Now that we've looked at different methods of synchronization of music to picture, next, we will look at visual synchronization methods from the Golden Age of Hollywood that are still used today.

Exploring visual synchronization methods used today

When we speak about visual synchronization methods, we're talking about using picture cueing accompanied by the metronome click. Since the Golden Age of Hollywood, visual synchronization methods have been used to record live orchestra music to picture. In this section, we will look closer at picture cueing in the olden days and how it's used today.

Picture cueing

Picture cueing is a visual synchronization method that uses superimposed **punches** and **streamers** to assist the conductor, during a live orchestra recording session, to synchronize the music to the picture. Punches and streamers are used especially when the music needs to flow, or have a "rubato" feel, and doesn't need to follow strict rhythmic pulses.

In the past, a streamer was created by etching a marker line in the celluloid film. This appeared as a diagonal line, superimposed over the movie, flowing from the left to the right side and followed by a punch:

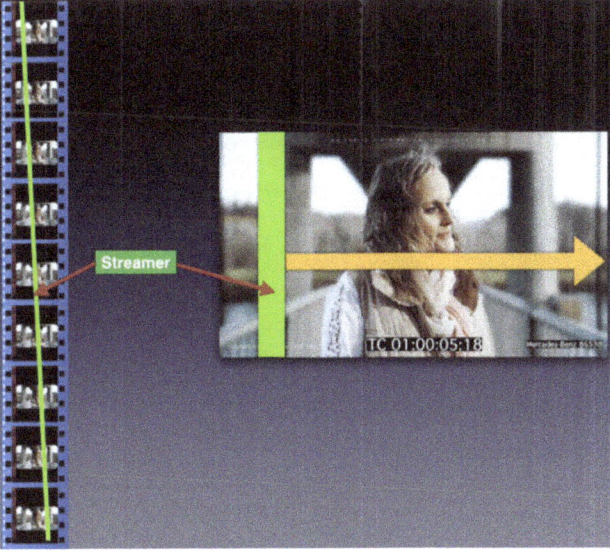

Figure 12.43: Streamer

In the past, a punch was created by making a hole in the middle of the frame. It was usually placed on the downbeat of a bar, on a hit point, or on the first beat of the count-in and at the point where the music needed to stop:

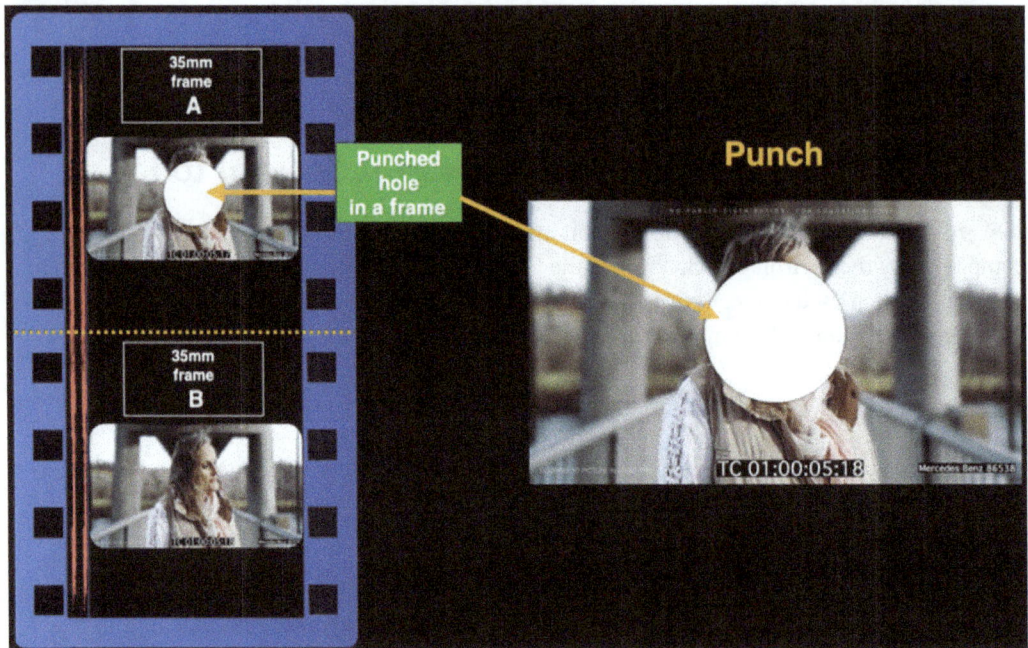

Figure 12.44: Punch

Flutters were a quick series of blinks that appeared as flickering lights and were created by punching multiple holes in the celluloid film. At different times, flutters were used in the following ways:

- As an indication of where the first beat in the bar should fall
- As an indicator to the conductor if they were early or late so that the conductor could catch up with the tempo
- As an indicator to the conductor that the music was about to start

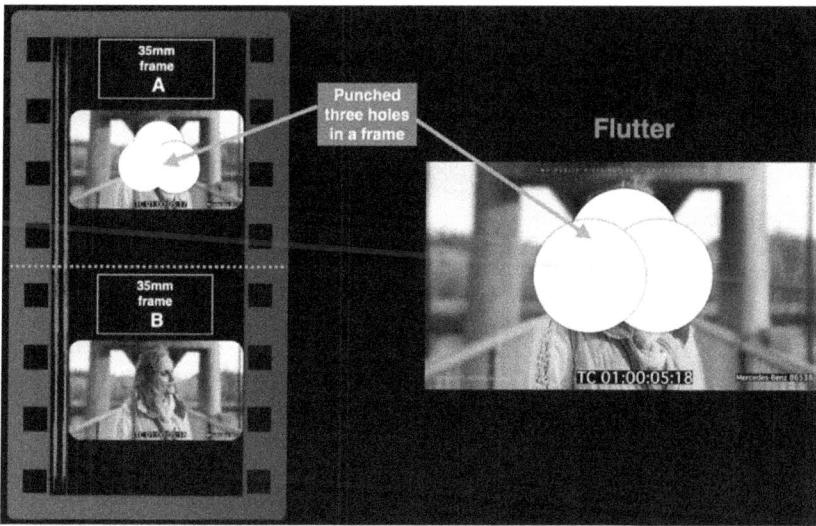

Figure 12.45: Flutter

Part of the picture cueing process also included implementing a digital metronome or click track, which we will look at next.

Digital metronome

Since the Golden Age of Hollywood, using a click track involved either recording the sound of the click track onto the celluloid film or punching holes in the frame. With the development of the digital metronome in the 1950s, the **Urei** company replaced the older, cumbersome ways of creating a click track. The digital metronome provided a steady click track to assist the recording session on the scoring stage. This device can still be found on some scoring stages today since it has proven to be more reliable.

Figure 12.46 is a depiction of a digital metronome:

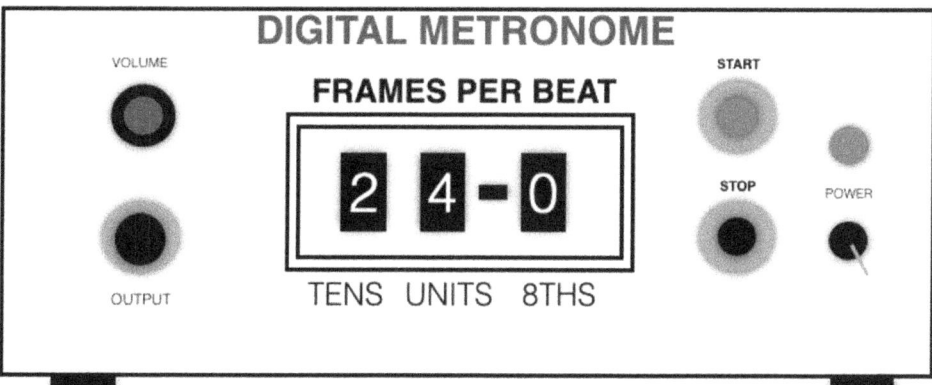

Figure 12.46: Digital metronome

The Urei metronome was calibrated as the numbers progressed in increments of a frame. The fpb mirrored the division of a frame into eight equal parts. The first two digits (24) in *Figure 12.46*, represent the tempo in fpb, while the third digit (0) is an eighth of a frame that was added to the tempo.

The following is a list of a few different bpm values and their equivalent fpb values:

- 24-0 fpb represents 60 bpm
- 24-1 fpb (24 and one-eighth frames per beat) represents 59.69 bpm
- 24-2 fpb (24 and two-eighths frames per beat) represents 59.38 bpm

Figure 12.47 provides a visual reference of the 8 possible settings of 24 fpb from 0 to 7:

Click (frames)	BPM
24-0	60
24-1	59.69
24-2	59.38
24-3	59.08
24-4	58.78
24-5	58.48
24-6	58.18
24-7	57.89

Figure 12.47: Digital metronome click frames to bpm conversions

As the numbers increase, the tempo decreases. The digital metronome continues from 25-0 and so on. For example, a Urei metronome setting of 12-0 fpb means that the metronome is set to 120 bpm and 2 beats occur per second.

The digital metronome assisted conductors during the recording of the orchestra to picture by helping to maintain a steady click track with no compromised synchronization. The audible Urei click track was a great way to keep the tempo between the orchestra, the conductor, and the film events in sync.

The click track was the audible part of synchronization. Today, on current scoring stages, we use the sound of the original Urei click track without the box as a digital recording in computer systems.

Implementing punches and streamers today

Today, when dealing with a digital film format, what was done manually is now done electronically by superimposing the punches and streamers onto the video. The punches are represented by a white circle, while streamers are yellow, green, and red by default. The film industry defined the default streamer colors and their specific function as a standard for picture cueing; these colors and functions are recognized on the scoring stage worldwide. In this section, we will review a general process of picture cueing today using punches and streamers.

The **yellow streamer** is the first streamer you will see. It is a reminder to the conductor of the tempo of the music and appears as a signal to the conductor that they need to be prepared and get ready for the recording. The streamer, on average, is 2 seconds long, but can be set up to any other specified time:

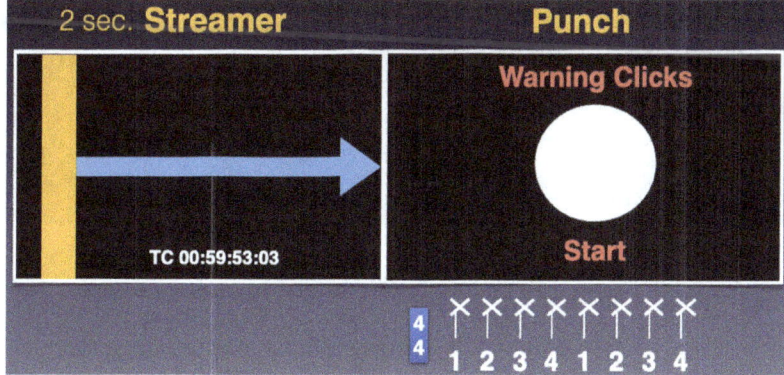

Figure 12.48: Yellow streamer

As it moves from left to right, eventually a **punch** appears marking the start of the warning clicks (also referred to as a warning clix). In most cases, the warning clicks section, commonly known as a count-in, is two bars long. The conductor will hear the warning clicks and start conducting following the click track.

The next streamer that follows is a **green streamer**, indicating that the music is about to start. It's followed by a punch on the first beat of a bar. When it reaches the right-hand side, it signalizes an upcoming first note of music as the downbeat:

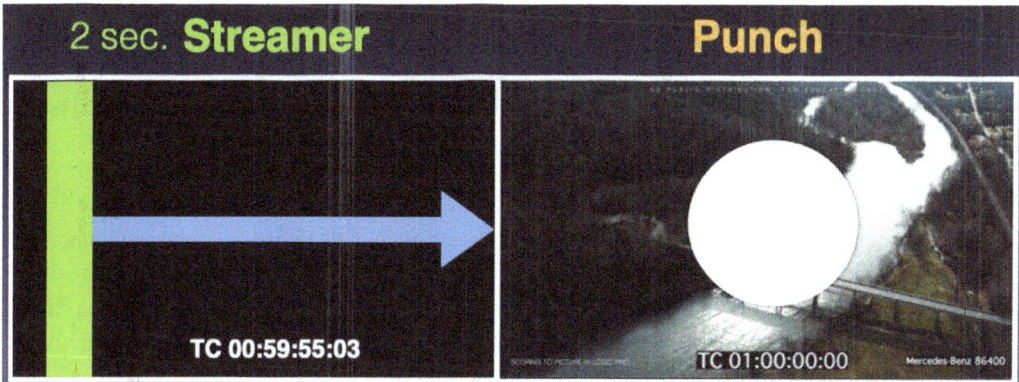

Figure 12.49: Green streamer

The green streamer can also appear followed by a punch to indicate additional hit points throughout the session:

Figure 12.50: Green streamer

Depending on the situation, flutters might be used, or additional green streamers may be added throughout the recording session.

At the end, to finalize the session, a **red streamer** is used to indicate the end of a scene or a cue, followed by a punch:

Figure 12.51: Red streamer

In addition to picture cueing on the scoring stage, this method can also be implemented in a home studio environment within Logic Pro. Logic Pro does not have a built-in feature of superimposing punches and streamers over the video, but you can purchase third-party software that can do this. This can assist film composers during film scoring tasks, for example, when recording single instrumentalists or small ensembles during a live recording session when recording music to picture, depending on your computer audio interface capabilities and setup.

Also, there are many other colors of streamers that can be added, superimposed, and specifically defined based on the needs of your recording session.

Summary

In this chapter, we explored techniques of advanced timings in film scoring. We reviewed how to calculate timings and how to structure a 30-second commercial. Additionally, we explored different methods and concepts to calculate tempo and how to synchronize music to picture.

Since the first chapter, we've learned how to score to picture in Logic Pro as well as gained a broader understanding of film music. Certainly, there's a lot to process and digest throughout all 12 chapters, but as you practice and implement the content that's been covered, you will gain the confidence and experience needed in your projects to reach the technical skill level required of a working Hollywood composer.

Studying film scoring and learning further how to use Logic Pro is a lifelong learning experience that takes time and practice, but it comes with many rewards and blessings. I hope that you've learned a lot and this textbook will continue equipping you and helping you to achieve only the best in your career.

Wishing you happy and successful film scoring!

Index

Symbols

2-pop 19, 21
   movie file, syncing with 91-94
2 second pre-roll 23, 24
3-pop 21
   movie file, syncing with 94-97
3 second pre-roll 24, 25

A

Academy Leader 18, 19
   2-pop 19, 21
   2 second pre-roll 23, 24
   3-pop 21
   3 second pre-roll 24, 25
   end pop 22
Adobe Premiere
   used, for reviewing SMPTE timecode 34-36
advanced timings, in film scoring
   structure and timings, outlining 350-353
audio
   extracting, from movie file 55, 56
audio branding 256

B

bar location
   movie file, syncing 109-111

basic mix
   finalizing 313-344
beat mapping 184
   entire MIDI region 199-202
   hit points 216-220
   single MIDI notes 192-199
Beat Mapping scene markers
   using 205-215
Beat Mapping track
   editing 204, 205
beats per minute (bpm) 364
BITC errors
   exploring 26-30
burnt-in timecode (BITC) 9-11, 16, 17

C

click book 365
composing process
   reviewing 258-299
countdown leader
   movie file, syncing with 84-90
cue sheets 8

D

dialog and temp music
  reviewing 36, 37
Digital Audio Workstation (DAW) 5
  timings, calculating 358
  timings, calculating in Logic Pro 358, 359
  timings, calculating with formulas 360-363
digital metronome 375, 376
Drop Frame (DF) 25

E

end pop 22
entire MIDI region
  beat mapping 199-202
errors in drop frame timecodes 25, 26
errors in non-drop frame timecodes 25, 26

F

film composer
  character qualities 12
  skills 13
film music 3, 4
  dealing, with tempo 154
film-music industry 4
  composed score 5
  history 4
flutters 374
frames per beat (fpb) 364
frames per second (fps) 44 363

G

Giant Beats Display 66, 67
Giant Time Display 66, 67
green streamer 377, 378

H

High-Pass Filter (HPF) 316
High-Shelf Filter (HSF) 338
hit points 124
  beat mapping 216-220
  defining 124

I

instrument track
  used, for creating tap tempo 184-192

L

layering instruments
  reviewing 258, 259, 300-304
leitmotif 11
Logic Pro
  movie file, opening 52-55
  spotting notes list, copying 126
  time signature, reviewing 224-230
Logic Pro LCD position display
  reviewing 158-162
Logic Pro session
  closing 51, 52
  opening 51, 52
  saving 51, 52
  saving, with movie file 63, 64
Logic Pro SMPTE display
  without subframes 67, 69
Logic Pro to picture
  movie file, importing 69
  movie, locking 78-81
  movie project settings, accessing 70-76
  movie project settings, reviewing 70-76
  Movie Track Info panel, accessing and reviewing 82

Movie Track Info panel, reviewing 82
project session, saving with movie file 82, 84
synchronization settings, accessing 77, 78
synchronization settings, reviewing 77, 78
syncing 69
Logic Pro, with different movie files
   syncing 84
   syncing, from bar location 109-111
   syncing, with 2-pop 91-94
   syncing, with 3-pop 94-97
   syncing, with countdown leader 84-90
   syncing, with multiple reels 97-106
   syncing, with SMPTE Offset View 107-109
Low-Pass Filter (LPF) 322

M

marker
   changing, to SMPTE view position 136, 137
   naming 131-136
   navigating with 145, 146
   renaming 131-136
marker positions
   reviewing 163-167
marker sets
   creating 147, 148
marker without rounding
   creating 126-131
Marquee Ruler 114
metronome (click track) 364
mix
   evaluating 306
movie
   locking 78-81
   watching, with metronome 154, 156
movie file
   aspect ratio, adjusting 62, 63
   audio, extracting 55, 56
   frame rate, setting up 57, 58
   importing 55, 69
   position, adjusting 58-60
   position, moving 58-60
   project session, saving with 82, 84
   sample rate, setting up 56, 57
   size, changing 60, 62
   used, for saving Logic Pro session 63, 64
movie project settings
   accessing 70-76
   reviewing 70-76
movie scene cut markers 143
   creating 143-145
   removing 143-145
Movie Track Info panel
   accessing 82
   reviewing 82
multiple reels
   movie file, syncing with 97
multi-tracks 344
musical choices
   versus technical choices 251, 257
Music Instrument Digital
   Interface (MIDI) 5
music role
   structuring 257
music spotting notes
   reviewing 124
music to picture synchronization
   methods 363
   35mm single frame film 364
   bpm, versus fpb 365, 366
   click book 365
   film lengths, displaying in Logic Pro 369-372
   frame click, displaying in Logic Pro 372, 373
   timings, calculating with fpb
      formulas 367, 369

N

Non-Drop Frame (NDF) 25

P

panning level for track
  setting 310-313
Pencil Tool 226
picture cueing 373, 374
picture template
  custom scoring, creating 111-122
pre-roll 23
punches 373, 374
  implementing 376-378

Q

QuickTime Inspector
  opening 40

R

red streamer 378

S

scene markers
  creating 138, 139
  versus SMPTE-locked markers 139-142
  versus standard markers 139-142
score to video
  exporting 344-348
Secondary Ruler 114
single MIDI notes
  beat mapping 192-199
SMPTE errors
  exploring 26-30

SMPTE-locked markers
  versus scene markers 139-142
  versus standard markers 139-142
SMPTE Offset View
  movie file, syncing with 107-109
SMPTE timecode 15
  reviewing 30-34
  reviewing, with Adobe Premiere 34-36
SMPTE view position
  marker, changing 136, 137
Society of Motion Picture and Television Engineers (SMPTE) 15, 16
sound
  shaping 313-344
spotting notes 8
spotting notes list
  copying, into Logic Pro 126
spotting session 6
  music composition 11
standard markers
  versus scene markers 139-142
  versus SMPTE-locked markers 139-142
stems 344
streamers 373
  green streamer 377
  implementing 376-378
  red streamer 378
  yellow streamer 377
structure and timing settings, film scoring
  outlining 350-353
  scenarios 354-358
structure and timing settings scenarios
  120 bpm and 3/4 time signature 354, 356
  120 bpm and 4/4 time signature 356
  192 bpm and 4/4 time signature 357, 358
synchronization settings
  accessing and reviewing 77, 78
sync pop 19

T

Tap Tempo
  creating, with instrument track 184-192
  using 156-158
technical choices
  versus musical choices 251, 257
temp music 6, 7
tempo
  adjusting, to match hit points 179-181
  film music, dealing with 154
tempo map
  creating 167-173
  creating, based on hit points 174-178
tempo mapping 167
tempo points 202
  editing 202-204
temp track 6, 7
time signature 223
  adding, to constant tempo 243-250
  adding, to marker positions 230-242
  in film music 224
  reviewing, in Logic Pro 224-230
timings, in DAW
  calculating 358
  calculating, in Logic Pro 358, 359
  calculating, with formulas 360-363
Track Alternatives 190

V

video file
  Audio Format setting 44
  components 40, 41
  Data Size setting 42, 43
  format 43, 44
  General 42
  Resolution section 42
  Video Details 44, 46
Vienna Ensemble Pro (VEP) 83
visual synchronization methods 373
  digital metronome 375, 376
  picture cueing 373, 374
  punches, implementing 376-378
  streamers, implementing 376-378
visual synchronization tools
  Beat Displays 66, 67
  Giant SMPTE Time 66, 67
  Logic Pro SMPTE display,
    without subframes 67-69
  reviewing 65
voiceover (VO) 257
volume level of tracks
  setting 306-309

Y

yellow streamer 377

www.packtpub.com

Subscribe to our online digital library for full access to over 7,000 books and videos, as well as industry leading tools to help you plan your personal development and advance your career. For more information, please visit our website.

Why subscribe?

- Spend less time learning and more time coding with practical eBooks and Videos from over 4,000 industry professionals
- Improve your learning with Skill Plans built especially for you
- Get a free eBook or video every month
- Fully searchable for easy access to vital information
- Copy and paste, print, and bookmark content

Did you know that Packt offers eBook versions of every book published, with PDF and ePub files available? You can upgrade to the eBook version at `packtpub.com` and as a print book customer, you are entitled to a discount on the eBook copy. Get in touch with us at `customercare@packtpub.com` for more details.

At `www.packtpub.com`, you can also read a collection of free technical articles, sign up for a range of free newsletters, and receive exclusive discounts and offers on Packt books and eBooks.

Other Books You May Enjoy

If you enjoyed this book, you may be interested in these other books by Packt:

The Music Producer's Creative Guide to Ableton Live 11

Anna Lakatos

ISBN: 978-1-80181-763-9

- Understand the concept of Live, the workflow of recording and editing Audio and MIDI, and Warping
- Utilize Groove, MIDI effects, and Live 11 s new workflow enhancements to create innovative music
- Use Audio to MIDI conversion tools to translate and generate ideas quickly
- Dive into Live's automation and modulation capabilities and explore project organization techniques to speed up your workflow
- Utilize MIDI Polyphonic Expression to create evolving sounds and textures
- Adopt useful techniques for production and discover the capabilities of live performance

The Music Producer's Ultimate Guide to FL Studio 21 - Second Edition

Joshua Au-Yeung

ISBN: 978-1-83763-165-0

- Get up and running with FL Studio 21
- Compose melodies and chord progressions on the piano roll
- Mix your music effectively with mixing techniques and plugins, such as compressors and equalizers
- Record into FL Studio, pitch-correct and retime samples, and follow advice for applying effects to vocals
- Create vocal harmonies and learn how to use vocoders to modulate your vocals with an instrument
- Create glitch effects, transform audio samples into playable instruments, and sound design with cutting-edge effects
- Develop your brand to promote your music effectively
- Publish your music online and collect royalty revenues

Packt is searching for authors like you

If you're interested in becoming an author for Packt, please visit `authors.packtpub.com` and apply today. We have worked with thousands of developers and tech professionals, just like you, to help them share their insight with the global tech community. You can make a general application, apply for a specific hot topic that we are recruiting an author for, or submit your own idea.

Share Your Thoughts

Now you've finished *Scoring to Picture in Logic Pro*, we'd love to hear your thoughts! Scan the QR code below to go straight to the Amazon review page for this book and share your feedback or leave a review on the site that you purchased it from.

`https://packt.link/r/1-837-63689-3`

Your review is important to us and the tech community and will help us make sure we're delivering excellent quality content.

Download a free PDF copy of this book

Thanks for purchasing this book!

Do you like to read on the go but are unable to carry your print books everywhere?

Is your eBook purchase not compatible with the device of your choice?

Don't worry, now with every Packt book you get a DRM-free PDF version of that book at no cost.

Read anywhere, any place, on any device. Search, copy, and paste code from your favorite technical books directly into your application.

The perks don't stop there, you can get exclusive access to discounts, newsletters, and great free content in your inbox daily

Follow these simple steps to get the benefits:

1. Scan the QR code or visit the link below

```
https://packt.link/free-ebook/9781837636891
```

2. Submit your proof of purchase
3. That's it! We'll send your free PDF and other benefits to your email directly

www.ingramcontent.com/pod-product-compliance
Lightning Source LLC
Chambersburg PA
CBHW060453300426
44113CB00016B/2577